THE CHURCH:
Selected Writings of Arthur Carl Piepkorn

**Edited and Introduced by
Michael P. Plekon
and William S. Wiecher
Afterword by Richard John Neuhaus**

**ALPB Books
Delhi, New York**

ALPB Books is a ministry of publication of the American Lutheran Publicity Bureau. ALPB Books publishes trustworthy theological and devotional books that are oriented to pastors and congregations at an economical price. The ALPB publishes *Lutheran Forum* and co-publishes PRO ECCLESIA quarterly and *Forum Letter* monthly.

The American Lutheran Publicity Bureau acknowledges those permissions given by others on pages 303-304 of this volume.

This volume is set in 10 pt. Palatino.

American Lutheran Publicity Bureau
PO Box 327
Delhi, NY 13753-0327
(607)746-7511

Publisher of *Lutheran Forum/Forum Letter*

Co-publisher of PRO ECCLESIA with the
Center for Catholic & Evangelical Theology

TABLE OF CONTENTS

PART II:
THE PARISH AT PRAYER

PART III:
MARY, ARCHETYPE OF THE CHURCH

AFTERWORD:

Introduction
ARTHUR CARL PIEPKORN:
Teacher And Father of The Church

by Michael Plekon
and William Wiecher

W hen Father Alexander Schmemann died on December 13, 1983, among all the words of the homilies and eulogies delivered, those of his parishioner, friend and colleague rang most true. Dr. Veselin Kesich, professor of New Testament spoke most briefly, simply yet eloquently:

> Fr. Alexander is known for his writings, and I would say that in his writings there are two themes permeating everything else: the themes of freedom and of joy. And not only in his writing but in his own life. He was a free man in Christ; he was a man full of joy.[1]

In North American Lutheranism of the 20th century the same could be said of Arthur Carl Piepkorn, the teacher and father of the Church who also died on December 13, but in 1973. Piepkorn was a free man in Christ, a man full of joy, just like Fr. Alexander Schmemann. The similarities between the two, despite obvious differences, are striking. Both were beloved pastors, renowned lecturers, and scholars.

Both served their churches with love and sacrifice, forming future pastors in seminary teaching, writing for the renewal of the liturgy and the life of faith, rather than for academic advancement. Both Fathers Piepkorn and Schmemann had little official support in their church, received much and vicious criticism and, in the end, were dismissed to the periphery by ecclesiastical administration. Neither formed "schools" of theological literature or of former students. Neither produced a systematic library of their own theological thinking like Barth, Florovsky or Rahner. Yet both were icons of faithful discipleship. Both lived out what they lectured, illuminating the life of the Church. Their legacy endures exactly where they would most have wanted — in their churches' renewed eucharistic life, in liturgy, prayer, study and in the pursuit of holy living by clergy, and laity alike. Both were filled with the freedom of Christ and the joy of the Holy Spirit. As A.M. Allchin has quoted Russian Metropolitan Evlogy on such saints as Francis of Assisi and Seraphim of Sarov, so too of Fathers Schmemann and Piepkorn.[2] Though in their lives here schism and division still separated their churchly existence, we cannot imagine such walls in the heavenly Kingdom. We cannot help but see them joined with all the company of heaven in eternal praise, thanksgiving and love, of the Holy Trinity, these two fathers and teachers of the Church East and West who spent their lives proclaiming, rediscovering and renewing the holy Church, the Liturgy, the Eucharist, Scripture and Tradition, the Mother of God and the life of holiness, for the life of the world.

Over the years many of us in the Lutheran movement within the Church catholic (Piepkorn's most basic ecclesial understanding) have been nourished by Fr. Schmemann's teaching, left in such writings as *For the Life of the World, Of Water and the Spirit, Church, World, Mission*, and *The Eucharist*, among others.[3] We have been encouraged, in the struggle to renew the liturgy and life of the Church, by his powerful essays on the problems of the Orthodox Church, from the early 1960s, all of which speak to the Lutheran Church in the 1990s.[4]

What Schmemann was (and is) first, for the Orthodox Church and for the greater Church catholic, Arthur Piepkorn also was, and is. And herein lies the impetus for the publication of this first volume of selections from his writings. Precisely, Piepkorn, like Schmemann, was a *father* and *teacher of the Church*. As Richard Neuhaus writes of him,

> No, there was nothing of himself that he would transmit, except insofar as he was the bearer of the tradition, of the sacred story. To learn from Piepkorn you would need the library, for he was the servant of a learned history. And you would need an altar and a pulpit, for the learning was nothing of real importance apart from the community of faith all of one's life in liturgy, or it is nothing of lasting interest.[5]

This first volume is all about the Church, as Piepkorn proclaimed the Creed's faith in her. That, as a Lutheran theologian, Arthur Piepkorn did have so much to say about the Church might seem both an aberration and a blessing. Not truly understanding the 16th century reformers assumptions and actual churchly practice, and ravaged by so much in the last several centuries: rationalism, pietism, the effects of the Reformed tradition both in Europe and here, Lutherans have come to suffer a profound ecclesial amnesia. The Church, thus, was reduced either to an invisible, over-spiritualized entity (taking part of Luther's writing for the whole) or merely the functional apparatus necessary for the preaching of the Gospel and administration of the sacraments. The Church became a pious (not even Platonic) dream or a barely tolerated polity, whose shape and action were matters of indifference.

Piepkorn is in fine theological fellowship in raising up again a veneration for, a glory in being the Church. Already in this century, one could hear the Holy Church and her catholicity celebrated by Gustaf Aulén, Nathan Söderblom, Yngve Brilioth, Gustaf Wingren, K.E. Skydsgaard, Peter Brunner, and Luther Reed, to name but a few.[6] More recently, the appropriation of the *Augsburg Confession*'s and Melancthon's *Apology*'s commitment to the catholic Tradition has had a notable procession of proponents. One thinks of Robert Jenson's general theological efforts as well as his more particular forays into the ecumenical impasse over the Church, the Ministry and the Mother of God. Carl Braaten has been a vocal defender of the particularity of the Gospel and the apostolicity of the Church.[7] Bruce Marshall, following Vladimir Lossky and Lindbeck, has offered a stunning vision of the Church's unity in and with the Gospel.[8] George Lindbeck himself has long been a teacher of the ecclesial basis of Scripture and doctrine and an astute interpreter of the growth of ecclesial understanding in the Lutheran-Roman Catholic and other ecumenical dialogues.[9] Bishop William Lazareth, influential in the generation of the "Lima Document" of the WCC Faith and Order, *Baptism, Eucharist, Ministry*, has also focused these ecumenical breakthroughs in ecclesial rediscovery for the Lutheran community.[10] Michael Root, Eugene Brand and Harding Meyer have also made like contributions.[11] Carl Volz and Karl Donfried have brought patristic and New Testament expertise to there discovery of the Church.[12] Still other efforts to rediscover the eucharistic nature of the Church, the sacramentality and incarnational reality of the Church, have been made within Lutheranism. Jesuit theologian Jared Wicks has made a remarkable excavation of Luther's overlooked understanding of the Church and sanctification as the work of the Holy Spirit.[13] In other churches, to the great work of Schmemann must be added the rich theological work of Paul Evdokimov, Vladimir Lossky, John Zizioulis, J.–M.R. Tillard, Louis Bouyer, Yves Congar and Avery Dulles, again, to cite only several.[14]

In this century's reappropriation of the Church's indispensability to the Gospel, among Lutherans, Arthur Carl Piepkorn has been both a distinguished and distinctive, if not always well recognized teacher and father. He consistently and with overwhelming detail revealed again the commitment of the 16th century reformers to the catholic tradition, abuses and errors corrected. Whether one hears the phrase echoing from Jenson and Gritsch or from Richard John Neuhaus or William Lazareth or George Lindbeck, it was Arthur Carl Piepkorn who, nearly fifty years ago began describing Lutheranism as the renewal and reforming movement within the Western catholic Church. It is of great interest to note that Piepkorn's contributions to the U.S. Lutheran-Roman Catholic dialogues, particularly his essays on Baptism, the Eucharist, Holy Ordination and the Sacred Ministry, meticulous in their exposition of the Lutheran Confessions' (and related writings of Luther, Melanchthon, Chemnitz, Gerhard and others) catholicity, i.e. their retention, preservation and celebration of the Church and her Tradition — were never *opposed* by other Lutheran participants in the dialogues. Theologians of different church bodies such as Warren Quanbeck, John Reumann, Kent Knutson, George Lindbeck, Kristen Stendahl, Joseph Sittler and Fred Kramer, did not formally, in print, that is, reject Piepkorn's fundamentally evangelical and catholic understanding of the Reformation and of Lutheranism's essential orientation and commitments.[15] The post-ELCA merger contestation between "evangelical-catholic" and "radical/denominational" groups of Lutherans have produced a very different kind of confessional conflict. It is not too much to say that the struggle is over the Church itself, over the Lutheran preservation or dismissal of the Church as believed in the catholic Tradition of the first Christian millennium and a half. Precisely here, Arthur Carl Piepkorn is very much the father and teacher of the Church. For him, the Lutheran Confessions are called "Symbols," truly confessions of faith in the Gospel and the Church. For Piepkorn the Church is one, holy, catholic and apostolic, as the symbol of Nicea-Constantinople confesses. The Church can also be described as paschal, sacramental, incarnational, and eucharistic, as Piepkorn does in the selected essays which follow. Never are doctrine, liturgy, and mission pitted against each other in Piepkorn's faithful teaching, as they frequently are today. Like Schmemann, Piepkorn rejected any reduction of the Church to one function. Never would he allow a part to be taken for the whole. Rather, the Church always appears as the Body of Christ, organically knit together of parts which formed a living community in communion with the Lord.

Nor can such communion with our Lord merely consist in mutually sectarian, isolated communities. Foremost, then, in the mind of Arthur Carl Piepkorn was the reunification of the Church — for the purpose of communing with our Lord; one body, one Eucharist, one

Lord — one Church. The breadth and depth of his voluminous collection of essays and monographs have at their core the conviction of the confessors at Augsburg:

> to employ all diligence, amicably and charitably to hear, understand, and weigh judgments, opinions and beliefs of the several parties among us, to unite the same in agreement on one Christian truth, to put aside whatever may not have been rightly interpreted or treated by either side, to have all of us embrace and adhere to single, true religion and live together in unity and in one fellowship and church, even as we are all enlisted under one Christ (Preface to the *Augsburg Confession*, 1530, 2-4).

For him the shape of American denominationalism, the schism of the Church, serves as a sad sign of the sin of humanity and as such, not an opportunity for triumphalism; rather, an opportunity for repentance and reconciliation. Sectarianism is not the spirit of the Christian Church, unity or fullness is. In other words, the essence of the Church lies in the Lord Jesus Christ as incarnated in its catholicity. For Piepkorn, the Bride's proclamation; The Word and Sacraments, liturgy, creeds, and the office of the holy ministry reveal the Church's catholicity (fullness) most clearly. This catholicity is nothing more than the ongoing sanctifying power of the Holy Spirit, as Piepkorn's own words convey in his article entitled "Why Lutherans should engage in conversation with Roman Catholics."

> Our common understanding of our Lord's incarnation by the Holy Ghost out of the Blessed Virgin Mary is such that we see the world in which we live as sacramental, a world in which God operates through material means and physical persons — the human proclamation of the word of God; a washing with water in the laver of rebirth; the eating and drinking of bread and wine that in the sacrament of the altar are the veritable body and blood of Christ; a human mouth speaking a word of binding or loosing that binds or looses in the presence of God; a ministry of men through which God communicates aid and help in our warfare against our native sinfulness and against the seductions of his foes and ours; a union of one man and one woman in marriage by which God discloses the secret of Christ and his bride the Church.

The articles selected span a period of 34 years and by no means encompass all his writings. We have chosen those writings which speak to his concern for the Church of Jesus Christ as the body of Christ in this time and space, birthed at Pentecost with an eschatological mission. Each Part encompasses the fullness of the Church's life, beginning with The Church and her Ministry. In this part the reader will discover Father Piepkorn's commitment to and knowledge of the Lutheran Confessions. As one deeply rooted in this 16th century confession, the

Confessions serve not as merely as piece of interesting history, a relic of sorts, or as eschatologically limited, but as a living tradition of great value to the ongoing mission and witness as a confessing movement within the Western Church. His very reference to these writings as "symbols" illustrate his conviction in their value for the present ecumenical task. Nor does he readily dismiss the sometimes troubling statements within these living symbols that are repugnant to modern protestant thought. Many of Fr. Piepkorn's critics of the past and present regarded him as a "romantic" with reference to his catholic contextual reading of the confessions. The reader will discover that for Father Piepkorn, the liturgy, creeds, the history of the first 1500 years of Christianity are not alien to the Lutheran symbols, for they speak clearly the living tradition of the saving Gospel of Jesus Christ for both present and future generations. Rigorously, Piepkorn demonstrated the interconnections of the body ecclesial in the historic extension of the catholic Tradition. The Lutheran Symbols, the Confessional documents themselves, are revealed to be producing nothing novel but always retaining the Tradition. Arthur Carl Piepkorn was to many, astonishingly catholic, and this was because he was so Lutheran. Consistently, as the essays demonstrate, he provided not only documentary textual support from the Confessions and from Lutheran theologians who were bound by the catholicity of them, but historical, practical instances of doctrine and ecclesial/liturgical supporting each other.[16]

In his essay entitled, "What The Lutheran Symbols Have To Say About The Church," (1955) the Church truly "exists." Therefore, the Church cannot be merely an invisible fellowship, nor a possession of a pious heart. The Church is no mere appendage to the mission of the Gospel. It is not an accident of history. Rather, the Church is the embodiment of the saving proclamation of Jesus Christ to the nations, the dwelling place of the Holy Spirit in history. This Church is the physical presence of Christ in this world and is not merely a matter of *adiaphora* of indifference. Nor is the structure of the Church's ministry merely up for grabs as he clearly reasons in "The Sacred Ministry and Holy Ordination in the Symbolic Books of the Lutheran Churches."

In "A Lutheran Theologian Looks at the Ninety-five Theses in 1967," Piepkorn creatively examines the Ninety-five theses on the 450th anniversary of the beginning of the Reformation. Moreover, in this chapter the ministry itself can never be taken apart from what the Church does as a community of believers in the communion of the holy things. In the 1938 article, "The Lutheran Church a Sacramental Church," which grew out of his parish experience, Father Piepkorn reflects on the sad state of the churches in the use of the means of grace and proposes a renewal of the churches by their returning to the riches of the Lutheran and truly Christian liturgical usages, by carefully discussing, baptism, holy communion and individual confession and absolution within the local worshiping communities. Finally, all this takes shape through our common heritage with those from whom we suffer painful separation; our Roman Catholic brothers and sisters. "Why Lutherans should engage in conversation with Roman Catholics" (1967) sagaciously engages the reader to ponder the importance of such conversations and the compelling need for these conversations to continue, not only on an official level, but also within our respective local communities.

The sharing of the "holy things" constitutes the Church. Through the Bride's liturgy, Word and Sacrament: The Parish At Prayer, the true catholicity and faithfulness of the Church's proclamation is seen. The wonderfully enriching article, "The Life of God in the Life of the Parish" makes a valuable insight, "In short, the parish derives its significance from the fact that it is the arena in which God establishes contact with man." Again,

> Our parishes will become more the church by the work of the Holy Spirit who alone creates the church. In a sense, however, we also have a part. By the power that He imparts, we can and should inhibit our native opposition to His work, make faithful use of the channels through which He has promised to communicate His life to us...

"The One Eucharist for the One World," written in 1972 reveals Piepkorn's growing affirmation of the Christian's faithful witness for justice in this increasingly "demonic" world. Piepkorn strongly reminds us of the transformational power of this chief sacrament of the Church. In this piece, he stresses the Father and His Son's compassion for the whole world by reminding the Christian of their calling within this world and culture of increasingly "undisguised nihilism." All Christians who share in the Holy Eucharist, Piepkorn states, "can, according to his vocation and influence and resources, conscientiously seek to redeem the area of his own influence for Christ whose advent into the world had as its aim the destruction of the works of the adversary." However, this concern for justice is not just blind ideology at work, but is solely grounded in the true incarnational presence of Christ in his Holy Supper; "assuming our common humanity, He united himself with all of humankind, so that there are no human limits to the identification of the Christ of the Eucharist with the one world of human beings."

The exegetical writing entitled, "Light and Glory: Devotional Reflections," reveals Piepkorn's ability never to divorce the text of Scripture from the liturgical setting of the Gospel's proclamation. Here he prayerfully comments on the Gospel text for the Feast of the Presentation of Our Lord. In great detail he examines each participant in this event and draws from them the implications for us today concerning our communion with our Lord Jesus. He comments, "What matters is that the Faith be carried on by men and women like St. Simeon. Men and women, who have the Word of God and *enough contact with God* to be sure of Him." Other selections in this part reveal the same, consistent need for exposure with Christ Jesus as he makes himself present through the Churches liturgy.

The last Part, Mary: Archetype Of The Church, deals with an area of passionate interest for Arthur Carl Piepkorn. Through Arthur Carl Piepkorn we receive a deep ecclesial appreciation for the Mother of God. It can be rightly claimed, we feel, that there have not been many Lutheran theologians, perhaps apart from Blessed Martin Luther himself, as interested in Mariology, as Father Piepkorn. Yet, for him, this was no mere hobby, an archaic interest or an exercise in theological correctness, but a faithful reexamination of Mary and her ministry in the history and life of the Church's proclamation. Throughout the Church's life, the Blessed Virgin Mary, who as Luther reminds us is crowned with the wonderful title, *Theotokos*, the Mother of God, stands as the archetype of the Church. She is the icon of the body of Christ, the icon of redeemed humanity, the new Eve, the image of communion with Christ to which we are all called through the sacrament of Holy Baptism. She is the bearer of the eternal Word. She is the icon of every Christian. Through the history of the Church she is venerated as a model of faithful discipleship. Through her, Piepkorn reminds us in his homily, entitled, "Blessed are Thou Among Women" (1958):

> The function of the Blessed Virgin Mary in the Sacred Scriptures in the history of salvation, and in the faith and worship of the Church, is to point to her Son ...She is the living and loving proof that when the time had fully come, God sent forth His Son, born of woman, born under the Law, to redeem those that were under the Law, so that we might receive adoption as children.

In another homily, "A Chapel Address on The Feast of the Annunciation" (1971), he affirms Mary as an icon of a redeemed and sanctified humanity, as one who says "Yes" to God and his grace for humanity, his Son Jesus Christ. Her yes was not the result of her power, but "action of divine grace going on for a long time. God's grace had prepared her for this hour." Likewise, for us who are baptized, "When the Word of God comes to us, the Lord who gave us the grace that has structured our lives in Christ so far is ready to give us the further grace that enables us to say our 'yes' to Him...." Like the Mother of God, Father Piepkorn embodied such spiritual God-Bearing himself.

In these selections, as in all his writings and sermons, the legacy of Arthur Carl Piepkorn stands in the tradition of being truly a teacher and father of the Church.

His mind was encyclopedic, as John Damm's memoir/appreciation at the Institute of Liturgical Studies of Valparaiso University (April

20-22, 1993) attests. His research projects, not only those reprinted here, but others, such as *Profiles in Belief* (1977) are examples of meticulous, yet vast study. But Piepkorn was not merely a collector or curator of the antique. As John Damm observed, he constantly brought the old and the new together, like the faithful scribe in the gospel of Matthew (13:52) read at the commemoration of theologians in the rite of the *Lutheran Book of Worship*. Father Arthur Carl, it would seem, handed over not himself but the rich gifts of Church and Gospel, of Liturgy and Doctrine. He brought them to life, not just back from the past, but right into the midst of where the hearer is. Readers of this volume indeed will hear themselves, their Christian life, the Church in which they participate all being addressed and quite vividly at that by Arthur Carl Piepkorn. Wherever one is, in the "Church of the West," (what he always called the Roman Catholic Church), in the Methodist, Presbyterian, Episcopal, Evangelical Churches, in the Orthodox Churches and, to be sure, in the Lutheran Churches, Piepkorn has a living word. It comes not so much from a historian, an educator, even an academic theologian. It comes from the altar, ambo and font where liturgy is celebrated; from the very life pulse, the heart of the Church's Life, her Word and Sacrament, her *liturgia*. From Arthur Carl Piepkorn, this living word of Gospel, Liturgy and Tradition comes from a priest, who lived and prayed well, a man of freedom amid much churchly anarchy and of joy despite adversity, a faithful teacher and father of the Church. Arthur Carl Piepkorn's writings are illustrative of the long time maxim of the Church, "*Lex orandi est lex credendi et agendi*" — The rule of prayer is the rule of belief and of action of the Church. Or simply what is prayed establishes what is believed. May this be for us, also.

Almighty God, your Holy Spirit gives to one the word of wisdom, and to another the word of knowledge, and to another the word of faith. We praise you for the gifts of grace imparted to your servant Arthur Carl, and we pray that by his teaching we may be led to a fuller knowledge of the truth to which we have seen in you Son Jesus Christ our Lord...[17]

ENDNOTES

1. Veselin Kesich, "Freedom and Joy," *St. Vladimir's Theological Quarterly* (28, 1) 41-42.
2. *The World is a Wedding: Exploration in Christian Spirituality* (NY: Crossroad, 1982) 80-81.
3. (Crestwood, NY: St. Vladimir's Seminary Press, 1988, 1974, 1979, 1988.)
4. "Problems of Orthodoxy in America, I The Canonical Problem, II The Liturgical Problem, III The Spiritual Problem" *St. Vladimir's Theological Quarterly*, 1964 (8, 2) 67-85; (8, 4) 164-85; 1965 (9, 4) 171-93. Also see his *Church, World, Mission* (Crestwood, NY: St. Vladimir's Seminary Press, 1979).

5. "Remembering Piepkorn," *Lutheran Forum* 1984 (18, 4) 15-18. The fuller text of Fr. Neuhaus' talk on the awarding of the first Piepkorn Prize forms the afterword in this volume.
6. To cite but a selection of their works: Yngve Brilioth, *Eucharistic Faith and Practice* (London: SPCK, 1930), Gustaf Aulén, *Reformation and Catholicity* (Philadelphia: Muhlenberg, 1961); Luther D. Reed, *The Lutheran Liturgy and Worship* (Philadelphia: Muhlenberg, 1947, 1959); K. E. Skydsgaard, *One in Christ* (Philadelphia: Muhlenberg, 1957); Gustaf Wingren, *Gospel and Church* (Philadelphia: Fortress, 1964); Peter Brunner, "The Realization of Church Fellowship," (and other essays) in *The Unity of the Church* (Rock Island, IL: Augustana, 1957).
7. *Lutheranism* (with Eric W. Gritsch) (Philadelphia: Fortress, 1976), *Christian Dogmatics* (ed. with Carl E. Braaten), esp. vol. 2, "The Holy Spirit" and "The Sacraments" (Philadelphia: Fortress, 1984), 105-78, 289-390; *Visible Words* (Philadelphia: Fortress, 1978); *Unbaptized God* (Minneapolis, Fortress, 1992), "An Attempt To Think About Mary," *dialog* 1992 (31), 259-64, "Sovereignty in the Church," in *The New Church Debate*, ed., Carl E. Braaten (Philadelphia: Fortress, 1983) 39-53; *Principles of Lutheran Theology* (Philadelphia: Fortress, 1983); *The Apostolic Imperative* (Minneapolis: Augsburg, 1985); *Justification: The Article By Which The Church Stands Of Falls* (Minneapolis: Fortress, 1992). For Jenson and Braaten, as well as others to be mentioned, also see their contributions to the two "Call to Faithfulness" conferences at St. Olaf College, published in *dialog* 1991 (30, 2) and *Lutheran Forum* 1992 (26, 4).
8. "The Church in the Gospel," PRO ECCLESIA 1992 (I, 1) 27-41.
9. *The Nature of Doctrine*, (Philadelphia: Westminster, 1984), "Lutheranism as Church and Movement: Trends in America Since 1980," *Gettysburg Lutheran Theological Seminary* Bulletin, 1991 (71), 43-59, "The Lutheran Doctrine of the Ministry: Catholic and Reformed, *Theological Studies* 1969 (30), 588-612. Also see his contributions to the St. Olaf conferences in the journals noted above, his "Confessions and Community: An Israel-like View of the Church," *Christian Century* (1990) (492-6 and essay in *The Role of the Augsburg Confession*, (Philadelphia: Fortress, 1980).
10. "Evangelical Catholicity: Lutheran Identity in an Ecumenical Age," in *The New Church Debate*, 15-38 and *Two Forms of the Ordained Ministry* (Minneapolis: Fortress, 1991).
11. Eugene Brand, *Toward a Lutheran Communion: Pulpit and Altar Fellowship* (Geneva: LWF, 1988); Harding Meyer and Heinz Schütte, "The Concept of the Church in the *Augustana Confession*," *Confessing the Faith* (Minneapolis: Augsburg, 1982) 184-88, Michael Root, et. al., "Communio/Koinonia: A NT/Early Christian Concept and Its Contemporary Appropriation and Significance," and Appendix 3 in William G. Rusch, ed., *Ecumenism: The Vision of the ELCA* (Minneapolis: Augsburg, 1990) 119-153 and "The *Augsburg Confession as Ecumenical Proposal*," *dialog* 1989 (28, 3) 223-32.
12. Karl P. Donfried, "A NT Scholar Looks at the Issue of Ministry," *dialog*, 1988 (27, 1) 8-16; "Implications of the Gospel: Some Hermeneutical and Ecclesiological Queries," *Word and World*, 1990 (10, 1) 70-80; Carl A. Volz, *Faith and Practice in the Early Church* and *Pastoral Life and Practice in the Early Church* (Minneapolis: Augsburg, 1983, 1990).
13. Jared Wicks, S. J., "Holy Spirit — Church — Sanctification: Insights from Luther's Instruction on the Faith," PRO ECCLESIA, 1993 (II, 2) 150-172. Mark Chapman and Leonard Klein, "'Evangelical Catholic' is Lutheran: A Response to Gerhard Forde," *dialog*, 1989 (28, 1) 60; Robert L. Wilken, "The Pastor as Icon," *dialog* 1993 (32, 1) 19-24; Leonard Klein, "If the Ministry is

Catholic: A View from Inside the Parish," *dialog* 1988 (27, 1) 34-39; Scott S. Ickert, "Nein! A Reply to Walter Sundberg," *Lutheran Forum* 1991 (25, 3) 34-38; Martin Heinecken, "Living by the Word of God: A Plea for a Distinctive Lutheran Identity," *Lutheran Partners,* 1990 (6, 5 & 6) 14-23, 18-27; Paul R. Hinlicky, "For the Church, Against the Quotas," Sharon Zanter Ross, "Holy Mother, the Church," and David S. Yeago, "Theological Impasse and Ecclesial Future," *Lutheran Forum* 1992 (26, 4) 64-68, 55-57, 36-45; Michael Plekon, "*Sola Ecclesia*: For the 'Churching' of the Church," and "Saying Yes to the Head and the Body," *Lutheran Forum* 1990 (24, 1) 14-17, 1992 (26, 2) 10-13.

14. Evdokimov, *The Sacrament of Love* (Crestwood, NY: St. Vladimir's Seminary Press, 1974), *The Art of the Icon: A Theology of Beauty,* (Redondo Beach, CA: Oakwood, 1990), *The Struggle with God* (Ramsey, NJ: Paulist, 1968); Vladimir Lossky, *The Mystical Theology of the Eastern Church, In the Image and Likeness of God* (Crestwood, NY: St. Vladimir's Seminary Press, 1976, 1974); John Zizioulis *Being as Communion,* (Crestwood, NY: St. Vladimir's Seminary Press, 1985); J.–M. R. Tillard, *Church of Churches* (Collegeville, MN: Michael Glazier/Liturgical Press, 1992); Avery Dulles, *Models of the Church* (NY: Doubleday/Image, 1987, expanded edition); Yves Congar, *The Mystery of the Church* (Baltimore: Helicon, 1961) and *The Church That I Love* (Denville, NJ: Dimension, 1969); Louis Bouyer, *Liturgical Piety* (South Bend, IN: University of Notre Dame, 1955).

15. See *Eucharist and Ministry: Lutherans and Catholics in Dialogue* IV, Paul C. Empie and T. Austin Murphy, eds., (Minneapolis: Augsburg, 1979) 36-43.

16. See *Eucharist and Ministry,* 101-19, 209-26; *Lutherans and Catholics in Dialogue* I-III, Paul C. Empie and T. Austin Murphy, eds., (Minneapolis: Augsburg, 1967) 125-47. Also see his "The Survival of the Historic Vestments in the Lutheran Church after 1555," Graduate Study No. 1 (St. Louis: Concordia Seminary, 1956).

17. From the *Lutheran Book of Worship,* copyright 1978. Collect of Theologians, p. 38.

PART I: THE CHURCH AND HER MINISTRY

WHAT THE SYMBOLS HAVE
TO SAY ABOUT THE CHURCH

It is not difficult to turn to the index of a modern edition of the *Book of Concord* and to discover therein the passages in the Lutheran Symbols which talk more or less explicitly about the church. That it is quite possible to read into these passages a very wide range of presuppositions is clear from the way in which different theologians have been claiming our church's Symbols in support of quite divergent, if not actually contradictory, opinions. But the articles of our creedal statements that the editors have headed, "Of the Church," or that bear similar titles are not all that the *Book of Concord* has to say about the church. In the roughly 250,000 words in the Lutheran Symbols there are about 800 references to "church" or a related term. Many of these are significant, if not decisive, for the construction of an ecclesiology of the Symbols.

It is a sound principle of interpretation that a document should be understood in the sense that the words conveyed to the people by and for whom it was originally written. To this principle the *Formula of Concord* (Ep Summary Concept 8) clearly commits us when it declares that the Creeds and the Fathers are witnesses of the manner in which those who were living at the time understood the Sacred Scriptures concerning the controverted issues. We are to understand and confess the Symbols in their original historic sense — that is, in the sense which the words and terms had when the documents in question were formulated, and not in the sense which some of the words and terms may subsequently have acquired through the dialectic of controversy. Thus we must not read into the Catholic Creeds as pre-Reformation documents the sense with which the Reformers may have invested certain of their terms; similarly we must not read into the particular creeds of the sixteenth century the sense with which subsequent systematizers of Lutheran doctrinal insights invested certain terms. It is worth keeping in mind that the Symbols were all written before 1580 and that the categories of the authors are not necessarily those of the evangelical Scholastics of the next century.

The reader who embarks with us on our quest will search in vain for certain familiar terms and categories in which we have learned to think and to talk systematically about the church. Nowhere do the Symbols describe the church either as *visibilis, sichtlich, sichtbar,* or as *invisibilis, unsichtlich, unsichtbar.* Far less is there an antithesis between a "visible church" and an "invisible church." Again, the reader will not find the *Kirche-Ortsgemeinde* antithesis, nor will he find a church *improprie dicta* opposed to the church *proprie dicta,* for while *proprie dicta* occurs several times, the closest that the Symbols come to the *improprie dicta* of the later dogmaticians is the term *large dicta* which AP X 10 derives from canon law. Furthermore, he will not find the familiar division into the "Church Militant" and the "Church Triumphant;" there is one casual passing reference to an "eternal church (*ewige Kirche*)" in the *Formula of Concord* (SD II 50), but otherwise the only church that the Symbols concern themselves with is the church that exists on earth in time. Again, we do not find "church" used as a synonym of what we mean by "denomination." The *Smalcald Articles* (Part Three VIII 4) speak of "the Pope's Church," but that is an ironical reference; and there is one reference to "our church (*unsere Kirche*)" in the *Formula of Concord* (SD X 3), but this may be an editorial oversight, inasmuch as the official Latin translation tacitly corrects it to "our churches." Another aspect that receives no stress is the description of the church as the bride of Christ — the sole explicit reference, a quite peripheral and unoriginal one, turns up in a collect of the *Traubüchlein* (16), which complete editions of the *Book of Concord* include as an appendix to the *Small Catechism.*

The Symbols come to us out of three clearly defined periods. For our purpose the first period begins in the second century and ends in the eighth. The *terminus a quo* is the remote ancestor of our Baptismal ("Apostles'") and Eucharistic ("Nicene") Creeds which we find in the Ethiopic version of the *Epistula apostolorum;* the *terminus ad quem* is the Bobbio Missal (Saec. VII/VIII) and a manuscript, *De singulis libris canonicis scarapsus* (710-724), of St. Priminius of Reichenau, which are the earliest witnesses to the present — that is to say, the medieval — developed form of the Baptismal Creed. The second era falls into the second quarter of the sixteenth century, from 1528 to 1537; here we shall find it convenient to take up separately the documents that come from the pen of Martin Luther of holy memory — the *Large* and the *Small Catechism* and the *Smalcald Articles* — and those which come predominantly from the pen of Philip Melanchthon — the *Augsburg Confession*, the *Apology*, and the *Tractate on the Authority and Primacy of the Pope*. The third era comes during the seventies of the sixteenth century, 1573 to 1579, and includes the *Epitome* and the *Solid Declaration* of the *Formula of Concord* and the *Preface to the Christian Book of Concord*.

I

A reference to "the holy church" enters the creeds at a very early date. The five-article creed in the Ethiopic version of the *Epistula apostolorum* (dated by scholars between 130 and 170)[1] confesses the Father, the Lord of the whole world, and Jesus Christ, our Savior, and the Holy Ghost the Counselor, and the holy church, and the forgiveness of sins (5). In the early North African baptismal rite between 198 and 200 Tertullian knows a necessary "mention of the Church."[2] The *Church Order* (around 215) of the Roman anti-Pope St. Hippolytus, as reconstructed from the Coptic, Arabic, Ethiopic, and Latin translations of the Greek original, included the question to the candidates for Holy Baptism: "Do you believe in the Holy Ghost in the holy church?"[3] Back in Africa, St. Cyprian of Carthage (died 258) in an undated letter to Januarius interprets the baptismal question thus: "When we say, 'Do you believe in eternal life and remission of sins through the holy church?' we mean that forgiveness of sins is not granted except in the church."[4] The creed of Marcellus of Ancyra (*Ankara*), set forth in the letter that he wrote to Julius of Rome in 341, reads at this point: "And in the Holy Ghost, holy church, forgiveness of sins, resurrection of flesh, life eternal."[5]

The present Baptismal Creed of the Western Church is immediately of Old Gallican origin, but it draws — so it would seem — rather heavily on Eastern sources. Thus the earliest form of the "Apostles' Creed" which contains the words *sanctam ecclesiam catholicam* is that which we can reconstruct from the *Competentibus ad baptismum instructionis libellus quintus de symbolo* (about 400) of Bishop Niceta(s) of Remesiana (Bela Palanka).[6]

In the creeds εκκλησια designates the church that adhered to the Apostolic tradition and traced its history genetically back to the holy Apostles, in contrast to the upstart heretical sects that claimed to possess the "correct" (that is, untraditional) interpretation of the written Scriptures. In the Creeds the term likewise designated the church in contrast to the sects that under Pneumatic and Enthusiastic leadership schismatically separated themselves from the church in their revolt against the sometimes less than morally perfect organizational administration.

The εκκλησια is the New Testament counterpart, the heir, and the fulfillment of the Old Testament *kahal* which the Septuagint versions renders εκκλησια. It is the church being realized *in acts* in worship, especially in Eucharistic worship. Since εκκλησια is a ready-made designation in Koine Greek (where it designates any kind of assembly) and in the LXX (where it designates both an assembly and the *Kultgemeinde*), catechists and preachers ought not to stress the etymology from εκ and καλεω, making εκκλησιζ identify a company of people called out from the *massa perdita* of the sinful world.

One of the prophetic Old Testament predicates of the New Testament church is holiness. St. Paul — following Old Testament precedent — calls the Christans αγιοι, often in a technical sense where the term is about the equivalent of "church members." The term survived in this sense for about a century, when it became ossified in a few formulas, like τα αγια τοιζ αγιοιζ in the Eastern Orthodox liturgy, until the Reformation, "saint" being reserved as a title for individuals of heroic virtue. The term αγια εκκλησια turns up for the first time in the title of the Letter of St. Ignatius of Antioch (died 117) to the Trallians, in the *Shepherd* of Hermas (Vision I, i, 6; I, iii, 4), which was written between 96 and 150, and in the title of the *Martyrdom of St. Polycarp of Smyrna* (156). In the creed the term is linked in the commentaries with the remission of sins on the one hand, while on the other it almost becomes a synonym for "Catholic." Thus the *Explanatio symboli ad initiandos*, a set of notes based on an extemporaneous instruction which St. Ambrose of Milan (333?-397) gave to candidates for Holy Baptism when they were having the actual text of the Baptismal Creed imparted to them, has this: "In *holy Church* and in *forgiveness of sins:* Believe therefore with faith that all your sins are forgiven. Why? You have read in the Gospel that the Lord says: 'Thy faith hath made thee whole'"(9).[7] On the other hand, St. Cyril had pointed out in his *Catechetical Lectures* (347/348) that the word εκκλησια can mean any kind of assembly and that therefore the term "holy" has been prefixed to differentiate the Catholic Church from "the meetings of the heretics, the Marcionites, and the Manichaeans."[8] In the same vein, St. Augustine has this comment on the words "holy church" in *De fide et symbolo* (393): "Unless the Christian Faith gather men together into a society in which brotherly love can operate, it remains less fruitful. Hence we believe *the holy church*, that is to say, *the Catholic Church*. Heretics and schismatics also call their congregations churches. But heretics do violence to the Faith by holding false opinions about God; and schismatics, although they believe as we believe, have broken away from brotherly love by wicked separations. Wherefore heretics do not belong to the Catholic Church which loves God; nor do schismatics, for the church loves it neighbor, and easily forgives his sins because it prays to be forgiven by Him who has reconciled us to Himself, blotting out all past transgressions and recalling us to new life."[9] A decade later Rufinus of Aquileia in his *Commentarius in symbolum apostolorum* (about 404) expands St. Cyril's references with additional specifications, interpreting the words "holy church" to require belief "in the existence of one holy church, that is, a church in which there is one Faith and one Baptism, and in which we believe in one God the Father, one Lord Jesus Christ, His Son, and one Holy Ghost," a church which is "without spot or wrinkle of treachery," and therefore different from the "churches" — actually "congregations of the malignant" — formed by Marcion, Valentinus, "Ebion," Mani, Arius, Paul of Samosata, Photinus, Eunomius, Donatus, Novatus, "and the rest of the heretics."[10]

The church is first called "Catholic" in St. Ignatius' Letter to the Smyrnaeans (8,2) — "wherever Jesus Christ is, there is the Catholic Church" — and in the *Martyrdom of St. Polycarp*, which is addressed to "the parishes of the Holy and Catholic Church everywhere" and which refers to the "Catholic Church throughout the inhabited (world)" (8, 1; 19, 2). In Latin we find the term in *Muratorian Fragment* (3) from the second or third century and in Tertullian (155?-222?). The term begins its development by being purely descriptive. *The* church exists wherever *a* church exists; the Catholic Church is the sum total of all the Christian communities and nothing more. By the end of the second century, however, the emphasis has begun to shift, and the additional connotation of "orthodox" has come to associate itself with the term "Catholic" over against the localized heretical aberrations. "Catholicity" next comes to be regarded as a necessary attribute of the church; as the church spreads out over the Mediterranean world and past its borders, this is looked upon as the expression of an inevitable destiny, and the universality of the church in subsequent decades is elaborated to cover not only geographical, political, and ethnic extension but also social comprehensiveness and the scope of the sins which the church condemns, remedies, and forgives.

From pre-Reformation times until the end of the nineteenth century, Western Christendom — including the authors of the Lutheran particular symbols — held that the Baptismal Creed described the church as a *sanctorum communio*. While interpretations differed in detail, *sanctorum* was consistently taken as a masculine and *communio* received a predominantly corporative interpretation. The evidence that has accumulated during the last two generations seems, however, to indicate the possibility that: (1) *sanctorum communio* was not originally an apposition to *sancta ecclesia catholica*, but a separate article of the creed; (2) *sanctorum* is not masculine, but neuter, and hence to be translated not "saints," but "holy things," that is, either the Holy Eucharist or the sacraments in general; (3) *communio* does not mean "communion with the saints" not does it designate a society or community, but it refers (like "one baptism for the remission of sins" in the

Eucharistic Creed) to the benefits that God confers upon those who participate in the Holy Eucharist (or the Sacraments generally).[11]

Ultimately, while to this writer the evidence for "communion of holy things" seems to be much stronger than the evidence for "communion of saints," both interpretations come out not too far apart. Even those who defend the latter interpretation must concede that "it can scarcely be doubted the *Communion of Saints* means much more than 'Church' in the creeds."[12] However the term is explained, *communio* must be taken in a dynamic rather than a static sense. It is a sharing, a taking part with other Christians, in the holy things that make them one, rather than a mere abstract being in association with other individuals. It is logically possible to think of the church as it is in an infinitesimally small moment of time. Theologically and actually it is not possible to do so. For in the church we live, we are part of a process, we are being justified before God by God; there is a constant forgiveness of the sins that we — who are simultaneously sinners and holy people — are constantly committing, and we who are being constantly *declared* holy by God's grace for Christ's sake through faith are constantly *becoming* holier by God's grace for Christ's sake through faith.

The "Nicene" Creed in the form in which we use it before the altar adds two other predicates of the church, "unity" and "apostolicity." The original Nicene Creed of 325 — based in turn upon an earlier baptismal confession — ended: "And in the Holy Ghost." This implied no lack of awareness of the church, for the Creed as received the Council of Nicaea added this damnatory clause: "The Catholic Church anathematizes those who say that there was a time when the Son of God was not, and that before He was begotten He was not, and that He came into being out of the things that are not, or who affirm that He is of a different υποστασιζ or ουσια or is created or changeable or alterable."

Whether the "*Nicaenoconstantinopolitanum*" stems from the Council of Constantinople of 381 or not is immaterial for our purpose. It was officially adopted by the Council of Chalcedon in 451 in substantially its present form, including the affirmation of faith in "one, holy, Catholic, Apostolic Church."

The "Nicene" Creed thus affirms the substantial unity of Christendom. This, it should be noted, is not an administrative or organizational unity, which the church of that time did not know except on a regional basis, but a unity of Sacraments, of worship, and of confession. All Christian churches had the same Eucharist, the same Baptism, the same system of discipline, the same ministry, the same Scriptures, the same Canon of Truth, the same tradition, and in these they had access to the same Christ, the same Holy Ghost, the same Father. The unity was not created by men — although churches and individuals could recede from it by schism, heresy, infidelity, and apostasy. The unity of the church was a *datum*, something given by God.

The apostolicity of the church was likewise an affirmation of the church's historic character. Actually it was a commitment to the Apostolic ministry, not in the sense of a theory of Apostolic succession through an unbroken chain of episcopal consecrations, but in the sense of a traceable linkage of ministerial tradition to a church founded by one of the Apostles. This served as at least a partial guarantee of the authenticity of the message proclaimed in the church, in contradistinction to the upstart schisms and heresies that adulterated the Christian message with human additions sanctified by the judicious citation of Scripture texts. The *purpose* of this commitment was the conservation of the Apostolic message and the Sacraments, although the *accent* was upon the sacred ministry as a means to this purpose, an accent that we find recurring in Article V of the *Augsburg Confession*. It remained for a later generation to transform the sacred ministry from a means into an end and to cite the Fathers of this period in a sense which they did not intend. At the same time, "apostolicity" is an empirical characteristic of the church.

Thus the Baptismal and the Eucharistic Creeds agree in their conception of a dynamic church which is simultaneously on the one hand empirical and phenomenal, perceptible with the bodily senses, and on the other hand spiritual, perceptible only in its effects.

This is likewise the conception of the Church Fathers of this period — including such significant contributors to developing ecclesiology as St. Cyprian of Carthage and St. Augustine of Hippo. The church which they envision falls into none of the neat categories that modern denominational ecclesiologists have constructed. It is a church that meets for instruction, for worship, for witness, for the administration of Holy Baptism, for the celebration of the Holy Eucharist, and for the exercise of church discipline. It is an organized church, with metropolitans and bishops and synods and priests and deacons and lesser orders of clergy from subdeacons to porters, and a laity. It is a historical church, with both an oral and a written doctrinal tradition going back to the holy Apostles, a rule of faith, a pattern of worship, a history of martyrs and confessors, and a growing body of theological literature. At the same time it is a supernatural, spiritual phenomenon, a breaching of the prison of time by the eternal Spirit of God, a living body of true believers, the mother of all the faithful. Its priests and bishops can justify their official status only by the faith of their hearts, the holiness of their lives, and the wisdom of their words; and the truth of their teaching can be tested by its congruence with the prophetic and apostolic Scriptures, understood as the church has always understood them.

The significant thing for us is that at this period the church senses no contradiction in the assertion of these at least paradoxical descriptions of herself, and almost any Church Father who discusses the topic at all can be quoted with apparent conclusiveness on behalf of either point of view by anyone who selects his evidence carefully enough.

II

The documents from the second period, from 1528–1536-37, which come from the pen of blessed Martin Luther, are all in German.

The plural *Kirchen*, where it stands by itself, usually means church buildings. *Unsere Kirchen* in the Introduction to the *Smalcald Articles* means ecclesiastical administrative units, which may range in size from a parish to a provincial or territorial church. In the *Smalcald Articles* (Part Two IV 4) *Kirchen* refers to other national churches: "The churches of the Greek and many other languages ... to this day have never been under the Pope."

The church is never described as *katholisch* in these documents, although in authorizing Bugenhagen to sign for him Brenz states that in his opinion the *Smalcald Articles* agree "with the conviction of the true and genuine Catholic Church." Here "Catholic Church" is the empirical, confessing church. In lieu of *katholische Kirche* we once find *ganze, heilige, christliche Kirche* (SA-II IV 3), when the Pope is accused of endeavoring to corrupt by every means at his disposal the whole, holy, Christian Church. *Heilige, christliche Kirche* occurs more frequently. The *Small Catechism* simply translates the Latin of the Apostles' Creed: *Ein heilige christliche Kirche, die Gemeine der Heiligen.* No deliberate alteration of meaning underlies the rendering of *catholicam* with *christliche*, and Luther, who is trying to avoid the use of foreign loan words as much as possible, had good fifteenth-century vernacular precedent. The official Latin version of the Creeds and the cathechisms retained *catholicam*, and so have a number of vernacular versions, including the Swedish (*allmännelig*). In teaching the *Catechism* we should therefore be careful not to suggest that the "holy Christian Church" is in any sense less empirical that the *sancta ecclesia catholica*, or that Lutherans regard the holy Christian Church as being less "Catholic" than other Christians do, or that the rest of Christendom regards the "Catholic Church" as less Christian than we do. If we use the concept *una sancta* as the designation for some kind of nonempirical church that can *only* be believed in and that has no tangible reality, we should realize that this is a systematic construct and that the church which the framers of both the Baptismal and the Eucharistic Creeds confessed is a church that is not only one and holy but also Catholic, and therefore empirical. The translation *Gemeine der Heiligen* goes back in the vernacular to Carolingian times.

The *Large Catechism* also refers in the Creed to *eine heilige christliche Kirche*, but uses another word in the apposition, *Gemeinschaft der Heiligen*. "A holy Christian Church" in three cases is a quotation of the Creed; one case is of particular interest because it affirms a relationship between the church and the Sacrament of the Altar: "Now the whole Gospel and the Article of the Creed, 'I believe a holy Christian Church, forgiveness of sins, etc.,' is put by the Word into this Sacrament and placed before us" (LC V 32). "The holy Christian Church" will not be destroyed as long as the world lasts (LC IV 50). It can well remain without a visible head and would probably have been better off so, had not such a head been created by the devil (SA-II IV 5).

Christliche Kirche alone occurs some eight times. Individual absolution is an office of the Christian Church (SA-III VIII 2). According to the *Taufbüchlein*, the Christian Church carries the little child to Holy Baptism, confesses before God that the child is possessed by the devil and is a child of sin and disgrace, and prays diligently for help and grace that through Baptism it may become a child of God (2). The Holy Ghost makes us holy through the Christian Church, the forgiveness of sins, the resurrection of the flesh, and everlasting life (LC II 40,41). The Papacy — not to be equated with the church which acknowledged the primacy of the Pope — is not a Christian Church; where Christ is proclaimed, there the Spirit makes, calls, and brings together the Christian Church, outside which no one can come to the Lord Jesus (LC II 44, 45). The apposition, *sanctorum communionem,* was added, in Luther's opinion, to indicate what "the Christian Church" is (LC II 49), cf. 37); he thus thinks of it as a post-Apostolic intercalation, a conviction in which the omission of the phrase in the *Commentarius* of Rufinus confirmed him.[13] It may be noted here that in the thinking of the Middle Ages *sanctorum communio* meant variously the communion of the Holy Sacraments of the church which the saints enjoyed (St. Ivo of Chartres;[14] Peter Abelard[15]), a sharing of the benefits of the departed saints with the others of the faithful who with the saints form one body (St. Thomas Aquinas, *Expositio super symbolum apostolorum*[16]), or the church as a corporate society (Amalarius of Trèves;[17] Magnus of Sens[18]). For Luther it is the community of holy ones in Christ characterized by, and realized in, mutual participation and self-giving. The element of faith is involved in as far as we must believe, sometimes in the face of apparently contradictory evidence, that the church with which we come into contact is one and holy and Catholic and Apostolic. The Holy Ghost creates holiness in us through the Word of God in the *Vereinigung* of the Christian Church (LC II 54). He initiates holiness on earth and increases it daily through these two things, the Christian Church and the forgiveness of sins; after we are dead, He will complete it in the twinkling of an eye and evermore preserve us through the two last things, the resurrection of the body and the life everlasting (LC II 59).

"Holy Church" occurs once: The holy church has obviously existed without a Pope for over 500 years at least. This reflects Luther's conviction that St. Gregory the Great was the last Bishop of Rome and Sabinian and Boniface III, St. Gregory's immediate successors, the first Popes.[19]

A synonym for "church" is *Christenheit*, with Luther in *Von den Konziliis und Kirchen* (1539) proposed as a substitute translation — along with *christlich Volk* — for the "un-German" and "blind" word *Kirche*.[20] In the *Large Catechism* he suggests that *Kirche* could best be rendered by *eine heilige Christenheit* (II 48). He also uses *Christenheit* as a synonym for *Gemeine* (with which he regularly reproduces the Greek εκκλησια in his German Bible), the holy community by which the Holy Ghost until the Last Day brings us to Himself and which He uses to exercise the Word, by which He creates and increases holiness (II 53). In Christendom everything is so ordered that we may there daily receive sheer forgiveness of sins through the Word and the signs, to comfort our conscience and to hold it upright as long as we live here. Our sins cannot harm us in Christendom, where there is sheer forgiveness of sins, both in the sense that God forgives us and in the sense that we mutually forgive, bear with, and raise up one another. But outside Christendom, where the Gospel is not, there is no forgiveness, just as there can be no holiness there (II 55,56). God has not yet brought His whole Christendom together nor has He fully distributed His forgiveness (II 61,62). Those who are outside Christendom, whether they be pagans, Turks, Jews, or false Christians and hypocrites, even though they believed in and adored but one true God, nevertheless do not know how God is minded toward them, cannot promise themselves either love or anything good from Him, and hence remain under eternal wrath and condemnation, for they have not the Lord Christ (II 66).

Since we do not know which of our fellow Christians are false Christians or hypocrites and which are true believers, the Christian must necessarily seek Christendom in the empirical church. This is borne out by the fact that we enter Christendom through Baptism (LC IV 81,87). Christian education of the young preserves God's Word and Christendom (V 86). Intolerable burdens and loads have been laid on Christendom (*Kurze Vermahnung zu der Beicht* 1).[21] Christ has put holy absolution into the mouth of His Christendom (14). Where we have "Christian Church" in the explanation of the Third Article in the *Small Catechism*, the original has *Christenheit*: "Just as He calls, gathers, enlightens, and hallows the whole of Christendom on earth and keeps it with Jesus Christ in the right and only faith, in which Christendom He daily forgives all sins liberally to me and all the faithful" (SC II 5). The *Taufbüchlein* prays that the candidate, having been separated from the number of the unbelieving, may be preserved dry and safe in the holy ark of Christendom (14). The Pope is not by divine right the head of all Christendom (SA-II IV 1); before the rise of the Papacy the bishops of all Christendom, like the Apostles before them, ruled the church jointly (SA-II IV 9).

Kirche by itself occurs rarely in the *Catechisms*, more frequently, in the *Smalcald Articles*. In the former it often refers to the church building (LC I 90; II 48; III 7; *Traubüchlein* 1,2,6). Luther wants to derive *Kirche* from the Greek κυρια, a false etymology (LC II 48). *Kirche* — that is, the Biblical εκκλησια means an ordinary assembly and ought to be specified as a Christian community or holy Christendom (*ibid*). The Holy Ghost accomplishes our sanctification through the community of saints or Christian Church, the forgiveness of sins, the resurrection of the flesh, and eternal life, by first of all leading us into His holy community and depositing us in the womb (*Schoss*) of the church, through which He preaches to us and brings us to Christ (LC II 37).

In the introduction to the *Smalcald Articles* a French visitor is described as having expected to find among the Lutherans of Wittenberg no church, no government, no marriage (*Bekenntnisschriften*, p. 411, line 4). We cannot carry out all the injunctions God has given us in the church, in government and in the home (p. 413, line 15). Holy Communion is the common Sacrament of the church, which no individual ought to use for his private devotion and play with at his own pleasure outside the fellowship of the church (SA-II II 9). (This is the famous passage which rejects the pretense that private Masses are justified because they give the celebrant an opportunity to receive the blessed Sacrament; it would thus seem that in Luther's mind the fellowship of the church is most fully realized when the Christian community celebrates the Holy Eucharist.) The Pope is the bishop or rector only of the church at Rome (SA-II IV 1). The Papacy exercises no useful function in the church, and the church must remain and exist even without the Pope (SA-II IV 6). *Kirche* is sometimes an administrative subdivision of the Catholic Church (SA-II IV 8,9; X 3). Yet it also designates the Catholic Church as such. Thus the church is best governed when we all live under Christ and the bishops keep diligently together in harmonious teaching, faith, Sacraments, prayer, works of charity, and so forth (SA-II IV 9). The Pope let himself be hailed as Lord of the Church (SA-II IV 13). He came to the aid of the poor church by inventing indulgences (SA-II IV 24); the irony is even heavier when Luther declares that what the Pope and his church decided and pronounced was to be regarded as Spirit and right (SA-III VIII 4). The church baptizes (SA-III V 4) and exercises the Office of the Keys (SA-III VII 1). Under no circumstances (*beileibe nicht*) must confession or absolution disappear from her midst (SA-III VIII 1). True Christian excommunication involves not admitting manifest and obstinate sinners to the Sacrament of the Altar or other communion with the church (SA-III IX). Even though papal bishops will not teach, baptize, administer the Holy Communion, or perform a single work or office of the church, and persecute those called to these offices, the church must not remain without clergy (SA-III X 2).

The title of *Smalcald Articles*, Part Three, Article XII reads: "Of the Church." In the article occurs the famous manifesto: "We do not concede that {the Papalist adversaries} are *the* church, and indeed they are not." The antithesis must be kept in mind. The adversaries profess to be *the* church and condemn as heretics all those not in communion with the Pope. That overweeningly proud insistence is here rejected categorically. By the same token, "we shall not listen to what they command or prohibit in the name of the church." It is in the context of this antithesis that the following statement must be interpreted: "A child of seven years" — the canonical minimum age of reason — "knows what the church is, namely, the holy believers and the 'lambs that hear the voice of their Shepherd.'" This is clearly not an exhaustive definition of the church; the sense of Luther's declaration is that the church is conditioned by adherence, not to the Roman See but to Christ.

An equivalent of *sanctorum communio* occurs only in the *Catechisms*, usually as quotations from the Baptismal Creed (SC II; *Taufbüchlein* 25; LC Second Introduction 13; II 47, 49). It is once equated with the Christian Church" (LC II 37), once described as a gloss or commentary on "the Christian Church" (II 49).

The documents under consideration do not explicitly relate the kingdom of God — about which they have much to say — to the church. Taking the statements about the kingdom of God or of Christ in these documents together (notably SC Introduction 23; II4; III 7,11; LC II 24, 30, 31; III 51, 53, 54), we can summarize thus: The kingdom of God is more inclusive than the church, because while the church exists in time, the kingdom of God is eternal. The church is the eschatological kingdom of God in its temporal aspect, but the line that divides the kingdom of God from the kingdom of Satan cuts across the church and even across the individual believer. It is to *Christians* that Luther says: "Thus you are still every day in the midst of the kingdom of the devil (*unter des Teufels Reich*), who does not rest day or night to catch you unawares, so that he can kindle unbelief and evil thoughts in your heart against ... all the commandments of God" (LC I 101). In its essence our flesh is lazy and inclined to evil, even though we have accepted God's Word and believe (LC III 63).

For the unity of the church the reference in *Smalcald Articles*, Part One, to the Lutherans and the Romanist party as *wir zu beiden Teilen* may be significant. Of the church's holiness the *Smalcald Articles* say that it depends not on vestments or humanly instituted ceremonies but that it consists "in the Word of God and the true faith" (SA-III XIII).

As we have seen, we initially enter the church, that is, Christendom, by Baptism (LC IV 2, 81); without Baptism and the Holy Eucharist there can be no Christian (LC IV 1). By the same token, we must be baptized, or we cannot be saved (LC IV 6). The survival of the church through the centuries is evidence that infant Baptism is pleasing to God; by way of example Luther cites Saint Bernard of Clairvaux from the eleventh century and Jean Charlier de Gerson and St. John Hus from the fourteenth (LC IV 50). Denial of the effectiveness or validity of infant Baptism overthrows the article: "I believe a holy Christian Church, the community of the saints, and so forth" (LC IV 51). Because children have been baptized and received into Christendom, they should also participate in the fellowship of the altar (LC V 87). The minimum requirement for admission to the blessed Sacrament in the sixteenth century was to have achieved the use of reason and to have an intelligent mastery of the text of the Decalog, the Creed, the Our Father, and the words of institution of Holy Baptism and Holy Communion, without formal explanations (SC Introduction 7-11). In practice, the Lutheran Reformers admitted children to their first Holy Communion at between seven and twelve years of age.[22]

The Church — *der gemeine Christenstand* (LC I 197) — consists of "preachers and Christians" (LC I 262); rector (*Pfarrherr*) and parishioners (*Pfarrkinder*) (LC Introduction 3); rector and people (SC Introduction 6); bishops, rectors, and preachers on the one hand and hearers on the other (SC Table of Duties). "Rector" is used even of the Pope as Bishop of Rome (SA-II IV 1). Our translation of *Pfarrer* as "pastor" betrays a subtle shift of emphasis away from the concepts of the *Book of Concord*. "Bishop" and pastor are equated (*Traubüchlein* 5), reflecting Luther's acceptance of the patristic doctine that originally priests and bishops constituted a single divine order (SA-III XI 1), which was later differentiated by human authority, and also reflecting his conviction that a parish with a pastor, one or more curates, and one or more congregations constituted an ecclesiastical unit. *Pfarrkinder* has as its correlative the spiritual fatherhood of the clergy, and the *Large Catechism* teaches that they who rule and preside over us through the Word of God are properly called spiritual fathers (I 158). Parochial jurisdiction is necessary and (divinely) commanded (SA-II III 18).

Luther always preferred the concrete to the abstract term. Hence he never wholly reconciled himself to *Gemeinschaft der Heiligen* and retained it in the *Large Catechism* only because people scent heresy when a word is changed in a familiar formula; he prefers *Gemeine der Heiligen*, a community in which there are altogether holy people, or, even more clearly, "a holy community" (LC II 49, 50). *Gemeine* is often synonymous with church (II 48), or Christendom (II 52: *Gemeine oder Christenheit*). When we commit ourselves to the *sanctorum communio*, we say in effect: "I believe that there is a holy little group and community of altogether holy people on earth, under one Head, Christ, called together by the Holy Ghost in one faith, sense and meaning, with manifold gifts, but harmonious in love, without divisions or schisms; of that community I am a part and a member, a partaker and associate of all the gifts it possesses, brought thither by the Holy Ghost and incorporated in it by having heard and by still hearing God's Word" (II 51, 52). The Holy Ghost carries on His work unceasingly until the Last Day; for that work He has ordered a community on earth through which He says and does everything (II 61).

In words reminiscent of St. Cyprian's dictum, "No man can have God for his Father in heaven who has not the church as his mother on earth," Luther describes the Holy Ghost's special community in the world as the mother who conceives and bears every Christian through the Word of God (II 42).

The imparting of the grace of God is not the responsibility only of the sacred ministry; the Gospel gives us counsel and aid against sin through the mutual conversation and consolation of brethren, as our Lord says in St. Matthew 18, "Where two or three are gathered together, and so forth" (SA-III IV).

In one crucial place the *Large Catechism* takes εκκλησια in a neutral sense. In interpreting the so-called stages of admonition, it declares that if the first two steps accomplish nothing, the plaintiff should take the case before the community, that is, either a secular or spiritual court (LC I 280). This has a significant bearing on the relevance of this passage to excommunication.

Two classes of people have severed themselves from the communion of the church: Those who have refused to make use of the means of grace — the sacred ministry of the Word, the Sacrament of Holy Communion, and holy absolution — and those who want to look for an obtain holiness not through the Gospel and the forgiveness of sins, but through their own works (LC II 56).

Summarizing: in the Symbols from Luther's pen we find ascribed to the church such a variety of attributes and activities that we cannot define the church either wholly in empirical terms or wholly in spiritual terms; both descriptions are correct, but neither must be affirmed in such a way that it excludes the other.

III

When we turn to the Symbols composed by Philip Melanchthon, a problem arises in the *Augsburg Confession*; here both the German and the Latin versions are equally authoritative, but frequently the plural of the one version corresponds to a singular in the other. Thus the marriage of priests would not seem to be disadvantageous to the churches (AC XXIII 17 Latin); the German has *gemeine christliche Kirche*. Burdens are laid on the churches (AC XXVIII 42); the

German has *die Christenheit*. The right kind of ordinances are appropriate for churches (AC XXVIII 55); the German has *die christliche Versamblung*. There is to be no disorder in the churches (*ibid.*); the German has *Kirche* (compare likewise the Latin and German in AC XXVIII 28,42).

"Churches" and "church" are also interchangeable in the *Apology*, Article XXIV, 44-51; the adversaries regard decorated altars, candles, and statues as ornaments of the churches, but the true ornament of the church does not consist of candles, golden vessels and similar ornaments — appropriate as they are — but pious, useful, and clear instruction, the devout use of the Sacraments, ardent worship and such things.

"Churches" sometimes means national or provincial churches (*Tractate* 12). Sometimes "churches" means the lay congregations as distinguished from the clergy (Ap IV 243). Over against the bishops, "churches" means the parishes with their clergy and lay congregations (AC XXVIII 22; compare both German and Latin). When the canonical bishops are enemies of the Gospel, the churches retain the right to call, elect, and ordain (*Tractate* 66), and they are forced with the participation of their own pastors (*adhibitis suis pastoribus*) to ordain pastors and ministers (72). The churches in the territories of the Smalcald League have cause enough why they will not acknowledge the papal ordinaries as their bishops (*Tractate* 79). The Council of Nicaea decreed that the bishops should be elected by their churches (*Tractate* 13), in contrast to the Pope's insistence in the sixteenth century that he alone could appoint bishops (*ibid.*). Again, it was anciently decreed that one bishop should ordain the ministers in many churches (*Tractate* 64). The impious Romanist bishops misuse the relief funds of the churches; thereby they defraud the church (*Tractate* 83).

"Our churches" is a common self-designation of the evangelical party. Of special interest is the statement: "In our churches there are no Anabaptists," where "churches" is equivalent to "geographical parishes" (Ap IX 2).

We find references to the "Roman Church," that is, the Western Church (AC *Epilog* to XXI; Ap. X 2), the "Latin" Churches (Ap XXII 4; *Tractate* 14, 15); the "West" (*Tractate* 14); the "East" (*Tractate* 12, 16); the "Greek," that is, the Eastern Church (Ap X 2), as well as to its national churches (Ap XXII 4; *Tractate* 15) and parishes (Ap XXIV 6). There is also a reference to the "Roman establishment" (*status Romanus*) (Ap XII 126).

The logical opposite of the territorial church is the Catholic Church. The Lutherans depart in their teaching in no way from the Catholic Church or even from the Roman Church (AC *Epilog* to XXI) — the conjunction of Catholic and Roman in contrast significantly identifies the Catholic Church as the totality of organized Christendom, with the Roman-Western Church a part thereof. The Lutherans dissent in no article of faith from the Catholic Church (AC *Preface* to XXII); in teaching, in dogmas, and even in ceremonies they receive nothing contrary to the Catholic Church (AC *Epilog* to XXVIII 5). The papalist bishops ought to rescind regulations contrary to the custom of the Catholic Church (AC XXVIII 72). In all these cases the German has *gemeine christliche Kirche;* in the second last case, the *editio princeps* had *heilige gemeine und catholica christliche Kirche* (*Bekenntnisschriften*, p. 136, line 19).

In the controversial doctrine of original sin the *Apology* stipulates that its opinion is not alien either to the Sacred Scriptures or the Catholic Church (II 32), or, more explicitly, Christ's Catholic Church (51). Similarly, the Lutherans' custom of holding on every holy day one common or public Mass, at which not only the celebrant but also members of the worshiping congregation receive the blessed Sacrament, is nothing against the Catholic Church (XXIV 6).

It is in the light of all these passages that we must interpret *Apology*, Article VII, 10: "The Creed says 'Catholic Church,' lest we understand the matter as if the church were an external political organization of certain people, rather than people scattered through the whole world, who agree with reference to the Gospel and have the same Christ, the same Holy Ghost, and the same Sacraments."

The Creed requires us to believe that there is a holy Catholic Church, but the impious are certainly not a holy church. The apposition that follows, *sanctorum communio*, is to be regarded as explaining what "church" signifies, namely, an assembly of holy people who have among themselves an association (*societatem*) of the same Gospel or the same teaching and the same Holy Ghost who renews, hallows, and governs their hearts (Ap VII 7).

In place of "Catholic" the *Apology* sometimes uses "Universal." The Lutheran teaching on justification before God by faith agrees with the Sacred Scriptures, the holy Church Fathers, and the Universal (*universa*) Church of Christ (IV 389). The Lutheran teaching on repentance affirms things true, pious, salutary, and necessary to the Universal (*universa*) Church of Christ (XII 3). The Lutheran teaching on good works contains comfort for the Universal Church (XX 9). Lutherans concede that the saints on earth pray for the Universal Church in general, and so do the saints in heaven, among them the blessed Virgin Mary (XXI 9, 10, 27). The consensus of the Prophets must be adjudged the consensus of the Universal (*universalis*) Church, and we concede neither to the Pope nor to the church the authority to contravene this prophetic consensus (XII 66).

Tota ecclesia may mean the same as *catholica* or *universa(lis) ecclesia*, although in this case the time aspect is more prominent. The whole church contradicts the adversaries when they say that the tinder (*fomes*) of original sin is a neutral thing (Ap II 42). The whole church asserts that we cannot satisfy the Law (Ap IV 66). The whole church confesses that eternal life is given by mercy, and by way of evidence St. Augustine, St. Cyprian, and the fathers are appealed to (Ap IV 322). On justification before God by faith (Ap IV 338; XXVII 13) and on the real presence of Christ's body and blood in the Holy Eucharist (Ap X 4), the Lutheran teaching is that of the whole church, in proof of which both Western and Eastern authorities are appealed to in the latter instance. The whole church throughout Europe knows what snares the Constitution *Omnis utriusque sexus* has laid for consciences (Ap XI 7). The Pope cannot by divine right be over the whole church, because the church — that is, the part represented in the College of Cardinals — elects him (*Tractate* 20), although he asserts his judgment ahead of that of the councils and the whole church (40).

In *Apology*, Article XXII, however, *tota ecclesia* means all orders in the church in contrast to a part of them. Christ instituted both parts of the blessed Sacrament not for part of the church — the presbyters alone — but for the whole church (1, 2, 4).

In the German *Augsburg Confession christliche Kirche* usually corresponds to the simple Latin *ecclesia*. The imperial invitation to the Diet of Augsburg in 1530 expressed the hope that as the whole empire is under one Christ, its member estates might once more live in "one association, church, and unity," as the German put it, or "in one *ecclesia Christiana*, unity, and concord," according to the Latin (AC Introduction 4). Thus, too, the German of Articles VII and VIII reads:

> It is also taught that there must at all times be and remain a holy Christian Church, which is the assembly of all the faithful among whom the Gospel is preached in purity and the Holy Sacraments are administered in accordance with the Gospel. For this is enough for the true unity of the Christian Church, that therein the Gospel is preached according to a pure understanding and the Sacraments are administered in accordance with the divine Word. And it is not necessary for the true unity of the Christian Church that humanly instituted ceremonies by everywhere uniformly carried out, as St. Paul says to the Ephesians in the fourth chapter: "One body, one Spirit, as you have been called to one hope of your calling, one Lord, one faith, one Baptism."
> Likewise, although strictly the Christian Church is nothing else than the assembly of all the faithful and the holy people, nevertheless, because in this life many false Christians and hypocrites remain among the pious, the Sacraments are uniformly efficacious, even though the priests through whom the are administered are not pious, as Christ Himself says: "The Pharisees sit on the seat of Moses and so forth" (AC VII 1 through VIII 2, German).

"Christian Church" describes the historic church, in which the priests were married (AC XXIII 10, German; the Latin reads "ancient church"); which profited by the skills and knowledge imparted in the monastic schools (AC XXVII 15, German); which the teaching about monastic perfection has scandalized (AC XXVII 48); in which justification before God by faith ought to be taught (*ibid.*); which has ordained Sunday for corporate worship (AC XXVIII 60); and the unity of which is not impaired by changes in human ordinances (AC XXVIII 74). The corresponding Latin portions all read merely *ecclesia*.

"Church of Christ" occurs frequently in the *Apology*. Sectaries who hold a doctrine of God other than that of the Sacred Scriptures and Nicene orthodoxy are outside the church of Christ (I 2). It must retain the Gospel (IV 120, 400; XX 44). It must not neglect the doctrine of justification before God by faith (Ap IV 377, 389). Christ, the Prophets, and the Apostles define it differently from the kingdom of the Pope (VII 27). Membership in it does not depend on national styles of dress (VII 34). Unbaptized children are outside of it; outside of it, too, there are neither Word nor Sacraments, because Christ gives rebirth through the Word and Sacraments (Ap IX 2). It has always felt that remission of sins is given *gratis* (Ap XX 14).

In the Augustana *Christenheit* reproduces not only the plural *ecclesiae* (AC XXVIII 28, 42) but also the singular *ecclesia*. According to St. Gregory, differences in humanly instituted ceremonies do not impair the unity of the *ecclesia/Christenheit* (XXVI 44); in it pious and learned persons have condemned the vicious lust of the bishops for political power (XXVIII 2); the bishops have burdened it with the slavery of the Law (39); they have given the impression that it needed a Levitical priesthood as in the Old Testament (62); these errors have woven themselves into it because the teaching of justification before God by faith was not clearly set forth (*ibid.*).

The *Apology* discusses the "signs" or "notes" of the church quite extensively in Article VII. These notes are the Word, the public profession of faith, and the Sacraments; hypocrites and evil persons are members of the church according to the external association of these signs (4, 19, 28). These notes identify the church as being a real society of true believers and righteous people scattered throughout the world; it is not a mere Platonic state (*Platonica civitas*), which has only ideal existence (20). In this connection, it may be noted that the Zwinglians made out the chief role of the Sacraments to be a means of identifying Christians; the Lutherans made this a minor function of the Sacraments (AC XIII 1). Some argued that to assign to the Sacraments a constitutive function in relation to the church prejudices the unique role of faith; the *Apology* answers that faith does not exclude the Word of God and the Sacraments, that faith is conceived out of the Word in the words of the Gospel and in the Sacraments and that accordingly we are to adorn the sacred ministry of the Word to the maximum extent (Ap IV 73).

According to the Scriptures, says Melanchthon, the church in the strict sense is that assembly of the Spirit-filled holy people and true believers in the Gospel of Christ in which the Gospel is correctly taught and the Sacraments are correctly administered (AC VII 1, Latin; Ap VII 1, 16, 28). In principle it is an association of faith and of the Holy Ghost in the hearts of its constituents (Ap VII 5), but it is also, though not exclusively (*tantum*), a body politic (*politia*) of good and evil people, an association of external matters and rites like other bodies politic (Ap VII 5, 29). With St. Paul we distinguish it from the people of God in the Old Testament in that the church is a spiritual people, that is, a people of God separated from the pagans not by civil ordinances but by the rebirth of the Holy Ghost (Ap VII 14, 16). The church in a true sense and in contrast to the kingdom of the devil is the kingdom of Christ (Ap VII 16, 17). While the evil members of the church are not the church, yet because the kingdom of God has not yet been revealed, they are mixed into the church, have the association of the external signs, and even bear offices in the church (Ap VII 17, 28). The church strictly is the pillar of the truth, but among its members will be weak persons who will erect perishable structures of straw upon the foundation, without, however, overthrowing the latter (Ap VII 20).

The church is built not on the authority of men, but on the sacred ministry of that confession of St. Peter in which he affirmed that Jesus is the Christ, the Son of God. Therefore our Lord is addressing St. Peter in the latter's capacity as a minister of Christ when He says: "Upon this rock," that is, upon this ministry (*super hoc ministerium*) (*Tractate* 25).

The church has its existence in time. It existed in the past, for the holy fathers wrote in the church (Ap IV 400). The church exists now. It will exist as long as the world stands (*perpetuo*, glossed by the German *alle Zeit*, should not be translated "forever;" (AC VII 1). The things that were done among the people of Israel were examples of those things that should take place in the future church (Ap IV 395). No matter how infinitely great the number of her wicked members may be, the church exists, and Christ will give her those things that He has promised (Ap VII 9); one of these promises is that the church will always have the Holy Ghost (21).

The church depends on Holy Baptism; if infant Baptism were invalid, the Holy Ghost would not be imparted, no one would be saved, and the church would disappear (Ap IX 3). Christ begets us anew through the divine, that is, spiritual, seed of the Word, not a *carnale semen* (Ap VII 14).

It is righteousness of the heart and the gift of the Holy Ghost that make us living members of the church (Ap VII 13; compare Ap IV135; IX 2). The *Apology* quotes Nicholas of Lyra with approval: "The church is not made up of people on the basis of either their ecclesiastical or secular power and rank ... but of those persons in whom is a true knowledge and confession of the faith and of the truth" (Ap VII 22). Yet the membership of the church includes pious, learned, and great men (AC XXVIII 2, 18); the situation of the times is reflected in the statement that Christian kings and princes are the chief members of the church (*Tractate* 54).

To safeguard the insight that the Sacraments do not depend for their validity on the faith or morals of the ministrant, the Lutherans condemn both the Donatists and the Lollard followers of John Wiclif for teaching that people sinned if they received the Sacraments from unworthy priests in the church (AC VIII 3; Ap VII 29, 30). Especially if they are not excommunicated, hypocrites and evil persons are members of the church according to the external association of the signs of the church (Ap VII 4, 9, 17); the church is aware of the impious teachers and wolves who will rage about (*grassantur*) within the church of the future (21).

Frequent reference is made to the customs (*Brauch, mos, exemplum, consuetudo*) of the church (AC XXII 4; XXIII 18; XXIV 35; Ap XXII 7; *Tractate* 70), of which some (like onerous episcopal legislation, the corporate invocation of the saints, and monastic vows) are of recent origin (AC XXVIII 72; Ap XXI 13; XXVII 66). The Sacrament of the Altar received the name of Eucharist in the church (Ap XXIV 76). The church instituted confession (AC XXV 12, German; the Latin has canon law say *humani iuris esse confessionem*). Yet individual absolution must be preserved and not be allowed to fall into disuse in the church (AC XI 1, German, where the Latin has *in ecclesiis*; Ap XI 1); it would be impious to take individual absolution out of the church (Ap XII 100).

While the church cannot dispense from a Commandment of the *Decalog* (AC XXVIII 33), the church did ordain the Lord's Day for public worship (60). Ceremonies and traditions in the church come in for frequent discussion (AC XXVI 15, German; XXVIII 11, 30, 39, Latin, where the German has *Christenheit*; Ap XV 31; XXIV 92; *Tractate* 11). The Lutherans want to retain the existing canonical form of church government, with its various grades of bishop and priest, even though these distinctions were made by human authority (Ap XIV 1, 2), as well as the ancient traditions made in the church for the sake of tranquillity and good order (AC XV 1; XXVI 40, 43, 44; XXVIII 53, 55, German, where the Latin has *ecclesiis*; Ap IV 234, 288; XV Title, 1, 13, 22, 38; XXVIII 15). The tranquillity and good order aimed at is not only or even chiefly within the parish or diocese, but at the level of provincial, national, and interecclesiastical relationships. The traditions cover everything from the order of service, the calendar, and the customary vestments and ceremonial to the disciplinary canons and the organization and administration of the church. The differences between the Eastern and the Western Church, as well as between the Lutheran territories and other Western provinces — at least at the level of the ordinary layman, priest, and bishop — were regarded by the *Augsburg Confession* as being primarily in the realm of custom and tradition rather than in the realm of doctrine (AC *Epilog* to XXI 2: *Tota dissensio est de paucis quibusdam abusibus, qui sine certa autoritate in ecclesiis irrepserunt*).

The church has had to bear the sacrilege of private Masses offered as propitiatory sacrifices for too many centuries (AC XXIV 18). The church has never required holy confirmation and extreme unction as absolutely necessary to salvation (Ap XIII 6). The church has suffered an injustice in connection with Holy Communion under one kind (Ap XXII 16).

Instruction in the church on faith and its righteousness, on Christian liberty, and on repentance is essential (AC XX 8, Latin, which twice has *ecclesia*, one occurrence of which is reproduced in the German by *christlich Wesen*; XXVI 20; XXVIII 48; Ap IV 119; XII 73; XV 32; XX 2; XXI 40, 44; XXVIII 7; see also Ap Introduction 16, 17; IV 83, 392; VII 20, 21; XII 66; XIV 4; XX 6; XXIV 65; XXVII 27; XXVIII 24). The church pronounces judgments on issues within the limits of the divine revelation (Ap XII 66, 67; XXII 15, 17; XXIII 68). She did not condemn the marriage of priests in the days of Jovinian (Ap XXIII 67); in the era of the Ecumenical Councils she did not recognize the primacy or superiority of the Bishop of Rome (*Tractate* 17). By refusing to submit to the judgment of Councils and of the whole church the Pope is making himself God (*Tractate* 40) and identifying himself as the apocalyptic Man of Lawlessness; and in refusing to have the controversy between the Lutherans and the Papalists judged in the prescribed fashion (*rite*), he is taking the right to judge away from the church (*Tractate* 49; compare 56).

The church is a confessing church (Ap IV 322, 344); during Whitsunweek she sings from the *Veni, Sancte Spiritus* the stanza, *Sine tuo numine nihil est in homine, nihil est innoxium* (AC XX 40, Latin); she prays in collects that end with the formula, "Through Christ, our Lord" (Ap IV 385); she preaches and administers the Sacraments through the sacred ministry, in that through the vocation of the church Christ calls men to act in His name and in His stead (Ap VII 28; XII 104). Hence no one should teach or preach publicly or administer any Sacraments in the church without a vocation in the prescribed order (*ordentlich; rite*) (AC XIV). The church has the right (*ius*) and the command to call, elect, select, appoint, and ordain sacred ministers, and no human authority can wrest this right from the church (Ap XIII 12; *Tractate* 67, 72). In a case of necessity — the example cited is an imminent shipwreck — even a layman (*etiam laicus*) can absolve and, by implication, baptize, since the keys are given to the whole church (*Tractate* 72). The Symbols at this point seem to argue that the whole church has all the powers of the sacred ministry, which she ordinarily imparts to those whom in compliance with God's will she calls, elects, and ordains. In these powers in a case of extraordinary necessity even a layman shares to the extent that an emergency requires.

Christ commanded St. Peter to rule the church by the Word (*Tractate* 30), yet the church is over the ministers (11). The concept of local jurisdiction is present but not stressed (Ap XII 106). An interesting passage is *Tractate* 65: "It is manifest that ordination imparted by a pastor in his own church (*a pastore in sua ecclesia*) is valid by divine right (*iure divino ratam*)." Thus the Symbols imply that candidates for the sacred ministry are ordained in the church of the ordinator.

The church administers holy absolution through the clergy (AC XII 2; Ap XII 20; *Tractate* 24, 60, 68). She administers discipline (Ap XII 7, 21, 120, 121; XV 39). Article XXVIII of the *Augsburg Confession* is a discussion of the *potestas ecclesiastica, Kirchenregiment*. The Symbol treats it as a real *potestas*, as real as the other *potestas* there discussed, the *potestas civilis*, although it operates on a different basis, with different means, for different ends.

Errors and vices have insinuated themselves into the church through lay ignorance, pastoral negligence, and satanic malice (AC XXIV 15, Latin; XXVI 1, 3; XXVII 48; XXVIII 62, Latin, where the German has *Christenheit*; Ap VII 32; XII 141; XIII 23; XVI 4; XX 4; XXI 40; XXVIII 16). The adversaries are disturbing the church with their impious dogmas (Ap XXI 43; XXIII 2; XXIV 92). The bishops are dividing the church (Ap XIV 2). The church suffers in being deprived of part of the Sacrament (Ap XXIII 6 *bis*). In the fourteenth and succeeding centuries darkness has been imported into the church through the canonical legislation of Boniface VIII, which has been a great plague to the church (*Tractate* 34, 37). Endless perils threaten to destroy the church (Ap VII 9). The church's welfare is something to be sought (Ap Introduction 16; XX 6; XXI 42), although the adversaries are not concerned about it (Ap XXI 42, 43). The pretensions of the Papacy are pernicious to the church (*Tractate* 4, 55, 59). The monks and bishops are defrauding the church by misusing the financial resources that she has to carry on her work (Ap XXVII 6; *Tractate* 80, 81, 83). Antichrist reigns within the church (*Tractate* 39, 40).

An instructive passage is *Apology*, Article IV, 232. In Colossians 3, when St. Paul speaks about αγαπη he is not thinking of personal perfection, but of the mutual organizational integrity of the church; so he commands that love be practiced in the church, lest the church burst into various schisms and factions and heretical movements arise out of the schisms. The sequence of events here sketched is significant; even more so is the fact that the *Apology* here espouses the sound patristic interpretation of αγαπη as the maintenance of fraternal concord within the church at every level rather than the practice of individualistic affection and charity. There are heretical movements in the historical church, many of them the result of the *odium doctorum* (242).

Faith is directly or indirectly involved in all the descriptions of the church strictly considered, but it is not in every case explicitly referred to: *Congregatio sanctorum in qua evangelium pure docetur et recte administrantur sacramenta* (AC VII 1, Latin; Ap VII 16); *congregatio sanctorum et vere credentium* (AC VIII l); *congregatio sanctorum qui vere credunt evangelio Christi et habent Spiritum Sanctum* (Ap VII 28); *congregatio sanctorum qui habent inter se societatem ejusdem evangelii seu doctrinae et ejusdem Spiritus Sancti, qui corda eorum renovat, sanctificat, et gubernat* (Ap VII 7); *die Versammlung aller Gläubigen, bei welchen das Evangelium rein gepredigt und die heiligen Sakrament laut des Evangelii gereicht werden* (AC VII 1, German); *die Versammlung aller Gläubigen und Heiligen* (AC VIII l).

This *congregatio* or *Versammlung* is the *vera ecclesia*. "True church" here has no denominational implication. The hypocrites and evil ones are associates (*socii*) of this true church according to the external rites, but they are not a part of the living body of Christ, as even the adversaries had conceded in agreeing that the wicked were dead members of Christ's body (Ap VII 12). St. Matthew (3:12) teaches that the true church will be separated from the people of the Jews (Ap VII 19). The true church is a pillar of the truth and does not err from the foundation (Ap VII 2). Wherever the true church is, there is necessarily the right of choosing and ordaining sacred ministers (*Tractate* 67). The one reference in the Symbols to the doctrine of the universal priesthood of believers asserts that St. Peter's word, "You are a royal priesthood," pertains to the true church; and since it alone has the priesthood, it certainly has the right to choose and ordain sacred ministers (*Tractate* 69). It should be noted that the priesthood is the common possession of the church and that individuals share in the common priesthood *as members of the church*, the new Israel.

The true church is also the body of Christ, and Christ is the church's Head (Ap VII 5, 12, 29; compare IV 400; *Tractate* 67). The *corpus Christi* has as its counterpart a *corpus diaboli* (Ap VII 29).

The distinction between the church in the strict sense (*proprie dicta*) and the church in the broad sense (*large dicta*; the Symbols do not use the term *improprie dicta*) was not new in the sixteenth century (Ap VII 28; compare 16). Canon law spoke of the church in the broad sense of the term as comprising good and bad people and affirmed that the evil ones were in the church *nomine sed non re*, whereas the good people were in the church *re et nomine* (Ap VII10).

The church is in a real sense the kingdom of Christ (Ap VII 16 *bis*, 17), although we cannot in this world equate the two (Ap VII 13, 17-19, 21). Because the kingdom of Christ is not revealed, the impious are mixed in with the church and hold offices in the church. The kingdom of Christ is a spiritual kingdom which consists in knowledge of God, fear of God, and faith in God and which is equated with the perfection of the Gospel and eternal life (Ap XVI 2, 7; XXVII 27). Christ by means of His Spirit is always giving life to His kingdom, whether it be revealed or whether it be hidden under the cross, for Christ is the same, who is now glorified, whereas before He was afflicted; with this the parables of Christ agree (Ap VII 18, 45). The kingdom of Christ in the empirical church is clearly scattered throughout the whole world, and today there are many churches in the Orient who seek neither ordination nor confirmation of orders from the Bishop of Rome (*Tractate* 16).

The unity of the church (*unitas ecclesiae*) is carefully differentiated from the organizational integrity of the church (*communis integritas ecclesiae*) and harmony in the church (*concordia, caritas, tranquillitas in ecclesia*). The use of *Einigkeit* in the German *Book of Concord* for both *unitas* and *concordia* has obscured this differentiation, although even here the genitive *der Kirche* is used where *Einigkeit* means *unitas* and the prepositional phrase *in der Kirche* is used where *Einigkeit* means *concordia* or its synonyms. Justus Jonas' paraphrase of the *Apology*, Article IV, 232 and 234, appears to be an exception, but the context, as well as the term *integritas*, clearly indicates that the external integrity of the church is intended. It was at this point that one of the sharpest differences arose between the evangelicals and the papalist adversaries. To the true unity of the church, said the former, it is enough to agree with one another in the teaching of the Gospel and in the administration of the Sacraments, and it is not necessary that human traditions — among which they included the polity of the church — be everywhere alike (AC VII 2; XXVI 44, quoting St. Gregory; XXVIII 74; compare Ap VII 33, 34, 46; XV 18). In setting up these minimum requirements for the church's unity, the Lutherans were not contemplating a humanly devised, external unification; they were talking about true, that is, spiritual, unity, without which faith cannot exist in the heart or the heart cannot be righteous before God (Ap VII 31). "Spiritual" in the vocabulary of the Symbols means "worked by the Spirit of God," hence the quotation from Ephesians 4 in *Augsburg Confession*, Article VII.

The objective of human institutions, ordinances, and ceremonies is organizational integrity and external union (or at least intercommunion) at the individual and corporate levels in the bonds of fraternal charity. Whereas *unitas* is God-given, Christians have a role in this lesser, external unification. If love were practiced, the churches would be made tranquil and peace would come to the State (Ap IV 236). The key words are *(bonus) ordo, (gute) Ordnung* (AC XV 1; XXVI 40; Ap IV

288; XV 1, 13; XXVIII 15), frequently coupled with *tranquillitas; integritas (communis)* (Ap IV 232, 234); *concordia* (AC Introduction *passim;* Ap IV 232); *dilectio (ibid.); reconciliatio* (AC Introduction 19, Latin); and ευταξια (Ap XV 22). (Compare AC Epilog to XXI, German.) The opposite of *concordia* and *integritas* is *dissensio, Zwiespalt* (AC Introduction 2, 6, German; Ap XII 90); *schisma, Trennung* (AC XXVI 43; XXVIII 78; Ap IV 232; VII 49; XXIII 59; *Tractate* 72); and *Unordnung* (AC XXVIII 55). The division between the papalist and Lutheran parties is at this stage a *dissensio,* a *schisma;* it has come about through the withdrawal of the Lutherans from obedience to the canonical bishops by the action of the Lutherans in ordaining priests of their own, but for this the impiety and tyranny of the bishops must be blamed (*Tractate* 72). Beyond schism lie factions and heresies (AC IV 232). In the use of the term "heretic" here (as in Ap IV 242), there is still primarily a sense of its etymological significance, "sectary, division maker," although elsewhere (AC I 5; Ap XXIV 96 of Arius for his Arianism) it is used of those who denied a cardinal doctrine of the faith.

We have thus seen that in the Melanchthonian documents the term "church" is used in a vast variety of ways that cannot be reduced to any simple pattern. The problem that we have here is real. The resolution of the problem may lie in the *Apology,* Article VII, 19. Christ, says Melanchthon, is talking about the way the church looks (*de specie ecclesiae dicit*) when He says: "The kingdom of heaven is like a net or like ten virgins." He would teach us that the church is covered up (*tectam*) by the vast number of evil people, so that this scandal does not offend the pious and so that also we might know that the Word and the Sacraments are effective even if they are ministered by evil people.

Summarizing: In this world we can hope to know only the church in her present aspect, hated by her foes, betrayed by the false sons within her pale, sore oppressed by the vast number of evil persons in her membership, rent asunder by schisms, distressed by heresies, weeping amid the toil and tribulation and tumult of her warfare. To want to know any other kind of church is presumption, a hankering after a *theologia gloriae* instead of the *theologia crucis* that is our earthly lot. The case of the church is parallel to that of the individual Christian. When we look at one another, each sees the other person in his unesthetic twentieth-century garb, with annoying mannerisms and habitual sins, with the constant dying of his mortal flesh apparent in wrinkling skin, trifocal spectacles, balding pate, hoarse voice, and the symptoms and syndromes of the ailments he describes. That person will be completely different in the resurrection, so completely different that our past experience furnishes no basis, according to the Scriptures, for imagining what he will be — or what even in this moment he really is in the sight of the heavenly Father, who, as He looks upon that person, sees him "in Christ."

IV

The ecclesiology of the *Formula of Concord* is significant not because it adds anything substantially new to the ecclesiology of the older Symbols — it does not — but because it comes out of a period in which the ecclesiological problem had been intensified by the march of events. The schism between the Lutheran and the papalist parties had hardened. The Scholastic theology against which the blessed reformers had protested had achieved an organizational embodiment at the Council of Trent in the Roman Catholic Church. The Lutheran movement had barely been rescued from disintegration by the valiant efforts of the theologians and princes. In the areas affected by the more radical reformations the fragmentation of Western Christianity was going on apace.

The plural *Kirchen* occurs frequently in the *Formula*. The introductions to the *Formula* and to the *Book of Concord* refer to "the churches in which the Apostles themselves planted the pure and unalloyed Word of God" (*Bekenntnisschriften*, p. 4, line 43; p.743, line 30). The term is used in a very general sense in Article X, when it is stipulated that the churches will not condemn one another because of difference in ceremonies when one has more or less of them (FC SD X 31). The sense is equally general in the declaration of Article VII that although our Lord spoke the words of institution but once, they are nevertheless effective down to the present day and until His advent and they bring about the presence of His body and blood in the Eucharist of the churches — which the Latin renders very significantly *per omnes mensas ecclesiae*, "throughout all the altars of the church" (FC SD VII 78). Provincial and national churches are clearly meant in the references to "entire churches within or outside the Holy Empire of the German Nation" in the introductions (*Bekenntnisschriften*, p. 11, line 55; p.756, line 5). A similar intention seems to be present in the reference to the pious and innocent people also in those churches "which have, to be sure, not come to an agreement with us" (*ibid.*, p. 12, line 8; p.756, line 19), and in the reference to the electors, princes, and estates which had permitted their churches to be reformed in accordance with the Word of God (FC SD Introduction 3).

Kirchen is used with specific reference to the Lutheran churches (FC SD VII 111), described as the churches of the *Augsburg Confession* (FC SD Summary Concept 2, 8; SD II 2, 73; SD VII 41), the pure churches (FC SD Summary Concept 9), the evangelical churches (FC SD Introduction 7; Summary Concept 11), the Reformed churches, which through their adoption of the *Augsburg Confession* are differentiated from the Papists and from other rejected and condemned sects and heresies (FC SD Summary Concept 5), the Christian churches

(*Bekenntnisschriften,* p.14, line 7; p. 760, line 3; FC SD Introduction 3), and "our churches" (*Bekenntnisschriften,* p. 4, lines 23 *et passim;* p.756, line 10; p. 758, line 20; FC SD Summary Concept 10). Only once is there a reference in the *Formula* — or anywhere else in the Symbols — to *unsere Kirche;* it occurs in Article X, where the adversaries of the truth are pictured as suppressing the pure doctrine either through force and coercion or through some slippery device and making it easy once more to insinuate their false doctrine into "our church" (FC SD X 3). This may not be the recognition of the denominational character of the Lutheran Church that it appears on the face of it to be. It may be a typographical or editorial error. The Latin significantly has the plural that we should otherwise expect, *ecclesias nostras,* and the German would become plural by the addition of an "n." Furthermore, the Leipzig Altzelle Interim of December 1548, which is the document that precipitated the Adiaphoristic Controversy settled by Article X, affected only one territorial church, the Church of Saxony.

There are two references to the "universal orthodox church of Christ (*allgemeine rechtlehrende Kirche Christi*)" in the introductions (*Bekenntnisschriften,* p. 3, line 46; page 742, line 11). Here the authors have in mind the historic orthodox church of the entire past. Specifically, the passage says that the evangelical churches recognized the doctrinal content of the *Augsburg Confession* as being the ancient consensus which the universal orthodox Church of Christ had believed and defended against many heresies and errors. With the qualification "primitive (*erste*)" and "ancient (*alte*)," the orthodox church is the church of the patristic era, when the Creeds were being formulated; the *Formula* rejects and anathematizes all heresies and errors which were rejected and condemned in the primitive, ancient orthodox church (FC SD Summary Concept 17).

Significantly, it is in Articles VII (on the Holy Eucharist) and VIII (on the Person of Christ) that we have references to the *whole* church. The Sacramentarian enthusiasts are poking fun in an inappropriate and poisonous fashion at the Lord Jesus Christ, at St. Paul, and at the whole church (FC SD VII 67). The similes used by the whole ancient church to illustrate the personal union of the two natures in our Lord are cited (FC SD VIII 64), and the Lutheran theologians appeal to the consistent rule of the whole ancient orthodox church that the two natures were conjoined in a personal union (57, 59, 61, 64).

"The Christian Church" is the historic church. The Catholic Creeds are clear and consistent denials of all those heresies which arose in the Christian Church (FC SD Summary Concept 4). In opposition to the anathematized heresy of Paul of Samosata, who denied the deity of our Lord, the Christian Church has always and simply believed and held that our Lord is both God and man (FC SD VIII 17). So, too, the pure doctrine of the Christian Church is appealed to in affirming the positive theses of Articles III (On the Righteousness of Faith) and IV (On Good Works) over against the negative antitheses (FC Ep III 3; IV 5) and again in setting forth the teaching about the Person of Christ (FC Ep VIII 4). "The Christian Church" includes the contemporary empirical church; we do not understand St. Matthew 28:19 as asserting that only the deity of our Lord is present with us in the Christian Church and community (*christliche Kirche und Gemein*) (FC SD VIII 77).

With one exception, *Christenheit* as a designation of the church occurs in the *Formula* only in quotations from the *Catechisms;* the exception is the description of anti-Trinitarianism as a new sect, previously unheard of in Christendom (FC Ep XII 29).

The *Catalog of Testimonies* sheds some light on the concept of the church in the minds of the authors of the *Formula* when it draws an interesting distinction by appealing to the ancient pure church and the Fathers (*Bekenntnisschriften*, p. 1103, lines 5, 11, 28; p. 1104, lines 1, 6; p. 1114, line 1) or the holy Fathers of the ancient pure church (*ibid.*, line 42). (The Latin uses the comparative *purior*, the "purer" church and fathers.)

The adjectival use of *Kirchen* in combinations is infrequent but instructive. We have *Kirchendiener* (*Bekenntnisschriften*, p.8, lines 4, 25; p.12, line 23; p.748, line 35; p.749, line 17; FC Ep XII 12; SD I 58; XII 16) in contexts that indicate that "ministers of the church" is clearly a technical term for the clergy, in distinction to teachers in *ludi* and *scholae* and theological professors, who could, like Melanchthon and Chemnitz at Wittenberg, be laymen. *Kirchendienst* (*Bekenntnisschriften*, p. 759, line 10; FC Ep XII 22; SD XII 30) is the sacred ministry, "the Word preached and spoken." *Kirchengebräuche* occurs in the title of Article X in the *Epitome* and *Solid Declaration*. *Kirchenlehre* occurs in the phrase *dieser Kirchenlehre halber* (rendered instructively in the Latin as *doctrinae capita in nostris ecclesiis hactenus proposita*) with reference to the Smalcald synod of 1537, which considered what was to be presented at the projected Council of Mantua with reference to the Evangelical position (FC SD VII 17). *Kirchenleher* designates "Doctors of the Church" (*Bekenntnisschriften*, p. 755, line 8; FC Ep VII 15; SD V 3; VIII 22; IX 1).

Gemeinschaft, "communion," occurs in Article VII. In contrast to Luther's conception of the meaning of *spiritualiter* as referring to the intangible and illocal mode of Christ's presence whereby He neither occupies nor vacates space, the Sacramentarians understand *spiritualiter* as meaning nothing more than the "spiritual" communion brought about when in spirit the truly faithful are by faith incorporated into Christ the Lord and become true "spiritual" members of His body (SD VII 104). A little farther on there is a reference to the godless epicureans and mockers of God's Word who are in the external communion of the church.

The church is viewed as a clearly historical and empirical phenomenon in passages that speak of the "primitive" church, that is, the church of the post-Apostolic period (FC Ep Summary Concept 3), or the "ancient" church, that is, the church which, assembled in the Second Ecumenical Council of Constantinople in 381, the Third Ecumenical Council of Ephesus in 431, the Fourth Ecumenical Council of Chalcedon in 451, and subsequent ecumenical and interprovincial councils, appealed to the Council of Nicaea and its Decree and Creed as a dependable and defensible witness to the truth (FC SD Summary Concept 5). A parallel passage embodies the observation that the ancient doctors of the church before and after Chalcedon in discussing the Incarnation frequently used the term *mixtio* as a synonym for *unio personalis* (FC SD VIII 18); they have in mind such men as SS. Athanasius, Gregory Nazianzen, Gregory of Nyssa, and Augustine. In contrast to the professors of heresy and false doctrine, the church of the era of the Catholic Creeds is described as the orthodox and genuine (*wahrhaftig*) church (FC Ep Summary Concept 3).

Kirche is sometimes a very general term. A criterion to be employed in judging humanly instituted rites and ceremonies is their probable usefulness (FC SD X 30) for building up (*Erbauung*) the church (9). Christ is present with His church and community on earth as Mediator, Head, King, and High Priest (FC SD VIII 78).

Kirche is a territorial church when St. Paul is described as recommending the article concerning Christian liberty most earnestly to his church in Galatia (FC SD X 15). The empirical church is obviously meant when the superscription of the Catholic Creeds declares that they are unanimously used (*einträchtiglich gebraucht*) in the church (*Bekenntnisschriften*, pp. 19, 21). The church has ministers who conceivably are not themselves regenerate, renewed, righteous, and pious (FC Ep XII 27). A church should not anathematize another because of a difference in quantity of humanly instituted ceremonies, as long as a united consensus exists in the doctrine and in all the articles thereof and in the right use of the Holy Sacraments (FC Ep X 7). Certain doctrinal positions are to be preserved with great diligence in the church (FC Ep V 2), whereas some other articles and tenets are intolerable (FC Ep XII 3; SD IV 2, 40). Unnecessary and unprofitable theological wrangling can confuse the church (FC SD Summary Concept 15). The church, according to her circumstances, can in Christian liberty elect to make use of one or more humanly instituted ceremonies (FC Ep X 12). The idea can be entertained in the church that human ordinances and institutions are divine worship or a part of it (FC Ep X 8). Such human ordinances have been introduced into the church in the interest of good order, Christian discipline, and evangelical well-being in the church (FC Ep X 1; SD X 1, 7). Such ordinances can be foisted on the church by coercion (FC SD X 15). The church is coordinated with such empirical phenomena as the state (*Polizei*), the government (*Regiment*), and the home (*Haushaltung*) (FC SD XII 2, 9).

There is no observable expansion of meaning when the church is described as the Church of God. The preaching of both the Gospel and the Law has existed in the Church of God from the beginning of the world and ought to continue to the world's end (FC SD V 23, 24). Heresies and errors contrary to the Catholic Creeds have been introduced into the Church of God, but we formally reject them (FC Ep Summary Concept 3). The publication of the *Apology* was designed to forestall the insinuation of anathematized errors into the Church of God under the pretext of the *Augsburg Confession* (FC SD Summary Concept 6). Confusion of Law and Gospel could reopen a door to the Papacy in the Church of God (FC SD V 27). In the pre-Reformation Church of God great controversies had occurred (FC SD Introduction 4). Uncertainty on the part of her clergy as to the substantial or accidental character of original sin will never help the Church of God achieve permanent peace (FC SD I 58). The issues decided by the *Formula* are of such importance that the rejected opinions neither can nor should be tolerated in the Church of God, much less defended or supported (FC SD Introduction 9). The enthusiasts are to be censured with all earnestness and energy for denying that God uses the means of grace in the work of sanctification and are not to be tolerated in the Church of God (FC SD II 80). The Church of God is to be protected against the Christological heresy of Zwingli's *alloeosis* doctrine (FC SD VIII 38). Blessed Martin Luther has extensively reminded the Church of God what one should believe about ceremonies (FC SD X 24). The rule, *Nihil habet rationem sacramenti extra usum a Christo institutum*, is a useful one in the Church of God (FC SD VII 86). The article of election provides glorious evidence that the Church of God will exist and persist against all the gates of hell; it also teaches which the right Church of God is, so that we shall not be scandalized by the great prestige of the false church (FC SD XI 50). The use of the "form of sound words" will obviate much quarreling and will preserve the church (Latin: the Church of God) from much scandal (FC SD IV 36).

The only reference to the church which suggests that she extends beyond time is a passing comment in Article II; by the public proclamation of the holy, sole-saving Gospel of God's eternal Son, our only Savior and Sanctifier Jesus Christ, God is gathering an eternal church for Himself out of the human race and works in the hearts of men true repentance and knowledge of sins and true faith in the Son of God, and God wills to call men to eternal bliss, draw them to Himself, convert, beget them anew, and hallow them through no other means than through His holy Word, in that we hear it preached or read it and in that we use the Sacraments according to His Word (FC SD II 50). "Church" is probably used in this passage in an imprecise sense.

The identity of the church with the people of God in the Old Testament is implied but not stressed (FC SD I 45; V 23, 24).

The church as the body of Christ likewise receives no emphasis. Article VII *rejects* the Sacramentarian Eucharistic theory set forth in the following undocumented quotation: "The bread is the communication of the body of Christ, that is, the bread is that by which the association with the body of Christ, that is, the church, takes place; or, the bread is the means by which the faithful are united to Christ, just as the Word of the Gospel, which is laid hold of by faith, is a means whereby we are united to Christ spiritually and are inserted into the body of Christ, that is, the church" (FC SD VII 59). The scope of this rejection is obviously not the identification of the church with the body of Christ, but the exclusive reference of a passage (1 Cor. 10:16) which speaks of the Eucharistic body of Christ to a spiritually conceived mystical body of Christ.

The *Einigkeit* that the *Formula* contemplates is not the *unitas ecclesiae* of the *Augsburg Confession,* Article VII. While the same noun is used in both cases in German, the *Formula* never uses it with the genitive *der Kirche,* nor does the Latin translation of the *Formula* ever render *Einigkeit* with *unitas.* Instead the Latin uses such words as *consensio* (*Bekenntnisschriften,* p. 4, line 38, *consensus* [FC Ep X 7], *pacificatio* [*ibid.,* p. 8, line 35], and *concordia* [*inter doctores ecclesiae* for *der christlicher Lehrer Einigkeit, ibid.,* p. 7, lines 13-15; again *ibid.,* p.15, lines 6-13], where the *Einigkeit/concordia* embraces non-Lutheran princes and estates; and FC SD Summary Concept 1, 14, where basic, enduring God-pleasing concord in the church is spoken of). The church is thus conceived of as an empirical entity larger than any intercommunicating segment. The oft-quoted passage in the Summary Concept article takes on new significance if this fact is kept in mind: "Basic, enduring concord in the church requires above all things that people have a succinct, unanimous concept and form, containing the common succinct doctrine which the churches of the true Christian religion confess, drawn together out of the Word of God, just as the ancient church universally had her specific symbols for this purpose. But such acceptance should not be given to private documents, but to such books that have been set forth, approved, and received in the name of the churches that confess one teaching and religion" (FC SD Summary Concept 1). In place of *Einigkeit* one finds on occasion another term, such as "peace" (I 58). The opposite of this *Einigkeit* is represented by "divisions"(*Zweispaltung, Bekenntnisschriften,* p. 747, line 6; FC SD I 58; or *Spaltungen, Bekenntnisschriften,* page 6, lines 49, 57; p.13, line 41; FC SD Introduction 7; Summary Concept 19; rendered in Latin as *dissidia, distractiones* and *dissensiones*). These terms are the ones used to describe the differences that have arisen among Lutheran theologians and that the *Formula* is trying to compose.

The break with that part of the medieval church which submitted to the papal hierarchy and became the Roman Catholic Church at the Council of Trent is described as *Trennung* (*schismata*) (FC Ep Summary Concept 4). The verb is used in the statement: "It is a difficult thing to separate oneself from so many lands and people and to affirm a particular teaching" (FC SD X 23). This would seem to make the actual schism between the Lutherans and the Roman Catholic Church begin with the rejection of the papalist bishops' authority and withdrawal from intercommunion with them. The decisive break can probably be dated to the Colloquy of Worms. The members of the Roman Catholic hierarchy are described as "enemies of the holy Gospel" (FC SD X 2) and as the adversaries (*Gegenteil*) of the Lutherans (XII 3).

For the opinions of those who refuse to accept the evangelical position the *Formula* uses such terms as "errors" (in the case of the enthusiasts, FC Ep II 13), "heresy" (for the denial of the deity of our Lord, FC SD VIII 17, and other false doctrinal systems rejected by the Catholic Creeds, FC SD Summary Concept 14), "heresies and sects" (to cover all those with whom the Lutherans were not in communion, FC SD Summary Concept 5), and "sects" (for sixteenth-century anti-Trinitarianism, FC Ep XII 29).

If there is a word in the *Formula* that corresponds to the developing concept of "denomination," it is *Religion*, both in compounds (*Religionsverwandte, Bekenntnisschriften*, p. 7, line 12; *Religionsstreite, ibid.*, p.6, line 30; FC SD XI 95), and in its simple uncompounded form. The Lutherans claim *Religion* for themselves (*Bekenntnisschriften*, p. 6, lines 7, 11; p.15, line 25), reserving "opinion" for the adversaries (*ibid.*, p.6, line 8). *Religion* describes the historic Christian faith (FC SD Introduction 1), which was abominably eclipsed under the Papacy but cleansed and purified on the basis of the Word of God by Dr. Luther of holy and blessed memory; the Lutheran system (FC SD Summary Concept 20); but also, when qualified by "opposing" or "papistic," the Roman Catholic system (FC SD X 5).

In the church there are laics (FC Ep Summary Concept 5; SD Summary Concept 8) and clerics; the latter, the ministers of the Word, preside over the community of God (FC SD X 10, 25). Together laics and clerics comprise the community of God, *die Gemeine Gottes* (FC Ep X 10; SD X 27), which the Latin usually reproduces as *ecclesia Dei*. This community exists in space and time (FC Ep X 4; SD X 9), but it cannot be narrowly equated with either a parish or a voluntary local congregation. It has, as the cited passages show, authority to alter humanly instituted ceremonies according to its best lights, as long as it does so in such a way that Christian charity and concern for the weak fellow Christian have full scope (FC Ep X 12; SD X 30). The term is almost interchangeable with "church" (FC SD VIII 77), as the Latin rendering indicates. Refusal to accept the public ministry of the spoken Word and Sacraments, reinforced with the written Word, is contempt both of God's Word and of God's community (FC SD II 57). In Article XII *Gemeine* is qualified by *rechte christliche* (Ep XII 9, 26; SD XII 34); the combination *rechte christliche Vorsamblunge noch Gemeine* also occurs (FC SD XII 14). This may reflect the language of the sectarians here condemned.

The *Formula* commits itself to the ecclesiology of the earlier symbols by citing their expositions of this article with approval (for instance in FC SD V 15; VII 11; X 19-22).

ENDNOTES

1. On the *Epistula apostolorum* see Johannes Quasten, *Patrology* (Westminster: The Newman Press, 1951), I, 25, 150-153, and the literature there cited.
2. Tertullian, *De baptismo*, 6.
3. Quasten, p. 191.
4. Cyprian, *Epistola LXX ad Januarium*, 2.
5. Epiphanius of Salamis, *Panarion*, LXXII.
6. The text of the Creed of Nicetas is reproduced from A.E. Burn, *Niceta of Remesiana* (Cambridge, 1905), p. lxxxiv, in F.J. Badcock, *The History of the Creeds*, 2d ed. (London: S.P.C.K., 1938), p. 72, and by J.N.D. Kelly, *Early Christian Creeds* (London: Longmans, Green and Co., 1950), p. 175.
7. R.H. Connolly (editor), *The Explanatio Symboli ad Initiandos* (Cambridge: University Press, 1952), p.10.
8. Cyril of Jerusalem, Κατηχησειζ φωτιξομενων, XVIII, 26.
9. Augustine, *De fide et symbolo*, X, 21 (Burleigh's translation).
10. Rufinus, *Commentarius in symbolum apostolorum*, 39.
11. The first commentator on the Baptismal Creed in modern times to revive the neuter interpretation of *sanctorum* seems to have been the Lutheran scholar Theodor Zahn, in *Das apostolische Symbolum* (Erlangen, 1893), pp. 88 ff. For recent discussions of this question and references to earlier literature, see Badcock, pp. 243-272; Kelly, pp. 388-397; and Werner Elert, *Abendmahl und Kirchengemeinschaft in der alten Kirche hauptsächlich des Ostens* (Berlin: Lutherisches Verlagshaus, 1954), pp. 5-16, 166-181.
12. Kelly, p. 390.
13. WA, 2, 190.
14. Ivo of Chartres, *Sermo XXIII* (Migne, *Patrologia Latina*, CLXII, 606): "'*Sanctorum communionem;' id est ecclesiasticorum sacramentorum veritatem, cui communicaverunt sancti, qui in unitate fidei de hac vita migraverunt.*"
15. Peter Abelard, *Explanatio symboli quod dicitur Apostolorum* (Migne, PL, CLXXVIII, 629-630): "Sanctorum communionem. *Hoc est illam, qua sancti efficiuntur vel in sanctitate confirmantur, divini scilicet sacramenti participatione; vel communem Ecclesiae fidem, sive charitatis unionem. Possumus et sanctorum dicere neutraliter, id est sanctificati panis et vini in sacramentam altaris.*"
16. Kelly, p. 394.
17. Amalarius of Trèves, *Epistola de caeremoniis baptismi* (Migne, PL, XCIX, 896): "Sanctorum communionem, *in vinculo pacis unitatem Spiritus servare credo.*"
18. Magnus of Sens, *Libellus de mysterio baptismi*, in Kelly, p. 394.
19. WA, 54, 229-230.
20. WA, 50, 624-625.
21. *Die Bekenntnisschriften der evangelisch-lutherischen Kirche, herausgegeben im Gedenkjahr der Augsburgischen Konfession 1930*, 2d ed. (Göttingen: Vandenhoeck und Ruprecht, 1952), p. 725. This edition (*Jubiläumsausgabe*) is hereafter referred to in this article as *Bekenntnisschriften*.
22. "Bugenhagen, in his introduction to Palladius' *Enchiridion* ... combines the examination of children and other communicants in that he declares the words of Luther's *Small Catechism* to be the confession upon which the child of eight years and the centenarian alike are admitted to the Communion....The children [in sixteenth-century Denmark] were often admitted to the Communion when they were only six to seven years of age" (Edmund Belfour, "The History of the Liturgy in the Lutheran Church in

Denmark," in *Memoirs of the Lutheran Liturgical Association* [Pittsburgh: The Lutheran Liturgical Association, 1906], II, 68-69). Of Sweden, Oscar Quensel says: "It seems that even eight and nine year olds were among the communicants as late as the 1570s" (*Bidrag till svenska liturgiens historia* [Upsala: Akademiska Boktryckeriet, 1890], II, 88). By way of documentation he quotes in note 2 on the cited page a rule of what appears to be the *Kyrkoordning* of 1571: "Again, no children younger than nine or at least eight years [are to be admitted to the Sacrament], because a younger child cannot have the requisite knowledge (*kunna föga beskedh weta*) about the Sacrament." By the end of the seventeenth century, in contrast, German Lutheranism had raised the age of Confirmation (and first Holy Communion), in some cases as high as 15 and 16 (Paul Graff, *Geschichte der Auflösung der alten gottesdienstlichen Formen in der evangelischen Kirche Deutschlands* [Göttingen: Vandenhoeck und Ruprecht, 1937-1939], I, 326). At the same time we also find an old Lutheran tradition which fixed twelve as the appropriate age in view of the account of the Child Jesus in the Temple at the age of twelve; it is demonstrable as late as 1750 (Karl Ramge, "*Die Sakramentsnot im Hinblick auf Taufe, Konfirmation und Beichte,*" in *Die Hochkirche*, XIV [1932], 124). Twelve is the age prescribed in the Schwäbish-Hall Church Order of 1615 (Graff, I, 314). Even as late as the beginning of the last century, children were still being admitted to Holy Confirmation (and Holy Communion) at the age of eight and nine "in many parts of Germany" (Fr. L. Rein[h]old, *Ideen über das Aeussere der evangelischen Gottesverehrung* [Neustrelitz, 1805], p. 179; quoted in Graff, II, 246). It is interesting to note that in his *Institutio christianae religionis* of 1536, John Calvin directed that "*puer decennis ecclesiae se offerret ... teste et spectante ecclesia profiterentur*" (quoted in Graff, I, 315, n. 2). While the Leipzig Altzelle Interim of 1548, which Melanchthon helped to draft, directed that Holy Confirmation be imparted to fourteen-year-olds, it explicitly stipulated: "*Doch soll diese Zahl der Jahre nicht also verstanden werden, dass nicht die Kinder auch in jüngern Jahren, so sie im Catechismo ziemlich unterricht sind, zur Beicht und Sakrament von ihren Aeltern sollen gebracht werden; sondern ihre Aeltern sollen sie zeitlicher zur Beicht und Sacrament gewöhnen, laut des Spruchs: lasset die Kinder zu mir kommen, solcher ist das Himmelreich. Aber die Confirmatio soll geschehen in verständigen Jahren, darin sie ihren Glauben und Zusage besser verstehen.*" Carl Gottlieb Bretschneider [ed.], *Corpus Reformatorum*, VII [Halle-in-Saxony: C.A. Schwetschke et Filius, 1840], cols. 200-201, 261.) Blessed Martin Luther is cautious on the whole issue; while refusing to affirm the necessity of the Eucharist in the case of children, he says in 1532 of 1 Corinthians 11:28: "*Non autem impedit quin etiam pueris possit sacramentum altaris dari*" (WA, *Tischreden*, 1, No. 365, p. 157). An undated utterance similarly says with reference to very small children (*kleinen Kinderlin*): "*Das ist Unrecht, dass sie es den Kindern nöthig zur Seligkeit achten, das Sacrament reichen; obs wol nicht Sünde sei, denn es S. Cyprianus auch gethan*" (WA, *Tischreden*, 6, No. 6777, p. 182). But in these passages he presumably has in mind the administration of Holy Communion to children under the age of reason, which contemporary law put at seven years. The entire question of the age of first Holy Communion in the practice of the Lutheran Reformers needs careful investigation.

THE SACRED MINISTRY AND HOLY ORDINATION IN THE SYMBOLICAL BOOKS OF THE LUTHERAN CHURCH

General. In the course of the confessional revival in the Church of the *Augsburg Confession* during the 19th and 20th centuries, Lutheran theologians interpreted the statements of the Symbolical Books about the sacred ministry in three typical ways.

Stated in an extreme form, the first view holds that the sacred ministry is only the activity of the universal royal priesthood of believers, the public exercise of which the Christian community has solemnly committed to certain persons merely for the sake of good order and efficiency. At the opposite extreme is the position which sees the sacred ministry as the contemporary form of the primitive apostolate and as the personal representation of Christ. A third view occupies the middle ground between these two positions and incorporates elements of both. It sees the sacred ministry as a divine institution that is essential to the church's existence. It regards the responsible public proclamation and application of the Gospel and the administration of the sacraments as the primary content of the sacred ministry. It looks upon ordination as the indispensable act of admission to the sacred ministry.

The modifications of these views are many. Each theologian believes that he has the authority of the Symbolical Books for his view. Almost all of the positions that Lutheran theologians currently take reflect to a greater or lesser degree the traditions of their own past which they are espousing or against which they are reacting.

2. *Sources.* The primary sources in the Symbolical Books for a doctrine of the sacred ministry are Articles 5, 14, and 28 of the *Augsburg Confession* (1530), Articles 13, 14, and 28 of the *Apology* (1531), Articles 4 in Part Two and 9 and 10 in Part Three of the *Smalcald Articles* (1536-1538), and the *Treatise on the Authority and Primacy of the Pope* (1537).[1] Except for the *Smalcald Articles*, which are by Luther, these are all from Philip Melanchthon's pen.

It is essential that one keep in mind the historical antithesis or at least the historical situation that conditioned a particular affirmation of the Symbolical Books.

3. *Lay people and clergymen.* The church consists of preachers and Christians (LC Decalog 262), rectors (*Pfarrherr*) and parishioners (LC Introduction 2-3); rectors and people (SC Introduction 6), bishops, rectors, and preachers on the one hand and Christians on the other (SC Table of Duties 2-3); laymen (FC Ep Summary Concept 5; SD Summary Concept 8) and the ministers of the Word who preside over the community of God (FC SD 10, 10). The presbyters are a part of the total church (Ap 22, 1.2.4). The church is more than (*supra*) the ministers; no minister has superiority or domination over the church at large (Tr 11).

4. *The divinely ordained purpose of the sacred ministry.* God instituted the sacred ministry (*ministerium ecclesiasticum; Predigtamt*) of teaching the Gospel and of administering the sacraments. His purpose in so doing is that men might obtain the faith that God forgives them by grace for Christ's sake through faith. The divine Word and the sacraments are, as it were, means by which God gives the Holy Spirit that works faith when and where God wills in those who hear the Word and receive the sacraments. The Lutherans reject the position that the Holy Spirit is received by purely interior preparation, meditation and activity without the external Word of God personally communicated through the sacred ministry (AC 5). The antithesis here is the asserted position of the Enthusiasts, who depreciated the sacred ministry.

The content of the sacred ministry is the responsible public proclamation of the Gospel and the administration of the Sacraments (AC 14; Ap 13, 7-9). It is not the offering up of an expiatory sacrifice which earns forgiveness of sins for the living and the dead. The sacred ministry (*Kirchendienst*) is "the Word preached and heard" (FC Ep 12, 22; SD 12, 30).

The obligation of the incumbents of the sacred ministry to proclaim and apply the Gospel of divine grace in Christ does not exclude the proclamation of the Word of God as judgment. On the contrary, it implies the latter as a necessary corollary of the sacred minister's primary task.

5. *The sacred ministry and the world*. The sacred ministry is part of the equipment of the church for an outreach into the world. God's gift of pastor-teachers to the church and their proclamation of the Gospel have in view the "edification" of the church (Tr 67). This is so not only in the metaphorical sense of the interior fortification of the church through an increase of devotion. It also looks to the literal building up of the church by the incorporation into it of those who are not as yet a part of it.[2]

6. *Functional and personal elements in the sacred ministry*. The Symbolical Books see the sacred ministry chiefly but not exclusively in dynamic and functional terms. Nevertheless, the Symbolical Books are conscious of the fact that apart from its incumbents the sacred ministry is an abstraction. "The authority of the *bishops* according to the Gospel is the authority or commandment to preach the Gospel, to retain sins, and to administer the sacraments" (AC 28, 5).[3] The ministry of the Word and sacraments is committed to *bishops as bishops* (AC 28, 21). "*Priests* ... are called to teach the Gospel and administer the sacraments to the people" (Ap 13,9). "The Gospel gives *those who rule over the churches* the command to teach the Gospel, to remit sins, and to administer sacraments.... This authority by divine right is common to *all who rule over churches*, whether they are called pastors, presbyters, or bishops" (Tr 60-61).

The church has the divinely imposed responsibility not merely of proclaiming the Gospel and administering the sacraments but also of choosing, calling, and ordaining fit persons to carry out these functions (Tr 67.72; Ap 13, 12 German). God gave to the church the concrete persons who discharge these functions, the "pastors and doctors" (*pastores et doctores*) that is, those who are engaged in the public and responsible "teaching of the Gospel" (*docendi evangelium*) (Tr 60-67).[4] We may have here a recognition that Eph. 4:11 by a kind of hendiadys is describing a single office with the words "pastors and teachers."

God wills to preach and to work through the human beings that the church has chosen and ordained to the sacred ministry (Ap 13, 11-12 German). Thus the incumbents of the sacred ministry are the human instruments through whom the Holy Spirit sanctifies and governs the church.

A minor problem arises on occasion when one tries to ascertain if "ministry" (*ministerium*) in a given passage means generally and abstractly the function of preaching the gospel and administering the sacraments — as it does frequently — or if it means concretely the incumbents of the sacred ministry as they engage in these functions. Sometimes, as in AC 5, 1 Latin and 28, 9, this is a matter of exegetical decision. Of interest is the fact that *Predigtamt* (literally, "the office of preaching") occasionally (for instance, AC 5,1 German and Ap 7, 20

German) has "the Gospel" or "the Gospel and the sacraments" as an explanatory apposition. To be effective, the Gospel must actually be preached and the sacraments must be administered. But these are precisely the functions the Symbolical Books attribute to the incumbents of the sacred ministry.

7. *The sacred ministry as service.* The sacred ministry is exactly a ministry (*ministerium; diakonia*), not a source of privilege, prestige, and power. The linkage of *ministerium* with *diakonia* goes back to the Vulgate of Eph.4:12. *Diakonia* has of course a very general and a technical sense ("a form of service") that does not refer to "deacons" in the strict sense which *diakonos* acquired in the later New Testament documents.

8. *The sacred ministry as an order in the church.* In order to give the sacred ministry an exclusively functional character and to eliminate distinctions between "lay people" and "ordained persons," some theologians have taken the position that the Lutheran view of the sacred ministry conceives of it only as a function of office that does not exist apart from its actual discharge, but never as an order in the church. The Symbolical Books, however, see the sacred ministry both as an office (*ministerium; Amt*) and as an order or estate (*ordo; Stand*) within the church (Ap 13, 11-12; 22, 13; 28, 13; SA III, 11, 1; compare SC Table of Duties 1, *heilige Orden und Stände*, "holy orders and estates"). This differentiation does not, of course, carry with it any narrowly clerical or hierarchical implications.

9. *The clergyman as the representation of God and of Christ.* In his proclamation and application of the Gospel and his administration of the sacraments, the officiant or celebrant acts in the place of God and in the stead of Christ (*vice Christi*), not in his own person (Ap 7, 28.47; 13, 12).

God preaches through the chosen clergy of the churches (Ap 13,12 German).

It is God Himself who baptizes (LC Baptism 10).

The absolution is to be believed as nothing less than a voice sounding from heaven (Ap 12, 40), that is, from God Himself. The confessor who administers absolution is ordinarily an ordained clergyman (Ap 12, 109, "the confession which is to be made to *priests*," and 176, "*the ministers of the Gospel* should absolve those who are converted;" Tr 60).

The Symbolical Books imply that the celebrant of the Sacrament of the Altar will be an ordained clergyman (AC 24,34 German, "the *priest* and others;" FC SD 7, 32, quoting Luther approvingly, "the *priests* who administer it.")[5] Christ binds His promise and activity in the Sacrament of the Altar to the speaking of the celebrant who consecrates the elements. "The words are spoken by the mouth of the *priest*, but by

God's power and grace through the words that he speaks, 'This is My body,' the elements set before us in the Supper are consecrated" (*gesegnet, consecrantur*, the Greek original of Saint John Chrysostom [347?-407] that the *Formula of Concord* here appropriates has *metarrhythmizei* [FC SD 7, 76; see also 77-78]).

The immorality or unbelief of an unworthy clergyman does not invalidate the Gospel that he preaches or the sacraments that he administers (AC 8, 1-3; Ap 7, 3.19. 28.47; LC Sacrament of the Altar 5.16; FC Ep 12, 27; SD 7, 32.89).

The Symbolical Books make frequent use of Luke 10:16 (AC 28, 22; Ap 7, 28.47; 12, 40; 28, 18-19): "He who hears you, hears Me." They see this passage as imposing on the clergy the obligation of teaching according to Christ's Word and not according to human traditions (Ap 28,19).

10. *Authority* (*potestas*). The authority of bishops (*potestas episcoporum*), the "power" of the keys (*potestas clavium*), or ecclesiastical authority (*potestas ecclesiastica*) is primarily the responsible public proclamation and application of the Gospel and the administration of the sacraments. These are described as the specific tasks and missions not only of an office in the church but of bishops and priests as public persons (Ap 13,9.12; 28,12).

The Symbolical Books accept the distinction between the authority of the clerical order (*potestas ordinis*) and the authority of jurisdiction (*potestas jurisdictionis*). The former is the competence of the pastor/bishop to do everything that he needs to do in order to proclaim and apply the Gospel and to administer the sacraments. The latter is his competence — to be exercised in accordance with the instructions contained in the Word of God — to excommunicate notorious evil livers and to reconcile them to the church again when they come to a better mind (Ap 28, 13).[6] The jurisdiction of the pastor/bishop in another place is seen as embracing reconciling sinners, rejecting doctrine that contradicts the Gospel, and excluding those whose impiety is a matter of public knowledge from the communion of the church by means of the divine Word alone, without human coercion. Herein the churches must obey them (AC 28, 20-21; SA III, 9; Tr 74).[7]

Minor episcopal functions, such as the administration of confirmation and the consecration of bells, do not, in the view of the Symbolical Books, require consideration (Tr 73).

11. *The sacred ministry as the identifying "mark" of the church (nota ecclesiae)*. Ap 7, 3 identifies the "signs" (*signa*) of the church as the Word of God, the response of the church to the divine gift in the form of its "profession" of confidence in Him, and the sacraments. Paragraph 20 of the same article calls the "pure teaching of the Gospel and the sacraments" the characteristic marks or "notes" (*notae*) of the church.

To be "signs" or "marks" of the church the Word of God must obviously be proclaimed and applied and the sacraments administered at concrete times and in concrete places. Since this proclamation and application of the Gospel and this administration of the sacraments is precisely the task of the sacred ministry, the sacred ministry itself becomes a "mark" or characteristic of the church.[8]

12. *The sacred ministry and the universal priesthood of the faithful.* The Symbolical Books nowhere attempt to derive the sacred ministry from the universal priesthood of the faithful.[9] The doctrine of the universal priesthood of believers had receded into minor importance — even for Luther himself — by the time the Symbolical Books were being framed. The classical prooftext for this teaching, 1 Peter 2:9, is cited only once in the Symbolical Books (Tr 69): "Since the church exclusively possesses the priesthood, it certainly has the right to choose and ordain its ministers."[10] It may be that the term "royal priesthood" is here best taken as another designation for the people (that is, the new Israel) of God: "Since only the church is the new Israel of God, it certainly has the right to choose and ordain its ministers." ("Church" here is obviously not to be equated with a local congregation.)

[handwritten margin note: is not the local congregation exclusively.]

[handwritten note between paragraphs: The concrete congregation is most surely "Church."]

The attitude of the Symbolical Books toward the Levitical ministry of the Old Testament is superficially ambivalent. They reject the late medieval suggestion that the Christian priesthood perpetuates the Levitical ministry as a function that earns the forgiveness of sins (AC 28, 39.61; Ap 13, 7; 24, 26.53-55), particularly when the obligation of sacerdotal celibacy is inferred from this thesis (Ap 23, 27. 41-42). At the same time the Symbolical Books identify the sacrifice of the Levites forecast in Mal. 3:3 with the sacrificial activity of those who preach the Gospel in the New Covenant and with the good works that this proclamation produces (Rom. 15:16) (Ap 24, 34).[11] The rejection of the Levitical ministry would seem to involve only the rejection of the misunderstanding and distortion or the function of the Levitical ministry as a service that earned forgiveness of sins. Again, the sacred ministry of the New Covenant is not bound to members of a single tribe functioning exclusively in one temple in a single Holy City; nor do they function by the leave of a single person, the bishop of Rome (Tr 25-26).

13. *The spiritual paternity of the clergy.* The clergy are spiritual fathers (LC Decalog 158-59). The use of *Pfarrkinder* (literally, "parish children") to describe the parishioners in the Symbolical Books has the fatherhood of the clergy as its correlative.

14. *The unitary character of the sacred ministry.* The Symbolical Books see the sacred ministry as unitary. There is basically only one holy order. That is the presbyterate-episcopate of the New Testament.

The Symbolical Books never call into question the existence of the sacred ministry itself by divine right (*jure divino*). What they do call into question is the postapostolic differentiation of grades within it by the separation of the presbyterate from the episcopate and, by implication, the subsequent introduction of the initially lay office of deacon into the major orders of the sacred ministry. These developments, they insist, exist only by human right (*jure humano*).

Regardless of their title, all ordained clergymen have the same basic authority to discharge the duties of their office (AC 28, 8.21; Tr 60-61.74). The terminology of the Symbolical Books reflects a recognition of an inevitable hierarchical structuring of any social institution like the church, but this does not have to do with inherent spiritual authority. They use the term "bishop" both for the head of a medieval diocese[12] and — on the analogy of the episcopal "parish-sees" (*paroikiai*) of the first three centuries — for the chief pastor of a town. They also use "rector" (*Pfarrherr*); "presbyter;" "pastor" (Tr 65); "preacher" (*Prediger*, especially to designate assistant clergymen); "priest" (*sacerdos/Priester*); and "minister" ({*Kirchen*}/*diener*) (See *Excursus I*, pp. 65-68).

15. *The diaconate and minor orders.* By the 16th century the diaconate had become a purely vestigial stage in the "course of honors" (*cursus honorum*) without any real function in the church in the Holy Roman Empire. The term *diaconus/Diakon* in the Lutheran documents of the 16th century (for example, Ap 13, 11 German) must be understood as referring to ordained priests serving as curates or assistants to the rector of a parish.[13]

The Symbolical Books were even less under constraint to discuss the lower orders of the clergy. These too had by the 16th century become only nominal stages in the process of becoming a priest. The tonsure was frequently received with no intention of taking higher orders in order to secure the valuable legal and canonical immunities that attached to clerical status.

16. *The adiaphoristic nature of church polity.* As long as the divinely ordained necessity of the sacred ministry is recognized and provided for, polity is an adiaphoron as far as the Symbolical Books are concerned.

Although the hierarchical structuring of the church is of human right only, the Symbolical Books affirm their preference for episcopal polity (Ap 14,1.5). The ideal is a universal episcopalism in which all bishops are equal in office, united in doctrine, belief, sacraments, prayer, and works of love (SA II, 4, 9).

17. *The authority of bishops.* Bishops have the right to establish regulations for the government of the church and for worship in the interest of good order, and the congregations and subordinate clergy

are bound in charity to obey such canons, but the bishops have no authority to make the salvation of the faithful dependent on obedience to such regulations nor may they properly institute any regulation and declare that observance of it earns forgiveness of sins (AC 28, 30-64). Change is of the nature of humanly established canons, and even the ceremonial injunctions of the Council of Jerusalem and the liturgical directives of the apostles were temporary in character (AC 28, 53-54.65-66; Ap 28, 16). The *Apology* sees the issue precisely as the question if the bishops have by divine right the authority to make laws the observance of which is useful for the attainment of everlasting life (Ap 28, 6). This it denies.

The authority of the bishops dare never conflict with the Gospel, and if the bishops teach or enjoin something that does contradict the Gospel (AC 28, 34), God has commanded the faithful not to obey (*ibid.*, 23-28, quoting the Sacred Scriptures, canon law, and St. Augustine; see also Tr 60-82).

18. *The secular power of hierarchs.* The Symbolical Books urge ecclesiastical authorities in the Holy Roman Empire — especially prince-bishops and prince-abbots — who also possess temporal power not to confuse the two (AC 28, 1-2). Both types of authority derive from God, but their ends are different (*ibid.*, 10-17). Pastors and bishops have no right to arrogate authority in temporal matters to themselves. Specifically, they have no divinely given authority in matters affecting matrimony and taxation (AC 28, 29; Tr 77-78.80-81; SC Marriage Booklet 1).

19. *Apostolic succession.* Without discussing the necessity of a succession of ministers, the Symbolical Books operate explicitly with the concept of a *de facto* succession of ordained ministers (SA III, 10; Tr 72, *adhibitis suis pastoribus*, "using their own pastors for this purpose").[14] It is noteworthy in this connection that Saint Jerome regards all presbyters as well as all bishops as "successors of the apostle" (*apostolorum successores*) (*Letter 146 [85] to Evangelus*, 1; Migne, *Patrologia latina*, 22, 1194). The bishops — that is, the pastors of town-dioceses — are the successors of the apostles in the government of the church (SA II, 4, 9).

The political situation in the 16th century throughout northern Europe — the domains of the King of Sweden excepted — made it a practical impossibility for the adherents of the *Augsburg Confession* to perpetuate the historic episcopate with apostolic succession.

20. *The papacy.* The papacy, in the sense of the Roman bishop's claim to universal primacy of jurisdiction, is a historical phenomenon that exists by human right only, not by divine right (Tr 1-21).

The bishop of Rome is by divine right the bishop and pastor only of the church of Rome. In addition he is the pastor of those who of their own will or through a political arrangement — that is, in both cases, by human right — have attached themselves to him (SA II, 4, 1). The papacy is not a universal institution; the Eastern churches have never been under the pope. In the patriarchate of the West, the medieval papacy did not exist for at least the first 500 years (*ibid.*, 4-5). The *Smalcald Articles* are dubious about the value of the papacy even as a humanly instituted symbol of Christian unity (*ibid.*, 7-8). As long as the pope insists on the last 17 words of *Unam Sanctam*,[15] he is the antichrist of 2 Thessalonians 2:4 (*ibid.*, 4.10-13).

There is no consensus of the fathers that would refer the rock of St. Matt. 16:8 to St. Peter, according to the *Treatise on the Authority and Primacy of the Pope*. But the *Treatise* agrees that St. Peter is the rock on whom the church is built, although he has this foundation-status because he is a "minister." Since the other apostles (and all clergy) received the same authority that Christ conferred on the prince of the apostles, "upon this rock" really means "upon this ministry" (Tr 22-29).

While Christ commanded St. Peter to shepherd and rule the church by means of the divine Word, this conferred on him no special superiority, since St. Peter had the Word only in common with the other apostles (Tr 30).

21. *The sacramental nature of order.* The term "sacrament" is applicable both to the sacred ministry itself and to ordination by the laying on of hands (Ap 13, 9-13).

22. *Ordination jure divino.* Ordination is effective (*rata*) by divine right (Tr 65). Obviously this implies as a lesser included principle that ordination itself is by divine right. Ordination can be called an adiaphoron only in a most narrow and technical sense.

The church institutes clergymen by divine command (Ap 13, 12). Because the authority to minister the Gospel exists wherever the church is, the church necessarily possesses the authority to choose, call, and ordain ministers (Tr 67). The churches are compelled (*coguntur*) to exercise this authority (Tr 72).[16]

The need for ordination that the adherents of the *Augsburg Confession* felt increasingly from the 1530s onward is reflected in the Ordination Register of Saint Mary's Church, Wittenberg, which provides data on 1,979 clergymen ordained between 1537 and 1560. Of these at least 1,025 (possibly as many as 1,069) are known to have been recruited from other professions and crafts, because the former profession or craft of the ordained is listed; 92 were former manual laborers.[17] It is possible that many more of the 900-plus ordinands had been recruited from other professions and crafts, since it is unlikely that all of them were university graduates.

The necessity of ordination was the issue in the famed "Freder ordination controversy" (1550-1556), which involved primarily John Freder (1510-1562) and the Pomeranian Reformer John Knipstro (1497-1556). A general synod of the clergy of Pomerania decided the controversy in 1556 by ruling that "the calling or election of a person (*vocatio vel electio personae*) must be distinguished from the ordination" and by committing itself to "the general rule of Luther" that "there must be a rightful vocation and ordination to the sacred ministry wherever the church of Christ is." The Wittenberg faculty, with Melanchthon concurring, rejected the position that ordination was an adiaphoron and held that Freder's vocation did not constitute an ordination.[18]

23. *The essentiality of ordination.* Only persons who are duly chosen, called, and ordained (*rite vocatus, ordentlicher Beruf*) are competent publicly and responsibly to proclaim the Gospel and to administer the sacraments (AC 14).

The verbs in AC 14 (*debeat/soll*) allow no option; they are the same verbs which describe the indispensable relation of good works to faith in AC 6. They have the force of the modern English "must" rather than "should."[19]

The *docent* ("they teach") with which the article begins, along with the location of the article among the doctrinal articles rather than among the reform (or "abuse") articles, indicates that the thesis of the article is a dogmatic statement.

That AC 14 implies ordination is clear from a number of facts:

First, it is the response of the Lutheran theologians to the charge that John Eck made in his *404 Propositions* that the Lutherans denied the existence of the sacrament of orders, called it a figment of human invention, and asserted that any layman at all can consecrate churches, confirm children, and so on (Wilhelm Gussmann, *D. Johann Ecks Vierhundertvier Artikel zum Reichstag von Augsburg 1530* [Kassel: Edmund Pillardy, 1930], nos. 267 to 268, pp. 134 and 177-78). The Lutheran response is that laymen are not admitted to the really crucial tasks of publicly and responsibly proclaiming the Gospel and of administering the sacraments.

Second, the word *rite* in *rite vocatus* implies in the normal terminology of the 16th century a formal ordination as something over and above a mere calling.[20]

Both *vocatio* ("calling") and *ordinatio* ("ordination") are extensively used in this period to describe the whole process of election and ordination.[21]

Third, the "canonical form of church government" (*politia canonica*) which Ap 28, 12 "does not reprehend," includes ordination.

Fourth, in 1530 there was still a ray of hope that the growing schism might be healed and that the bishops might consent to permit the proclamation of the Gospel. Under these circumstances the *Augsburg Confession* would not have proposed pretermitting ordination.

Fifth, the *Confutatio pontificia* accepted Article 14 in principle. It would not have done so if it had understood the article as suggesting that ordination was not necessary. The particular point on which the *Confutatio* insisted was that a bishop perform the ordination. This is clear from the *Apology* on Article 14. The first draft formulates the proviso in these words: "that ordination be performed by bishops (*ut ordinatio fiat ab episcopis*)." In its final form the *Apology* restates the proviso: "as long as we use canonical ordination (*si tamen utamur ordinatione canonica*)." The *Apology* makes it clear that it has no quarrel with ordination or even with episcopacy, but that episcopal ordination is not available to the proponents of the *Augsburg Confession*. The implication is that they may have no alternative but to avail themselves of ordination by clergymen in presbyter's orders. The number of such ordinations prior to 1530 was very small; indeed, regular ordinations in the Church of the *Augsburg Confession* did not begin until 1535 and on a large scale not until 1537.

Sixth, Ap 13, 11-12 relates the sacred ministry to ordination by using the term *ordo* for both.

Seventh, the edition of 1540 explicates Melanchthon's intention by adding after *vocatus*: "as St. Paul commends St. Titus to appoint presbyters city by city (*sicut et Paulus praecipit Tito, ut in civitatibus presbyteros constituat*)" (CR 26, 360).[22]

Eighth, when the Greek translation of the *Augsburg Confession* was drawn up in 1559, it added to *rite vocatus* in Article 14 the words *pros ten hyperesian* ("to the ministry"). In 1584 the Lutheran theologians of the University of Tübingen published their correspondence with His All-Holiness Jeremiah II, the ecumenical patriarch. In 1576 Jeremiah had indicated his understanding of the *Augsburg Confession* by paraphrasing the Greek translation at this point: *ei me hypo ton tachthenton enthesmos pros tauten ten hyperesian* ("except by those who have lawfully been instituted for this service"). In this sense he approved the article. Martin Crusius (1526-1607) significantly translated this phrase into Latin in these words: *nisi rite vocatus et ordinatus ad hanc functionem* ("unless he has been duly called and ordained to this function"). In 1577 Luke Osiander the Elder (1534-1604) and Crusius included in their summary of the areas where Jeremiah and the Lutherans agreed, the thesis "that it must not be granted to anyone to take to himself the office of teaching or administering the holy sacraments in the church unless he be lawfully called (*me nomikos klethenta*), but that in a case of necessity even a layman can rightfully baptize." How they understood this is apparent from their description of a Lutheran ordination: "In a well-attended assembly of the people, after a sermon has been preached and a number of prayers said pertaining to this matter, the candidates are ordained (*cheirotonountai*) by the bishop of the place, with one or more sacred ministers assisting, and then [the newly ordained clergyman] assumes the care of the church committed to him" (*Acta et scripta theologorum Wirtembergensium et Patriarchae Constantinopolitani D. Hieremiae, quae utrique ab anno MDLXXVI usque ad annum MDLXXXI de Augustana Confessione inter se miserunt, graece et latine ab iisdem theologis edita* [Wittenberg: Haeredes Johannis Cratonis, 1584], pp. 104-105.148.176).

24. *The ordination rite and the imposition of hands.* Ordination need not be an elaborate ceremony. Originally ordination was a simple rite in which a bishop laid hands on the candidate (Tr 70).[23] Ap 13, 12 sees the imposition of hands in ordination as an integral part of what it is ready to call "the sacrament of orders."[24]

25. *The minister of ordination.* The differentiation of grade between bishop and presbyters is not by divine right (Ap 14, 1; Tr 65), and therefore by divine right presbyters have the authority to ordain. An ordination that a pastor performs in his own church upon qualified candidates is valid by divine right (Tr 65).

When canonical bishops have become heretics or refuse to ordain, "the churches are compelled by divine right to ordain pastors and ministers, using their own pastors for this purpose (*adhibitis suis pastoribus*)." Significant is the bracketing of "calling, choosing, and ordaining" under the singular noun *jus* in Tr 67 and of "choosing and ordaining" again under the same singular noun in paragraphs 67, 69, and 72.

Ordination by the existing bishops is permissible for the sake of love and good order, but it is not necessary (SA III, 10, 1). Under the circumstances, the adherents of the *Augsburg Confession* ought and propose to ordain fit persons to the sacred ministry. This procedure conforms to the primitive practice of the church at Alexandria, as St. Jerome reports, while canon law affirms that the validity even of a heretical ordination must be conceded (*ibid.*, 3) (See Excursus II, pp. 68-71).

26. *The "ineradicable mark" (character indelebilis) of ordination.* The Symbolical Books do not address themselves to the somewhat metaphysical question of the "ineradicable mark" (*character indelebilis*) of ordination. In actual practice, the ecclesiastical authorities in the churches of the *Augsburg Confession* did not reordain those who had received holy orders in the medieval church. The present writer knows of no instance in the 16th century of the reordination of a clergyman who had received holy orders in the Church of the *Augsburg Confession*,

had laicized or apostatized, and then sought readmission to the exercise of the sacred ministry.

27. *The competence of laymen as sacramental ministers.* While the ordinary minister of Baptism and reconciliation/absolution is an ordained clergyman, the Symbolical Books, following a pseudo-Augustinian tradition of medieval canon law, allow a layman to be the extraordinary minister of these sacraments in a life-and-death emergency (Tr 67).

It is noteworthy that this passage does not accord a layman the authority to consecrate the Eucharistic elements even in a life-and-death emergency. That a layman may not presume to do so is not in the premises wholly an argument from silence. The Eucharist is not as indispensably necessary as Baptism or reconciliation with the church (absolution).[25]

The Symbolical Books concede to matrimony the status of an inferior sacrament (Ap 13, 14). While they do not discuss the question of the minister of marriage, Lutheran theology has always held that the contracting partners are the ministers of matrimony. The clergyman who presides at the liturgical exchange of their expressions functions (1) as a witness and (2) as the public representative of the church competent to impart the "priestly blessing" (*benedictio sacerdotalis*), as it came to be called.

EXCURSUS 1:
THE PRIMITIVE AND MEDIEVAL CHURCH ON THE IDENTITY OF BISHOPS AND PRESBYTERS

The Biblical evidence alleged in favor of the original identity of the episcopate and the presbyterate has been often rehearsed: The reference to bishops and deacons, with no mention of presbyters, in Phil. 1:1; the reference to the same officials of the Ephesian church as presbyters and bishops within the space of 12 verses in Acts 20:17-28; the reference to the presbyters that Titus had instituted in Crete as bishops (Titus 1:5-7); the listing of canonical qualifications for bishops and deacons but not for presbyters in the Pastorals; the designation of the authors of 2 and 3 John and of 1 Peter as presbyter and copresbyter (2 John 1; 3 John 1; 1 Peter 5:1);[26] and the reference to presbyters but not to bishops in James.

The situation is not much different in the period of the Apostolic Fathers. In 1 Clement (about 96) the leaders of the Christian communities are bishops and deacons (42, 4.5); presbyter seems to be the synonym of bishop at least in 44, 5 (see verses 1 and 4); 47, 6; 54, 2; and 57, 1. The community of the *Didache* (first half of the second century) also operates with bishops and deacons (15, 1). The presbyters are named as the ruling officers in the *Shepherd of Hermas* (about 150) (Vision 2,4,2.3 [see 2, 2, 6; 3, 7, 8; 3, 9, 7]; apostles, bishops, teachers, and deacons appear in 3, 5, 1; bishops and *philoxenoi* [literally, "stranger-lovers"] appear in *Similitude* 9, 27, 2). There are presbyters and deacons at Smyrna and at Philippi according to the *Letter* of St. Polycarp (69?-155?) 5,3; the address and 6,1 speak only of presbyters; the reference to Valens the presbyter in 11, 1 does not help us; St. Polycarp himself is called bishop only in the subsequently added titles of the *Letter* and of the *Martyrdom*. Presbyters are the ruling officers in 2 Clement 17, 3 (about A.D. 150). Presbyter is a synonym of bishop in St. Irenaeus of Lyons (130?-200?), *Against the Heresies* 3, 2, 2 (see 3, 3, 2) and 4, 26, 5 (Migne, *Patrologia graeca*, 7, 847.848.1055); in Eusebius, *Church History*, 5,24 (Migne, *Patrologia graeca*, 20, 505), quoting St. Victor of Rome (died 198); and in St. Clement of Alexandria (150?-215?), *Quis dives salvetur?*, 42 (Migne, *Patrologia graeca*, 9, 648). The *Letter* of St. Firmilian of Carthage (died 268), reproduced in St. Cyprian's correspondence as *Letter* 75, 4.7 (Migne, *Patrologia latina*, 3,1206.1209), can also be cited.

St. John Chrysostom recognizes the synonymity of presbyter and bishop in the New Testament in his *Homilies on Philippians* (on 1:1) (*Interpretatio omnium epistolarum Paulinarum per homilias facta*, ed. Frederick Field, 5 [Oxford: J. Wright, 1855], 8). So does Theodoret (393?-458?) in his comments on Phil. 1:1 and 1 Tim. 3:1 (Migne, *Patrologia graeca*, 82,560.804), as well as Oecumenius (6th century) in his *Commentary on the Acts of the Apostles* (on 20:17) (Migne, *Patrologia graeca*, 118, 255) and Saint Maximus the Confessor (580?-662) in his *Scholia on "Concerning the Divine Names" of Dionysius the Areopagite*, 1,1 (Migne, *Patrologia graeca*, 4, 185).

St. Jerome (342?-420) sets forth his position unambiguously in his *Letter 146 (85) to Evangelus:* "The apostle clearly [teaches] that presbyters are the same as bishops.... Listen to another bit of evidence in which it is most clearly proved that the bishop and the presbyter are the same.... But at a later date the choice of one who was placed ahead of the others was undertaken as a remedy against schisms, lest some one person by attracting a following would rend the church of Christ. Thus at Alexandria from St. Mark the Evangelist down to the bishops SS. Heraclas [died 247] and Dionysius [died 265], the presbyters always chose one of their own number whom they would place on a higher level and call bishop, just as if an army were to make an emperor, or deacons would choose out of their midst one whose diligence they knew and call him archdeacon. For, apart from ordination, what does a bishop do that a presbyter does not do?"[27]

In his *Commentary on Titus* (on 1: 5) he states: "The presbyter accordingly is the same as a bishop, and before rivalries came about in our religion through diabolical impulse and they would say among the people, 'I am of Paul,' 'I am of Apollo,' 'I am of Cephas;' the churches were governed by a common council of presbyters. Later on some individual believed that those whom he baptized were his, not Christ's, and it was decreed in the whole world that one of the presbyters should be chosen and placed over the rest and have the care of a single church and the seeds of divisions be removed. If anyone should think that this opinion, that the bishop and the presbyter are one and that the one designation refers to his age and the other to his office, is our own and not that of the Scriptures, let him read again the words of the apostle when he speaks to the Philippians.... Philippi is one city of Macedonia, and certainly in a single city there could not have been a number of bishops, as they are called. But because at that time the same persons were called bishops and presbyters, he speaks on that account without distinction about bishops as he does about priests.... On that account these things [are so] as we demonstrated that among the ancients presbyters and bishops were the same but gradually, in order that the emerging shoots of dissension might be plucked out, the whole responsibility was transferred to a single person. Therefore as the presbyters know that they are subject to the one who has been placed over them by an ecclesiastical custom, so the bishops should know that they are greater than presbyters more through custom than through the verity of an ordinance of the Lord and that they [all] ought to rule the church in common."[28]

"Among the ancients bishops and priests [were] the same,"[29] St. Jerome says in his *Letter 69 to Oceanus*, 3.

A relic of the old tradition emerges as late as the turn of the fifth/sixth century when the fourth of the Egyptian canons pseudonymously attributed to St. Hippolytus directs: "When a presbyter is ordained, all things concerning him shall be done as concerning a bishop, except taking his seat on the throne. And the bishop's prayer shall be said over him entire, except the name of 'bishop.' The bishop is in all respects the equivalent of the presbyter except in regard to the throne and ordination, because he was not given authority to ordain."[30]

St. Isidore of Seville (560?-636) in chapter 7 (*"De presbyteris"*) of his *De ecclesiasticis officiis* sees the authority to ordain and consecrate reserved to the bishops "to prevent a challenge to the discipline of the church by many to destroy its harmony and generate scandals," and he sees the New Testament addressing bishops under the designation presbyters and comprehending presbyters under the name of bishop.[31]

Amalarius of Metz (780-851?) in chapter 13 (*"De presbyteris"*) of the second book of his *De ecclesiasticis officiis* commits himself to the view of St. Ambrose in his treatise on the letters to Saint Timothy, that in ancient times presbyters were called both bishops and presbyters and to the now familiar view of Saint Jerome as expressed in his *Commentary on Titus* and in his *Letter 146 (85) to Evangelus* (Migne, *Patrologia latina*, 105, 1088 to 1091). According to Ludwig Ott[32] even John Duns Scotus (1264?-1308) allowed a certain probability to St. Jerome's view.

The question of the divine origin of the episcopate was extensively argued at Trent, and that council did not undertake to define the preeminence of bishops of presbyters with reference to the power of jurisdiction and the power of consecration in terms of either divine or human-ecclesiastical law.

EXCURSUS II:
THE MINISTER OF ORDINATION IN THE PRIMITIVE AND MEDIEVAL CHURCH

The earliest description of an ordination that has survived from the early church is in the *Apostolic Tradition* ascribed to St. Hippolytus of Rome (died 235). By this time the monarchical episcopate had been introduced in the church of the city of Rome.

In the era prior to the introduction of the monarchical episcopate, ordination would have been imparted by members of the local college of presbyter-bishops. Rome prior to the middle of the second century would have been a case in point.

In the second century it appears that the local college of presbyters instituted the bishop at Alexandria and Lyons.

Canon 13 of the Council of Ancyra (314), approved by St. Leo IV, bishop of Rome from 847 to 855, provided that neither *chorepiscopi* nor city presbyters may ordain presbyters or deacons outside their own *parochia*, unless the bishop has granted permission in the form of a letter for them to do so.[33]

According to Blessed John Cassian (360 to 435), the Egyptian presbyter-abbot Paphnutius ordained his successor, the abbot Daniel, to both the diaconate and the presbyterate.[34]

Even prior to their respective consecrations as bishops, SS. Willehad (730-789) and Liudger (774?-809) were administering ordination to the presbyterate in their missionary districts.

In his *Vita Sancti Willehadi*, 5, Saint Ansgar writes: "In the year of the Lord's incarnation 781, and in the fourteenth year of the reign of the noted prince Charles ... the servant of God Willehad began to build churches throughout Wigmodia [a district of Lower Saxony] and to ordain presbyters over them who would freely confer on the peoples [of the area] the counsels of salvation and the grace of Baptism."[35] Section 8 of the same biography recounts that in 785 St. Willehad "restored the churches that had been destroyed, and appointed approved individuals to exercise authority over the individual localities who would give to the peoples [of the area] the counsels of salvation."[36] St. Willehad was not consecrated a bishop until 787.

Altfrid (died 849), second bishop of Mimigernaford (Münster-in-Westfalen) and the successor of its founder, Saint Liudger, writes in his *Vita Sancti Liudgeri*, 19: "He baptized one Landric, the son of a certain prince [of Helgoland], and ordained him a presbyter after he had instructed him in the Scriptures."[37] Section 20 of the same biography states that Saint Liudger, "in his accustomed fashion, with all longing and concern strove to do good to the rude peoples among the Saxons by teaching them and, after the thornbushes of idolatry had been rooted out, to sow the Word of God diligently in place after place, to build churches, and to ordain presbyters whom he had educated to be co-workers with him [in proclaiming] the Word of God in each of these places." During this period St. Liudger declined episcopal rank humbly (*pontificalem gradum humiliter*) and tried to persuade disciples of his to receive episcopal orders in his stead; he yielded only later to the arguments of Bishop Hildibald of Cologne and allowed himself to be consecrated.[38]

Following the lead of Hugo of Pisa (Huguccio; died 1210), many medieval canonists took the position that a simple presbyter was competent to ordain to the presbyterate if the pope empowered him to do so.

Concretely, the bull *Sacrae religionis* of Boniface IX, dated Feb. 1, 1400, provides: "We ... grant ... [to] the same abbot [of the Monastery of SS. Peter and Paul the Apostles and of St. Osith the Virgin and Martyr, of the Order of Canons Regular of St. Augustine, in Essex in the diocese of London], and [to] the abbots of the same monastery who are his successors for the time being in perpetuity, to have the power freely and licitly to confer on all professed canons, present and future, all minor orders, as well as the subdiaconate, the diaconate, and the presbyterate, at the times established by the law, and that the said canons promoted in this way by the said abbots are able to serve freely and licitly in the orders so received, notwithstanding any conflicting constitutions, apostolic and others, whatsoever, put forth to the contrary and reinforced with any degree whatever of firmness."[39] Because of the objection of Bishop Robert of London, who had the right of patronage in the monastery named, the same pope on Feb. 6, 1403, in the bull *Apostolicae sedis* withdrew the permission granted in *Sacrae religionis*, again specifying that the privilege had authorized the abbots of the monastery to confer orders through the presbyterate.[40]

In the bull *Gerentes ad vos*, Martin V on Nov. 16, 1427, conferred on the abbot of the Cistercian monastery at Altzelle in Upper Saxony the license and faculty "of conferring on each of the monks of the same monastery and on persons subject to you, the abbot, all holy orders, without in the least requiring a license to do this from the diocesan of the place, notwithstanding any constitutions and ordinances, apostolic and otherwise, to the contrary."[41]

On Aug. 29, 1489, Innocent VIII, in the bull *Exposcit tuae devotionis*, conferred on Abbot John of Cîteaux and on "the four other aforesaid abbots of [La Ferté, Pontigny, Clairvaux, and Morimond], and to their successors [authority] freely and licitly ... to confer lawfully upon any monks so ever of the said order, as religious of the aforesaid monasteries whom you shall find qualified therefore, the orders of the subdiaconate and the diaconate."[42]

As conservative a Roman Catholic dogmatician as Ludwig Ott sees this authorization of presbyters to impart orders as posing a question that demands one of two answers: (1) Either the popes of the 15th century "were victims of the erroneous theological opinions of their times;" or (2) "a simple priest is an extraordinary dispenser of the orders of diaconate and presbyterate, just as he is an extraordinary dispenser of confirmation. In this latter view, the requisite power of consecration is contained in the priestly power of consecration as *potestas ligata*. For the valid exercise of it a special exercise of the papal power is, by divine or church ordinance, necessary."[43]

With reference to the first answer, at least one Roman Catholic scholar holds that if the popes in question had erred in giving these faculties, the erring pope "in his official capacity as pope [would have] imposed material idolatry on those of the faithful who sought the ministry of men ordained in virtue of these bulls."[44] The final clause of the second answer is for a Lutheran, of course, not a necessary conclusion.

While a Lutheran will not insist that "ordinary minister" necessarily implies an "extraordinary minister" in certain circumstances — although this might very well be a legitimate inference — he observes that the bull of union of the Armenians (*Exsultate Deo* of Nov. 22, 1439; Eugene IV and the Council of Florence) declares with reference to the sacrament of order: "The ordinary minister of this sacrament is a bishop (*ordinarius minister huius sacramenti est episcopus*)."[45]

Gabriel Vázquez (1549-1604) asserts that Benedictine presbyter-abbots and Franciscan presbyter-missionaries in India had received authority to administer the sacrament of orders, but this statement still lacks documentation.[46]

While the historical evidence inclines most Lutherans to deny that the diaconate was originally an integral part of the clerical office, the Roman Catholic inclusion of the diaconate among the authentically sacramental grades of the clerical estate is not wholly without significance for the present discussion. If the making of a deacon is part of the single sacrament of order, it would seem to be important that in the case of the diaconate the minister of the sacrament has had to be a person in episcopal orders.

Granted the unity of the sacrament of order that Roman Catholic theology asserts, a Lutheran sees a number of questions arising. For instance, if there is only one sacrament, why should a minister who is competent to administer part of the sacrament not be competent to administer the whole sacrament? Concretely, if a priest is competent to ordain to the diaconate, why is he not intrinsically competent to ordain to the presbyterate? If the episcopal order is competent to coopt additional members of the order and if in emergencies laymen can by baptism coopt, as it were, additional members of the one holy catholic and apostolic church, why cannot the presbyterate function similarly, at least in a case of necessity? Again if a presbyter is competent to administer one properly episcopal function, namely confirmation, why is he not competent to administer another properly episcopal function, namely ordination?

If it be argued that to concede the validity of presbyteral ordinations to the presbyterate is depriving the bishop of a privilege that is exclusively his, a possible answer is that the alienation of an exclusive privilege is not something unique in the experience of the episcopal order. Once the monarchical bishop had established his preeminent authority, he was for a long time normally the only person that administered Baptism, a privilege that he ultimately came to share with the presbyters. Until the fifth century it was his exclusive prerogative to preach during the Sunday Eucharist; this prerogative too he had to share with the presbyters. Until the tenth century he alone administered absolution to the penitents who were undergoing public discipline; thereafter this became a competence of the presbyters as well. The once exclusively episcopal privilege of administering chrismation was widely delegated io presbyters in the Eastern Church at an early date. In more recent times the administration of the parallel Western ceremony of confirmation has ceased to be the exclusive province of the bishop in the Roman Catholic Church.

The Lutheran Church does not equate any ecclesial community — its own, the Roman Catholic (SA III, 12, 1) or any other large or small — with the one holy catholic and apostolic church. It respects the right of the Roman Catholic Church to determine the canonical licitness of the ordinations performed within that communion and does not seek to impose Lutheran standards of canonical licitness upon the Roman Catholic community. By the same token it reserves to itself the right to establish its own standards of canonical licitness in the case of ordinations on those points where the divine law (*jus divinum*) makes no prescriptions and to reject those of other denominations as binding in matters that cannot be established as being of divine right.

ENDNOTES

1. This article uses the following abbreviations: AC, *Augsburg Confession*; Ap. *Apology of the Augsburg Confession*; SA, *Smalcald Articles*; Tr, *Treatise on the Authority and Primacy of the Pope*; SC *Small Catechism*; LC, *Large Catechism*; FC, *Formula of Concord*; Ep. *Epitome*; SD, *Solid Declaration*; WA, *Weimarer Ausgabe*, the critical edition of Martin Luther's works; CR, *Corpus Reformatorum* (for the works of Philip Melanchthon).

2. LC Our Father 52-54: "So that we who have accepted [the divine Word] may remain with it and daily increase in it and that it may find a response and acceptance among others and go mightily throughout the world, so that the Holy Spirit may lead many to come to the kingdom of grace and become partakers of salvation;" "that [the kingdom of God] may come to those who are not yet in it;" "that the Gospel may be purely proclaimed throughout the world." Of interest is the stress in the Wittenberg ordination formularies of the late 1530s (WA 38, 423-33) on ordination as the fulfillment of the petition that Christ commanded His disciples to offer, imploring the Lord of the harvest to send out laborers into the plentiful harvest (Matt. 9:37-38; see John 4:35). The prayer of the rite invokes the Holy Spirit to the end that God's ministers may be His evangelists with great masses of people (*scharen/hauffen*) (*ibid., 429, 6-430, 13*).

3. "According to the Gospel" is in the Symbolical Books as a synonym for "by divine right (*jure divino*)" (AC 28,21 Latin; see also Tr 60.61 and SA II, 4,1).

4. At another place, however, outside the Symbolical Books, Melanchthon would differentiate the authority to teach the Gospel (*potestas docendi evangelium*) from the authority to govern the church (*potestas gubernationis ecclesiae*). The former is common to the clergy and to the *doctores* (like himself); the latter — the administration of the church (*administratio ecclesiae*), which includes the administration of the sacraments (*administratio sacramentorum*) — belongs to the clergy alone (CR 24, 313).

5. The case (1531) of John Sutel in Göttingen makes it clear that in the mind of the early Lutheran community the mere possession of a call without a public ordination through the laying on of hands did not authorize the recipient to preside over the Eucharistic assembly and pronounce the formula of consecration. Luther counsels Sutel to refrain from celebrating the Sacrament of the Altar until he "publicly before the altar with prayer and the laying on of hands receives from the other clergymen the evidence [of the legitimacy of his status] and authority to celebrate the Sacrament of the Altar" (*tum publice coram altari a reliquis ministris cum oratione et impositione manuum testimonium accipies et autoritatem coenae tractandae* [WA Br 6, 43-44]).

6. These *potestates* correspond to the authority to sanctify and the authority to rule.

7. The authority to proclaim the Gospel and to administer sacraments implies the authority to ordain. In the *Loci communes* of 1538 and 1541 Melanchthon includes in the authority of the clerical order (*potestas ordinis*) the command to call — in the broad sense that includes ordaining — ministers (*mandatum vocandi ministros*) (CR 21, 501). So does the *Confessio Saxonica* of 1551 (CR 28, 413, *ordinare ministros rite vocatos*, "to ordain rightly called ministers").

8. See also Luther, *Von den Conciliis und Kirchen*, WA 50, 632, 35-633, 11.

9. The Wittenberg ordination formula H of the late 1530s stresses that the sanctification represented by the vocation into the holy and divine ministry is a second sanctification, the first being through the divine Word and the Sacrament of Baptism (WA 38, 424, 23-425, 5.28-34).

10. The only other passage in Melanchthon's works known to this writer in which the church's authority to choose and ordain clergymen is related to I Peter 2:9 is in his *Loci communes* of 1535. Here he argues not only from the cited passage, but also from Ephesians 4:8. The priesthood (*sacerdotium*) in this passage is the authority to administer the Gospel (*jus administrandi evangelii*); thus it includes the church's right and obligation to administer the Gospel by calling fit persons into the service of the Gospel (CR 21, 505).

11. This is, of course, wholly consistent with the transfer in 1 Peter 2:9 of the title "a kingdom of priests and a holy nation" of Ex. 19:6 from the Israel of the Old Covenant with its Levitical priesthood to the Israel of the New Covenant.

12. Although it was not unusual for some bishops, for example both Archbishop Gebhard II von Waldburg (1547-1601) of Cologne and his successor in the archsee, Archbishop Ernest of Bavaria (1554-1612), to be only in priest's orders.

13. In the fourth century St. Jerome in *Letter 146 (85) to Evangelus* was making the point that there is a primordial difference between the presbyter-bishops on the one hand and deacons on the other (Migne, *Patrologia latina*, 22, 1193-94).

14. It is regrettable that the important words *adhibitis suis pastoribus* are omitted in the German translation as well as in Theodore G. Tappert (translator-editor), *The Book of Concord* (Philadelphia: Muhlenberg Press, 1959), p. 332.

15. "Further, we declare, state [and] define that for every human being it is absolutely necessary for salvation to be under the bishop of Rome *(Porro subesse Romano pontifici omni humanae creaturae declaramus, dicimus, diffinimus omnino esse de necessitate salutis)*" (Henry Denzinger, *Enchiridion symbolorum definitionum et declarationum de rebus fidei et morum*, 32d edition by Adolf Schönmetzer [Barcelona: Herder, 1963; hereafter cited as Denzinger-Schönmetzer], no. 875).

16. Preaching on Acts 13:1 ff., Luther had declared in 1524: "One must not act on God's behalf unless one is called and ordained by God.... I preach in that name, because I have been ordained thereto *(Nemo in causa Dei agere debet, nisi sit vocatus et ordinatus a Deo ... Ego praedico in eo nomine, quia ordinatus ad hoc)*" (WA 17, 1, 508, 10-11; 509, 16-17).

17. See *Bekenntnisschriften der evangelisch-lutherischen Kirche herausgegeben im Gedenkjahr der Augsburgischen Konfession 1930*, 5th ed. (Göttingen: Vandenhoeck & Ruprecht, 1963), p. 501, n. 1.

18. James Henry Balthasar, *Erste Sammlung einiger zur Pommerischen Kirchen-Historie gehörigen Schriften* (Greifswald: Andreas Buss, 1723), p. 114. See the comprehensive excursus on the controversy in Hellmut Lieberg, *Amt und Ordination bei Luther und Melanchthon* (Göttingen: Vandenhoeck & Ruprecht, 1962), pp. 360-71.

19. See, for example, the letter *Ejus exemplo* of Innocent III to the archbishop of Tarragona (the profession of faith of Durandus of Huesca) (1208): "*Non potest nec* debet *eucharistiam consecrare ... nisi sit presbyter ... regulariter ordinatus* (No one can or may consecrate the eucharist ... unless he is a priest ... regularly ordained)" (Denzinger-Schönmetzer, no. 794).

20. See Hans Asmussen, *Warum noch lutherische Kirche? Ein Gespräch mit dem Ausburgischen Bekenntnis* (Stuttgart: Evangelisches Verlagswerk, 1949), pp. 182-86; Ernst Sommerlath, "*Amt und allgemeines Priestertum,*" *Schriften des Theologischen Konvents Augsburgischen Bekenntnisses*, 5 (Berlin: Lutherisches Verlagshaus, 1953), 57-58.64; and Martin Dörne, *Lutherisches Pfarramt: Rechenschaft und Wegweisung* (Leipzig: A. Deichert, 1937), pp. 14-15. For a medieval example of the use of *rite* see chapter 1, *De fide catholica*, of Lateran IV (1215): "[*Hoc*] *sacramentum nemo potest conficere nisi sacerdos qui rite fuerit ordinatus* (No one can confect [this] sacrament except a priest who has been duly ordained)" (Denzinger-Schönmetzer, no. 802).

21. A not untypical statement is one that Luther makes in a sermon of 1524: "*Sed nos qui jam habemus ministeria commendabimus in nostrum ministerium... Si ... scimus pium hominem, extrahimus eum et damus in virtute verbi quod habemus auctoritatem praedicandi verbum et dandi sacramenta. Hoc est ordinare.* (But we who already have ministries will recommend [others] into our ministry.... If ... we know a devout man, we take him out and by virtue of the Word that we possess we give him the authority to proclaim the Word

and to administer the sacraments. This is what it means to ordain)" (WA 15, 721, 1-5).

22. The bearing of this becomes clearer from another statement of Melanchthon in his disputation *De politia ecclesiae seu ministerio et ordinationibus* (date uncertain): "*Jus vocandi et eligendi ministros pertinent non tantum ad populum, sed Paulus jubet Titum constituere presbyteros, et Timotheo scribit: Nemo cito manum impone. Necesse est igitur, pastores a pastoribus ordinari ... Pugnat cum jure divino et cum veteri ecclesia* demokratia *in qua populus ad se rapit electionem, sine judicio et approbatione pastorum* (The right of calling and choosing ministers [of the church] belongs not only to the people, but St. Paul directs St.Titus to appoint presbyters, and he writes to St. Timothy, 'Do not lay hands on anybody rashly.' It is accordingly necessary that pastors be ordained by pastors ... The kind of democracy in which the people snatch the election [of clergymen] to themselves without the judgment and the approbation of the pastors is in conflict both with the divine law and with the ancient church)" (CR 12, 490).

23. The "custom" referred to in this passage was not ordination but the mode of electing and ordaining/consecrating the pastor/bishop. The first antithesis is between the election of the pastor by the people of the parish/diocese and the arbitrary selection of the pastor by higher authority. The second antithesis is between the simple primitive rite and the elaborate ceremonies into which ordinations and consecrations had developed in the late Middle Ages. The Wittenberg ordination rite of the late 1530s (WA 38, 423-33) called for the ordination to take place within a celebration of the Holy Eucharist and consisted of seven elements: (a) corporate prayer for laborers in the Lord's harvest; (b) *Veni Sancte Spiritus* with versicle, response, and the Whitsunday collect; (c) lessons; (d) obligation of the ordinands to the sacred ministry; (e) imposition of hands by the ordinator and the assistant ministers with the Our Father and an invocation of the Holy Spirit upon the ordinands; (f) "Go then and tend the flock" (1 Peter 5:2-4) as a votum; (g) blessing of the newly ordained clergymen with the sign of the holy cross. There is some variation in parts and sequence among the four surviving rites.

24. Compare Luther's statement in his *Commentary on Genesis* (on 28:17): "*Impositio manuum non est traditio humana; sed Deus facit et ordinat ministros* (The laying on of hands is not a human tradition; on the contrary, God makes and ordains ministers [of the church])" (WA 43, 600, 25-26).

25. For that reason the opinion of the Church of the *Augsburg Confession* of this period holds that a layman may not celebrate the Eucharist even in an emergency (WA Br 7, 338-39, 365-66; WA Tr 5, 621, no. 6361). The assertion has repeatedly been made (for example, by Robert E. McNally, *The Unreformed Church* [New York: Sheed and Ward, 1965], p. 134, and by Clyde Leonard Manschreck, *Melanchthon, the Quiet Reformer* [New York: Abingdon Press, 1958], p. 72) that Melanchthon, the lay author of the *Augsburg Confession*, the *Apology*, and the *Tractate*, presumed to celebrate the Eucharist in Wittenberg in 1521. This assertion is based on a misunderstanding of a Latin account of Melanchthon's attendance with his students at a celebration of the Eucharist in which both kinds were distributed to the communicants. Melanchthon says explicitly of himself: "I do not possess the authority to administer the sacraments (*Non habeo administrationem sacramentorum*)" (CR 24, 313).

26. The textually dubious *episkopountes* ("exercising oversight") in 1 Peter 5:2 would, if it were original, not be without significance in this connection.

27. *"Apostolus perspicue [docet] eosdem esse presbyteros quos episcopos ....Quod autem postea unus electus est, qui caeteris praeponeretur, in schismatis remedium factum est, ne unusquisque ad se trahens Christi ecclesiam rumperet. Nam et Alexandriae a Marco evangelista usque ad Heraclam et Dionysium episcopos, presbyteri semper unum ex se electum, in excelsiori gradu collocatum, episcopum nominabant, quomodo si exercitus imperatorem faciat; aut diaconi eligant de se, quem industriam noverint, et archidiaconum vocent. Quid enim facit excepta ordinatione episcopus, quod presbyter non faciat?"* (Migne, *Patriologia latina*, 22, 1193-94).

28. *"Idem est ergo presbyter qui et episcopus, et antequam diaboli instinctu studia in religione fierent, et diceretur in populis, 'Ego sum Pauli, ego Apollo, ego autem Cephae,' communi presbyterorum concilio ecclesiae gubernabantur. Postquam vero unusquisque eas quos baptizaverat suos putabet esse, non Christi, in toto orbe decretum est, ut unus de presbyteris electus superponeretur caeteris ad quem omnis ecclesiae cura pertineret, et schismatum semina tollerentur. Putet aliquis non Scripturarum sed nostram esse sententiam, episcopum et presbyterum unum esse, et aliud aetatis, aliud esse nomen officii, relegat apostoli ad Philippenses verba dicentis... Philippa una est urbs Macedoniae et certe in una civitate plures, ut nuncupantur, episcopi esse non poterant. Sed quia eosdem episcopos illo tempore quos et presbyteros appellabant, propterea indifferenter de episcopis quasi de presbyteris est locutus.... Haec propterea, ut ostenderemus apud veteres eosdem fuisse presbyteros quos et episcopos; paulatim vero ut dissensionum plantaria evellerentur ad unum omnem sollicitudinem esse delatam. Sicut ergo presbyteri sciunt se ex ecclesiae consuetudine ei qui sibi praepositus fuerit esse subjectos, ita episcopi noverint se magis consuetudine quam dispositionis dominicae veritate presbyteris esse majores, et in commune debere ecclesiam regere"* (Migne, *Patrologia latina*, 26, 597-98).

29. *"Apud veteres iidem episcopi et presbyteri [fuerunt]"* (Migne, *Patrologia latina*, 22, 656).

30. Quoted in the translation of Francis Crawford Burkitt in Walter Howard Frere, "Early Ordination Services," *Journal of Theological Studies*, 16 (1914-1915), 345-47.

31 *"Ne a multis ecclesiae disciplina vendicata concordia solveret, scandala generaret."* For the whole passage, see Migne, *Patrologia latina*, 83, 787-88.

32. Ludwig Ott, *Fundamentals of Catholic Dogma*, trans. Patrick Lynch, ed. James Bastible, 6th ed. (St. Louis: B. Herder Book Company, 1964), p. 453.

33. John Dominic Mansi, *Sacrorum conciliorum nova et amplissima collectio*, 2 (Florence: Antonius Zatta, 1759), 517. The occasion of this 18-bishop council is uncertain and the canons (including this one) appear in various forms (see *ibid.*, cols. 525 and 531). Whatever the text of the canon may originally have been, it is noteworthy that a later generation saw nothing inappropriate about the version here cited.

34. *"Merito puritatis ac mansuetudinus [Danihelis] a beato Pafnutio solitudinis eiusdem presbytero ... ad diaconii est praelectus officium. In tantum enim idem beatus Pafnutius virtutibus ipsius adgaudebat, ut ... coaequare sibi etiam sacerdotii ordine festinaret, siquidem ... eum presbyterii honore provexit* (In view of [Daniel's] purity and gentleness the blessed Paphnutius, the presbyter of the same desert monastery ... preferred [Daniel] to the office of deacon. Indeed, the same blessed Paphnutius rejoiced in [Daniel's] virtues to such a degree, that ... he hastened to put [Daniel] on a par with himself even in the order of the priesthood, inasmuch as ... he advanced him to the honor of the presbyteral office.)" John Cassian, *Conférences*, IV, 1, ed. E. Pichery (Paris: Les Éditions du Cerf, 1955), p. 167.

35. *"Anno incarnationis Domini 781, regni vero memorati principis Karoli 14mo ...
servus Dei Willehadus per Wigmodiam ecclesias coepit construere ac presbyteros
super eas ordinare, qui libere populis monita salutis ac baptismi conferrent
gratiam"* (George Henry Pertz, ed., *Monumenta Germaniae historica:
Scriptores*, 2 [Stuttgart: Anton Hiersemann, 1963], 381, 48-50).
36. *"Ecclesias quoque destructas restauravit, probatasque personas qui populis monita
salutis darent singulis quibus locis praeesse disposuit"* (*ibid.*, p. 383, 1-3).
37. *"Cuiusdam etiam eorum principis filium, Landricum nomine, accepit a fonte; quem
sacris literis imbutum ordinavit presbiterum"* (*ibid*, p. 410, 35-36).
38. *Ibid.*, p. 411, 11-22. The quoted passage reads in the original: *"More solito cum
omni aviditate et sollicitudine rudibus Saxonum populis studebat in doctrina
prodesse, erutisque ydolatrie spinis, verbum Dei diligenter per loca singula serere,
ecclesias construere, et per eas singulos ordinare presbiteros, quos verbi Dei
cooperatores sibi ipsi nutriverat."*
39. *"Nos ... ut idem abbas et successores sui in perpetuum abbates eiusdem monasterii
pro tempore existentes omnibus et singulis canonicis praesentibus et futuris
professis eiusdem monasterii omnes minores necnon subdiaconatus, diaconatus
et presbyteratus ordines statutis a iure temporibus conferre libere et licite valeant
et quod dicti canonici sic per dictos abbates promoti in sic susceptis ordinibus libere
et licite ministrare possint, quibuscumque constitutionibus apostolicis et aliis
contrariis in contrarium editis quibuscumque quacumque firmitate roboratis
nequaquam obstantibus ... indulgemus"* (Denzinger-Schönmetzer, no. 1145).
40. Denzinger-Schönmetzer, no. 1146.
41. *"Singulis monachis eiusdem monasterii ac personis tibi abbati subiectis omnes
etiam sacros ordines conferendi, dioecesani loci licentia super hoc minime
requisita, constitutionibus et ordinationibus apostolicis ceterisque contrariis
nequaquam obstantibus"* (Denzinger-Schönmetzer, no. 1290).
42. *"Quibuscumque dicti ordinis monachis, aliis vero quatuor abbatibus praefatis ac
eorum successoribus, ut suorum monasteriorum praedictorum religiosis quos ad
id idoneos repereritis, subdiaconatus et diaconatus ordines ... rite conferre ... libere
et licite"* (Denzinger-Schönmetzer, no. 1435). The diaconate was conferred
in Rome at least as late as 1662 with the apparent knowledge and approval
of the pope (Corrado Baisi, *Il ministro straordinario degli ordini sacramentali*
[Rome: Libreria Cattolica Italiana, 1935], pp. 16-24). Elsewhere Cistercians
made use of the permission until it began to fall into desuetude in the 18th
century, and an order for the ordination of a subdeacon and deacon is still
a part of the most recent edition (1949) of the *Rituale Cisterciense* (Denzinger-Schönmetzer, p. 352).
43. Ott, p. 459.
44. Alban Baer, art. "Abbot, Ordination by," in H. Francis Davis, Aidan Wil-
liams, Ivo Thomas, and Joseph Crehan, eds., *A Catholic Dictionary of
Theology*, 1 (London: Thomas Nelson and Sons, 1962), 4.
45. Denzinger-Schönmetzer, no. 1326. Canon 951 of the 1917 Code of Canon
Law makes the point that a consecrated bishop is the ordinary minister of
holy ordination, but it contemplates an extraordinary minister who may
lack the "mark" of a bishop (*charactere episcopali careat*) but who "may
receive either from the law (*a jure*) or from the Apostolic See by a special
indult the authority (*potestatem*) to impart certain orders" (*Codex juris canonici
Pii x Pontificis Maximi* [Rome: Typi Polyglotti Vaticani, 1923], p. 264).
46. *Disputationes in partem tertiam Summae theologicae S. Thomae*, disp. 243, c. 4,
cited by Piet Fransen, art. "Ordo," in Josef Höfer and Karl Rahner, eds.,
Lexikon für Theologie und Kirche, 7 (Freiburg: Verlag Herder, 1962), 1216.

THE LUTHERAN CHURCH — A SACRAMENTAL CHURCH

Christianity is in its historic aspect essentially sacramental, and until the day of the Swiss Reformers non-sacramental Christianity of the sort that went out of Geneva would have been utterly unthinkable. The ancient Creeds are thoroughly sacramental. Quite apart from its genesis as a baptismal symbol and the consequent association of sacramental ideas with its use, the Apostles' Creed has a phrase that the early Church frequently invested with a meaning different from that which a later age gave it, "*communionem sanctorum*," taken not as a masculine, "communion of saints," but as a neuter, "communion of holy things," i.e., a sacramentally established fellowship. Variant versions of the baptismal symbol add great support to this theory. The Nicene Creed relates the "forgiveness of sins" to sacramental experience through its declaration, "I acknowledge one Baptism for the remission of sins." By its acceptance of the Catholic Creeds and by its identification of its doctrine with that of the historic Catholic Church, the Lutheran Church is, of course, committed to the same position as that of the ancient Church.

Our sacramental thinking is necessarily affected by the fact that "sacrament" in the sense in which theology uses it is not a scriptural term. Although the word which the Greek uses for sacrament, *mysterion*, is employed some thirty times in the New Testament, mostly in the Pauline Epistles, and but three times in the Gospels, *mysterion* as the equivalent of "sacrament" as either we or the Latin Church define it is not employed by the sacred writers. In discussing the nature and number of the sacraments, therefore, we are dealing not with inspired definitions but with the arbitrary ecclesiastical distinctions. The history of this point is a bewildering mélange of conflicting opinions. St. Thomas of Aquino and the Council of Lyons in 1274 fixed the number at seven in which they were followed by the Greeks since the days of Michael Palæologus and in the West by Trent. The question was reopened at the time of the Reformation, and while the *Apology of the Augsburg Confession* declared in favor of three primary Sacraments — Baptism, Eucharist, and the Absolution — it recognized the possibility of secondary sacraments, a name it was perfectly prepared to give to Marriage, Ordination, Confirmation, and Unction, provided these were understood evangelically and accurately differentiated from the three chief Sacraments. Article XIII of the *Apology*, *De numero et usu Sacramentorum*, is herein significantly in agreement with the most influential symbol of the Middle Ages, the so-called *Innocentianum* of 1213.

I

The Sacrament of Holy Baptism still enjoys its ancient place of prominence in the Lutheran Church. We have our people indoctrinated on this point sufficiently well that even if they neglect every other religious duty they still frequently bring their children to be baptized or at least do not interpose any serious objection when they are urged or invited to bring their children to the laver of regeneration.

It is to be feared, however, that we have allowed our people to water down their sacramental belief. Speaking on the basis of a missionary ministry on the frontier of Minnesota's Iron Range mining towns, in the course of which Holy Baptism was administered to 138 candidates in thirty-eight months, the viewpoint was often expressed that Baptism was a sort of formal giving of a name, the symbol of entrance into the Church, and a magical procedure that brought the child good luck, but uniformly there appeared little sense of the need for the prompt application of this Holy Sacrament to a newborn child.

It was anciently the custom to baptize the child within the first week of its earthly life, and in parts of Germany at least it was the normal thing for a long period after the Reformation to baptize a child on the day of birth. While examining a considerable number of Pomoranian church books with a view to verifying certain data about my ancestry, I found page after page of baptismal entries extending well over a century with only occasional birthdates supplementing the register of baptisms, simply because it was taken for granted that the child would be reborn into heaven's kingdom the same day that it saw the light of day on earth. Similarly we remind ourselves that Martin

Luther, born an hour before midnight in Eisleben on November 10, 1483, was hurried to the still unfinished church of SS. Peter and Paul the next morning and baptized with the name of the Saint whose day was being kept, S. Martin of Tours, the greatest saint of France. If quite such holy celerity is possible in this day of hospital deliveries, or if it is absolutely desirable, is, we concede, open to serious question, but certainly our normal practice, which sees nothing unusual in waiting several weeks or even several months before bringing a child to Our Blessed Lord in Holy Baptism, is open to far more serious question. That our current procedure can breed a smug casualness and a careless and negligent attitude toward the Sacrament is beyond question. While custom plays in to a very great extent, the fact remains that patient pastoral admonition can work wonders in bringing about a reformation of practice.

A particular area of consciousness that needs to be deepened is the propriety and method of lay baptism. Too many children are still permitted to die unbaptized because the pastor was called too late and the standers-by, for all their Lutheran background, were either too ignorant or too hesitant to exercise their privilege of administering emergency Baptism. Here again the only remedy is patient instruction. The entire subject should be thoroughly discussed at least once a year in the presence of the whole congregation; children in the confirmation classes should be required to describe in detail what they would do if they were confronted with such an emergency, until every child is familiar with the formal and material essentials of a valid Baptism and would know how to go about administering it. If such instruction be given, the embarrassing question of the eternal destiny of unbaptized infants would be asked far less frequently.

Baptism is the sacrament of entrance into the Church, and for symbolical reasons alone it should therefore, except where grave cause of an emergency nature prevents, be administered in church. Nothing deepens the consciousness of having been baptized more than seeing the Sacrament administered, and it is a tragic thing that there are congregations where children grow up to maturity without ever having witnessed the administration of Holy Baptism. The Lutheran conception of the congregation's function in the administration of the Sacraments endorses the procedure of baptizing children *in facie ecclesiae* and where the custom has been allowed to fall into disuse, it should by all means be restored as rapidly as may be. Baptism in a home, often in the midst of the conviviality of the impending christening feast, can never recapture the solemnity and seriousness of a church Baptism, nor can it possess the pedagogical value that the latter possesses.

By the end of the Middle Ages, the simple administration of water to a candidate in the name of the Father and of the Son and of the Holy Ghost had been overlaid with an astonishing quantity of ceremonial. There were anointings, signings with the holy cross, candles, salt, honey, anointing with the spittle, exorcisms, and breathing into the candidate's nostrils — so much that the essentials were almost totally obscured. Nevertheless, the sacramental life of the beholder is edified if there be a reasonable amount of ceremonial. Where vestments are in use, the conventional service vestment at the very least should be employed. Where the stole has been restored, a white or white-and-violet stole has a beautiful and significant meaning. The westward position at the renunciations and the altarward turning for the questions on the creed are profoundly impressive. The use of an initial exorcism is thoroughly Lutheran: "Depart, thou unclean spirit, and give place to the Holy Spirit." The triune affusion of water is both confessional and a source of added certainty. The use of the white baptismal mantle as it has survived in some parishes is worthy of more general introduction. The impressive giving of the candle to the candidate or chief sponsor with the words: "Receive the Light of Christ and see that thou keep unspotted by thy baptismal purity," needs but to be demonstrated to make its appeal.

One of the best ways of becoming conscious of our own Baptism is to be required to assume the serious responsibilities of being a sponsor. It is to be feared that we have become rather liberal in the matter of admitting sponsors at Lutheran baptisms. The *Small Catechism* in its preface quite clearly implies that the right to be a sponsor is reserved to active communicants, that none but active communicants should be admitted to this office. And, after all, only an active communicant could, without stultifying himself, seriously and honestly make the engagements to which a Lutheran sponsor commits himself. A pagan or a non-Lutheran Christian would be sadly at a loss trying to fulfill the requirements of sponsorship, should he ever begin to take them seriously. Our people should and can be taught that they must not embarrass themselves, their friends or relatives, and their pastor by presenting non-Lutherans as sponsors, and that in this, as in other rites where the Church plays a part, no definitive arrangements should be made without the pastor's knowledge and approval.

"What does such baptizing with water signify?" the *Catechism* inquires. "It signifies that the old Adam should by *daily* contrition and repentance be drowned and die with all sins and evil lusts and, again, a new man *daily* come forth and arise, who shall live before God in righteousness and purity forever." Baptism, it is true, is applied but once in a lifetime and its repetition would be sacrilege, but once applied it should not thenceforward be forgotten. A framed baptismal certificate is one of the finest things that can be hung on the wall of a nursery,

Dr. Francis Pieper used to insist in his classes in pastoral theology, and unquestionably he was right, but we are reminded of Gertrude Stein's comment about pictures on the wall *(Autobiography of Alice B. Toklas)* to the general effect that after a picture has been hanging on the wall for a certain length of time it gradually fades into the wall paper. Rome has met the problem by the use of Holy Water as a reminder of Baptism, but except for the fact that we neglect it, we have a far better way of reminding ourselves suggested in our *Small Catechism*. The head of the family is directed to instruct the members of his household to bless themselves morning and evening after this fashion; "In the morning when you get up, and in the evening when you retire, you shall bless yourself with the Sign of the Holy Cross and say, 'In the Name of the Father and of the Son and of the Holy Ghost. Amen.' Then, kneeling or standing, repeat the Creed and the Lord's Prayer; if you wish, you may also say the little prayer, *I Thank Thee.*" Let me call attention to the relation between this brief office and the Sacrament of Holy Baptism. The blessing with the sign of the holy cross corresponds to the signing with the holy cross at Baptism with the formula: "Receive the sign of the holy cross, both upon the forehead and upon the breast, in token that thou hast been redeemed by Christ the Crucified." The invocation, "In the name of the Father and the Son and the Holy Ghost," reminds us that we were baptized into that name. The Apostles' Creed has always been the ancient baptismal symbol, as the Nicene Creed has been the ancient Eucharistic confession, and its use is designed to remind us of Holy Baptism's divine gift of faith. The "Our Father" recalls that in order to implore the blessing of Almighty God upon us, the minister laid his hands upon our head and bade the congregation pray with him the *Paternoster* with special intention for our eternal salvation. If thus at morning's dawn we consecrate ourselves anew to God and at nightfall plead again the perfect sacrifice of Christ, into whose death we have been baptized and into whose new divine life we have been engrafted, Baptism will mean more to us than a rite and we shall experience the constant power of the new birth's sanctifying operation. There will then be no hiatus between infant baptism and what Hallesby and others call adult "conversion."

II

Less encouraging is our state with reference to the Sacrament of Holy Communion, in which we have departed far from the example of the ancient Church. Without harking back to apostolic times, when the disciples of Our Lord continued diligently in daily breaking of bread, and considering only the norm of practice proposed by the Lutheran Confessions, how many parishes can affirm that the proud boast of Article XXIV of the *Augsburg Confession* describes their current practice: "Falsely are our churches accused of abolishing the mass; for the mass is retained among us and celebrated with the highest reverence...We hold one Communion every holy-day, and, if any desire the Sacrament, also on other days, then it is given to such as ask for it"? Another authoritative document in the *Book of Concord* is the *Apology of the Augsburg Confession*, in which Article XII re-echoes the words of the Augustana: "At the outset we must again make the preliminary statement that we do not abolish the Mass, but religiously maintain and defend it. For among us masses are celebrated every Lord's Day and on the other festivals, in which the Sacrament is offered to those who wish it." From this it is clear — and this is abundantly supported by the evidence of the sixteenth century Church Orders — that in the mind of the Reformers the normal chief parochial service in the Lutheran Church, as it has been and is in the Latin Communion, in the Orthodoxy, and in the separated far Eastern Churches, would include the celebration of the Blessed Sacrament. Normally, no Sunday or major festival was to go by without the opportunity for Christians to receive the Holy Communion and when necessity or devotion drove them to the Altar for the Bread of Angels, they were to be accommodated with as many additional masses as their need and desire called for. The Lutheran ideal is therefore not four Communion services a year, or six, or twelve, or fifteen, but some sixty at the least. And until that ideal is more generally realized it is idle to speak of sacramental life among us — the only proper description of our present state is sacramental starvation.

What has been said of the frequency of celebration applies with equal force to the frequency of reception. With shame I must confess of my synod that the average annual number of communions per communicant is barely 2.04, while the only moderately large group in the Synodical Conference that has succeeded in rising above this tragically low level of sacramental spirituality is our negro mission, the parishes of which show an average of about four. We stand arraigned, accused, and condemned by the *Catechism* which we teach our children: "Except a man receive the Sacrament at least some four times a year, it is to be feared that he despises the Sacrament and is not a Christian."

At least four times a year! I would have you remember the history behind that "at least." Luther was a realist, aiming for achievable goals. A misdirected sense of awe-struck reverence had created a public opinion which frowned on the reception of the Sacrament more frequently than once a year, at Easter-time, and it was Luther's hope that this once-a-year reception might gradually be raised to at least once-a-quarter. But Luther also recognized that this finally represented also a minimum of spirituality, and that reception of the Blessed Sacrament once a quarter was the absolute least to maintain any semblance of sacramental life.

We lack even that minimum. We deplore it, we discuss it, we read papers about it, we published articles about it, we write pamphlets about it, and the average refuses to rise. Why? Let me speak frankly. What do we know about the advantages of frequent reception? The average Lutheran pastor himself is barely able to maintain the four-times-a-year minimum and vast quantities of our clergy fail to maintain it. Obviously, the first step toward remedying this situation is to secure some first-hand experience with our subject before we try to chant its virtues to others.

Secondly, and just as obviously, let us give our people the opportunity to receive Holy Communion frequently, and they will infallibly receive more frequently. I know of no church — and this matter has interested me for a long time — which has accompanied an increase in the number of celebrations with conscientious sacramental preaching, and which has not recorded a perceptible increase in the average annual number of communions per communicant. We may not be able to achieve the goal of weekly celebrations of Holy Communion at a single step. Not one congregation in a hundred is prepared for it. But we can stop making our communion services vestigial appendices of our Sunday services; we can stop relegating them to evenings; we can discourage the exodus of worshipers before the Preface on Communion Sundays. We can from year to year increase the number of communions, until we have reached the point where some Lent we can begin to celebrate every Sunday, and finally secure a resolution to this effect: "Resolved, that Holy Communion shall be celebrated in this church whenever communicants have announced their intention of receiving the Blessed Sacrament." We have demonstrated to ourselves the feasibility of introducing weekly communions in a convert congregation with a communicant membership of thirty-five. As the practice grows more general, its introduction will become the easier, and we shall see the dawn of a sacramental springtime in our Lutheran Church.

Thirdly, and again obviously, we can set our people a good example. The idea of self-communion will come as a shock to some of you. To others, especially to those of the Swedish tradition, it will occasion no surprise. Yet self-communion is the most natural thing in the world. If we believe that it is not we, but Christ who consecrates, as St. Augustine says, are we who minister God's gift better than or any different from those to whom we offer it, that we can not accept Our Lord's invitation, "Take eat...Take drink"? The practice has, for one thing, the endorsement of the ancient Church. The best consensus of the Fathers, furthermore, interprets the accounts of the institution of the Holy Communion as indicating that Our Blessed Lord Himself received the Eucharistic Sacrament on the night before He suffered. Clerical self-communion has the specific endorsement of the Lutheran Confessions, Thus the official German version of the Augustana, Article XXIV, "Of the Mass," declares: "The Mass is not to be a propitiatory Sacrifice for others, living or dead, but a Communion at which the priest and others receive the Sacrament." The German edition of the *Apology* implies the same thing when it declares (Article XII, Of the Mass): "The fact that we hold only public or common masses, at which the people *also* receive, not solitary masses, is no offense against (the practice of) the Catholic Church." Clerical self-communion was the general custom of the Lutheran Church in the period of the Reformation and afterward. Implied in most Church Orders, it was specifically directed in Wittenberg 1523, Hartzgerode 1534, Merseburg 1544, Anhalt 1548, Lemburg, Ulm and others. Anhalt 1532, for instance, states: "Let the priests be always fasting (before celebrating) and temperate (after celebrating) that the Sacraments be not dishonored." It has never ceased being the custom of the Church of Sweden, and the right to self-communion has been restored to the priesthood of the Danish and Norwegian Churches. It has the assent of the chief doctors of the Lutheran Church, among them Luther, Gerhard, Quenstedt, Baldiun, and the casuist, Dedekennus.

Quite apart from the value it possesses as an example for his flock, the pastor needs self-communion disparately for his own spiritual life. Martin Luther's Christian Questions apply to him also, and with redoubled force. Above and beyond his flock he should be moved by both the command and promise of Christ to receive frequently. Upon him there lies a burden of concern and trouble that his people will never know and that should incite him to flee often to the everlasting arms that enfold him in the Sacrament of the divine compassion. He too is a creature of flesh and blood, he too lives in a world of sin and temptation, and he too has the devil always with him, who, with his lying and murdering day and night, will let him have no peace within or without. And if the contemplation of these considerations should move the laic to go to the Lord's Table, shall it move the minister of the Lord's Table less powerfully?

This does not mean, of course, that the Sacrament is to be received without preparation and without consideration. The divine mandate must be observed: "Let a man examine himself and so let him eat of that bread and drink of that cup." Few things are ultimately a subtler negation of the sacramental principle than open communion, the reckless and careless offering of the Body and Blood of Our Lord to all who chance to be present in the church at the moment and experience an emotional desire to receive. The Sacrament calls for spiritual preparation, and we commend with all honor and respect those saintly souls who prepare themselves a week in advance for the reception of Our Lord's Supper. We can not examine ourselves too thoroughly nor judge ourselves too rigorously nor repent too contritely. And when we have examined and judged and repented to the utmost, we must still come to our Eucharistic King with the prayer of humble access: "Lord, I am not worthy that Thou shouldest come under my roof, but speak the word only and my soul shall be healed."

One point of preparation is emphasized by our *Catechism*, the desirability of receiving the Holy Communion fasting, which, by the consent of the undivided Church of the East, the Far East, and the West, means going without food or drink from the midnight previous, not because God is mollified by a growling stomach, but because by a body kept under, the soul is made freer. Fasting is not an unpleasant chore or a Pharisaic rule to one who lives the sacramental life, but an act of devotion that we joyously perform that we may the more lovingly go forth to meet our Heavenly Bridegroom.

The *Catechism*'s emphasis upon the forgiveness of sins that we receive in the Holy Sacrament — a necessary emphasis in the days when the Mass was regarded as a propitiatory sacrifice for the sins of the living and the dead — has, in one of the amazing perversions that popular thinking sometimes undergoes, made Holy Communion for many Lutheran Christians nothing more than the last act in a periodic orgy of repentance and contrition and remorse. But the Sacrament is more than a seal of absolution, pardon, and remission. It is a Eucharist — a giving of thanks, the most perfect oblation of gratitude that we can offer. It is a Commission — the most intimate fellowship and union with our Saviour into which sinful man can enter. It is a Medicine of Immortality — the immortal body of the conquering Christ fortifying and strengthening us with all virtue and power and strength and grace. It is Christ coming to men — more than that, it is Christ coming to me, to become mine and to make me His.

Lutheran theology rightly reprehended everything that reeked of propitiatory sacrifice in the medieval mass, and yet certain sacrificial connotations in the celebration of the Eucharist are inescapable. In the offering of the oblations for the double purpose of the celebration of the Sacrament and the relief of the needy (with later the substitution of money for the gifts of bread and wine), these oblations are but symbols of the fact that at the altar we offer and present to God ourselves, our souls and bodies, to be a reasonable, holy, and living sacrifice, most humbly beseeching Him that all they who receive the Holy Communion may *worthily* receive His body and blood and be fulfilled with grace and heavenly benediction.

The Holy Communion is a tremendous stimulus to prayer and intercession. At no time do we come closer to Calvary and to its unique and everlasting atonement than in that memorial which Christ hath commanded and ordained, the showing forth His death until He comes again, showing it forth as a remembrance to the Father, to ourselves and to mankind, and then and there, having in remembrance His

Blessed Passion, mighty Resurrection, and glorious Ascension, we join our imperfect pleading of His merits to His heavenly mediation and beseech the divine compassion to vouchsafe that by faith in His blood we and His whole Church may obtain remission of sins and all other benefits of His passion. The Letter to the Hebrews instructs us that the Day of Atonement's sacrifice was not ended with the slaying of the sacrificial victim, but needed the pleading of that act before the mercy seat to give it value; and even so Our Lord, having once and for all, by His one oblation of Himself once offered, made a full, perfect, and sufficient sacrifice, oblation and satisfaction for the sins of the whole world, has entered in the most holy place on high and ever liveth to plead that His most precious oblation for us and in our behalf. And so in the transcendent miracle of the Holy Sacrament we stand in the presence of Calvary's sacrifice, the body that was given for our transgressions and the infinitely precious blood shed for our sins, and plead Christ's merits for that which we most need and desire.

III

We come now to what the *Apology* calls (Article XII, 41) *sacramentum poenitentiae*, the Sacrament of Penance, the third major Sacrament of Lutheranism. Article XI of the Augustana, fortified by Article XXV, declares: "Sacerdotal absolution is to be retained in the churches, although an enumeration of all sins is not necessary....Confession is not abolished among us. The body of Christ is given only to those who have previously been heard and absolved." No more enthusiastic endorsement of private confession has ever been enunciated than the statement of Luther: "I will not allow anyone to deprive me of private confession, nor would I exchange it for all the treasures of the whole world, for I know what strength and consolation it has given me. No one knows the power of private confession, except he be compelled frequently to fight and wrestle with the devil. I had long since been conquered by Satan and liquidated, had I not been preserved by confession." And Luther practiced what he preached; every seven to fourteen days he would go to his father confessor, John Bugenhagen, rector of St. Mary's Wittenberg, and confess his sins.

And indeed the sacramental life without sacramental confession is unthinkable. The need of something of the sort is inescapable, and even our makeshift substitutes testify against us. Private announcement for Holy Communion has in America come to be in many places a vestigial remnant of private confession. The confessional service is but Pietism's substitute for private confession. The fine Scandinavian custom of having each communicant kneel before the priest to receive personal and individual absolution is but a remnant of private confession, when the penitent received not only individual absolution but also made an individual confession. There is nothing that will hold our young people closer to the Church than intelligently handled private absolution. It will give the pastor a far more personal contact with his people than all the calling he can do and all the guilds he can organize. If young people are trained from an early age to make their confession privately at regular monthly intervals, we need have little fear of their not surviving the period of adolescence with faith unshaken.

Lutheranism can make the greatest contribution to Protestantism just on this point, for Lutheranism has the sanest and most Scriptural doctrine of confession of any Church. We force no one to enumerate his sins; we make confession contingent upon the individual's willingness, except in matters of public scandal; we absolve without condition and without penance; yet we can offer personal, individual, operative absolution. We have all of Confession's blessings, none of its banes.

It goes without saying that the seal of confession must not only be inviolable, but it must be known to be inviolable and irrefragable. The confessor must, above all, be discreet. Good and discreet confessors are not born, they are made, made by the Holy Ghost and by careful and prayerful preparation and by consecrated study and pervasive humility.

What we have said of Holy Communion applies to Holy Absolution. We can best preach by example, and we can best be convinced of the virtue of sacramental life by living sacramentally ourselves. As much as the most sinful penitent in his flock, the pastor needs a confessor, one to whom he goes not only for counsel and advice, not only for discussion and exchange of ideas, but for absolution, pardon, and remission of his sins, and the pastor's care of his own soul calls for the grace of confession as a primary means to prevent the possible catastrophe that he who has preached to others should himself be a castaway.

One specific phase of Confession remains to be considered. The greatest pastoral Theologian has indicated the best procedure in the case of sick calls when He told the paralytic that they lowered through the roof at His feet: "Son, be of good cheer, thy sins be forgiven thee." It should be the most natural thing when making a sick call — we think of course of the initial call upon a genuinely sick parishioner — to hear the patient's confession first of all, and our people should be taught to regard it as the first thing to be done when the pastor calls on a sick person that the latter make his confession. From every angle, it commends itself as the most effective way to combat the effect of illness upon the individual's soul.

A LUTHERAN THEOLOGIAN LOOKS AT THE NINETY-FIVE THESES IN 1967

The fact that 1967 is being celebrated as the 450th anniversary of the beginning of the Reformation that radiated from Wittenberg in the sixteenth century adds to the annual ambivalence with which a Lutheran theologian normally faces the last day of October.

It is not so much a matter of the date as of the document that the date emphasizes. The difficulties connected with the date he takes in his stride. He knows that the keeping of October 31 in his tradition seems to have developed out of a little classroom ceremony that Philip Melanchthon initiated — a professiorial commemoration prompted by collegial piety.[1] He knows that most of the early liturgical commemorations of the Reformation were annual remembrances of the introduction of the evangelical religion in the respective town or territory. He knows that 1617 became the first centennial of the Reformation because by then there was a weary recognition that the breach in the Western patriarchate promised to be permanent and that an interprovincial and international birthday of the evangelical movement was a felt need among at least some adherents of the *Augsburg Confession*. (He also knows that at that very time the "hawks" of the seventeenth century were on the verge of devoting three decades to a series of gory and futile wars designed to prove that the force of arms could — or could not — reunite the Western *corpus christianum*.)

He is not greatly distressed by the arguments that October 31 may perpetuate a historical error and that he ought really observe November 1, or that the ninety-five theses may actually not have taken their extant form before December of 1517. Again, he is fully aware that the surviving evidence does not establish beyond historical doubt that Augustinian Hermit Martin Luther really nailed the ninety-five theses to the north door of the Church of All Hallows in Wittenberg on October 31, 1517, and may merely have mailed them to his ecclesiastical superiors on that day. But the Lutheran theologian also knows that the counterarguments are ultimately just as indecisive. Thus he is likely to be satisfied with the view that in either case Luther can truthfully be said to have posted the theses.

Nor does your Lutheran theologian feel the distress over against the Lutheran Reformation that some Anglo-Catholics have felt over against the Henrician Reformation in England. Your Lutheran theologian regrets profoundly, of course, that the external unity of the empirical Church, already torn by the schisms with the various Eastern Christian Churches, underwent further rending. Yet he feels that the breach was not something which the Lutheran Reformers designed or for which they were exclusively or even extensively responsible. Without making any concession to historical determinism, he is likely to believe that in the premises — the sociopolitical situation that had been developing for over a century and the concrete personal factors in the formula, the Hohenzollern prince-bishop-archbishop-primate, the stubborn son of upward mobile Hans and Margaret Luther, the Medici pope, the Wettin rulers of Saxony, the ordinary of the diocese of Brandenburg, the spectacularly successful indulgence preacher, the Dominican general, the Ingolstadt professor who forged the weapons of theological debate — a cataclysmic rupture would have been avoided only by a direct divine intervention. Ultimately, he feels, the Lutheran Reformation, precisely because it was a reformation, had aspects that deserve celebration and expressions of gratitude to God.

Nor is your Lutheran theologian too much dismayed by the reflection that some other date than October 31 would have been more appropriate — say June 25, the day in 1530 when the Saxon chancellor Christian Beyer read the *Augsburg Confession* before the assembled estates of the Holy Roman Empire of the German Nation. For after all, your Lutheran theologian feels, once the Lutheran community decided to celebrate the Reformation, the date became of minor moment. We keep the Nativity of Our Lord Jesus Christ on December 25. Monarchs celebrate their official birthdays on a day when they can at least hope for good weather for their presumably rejoicing subjects. The rubrics permit commemorating the dedication of a church on any suitable date if some other commemoration permanently impedes a celebration on the actual anniversary.

The problem, this writer would repeat, is not the date but the document. Reformation Day is bound to the ninety-five theses. These theses, your Lutheran theologian notes, are the program for a disputation that was never held. Unlike the *Small* and the *Large Catechisms* and the *Smalcald Articles* — also works of Luther — the ninety-five theses did not find a place among the symbolical books of the Lutheran community. Indeed, unlike *De servo arbitrio* and *De votis monasticis judicium*, they are nowhere cited in the Lutheran symbols as supporting documentation to illustrate at length a point that the symbols make in more summary fashion. Again, while the Lutheran symbols quote significant portions of *Vom Abendmahl Christi Bekenntnis*, for example, they do not quote or even demonstrably allude to the theses.

Beyond that, the theses appear to say either too much or too little. That they say too little is suggested by the fact that Luther himself felt that he had moved beyond the position of the theses and the explanatory *Resolutiones* by 1520; he writes in that year that he wishes that all he had written on indulgences might be burned and that a single proposition might replace them: "*Indulgentiae sunt adulatorum Romanorum nequitiae.*"[2] They say too much in that they affirm attitudes toward the pope, toward purgatory, and toward indulgences themselves that a contemporary Lutheran cannot bring himself to affirm. The fundamental problem for the Lutheran lies in the basic assumption that the theory of a penal purgatory developed, that every forgiven sin — venial sins forgiven by their very definition, mortal sins forgiven either in the tribunal of penance or in response to an act of perfect contrition — has a specific but incalculable residual element of temporal punishment that either satisfactions in this life or satispassions in purgatory must expiate. For this the Lutheran finds persuasive evidence neither in the Sacred Scriptures nor in the primitive Church's understanding of the divine revelation.[3]

Nevertheless, your Lutheran theologian cannot deny that the theses were in a very real sense the catalyst that precipitated the Lutheran Reformation,[4] and for that reason alone they call for special attention in 1967.

For a fuller understanding of Luther's position as sketched in the theses, we have a number of subsidiary documents.

Most important are the *Resolutiones disputationum de indulgentiarum virtute* of 1518,[5] a thesis-by-thesis commentary on the earlier bare-bones statement upon which this paper draws heavily. The *Resolutiones* are our clue to the widely-varying degrees of intensity of Luther's conviction over against the different theses. Again, in the *Resolutiones* we have without doubt the documentation that Luther would prudently have collected before offering his theses for public disputation. (That he had expanded and refined this documentation in the course of the intervening months is likewise obvious.)

From an earlier date we have his *Sermo de indulgentiis pridie Dedicationis*,[6] conventionally taken as preached on All Hallows' Eve (October 31), 1516; the concluding paragraph of his sermon on St.

Matthias' Day (February 24), 1517;[7] and from a later period his popular *Sermon von dem Ablass und Gnade* of 1518,[8] which went through twenty-two editions; the *Asterisci Lutheri adversus Obeliscos Eckii* (March[?] 1518),[9] and his defense against a countertreatise by John Tetzel, *Eine Freiheit des Sermons päbstlichen Ablass und Gnade belangend* (June, 1518).[10]

With the perspective of four and a half centuries, your Lutheran theologian finds both positive and negative elements in these documents, and pre-eminently in the ninety-five theses.

In all these documents Luther writes as an intentionally Catholic theologian who could rightly point out that he had his ordinary's imprimatur — not hastily given, either — both for the *Sermon von dem Ablass und Gnade* and for the *Resolutiones disputationum de indulgentiarum virtute* (and with the latter, for the ninety-five theses that the latter incorporated). Nevertheless, even though he could justifiably argue that ecclesiastical authority had not decided all the issues quite as definitely as his opponents imagined, Luther confessedly stood in opposition to the theological consensus of his age. One must also concede that not all the biblical evidence that Luther cites will stand twentieth-century exegetical scrutiny. His logic is sometimes more ingenious than persuasive. The historical facts that he alleges are, upon examination, not as decisive in every case for us as they seem to have been for him. (That one can say the same things, sometimes with greater justice, of his adversaries' contributions to the controversy does not alter the facts as far as Luther is concerned.)

At the very least, Luther's act in offering the theses was either an example of great courage or of great rashness. We can accept at face value his innocent evaluation of Leo X as *"pontifex optimus ... cuius integritas et eruditio delitae sunt omnibus bonis auribus"* and as *"ille suavissimus homo."*[11] We can do the same in the case of his protestations that he did not at the time realize how deeply the primate of Germany was involved in the indulgence operation himself. We can do the same with his declared conviction that he needed only to call Archbishop Albrecht's attention to the scandalous contents of the *Instructio* published under his name and coat of arms and Albrecht would at once prohibit its further circulation. But it needs to be remembered that in his attack on indulgences the Augustinian Hermit was involving himself not only with the pope and with the primate of Germany but with the prince on whom he depended for personal protection. The right to offer indulgences to the faithful who came to venerate the relics in the electoral Chapel of All Hallows in Wittenberg dated back to Boniface IX (1389-1404).[12] Luther's own elector, Frederick the Wise, was no mean collector of indulgenced relics himself. According to the catalog that Luke Cranach the Elder illustrated in 1509, the *Wittemberger Heiligthumsbuch*, the elector had expanded the collection that he had inherited to a total 5,005 items, with the possibility of 1,443 years of indulgence.[13] Nine years later, the size of the collection had grown to 17,443 items, carrying with them the possibility of the equivalent of

127,709 years and 116 days of public penance in the primitive Church's fashion.[14] Luther's *Sermo de indulgentiis* had, he himself ruefully remarked, gained scant thanks from the elector.[15] Luther knew how much the university at which he taught depended on the revenues of the chapter of All Hallows' Chapel.[16] For him to have taken publicly the position toward which he had increasingly felt himself pushed for two years is a tribute to his integrity.

Again, the Lutheran theologian can only commend Luther's pastoral concern for the faithful whom both the exaggerations of the indulgence preachers and their own mistaken expectations had betrayed into committing mortal sin without repentance. Similarly, he can only laud the genuine desire to preserve the visible head of the Church and the respect that the priesthood still enjoyed from the calumnies and the cynical questions that fell from the lips of the laymen (theses 81-90), whose disposition to anticlericalism the *"effusa licentia praedicandarum veniarum"*[17] had only heightened and confirmed. Likewise, he can only praise Luther's recognition of his own fallibility, along with his disclaimer of heresy as a necessary consequence (*"errare quidem potero, sed haereticus non ero"*)[18] and his determination not to accept the "mere opinions" of the Schoolmen and the canonists, which are "maintained without text or proof," as intrinsically decisive.[19] He would feel that Luther was justified in insisting that the precise value of an indulgence is not something that can be specified with the precision that some of the indulgence preachers appear to have claimed.[20] The Lutheran theologian will stand with Luther in his rejection of a penal purgatory, although he may doubt that Luther, even with all his reservations, could be quite as certain as he ultimately appears to have been in 1517 about the nature of the cleansing process in the intermediate state.

The Lutheran theologian must hail with unqualified endorsement the opening thesis, asserted without any doubt: "When our Lord and Master Jesus Christ said, 'Repent,' he willed the entire life of believers to be one of repentance." This repentance Luther sees as a "transmentation," the assumption of another mind and feelings, the recovery of one's true senses, the transition from an awareness merely of earthly matters to a knowledge of spiritual things, a change of heart that results in a hatred of sin. This repentance involves the totality of life and the totality of Christians; it must mark the life alike of the king in his purple robes, of the priest in his sacerdotal ornaments, of the monk in his cell, and of the beggar in his poverty. Repentance is our own response of self-displeasure to our own perennial prayer, "Forgive us our debts."[21]

Your Lutheran theologian rejoices in the polar stress of the second and third theses, which on the one hand sees the repentance that our Lord calls for as transcending the transaction that takes place in the confessional between the confessor and the penitent, and on the other hand as affirming that this repentance cannot be solely something within. To prove its worth, it must find outward expression in a fasting that includes all chastenings of the flesh, in a prayer that includes every spiritual pursuit in meditation, reading, listening, and petitioning, and an almsgiving that includes every service to one's neighbor.[22]

The Lutheran theologian will acknowledge the rightness of the realistic insight — nourished by the cited examples of Sts. Augustine of Hippo and Bernard of Clairvaux — that true interior repentance, in the form of an unremitting hatred of our native self-centeredness, must last as long as life itself.[23]

He will concur in Luther's conviction that the only penalties which the Church can really remit are those which the Church itself has imposed (thesis 5) and that beyond such remission the Church's action can only be a declaration that God has remitted the guilt (thesis 6). But at a time when the sacrament of repentance has become something of a formality in most Lutheran Churches most of the time, he might well urge Lutherans to reconsider the virtue of the sacerdotal declaration of pardon in the name of Christ who gives the priest his authority (thesis 7). "As a general rule we are not sure of the remission of guilt, except through the verdict of the priest," for there is no peace until we are sure that the remission of sin is for us.[24]

He will also concur in Luther's conviction that the Church ought not to seek to impose canonical penalties on the dying or reserve them to a penal purgatory where the departed are beyond the jurisdiction of the empirical Church (theses 8-13). He will regard it as a legitimate thesis that "any truly repentant Christian has a right to full remission of penalty and guilt, even without indulgence letters" (thesis 36), and that "any true Christian, whether living or dead, participates in all the blessings of Christ and the Church, and this granted him by God, even without indulgence letters" (thesis 37).

He appreciates the insistence on faith as a condition of the fruitful use of the means of salvation that comes through so strongly and clearly. For example:

LW. 31:193

> Faith is necessary everywhere. You receive as much as you believe. And this is what I understand it to mean when our teachers say that the sacraments are efficacious signs of grace not because of the mere fact that the sacrament is performed but because it is also believed, as St. Augustine contends.[25] ...So also here. Absolution is efficacious not by the mere fact that it takes place, no matter who finally does it and whether he errs or does not err, but because it is believed.[26]

Yet as Luther himself points out, "declare" and "approve" are "too modest" to be quite adequate as verbs that describe the process of pardon.

> The judgment of the keys is necessary, so that a man may not believe in himself, but rather trust in the judgment of the keys of the Church, that is, of the priest. And it makes no difference to me if the one who bears the keys is unlearned or flippant. The penitent can believe, not on account of the priest or his

authority, but on account of the word of him who said and who did not lie, "Whatever you shall loose and so on." For those who believe in that word the authority of the keys cannot err. The keys err only for those who do not believe that the absolution of the priest is valid.[27]

Your Lutheran theologian will approve the opposition of the theology of the cross to the theology of glory.

A theologian of the cross (that is, one who speaks of the crucified and hidden God) teaches that punishments, crosses, and death are the most precious treasury of all and the most sacred relics which the Lord of this theology himself has consecrated and blessed, not alone by the touch of his most holy flesh but also by the embrace of his exceedingly holy and divine will, and he has left these relics here to be kissed, sought after, and embraced.... A theology of glory does not recognize, along with the Apostle, the crucified and hidden God alone [1 Cor 2:2] ....Disagreeing with the theologian of the cross, [the theologian of glory] defines the treasury of Christ as the removing and remitting of punishments, things which are most evil and worthy of hate. In opposition to this theologian of the cross defines the treasury of Christ as impositions and obligations of punishments, things which are best and most worthy of love.[28]

With great enthusiasm the Lutheran theologian concurs in the assertion of thesis 62 that "the true treasure of the church is the most holy gospel of the glory and grace of God." The *Resolutiones* explain: "The gospel is a preaching of the incarnate Son of God, given to us without any merit on our part for salvation and peace. It is a word of salvation, a word of grace, a word of comfort, a word of joy, a word of the bridegroom and the bride, a good word, a word of peace."[29]

In this connection he will note appreciatively the adumbration of what Lutherans have come to call the "law-gospel polarity," which capsules major emphases of the biblical revelation.

Through the law [Luther observes in his comment on thesis 62] we have nothing except an evil conscience, a restless heart, a troubled breast because of our sins, which the law points out but cannot take away. Therefore for those who are overwhelmed by sadness and in dire despair, the light of the gospel comes and says, "Fear not" [Is 35:4], "Comfort, comfort my people" [Is 40:1], "Encourage the fainthearted" [1 Th 5:14], "Behold your God" [Is 40:9], "Behold the lamb of God, who takes away the sins of the world" [Jn 1:29], Behold that One who alone fulfills the law for you, whom God has made to be your righteousness, sanctification, wisdom, and redemption, for all those who believe in him [1 Cor 1:30]....The true glory of God springs from this gospel.[30]

All this, however, lies 450 years in the past, a past that cannot be reversed or undone. It is an oversimplification, but not a wholly untrue observation, which sees in the various "reformations" of the sixteenth century — that of Trent, that of Luther and his associates, that of Henry VIII and Edward VI and Elizabeth I, that of Zwingli and Oecolampadius and Bullinger and Calvin and Knox, and the radical reformation of the Anabaptist left wing — the institutionalization in confessional traditions of emphases that the pre-Reformation Western Church held in a progressively more uneasy and growingly intolerable tension. Each confessional tradition was right not only in what it shared in common with the others, but also in the insights which it particularly perpetuated, but each became increasingly wrong in its unbalanced (and sometimes absolutized) stress on its privileged insights as it continued in isolation from the other confessional traditions.

Concretely, in the issues that divided the adherents of the Apostolic See and the Lutheran Reformers, we have a perpetuation and an institutionalization of the juridical stress in the Tridentine Reformation and a perpetuation and an institutionalization of the evangelical stress in the Lutheran Reformation. The transcending of the differences that nearly 450 years of mutual isolation have rigidified will lie in a recovery of the complementarity of the valid basic insights that are at the root of each confessional tradition's emphases and in a revision of the confessional vocabularies that sometimes occlude for the other partner in the dialogue the basic validity of a given confessional tradition's emphasis.

The Lutheran theologian rejoices in the conclusions of his Roman Catholic counterparts as they have addressed themselves in recent years to various aspects of indulgences. Here a de-emphasis of the juridical aspects and of the quantifiability of either the punishment or the satisfaction. There a stress on the fact that neither the Church nor the penitent can determine the value of any act of repentance in the sight of God. In another context the assertion that the Church can only intercede for the penitent in the consciousness of her solidarity with her Head and of the perennial value of His once-and-for-all atonement. Elsewhere still in the observation that references to the merits of Christ and of the saints do not in any sense involve the association of two entities of equal value. Or in the emphasis on the sovereignty of the divine will and action. Or in the declaration that repentance is always a response to the divine judgment and the divine grace and that the virtuous acts that a penitent Christian performs are always theologically subsequent to his renewed commitment to a God who continues to love us even when our sin has offended His justice. Or in the assertion that a Christian can never claim forgiveness as a matter of right but only as a gift rooted in the atonement that God Himself accomplished in Christ. Or in the affirmation that whatever we do as the expression of our repentance in thought, in word, or in act is part of the imitation of Christ to which God has called us in baptism. Or in such evaluations of the historical realities as the declaration that, while the theories of indulgences that John Tetzel actually advanced can be defended technically, his practice — even though widely approved by ecclesiastical authority — had extensively become something sub-Christian.

If all of us — Lutherans no less than Roman Catholics — can recover for ourselves and for the Church militant of which we are a part the real significance of the beginning and the ending of the ninety-five theses, the 450th observance of the beginning of the Reformation that began at Wittenberg will not have been in vain after all:

> In the Name of Our Lord Jesus Christ. Amen.
> When our Lord and Master Jesus Christ said, "Repent" [Mt 4:17], he willed the entire life of believers to be one of repentance (thesis 1)....
> Away then with all those prophets who say to the people of Christ, "Peace, peace," and there is no peace! [Jer 6:14] (thesis 92).
> Blessed be all those prophets who say to the people of Christ, "Cross, cross," and there is no cross! (thesis 93).
> Christians should be exhorted to be diligent in following Christ, their Head, through penalties, death, and hell (thesis 94);
> And thus be confident of entering into heaven through many tribulations rather than through the false security of peace [Acts 14: 22] (thesis 95).

ENDNOTES

1. D. *Martin Luthers Werke: Kritische Gesamtaugabe* (Weimar, 1883-) 1, 230. Here after this edition is abbreviated WA.
2. *"De indulgentiis ante duos annos scripsi, sed sic, ut me nunc mirum in modum poeniteat editi libelli. Haerebam enim id temporis magna quadam superstitione Romanae tyrannidis, unde et indulgentias non penitus reiiciendas esse censebam, quas tanto hominum consensu cernebam comprobari. Nec mirum, quia solus volvebam saxum. At postea beneficio Sylvestri {Prieratis} et fratrum adiutus, qui strenue illas tutati sunt, intellexi, eas aliud non esse quam meras adulatorum Romanorum imposturas, quibus et fidem dei et pecunias hominum perderent. Atque utinam a Bibliopolis queam impetrare et omnibus qui legerunt persuadere, ut universos libellos meos de indulgentiis exurant et pro omnibus quae de eis scripsi hanc propositionem apprehendant:* INDVLEGENTIAE SVNT AD-LATORVM ROMANORVM NEQVICIAE" (*De capivitate Babylonica ecclesiae praeludium* [1520], WA 6, 497, 9-23). Nevertheless, Luther still appeals to the ninety-five theses and to the *Resolutiones* (*ibid.*, 543, 5-7; 548, 18-20; 549, 15).
3. However, in the *Resolutiones* Luther already holds that the bishop of Rome as late as the episcopate of St. Gregory the Great "had no jurisdiction over other churches, at least not over the Greek Church" (WA 1, 571, 16-18). In quoting the text of the ninety-five theses and the *Resolutiones*, this paper generally follows the translation of Charles M. Jacobs, as revised by Harold J. Grimm, for the former, and of Carl W. Folkemer for the latter, as contained in the American edition of *Luther's Works* 31, *Career of the Reformer* 1, edited by Harold J. Grimm (Philadelphia, 1957) 25-33, 83-252.
4. So Luther himself. In *Wider Hans Worst* (1541), he rehearses the events of 1517 — not without evidence of some lapses of memory concerning happenings that took place nearly a quarter of a century before — and declares: "*Dis ist der erste, rechte grundliche Anfang des Lutherischen Lermens*" (WA 50, 541, 7.21). But it should be noted that Luther is attemptimg to exculpate his late lord, the elector Frederick the Wise, from the charge of Duke Henry of Brunswick-Wolfenbüttel. Frederick, said Duke Henry, had been responsi-

ble for the "Lutheran upheavals." Luther puts the blame for them on Archbishop Albrecht of Mayence and John Tetzel.

5. WA 1, 525-628.
6. WA 1, 94-99.
7. WA 1, 141, 22-38.
8. WA 1, 243-46. In spite of the title and the opinion of the editors of the Weimar edition, Luther may never have actually preached the contents of this treatise.
9. WA 1, 281-314. The traditional date of August 10, 1518, is almost certainly wrong; see *ibid.* 279-80.
10. WA 1, 383-93.
11. WA 1, 573, 17-19.
12. Matthaeus Faber, *Schlosskirche* (1717) pp. 48ff., 67ff., cited in E. G. Schwiebert, *Luther and His Times: The Reformation from a New Perspective* (St. Louis, 1950) 312.
13. Schwiebert, *ibid.*
14. Schwiebert, *ibid.* According to Roland H. Bainton, *Here I Stand: A Life of Martin Luther* (New York, 1950) p. 71, the collection had grown by 1520 to 19,013 items with an indulgence potential of 1, 902,202 years and 270 days.
15. Bainton, p. 71.
16. See Heinrich Boehmer, *Road to Reformation,* translated from the German original by John W. Doberstein and Theodore G. Tappert (Philadelphia, 1946) p. 177.
17. WA 1, 652, 32.
18. WA 1, 530, 11.
19. WA 1, 530, 4-8.
20. Luther's vehement 32nd thesis, *"Dammabuntur in aeternum cum suis Magistris qui per litteras veniarum securos sese credunt de sua salute,"* is the strongest statement of his position. It is directed, as the American edition of *Luther's Works* (31, 179, 61) points out, against those "who permitted the ignorant masses to believe that the purchase of indulgences made them sure of salvation and free from guilt before God, instead of free from punishments imposed by the church."
21. WA 1, 5530, 16-531, 18.
22. WA 1, 531, 20-533, 33, especially 532, 12-27.
23. WA 1, 533, 35-534, 18.
24. *"Ordine generali non est nobis certa remissio culpae nisi per iudicium sacerdotis"* (WA 1, 541, 20-21).
25. Luther has in mind St. Augustine's *Tractate* 80 on Jn 3: *"Unde est tanta virtus aquae, ut corpus tangat et cor abluat, nisi faciente verbo, non quia dicitur, sed quia creditur?"* (PL 35, 1840).
26. WA 1, 595, 4-8.
27. WA 1, 594, 31-37.
28. WA 1, 613, 23-28; 614, 17-18. 22-26.
29. WA 1, 616, 20-23.
30. WA 1, 616,27-34. 39.

WHY LUTHERANS SHOULD ENGAGE IN CONVERSATION WITH ROMAN CATHOLICS

These reflections do not propose to justify conversations with fellow Christians in general. The obligation to encourage, to instruct, to listen to, to warn, to admonish, to comfort, and to strengthen one another, even across denominational barriers, is so deeply rooted in the written word of God that it needs no justification. To the extent that we are fellow Christians at all, we have by definition functions in the same body, we share the same Spirit, a common Lord, a common confidence in his grace, one baptism for the forgiveness of sins, a single heavenly Father in Christ his Son, and we have a common hope of being made like our Lord and of seeing him as he is. These are all matters that we need to talk about with one another, for this common communication of the word of God is one of the ways that the Holy Spirit uses to build the one, holy, catholic and apostolic Church and to accomplish his saving and transforming work.

These reflections are designed to provide an answer to the question: Why should Christians of the *Augsburg Confession* engage in conversations specifically with the Christians who acknowledge the authority of the Bishop of Rome?

The answer, it seems to me, is contained in part already in the question when it is put in these terms. Lutherans have a responsibility to engage in conversations with Roman Catholic fellow Christians precisely because they committed themselves to the *Augsburg Confession*. One of the reasons for drafting the *Augsburg Confession* was the existence of "dissension concerning our holy faith and the Christian religion," and one of the reasons for the imperial assembly at which the Lutheran princes and estates presented the *Augsburg Confession* was "to employ all diligence amicably and charitably to hear, understand, and weigh the judgments, opinions and beliefs of the several parties among us, to unite the same in agreement on one Christian truth, to put aside whatever may not have been rightly interpreted or treated by either side, to have all of us embrace and adhere to a single, true religion and live together in unity and in one fellowship and church, even as we are all enlisted under one Christ" (Preface to the *Augsburg Confession*, 2-4). The turns of phrase in this statement are those of the Emperor Charles the Fifth, but the Lutheran party made them its own. Those who today subscribe to the doctrinal content of the *Augsburg Confession* must regard this objective as a piece of unfinished business, to be worked at whenever the opportunity presents itself.

Lutherans and Roman Catholics have so much in common!

For one thing, they have fifteen hundred years of history that belong equally to both. Lutherans do not think of the Church as something that goes back only as far as Augsburg, any more than Roman Catholics think of the Church as something rooted only in the Council of Trent. But everything that lies beyond Augsburg and Trent is common property. The fifteen centuries that Lutherans and Roman Catholics share as a common heritage are inextricably a part of the faith of each, of the worship of each, and of the theology of each.

Let us Lutherans — since I am addressing myself chiefly to my coreligionists — look at our own heritage. We share with the Roman Catholic Church the four great creeds — the three so-called Catholic Creeds and what has been called the "fourth ecumenical confession," the *Te Deum laudamus*. Both our Churches have built our confession and our theology on the Nicene-Constantinopolitan Creed that we both confess before our altars at celebrations of the Holy Eucharist. Authentically ecumenical though this creed is, binding together the Western, the Eastern Orthodox, and even the ancient non-Chalcedonian branches of the Church, we Westerners — we Lutherans and Roman Catholics — say it, for good or for ill, in our own peculiar Western way. We normally use the first person singular "I believe" rather than the Eastern first person plural "We believe" and we affirm the fateful (and sometimes misleading) Western addition in the article on the Holy Spirit, "Who proceeds from the Father and the Son." The so-called Athanasian Creed that we both use — and in the United States we are almost the only denominations that do use it — as a fifth- or sixth-century strictly Western creed that the East does not know. The so-called Apostles' Creed in the form in which we have it is a product of the seventh century in the West. The *Te Deum laudamus* is Western both in its ancient constituent elements and in its final sixth-century form.

The same thing is true of our worship. Our calendars disclose the same structure and by and large they have even the same dates for the commemorations. The Common Service of the Lutheran Church is the Western Eucharistic rite, with some moderately late medieval features at that. This is true in the sequence of parts — Invocation, Confession, Introit, *Kyrie eleison, Gloria in excelsis,* Collect, Epistle, Psalmody, Gospel, Creed, Offertory, Great Intercession, Preface, *Sanctus and Benedictus qui venit,* Consecration, *Pax, Agnus,* Distribution, Thanksgiving, Blessing.

It is true of the texts as well: With minor dislocations the overwhelming majority of introits, graduals, tracts, alleluia verses, epistles, and gospels are common to both rites. This is strikingly true in the case of the collects; again with minor dislocations we have almost the same Sunday collects (and many of the same festival collects) from one Advent to another. Lutherans in particular will do well to remember that these ancient prayers from the so-called Leonine, Gelasian, and Gregorian sacramentaries are, in the form in which we both have them, deliberately and pointedly anti-Pelagian in their theology, with a repeatedly stressed reluctance to "put their trust in anything that we do" and an equally emphatic appeal to God's grace that is most evangelical.

The same thing goes for our hymns. Take either the *Service Book and Hymnal* or *The Lutheran Hymnal* and note the number of pre-16th century authors: Peter Abelard, Adam of St. Victor, St. Ambrose, St. Bede the Venerable, St. Bernard of Clairvaux, Bernard of Cluny, St. Venantius Fortunatus, St. Francis of Assisi, St. Gregory the Great, Aurelius Prudentius, Girolamo Savonarola, Celius Sedulius, St. Theodulf of Orléans, St. Thomas Aquinas, and the authors of *Christ ist erstanden, Dies irae, Kyrie Fons bonitatis, Veni Creator, Veni Sancte Spiritus, Veni veni Emmanuel, and Victimae Paschale* — all of which Lutherans sing without the least sense that they are alien imports.

Equally instructive are the appeals to the authentic (and to the pseudepigraphic) writing of the fathers and theologians of the Western Church in the Lutheran Symbolic Books — St. Ambrose, St. Augustine, St. Bernard of Clairvaux, St. Francis of Assisi, St. Gelasius, Jean le Charlier de Gerson, St. Gregory the Great, St. Jerome, St. Hilary of Poitiers, Hugh of St. Victor, St. Leo the Great, Peter Lombard, and St. Thomas Aquinas.

Unlike some other reforming traditions, when Lutherans have taken their tradition seriously, they have taken history seriously. The Christian proclamation and teaching of the apostolic era has always had a privileged status in the Lutheran community as the criterion of subsequent proclamation and theology. But Lutherans have never attempted to turn the clock back, to wipe out the centuries that have intervened in God's providence since the year 100, and to reproduce the apostolic environment in worship or in theology. They have respected all time as the arena in which God works and reveals himself and in which the Holy Spirit has been leading the pilgrim People of God into the fullness of the truth of the revelation which he inspired.

All the centuries that we have in common, together with all their saints and with all their achievements and with all their teachers and with all their warning mistakes, are part of our tradition. We do not approve of everything that men did in those fifteen hundred years in the name of the Church — as little as approve without exception our confessional history during the last four hundred years — but again for good or for ill, those fifteen hundred years have helped to inform us as we are today. They have entered into the corporate memory of both Lutherans and Roman Catholics. They are a part of the rock from which both of us were hewn, of the quarry from which both of us were digged. We have come by our common Catholic theology via the same route. We both see the Trinitarian and Christological definitions of the first four ecumenical councils as irreformable. We both see the Church and her ministry as part of the Gospel and as institutions through which the Holy Spirit communicates himself and his grace.

Our common understanding of our Lord's incarnation by the Holy Ghost out of the Blessed Virgin Mary is such that we see the world in which we live as sacramental, a world in which God operates through material means and physical persons — the human proclamation of the word of God; a washing with water in the laver of rebirth; the eating and drinking of bread and wine that in the sacrament of the altar are the veritable body and blood of Christ; a human mouth speaking a word of binding or loosing that binds or looses in the presence of God; a ministry of men through which God communicates aid and help in our warfare against our native sinfulness and against the seductions of his foes and ours; a union of one man and one woman in marriage by which God discloses the secret of Christ and his bride the Church.

Because of the commitment to our respective symbolical documents, it is true, in spite of serious and formidable differences, that, as we penetrate one another's understanding of our common heritage, there are emerging on balance more agreements and fewer differences in crucial issues between the Lutherans of America and the Roman Catholics of America than between the Lutherans of America and the other major Western denominations in this country.

In the interpretation of this common heritage to ourselves and to one another we both have enough to say and enough to hear to make conversations eminently valuable!

But if we Lutherans and Roman Catholics need to engage in conversation with each other because of the fifteen hundred years of history we have in common, we need no less to engage in conversation because of the more than four hundred years of separation, which have sometimes threatened to devour our common patrimony. For these have been unhappy centuries, tinged by mutual acrimony and darkened by mutual anathemas. We both have suffered because our isolation from one another has deprived us of the counsel and admonition of the other party. Excrescenses and the unbalanced exaggerations of valid insights have threatened each of us with the serious impairment of part of our Christian substance. Because the vocabulary of mutual communication most of the time contained only the inflammatory words of critical accusation and shrill condemnation, we often failed to take seriously what the party was really telling the other.

Some aspects of Roman Catholicism that most affront Lutherans are, humanly speaking, there because we and our forebears did not know how to warn effectively against them across the wall between us. In the very nature of the situation, each of us can see the faults of the other better than our own, but it is no less true that some of the Lutheran emphases that have most affronted Roman Catholics are formulated in the way that they are because in our separation from our Roman Catholic fellow Christians we did not have their fraternal counsel to inform us.

It is impermissible to speculate on what might have happened had the breach that finally came into the open in the sixteenth century not taken place. It is unlikely at least that we should have developed quite as many different theological vocables and deposited quite as many different theological premises as we have done. In any case we can learn more than most of us have done from the period between 1520 and 1550 in the Holy Empire. It was a period in which the lines between the Lutherans and the supporters of the Roman See had not yet hardened and solidified, as they were to do in the second half of the second century. The definitive breach had not yet come, the situation still possessed a degree of fluidity, a considerable amount of relatively free communication was going on in a great many communities between the two parties.

In case after case it is demonstrable that this contact produced a significant moderation of extreme positions, sometimes to the extent that it is almost impossible to identify from his printed sermons of this period the party to which a given clergyman was committed. There were many instances of the joint use of Church facilities without friction. In still other cases intercommunion, at least on an informal and practical basis, was achieved. When the political authorities on both sides began to enforce the definitive break of 1563, these experiments in communication and comity were more or less severely proscribed. But they do provide the basis for a measure of optimism that a serious probing of positions undertaken in an atmosphere of mutual confidence could help to narrow the chasm that over four hundred years of separation have created. In any case, we on both sides have an obligation to ourselves and to one another not to let four hundred years of separation further destroy the common base of the previous fifteen hundred years of association.

It is of course important that the conversations in which we engage are not limited to officially prescribed meetings between small panels of theologians and ecumenists gathering together for three days twice a year. Such official conferences, valuable and necessary as they are, need to be matched by hundreds of parallel conferences of informed, responsible, and concerned clergymen and laymen, gathering together in small enough groups to permit the intimacy essential to effective discussion and over a long enough period of time and often enough that mutual confidence in the integrity of the other participants becomes an experience of the heart and is not merely an attitude of the head. These conversations need to be reinforced in turn with cooperative ventures in projects of mutual interest that both can undertake without violation of conscience, as well as with meaningful contacts with the other party actually at worship.

Whether or not the task of reconciliation is ultimately possible no one can say. It certainly will not be either easy or rapid. We have not as yet wholly transcended the developments that made the Lutheran and the Tridentine reformations of the sixteenth century necessary and contributed to the shattering violence of the rupture when it came. Over 400 years of separation and of misunderstanding have added to the difficulty as well as the urgency of the present task.

But the urgency of the task is there. We must undertake it. Humanly speaking, the credibility of the Gospel of God's grace *in* Christ that both Lutherans and Roman Catholics proclaim is involved. If we try to see our problem from God's side, none of us can believe that Christ wills his followers to be divided from one another by mutual acrimony and anathemas. Ultimately, of course, the solution must come from the divine side, but God will bring it about through Christians whom he summons and whom he has made ready to undertake it.

As we respond to his call and to his grace, we must pray for the solution not only with our lips but also with our labors. The ancient ending of the collects that are part of our common tradition suggests both the pattern and the manner of the final fulfillment (as we remember that the "oneness of the Holy Spirit" is that of which Ephesians 4, 3-6 speaks): *through Jesus Christ, your Son, our Lord, Who lives and reigns with You, O Father, in the oneness of the Holy Spirit, God, for ever and ever, Amen.*

PART II:
THE PARISH
AT PRAYER

THE LIFE OF GOD IN THE LIFE OF THE PARISH

Basically a parish is a piece of land. We are familiar with the secular use of the term from the designation "parish" which the state of Louisiana uses in place of the more familiar "county," and from the German equivalent *Gemeinde* understood as the territorial subdivision of a *Kreis*. Technically, it is the piece of land for which a pastor has the responsibility of furnishing the ministrations of the holy religion. In spite of this religious connotation, the factors which led to the gradual development of the parochial system in Western Christendom in the early Middle Ages were to a very large extent secular and fiscal, involving such things as the right to receive certain income and the duty to meet certain fiscal obligations. The ancient English ceremony of "the beating of the bounds" usually connected with the Rogationtide procession from the ninth to the seventeenth centuries had as a purpose impressing the locations of the landmarks that defined the limits of the parish as ineradicably as possible upon the minds of the young. The boundaries were solemnly beaten with willow rods, and youngsters of the parish on occasion were themselves beaten or soundly bumped on the ground at the boundary to make sure that they would not forget the spot.

Yet in spite of all of this the parish is not merely so many acres or so many square miles of territory. Its real significance lies in its relation to the church's ministry. A parish is a piece of land in which the ministers of Christ responsibly proclaim the Word of God and administer the Christian mysteries and in which by these means the Holy Spirit continues to govern and to sanctify the church in that place.

Here in the washing of rebirth the Holy Spirit makes Christians out of pagans and makes God's chosen in every generation the contemporary participants in the once-for-all act of Our Lord Jesus Christ for the salvation of the whole world.

Here God deals with men through His ordained servants with the same validity and certainty as if He acted in His own person, when they exclude manifest and impenitent sinners from the Christian community and absolve those who repent of their sins and are willing to amend.

Here at the command of the world's Redeemer, His Body and Blood become the food of Christians for the forgiveness of their sins, for the gift of God's own divine life, for their everlasting salvation, for the increase of their faith and for the heightened fervency of their mutual love.

Here, as God through his church calls new candidates into the sacred and lifelong ministry of reconciliation and of oversight, his ordained representatives commit to these new officers of the *militia Christi* the authority to proclaim the Word of God, to remit and retain sins, and to administer the Sacraments.

Here Christian men and women whom God has called to life together by their mutual consent in Holy Matrimony initiate a new cell of the church and in their life of mutual love and concern enact the mystery of the bond that unites the Heavenly Bridegroom with His bride the church.

Here at God's command instruction in the divine and saving Truth is imparted to those who desire admission to the Sacrament of the Altar.

Here at the Holy Spirit's direction the cross of sickness is sanctified where it is not taken away, and the sins of the contemporary counterparts of the paralytic on his pallet are forgiven by the ministry of God's ministers.

Here in the words which the Holy Spirit imparts and hallows to be His own words, the mutual conversation and consolation of brothers and sisters in Christ takes place as part of the Gospel's counsel and aid against sin.

Here the words of divine witness and admonition are spoken by human lips for the edifying of God's building and for the purging of God's vineyard.

In short, the parish derives its significance from the fact that it is the arena in which God establishes contact with man. It is a symbol of the divine primacy and the divine initiative in our transformation from sinners to saints.

God has willed and ordered and instituted all things with reference to people, men and women and children who can and do receive the gift of faith and can and do respond with faith in the relationship of faith, who can and do receive the gift of grace and can and do react by saying grace, who by God's design and God's enabling can and do reply to God's sacraments of pardon with their sacrifice of praise, who can and do hear the Word of God that is proclaimed, who can be and are reborn through Holy Baptism, who can and do receive the forgiveness of their sins in the sentence of Holy Absolution, who can and do receive the Body and Blood of Our Lord in the Holy Eucharist, who can be and are made able ministers of the New Testament and priests of Christ's Holy Church, who can be and are united in Holy Matrimony, who can and do receive instruction in the Mysteries of the faith, who can be and are minister to when they are ill, who can be and are consoled and confirmed and comforted by their mutual words and witness. Even the essentiality of people, however, is still secondary to the primacy of God in the life of the parish. Although a parish without people is only a piece of geography, the people are the material on which and through which God works.

The church is prior to the Christian. A person becomes a Christian by being made a member of the church. God's eternal choice of His own is not conditioned by a higher standard of morality or a greater measure of piety than others can muster; it implies first and foremost and altogether a gracious act of God. This fact negates the shallow view of the church which makes it merely an association of like-minded people who have a particularly great interest in religion. It is God who chooses us, not we Him. By the same token, the term "in Christ" cannot be limited to the relation between Christ and the individual. "We being many are one body in Christ and every one members of one another"(Romans 12:5).

The Christian people in the parish, those who are gathered by and around the Sacred Ministry of the Word of God and of His Holy Sacraments together with those who exercise the Sacred Ministry of the Word of God and of the Holy Sacraments according to their vocation, are the church. This statement is true without qualification, even though it exhibits a certain ambivalence. While such a community in any given place is of necessity only a part of the one, holy, catholic and apostolic church, quantitatively considered, in that place such a community *is* the one, holy, catholic and apostolic church, qualitatively considered, and everything that can be said qualitatively about the one, holy, catholic and apostolic church can be said about such a community.

Thus the Christian people — laity plus clergy — transform, as it were, the secular and geographical community of the parish into the spiritual and holy community of the church. These people also give the spiritual, holy community its empirical aspect. It is through them, and through them only, that by God's design the church can be heard and seen and perceived, can become a focal point, can become the growing edge, can absorb others into the community, can become the workplace of God.

This community paradoxically is perfect and imperfect. On the one hand, the foundation of God stands sure — the Lord knows who His own are. It has all the elements that are required for its function, *de jure* at least, if not *de facto*. Yet the number of those whom God desires to bring into the holy community is never complete until He finally will complete it at His Son's final Epiphany. Again, we cannot assume that every person in this community is in deed as well as in name — as medieval canon law and the Lutheran Symbols put it — in the church. The parables of the net and of the ten virgins remind us that among those who are members of the church in name there may be those who are not members in deed, or, put in other terms, that there may be members of the community who are members only according to the external association in rites and ceremonies but not in the prior and principal association of the Holy Spirit and of living faith. The history of the church teaches us that the number of these secular members, these satellite and parasitic fellow-travellers may be so great at times as to occlude and cover up those who are in the church in deed as well as in name. We all need to remind ourselves, however, that the line of demarcation runs not only between members of the church but also through them, even through those who have been transplanted from the kingdom of darkness into the light of the kingdom of God's dear Son and who as members of God's new Israel share in His people's holiness and in the priesthood of His sacred sacerdotal college. For we are all of us always imperfect in our faith and in our love.

Here then is the basis for rejecting some of the common misconceptions about the church, misconceptions that are often as potent in the church as outside it.

The church is not a building, any more than the pastor is a parsonage. The building has symbolic value as the house of God in the parish of human houses. The building has a practical value as the place where the community of God meets for worship, for instruction and for fellowship. In both roles the building rightly levies on the best that the community can provide in skill, in beauty and in artistry. But the real church is the fellowship itself, which was there before the building and which would continue even if the building were destroyed.

Again, the church is not a society of good people, or an association of people who have the same color of skin, pay income taxes in the same bracket or vote the same political ticket. It is the company of those who know their need for forgiveness and who are aware that God has forgiven them in Christ.

Again, the church is not a school for those who want to take courses either in religion or in morals, but a community of love, the family of God whom He has called to sonship in His Son and to whom He has revealed His love and His will for their lives and for the whole world.

The mission of the parish thus is not to preserve the local branch of a venerable institution with a tradition that is of social and ethical importance to our culture. It is not there to oil ecclesiastical machinery or to solicit new people to join an organization. Its task is to communicate the life of God to a world of men that He has redeemed at the infinite cost of His Son's sacrifice. Hence its activities are designed not to keep people busy, but to keep them faithful to their calling. The ultimate value of its activities must be measured in the degree to which they equip the people of the church for their task of representing God in and to the World. This is true even of its services, which, essential as they are, are still only means to an end. An automobile does not exist for the purpose of being filled up with gasoline and oil and water — even though it cannot operate with these — but to provide transportation.

By the same token, the mission of the individual Christian is not fulfilled in writing a check but in offering his life, not in attending church on Sunday but in being the church seven days in the week, not in furnishing fiscal support to the clergy and the other full time workers, or engaging in church activities, but in serving as a channel for the life of God and the love of God to reach other people.

Our parishes will become more the church by the work of the Holy Spirit who alone creates the church. In a sense, however, we also have a part. By the power that He imparts, we can and should inhibit our native opposition to His work, make faithful use of the channels through which He has promised to communicate His life to us, and respond cheerfully to the good inspirations that He puts into our hearts.

There is no part of the parish that cannot be said to be "of God." It is anchored in the soil of God's creation; it is utterly dependent upon the material means that He has designed; it is bound to the eye and the ear and the lip and the larynx, the hand and the lungs and the nervous system; and in its holiest rites it uses such homely and creaturely things as water and bread and wine.

The parish exists by and for God's redemptive and His hallowing activity. Its clergy are not their own masters nor are they servants of the parishioners — they are "God's fellow-workers" (I Corinthians 3:9). The people, even as Christians, are not the creatures of the clergy; they are God's vineyard and God's building. Because the parish is of God it is set apart from all other groups, actually as well typically. Its cohesion does not depend primarily on its possession of a common ceremonial or a common constitution or a common ritual, but upon the fact that it has a common Lord, a common commitment to Him, a common Baptism into Him, a common vocation from Him, a common hope through Him, a common God and Father Who is above all and through all and in all. Its hope is for all men and for all creation (Colossians 1:23).

Its unity is not predicated upon uniformity but upon community. This is the thrust of all the images that the New Testament employs — a marriage, a building, a household, a body. Its unity is not dissolved by the number or the diversity of parishes. Each parish is a finished picture of the whole church. Each fully represents the purpose of the whole. The whole church is in every part.

A household (Galatians 6:10) is a unit because it has a common parentage. As elements of a household, members of a parish have a special responsibility toward one another based on their common spiritual parentage.

The parish is the bride of the Christ. "I espoused you to one husband," St. Paul writes to the Corinthian community, "that I might present you as a pure virgin to Christ," and when he asserts that the head of a woman is the man, it is not because St. Paul's background is oriental and his era ancient, but because in Holy Matrimony woman is the type of the church and the man the type of Christ.

The solidity of a building ultimately depends not on the workman but upon the foundation. "According to the grace of God ... I laid a foundation which is Jesus Christ," St. Paul can say (I Corinthians 3:10-11), and he can call himself a "wise architect" without a trace of boasting, for the simple reason that the choice of the right foundation involved a rejection of everything that he as an individual might have chosen apart from the grace of God.

Whatever else the picture of the parish as a body may convey, it describes the parish less as an organization that as an organism, a thing endowed with life and with life's possibilities for growing, developing and propagating. This life is not from within the members themselves, as though they were self-propagating, but it is from God. The widely prevalent delusion that righteous living is the thing that builds the church is devastating, because it puts men, rather than the true Maker and Builder, God, in the position of seeming to initiate and motivate the growth of the church. St. Paul does not urge his readers to do good works in order to bring about the perfect society, but because they have become and are members of one another in Christ. Apart from the church, he knows nothing of a body of which we are members, a bride betrothed to the Lord Jesus, an edifice in which we are stones. He knows nothing of a life of faith apart from the church. The members of the church have life only because they are members of the body. The life of faith begins when a person becomes a member of one body that is the church and continues only so long as this membership in the church continues.

As the qualities of the whole church are present in each parish, so the qualities of each parish are present in each parishioner, lay or clerical. Christians are "holy," that is they have been separated form the world for a religious purpose, because they are "in Christ," and because "if the root be holy, so are the branches" (Romans 11:6). Holiness entails a responsibility to life in accordance with this fact: "Walk worthy of the vocation with which you have been called" (Ephesians 4:1).

We now consider the channels through which the life of God becomes the life of the parish.

The one inclusive means, the preeminent channel, *the instrument* in a peculiar sense is the Word of God. Upon His apostolic delegate His Son laid the imperative of teaching all the things that He had commanded the Twelve while they were with Him. This command is still an imperative upon those who represent Him. It involves the use of more than merely verbal symbols; it goes beyond mere speaking or mere hearing or mere reading. It engages and preempts the skill of the graphic and the plastic artist, of the musician and the dramatist, of the architect and the craftsman, of the engineer and the builder, of the designer and the technician.

At the level of communication through verbal symbols this Word includes the "alien" word of wrath and judgment as well as the "proper" word of reconciliation and forgiveness. It requires the members of the holy community of the parish to communicate within the outside its circle the total word with the greatest possible degree of relevance and concreteness. The parish is to speak it not only in the sermon of its responsible mouthpieces, the clergy, but the Word of God is to be spoken in every occasion for public and private instruction, for private counseling and spiritual direction, in the church building and in the homes and places of daily occupation of the members of the parish, in guilds and in committees, in formally structured and wholly unstructured situations — wherever the dynamic power of the group can be harnessed to its communication.

The Word of God is to be spoken by each member of the community according to his competence and vocation, remembering that while the public and responsible proclamation of the Word of God is the task of the called and ordained servant of that Word, the witnessing of and to the Word of God is the common task of every Christian. This reaches into his daily life; God in His saving act in Christ in every political, domestic, economic and social structure of which we become a part.

Since the sermon is not a formulation of the preacher's ideas about God and religion, but the witness of the entire parish to itself and to the world, a rotating panel of parishioners changing from week to week might well be enlisted to meet with the pastor to discuss what was ultimately their sermon and to help him find answers to such questions as: Did the sermon have anything to say? Where did it fail? How could it have been improved in terms of clarity and relevance to those who heard it? What about the text for the next Sunday? In this way the sermon would become less the prophetic voice of a man, but more the voice of God speaking through the community.

The life of God in the parish implies that the members of the church according to their ability and competence recognize their responsibilities in assisting in the conduct of the service and in the provision of services in the absence of the pastor. Specifically, such responsibilities would include the reading of the lessons, ministering about the altar, and officiating at choir offices.

Both our membership in the church and the unity of the church go back to Holy Baptism, "for in one Holy Spirit we were all baptized into One Body" (I Corinthians 12:12). Holy Baptism is to be stressed as necessary to salvation and to the new life in Christ, and as a transformation of our relationship to the body of Christ, translation into God's kingdom, being grafted into the true Vine outside of which we can do nothing. This new relationship is to be renewed daily; daily we are to creep back to the font; by daily contrition the old Adam or the old Eve is to be drowned and die with all sins and evil lusts, and the new man or the new woman is daily to come forth and arise, beginning in time the life in righteousness that shall never end.

Practically, Baptism is to be administered at the earliest possible time. The Easter and Pentecost vigils should be used for adult baptisms. Occasionally at least Holy Baptism should be administered at a parochial celebration of the Holy Eucharist, to signify that every Baptism is a ministry in which both God and the church — the latter through the officiant and the sponsors, who are invariably to be communicants of the Lutheran church — are both engaged. The fullest feasible use of baptismal symbolism recommends itself: the font, if possible, near the entrance of the church; the entry into the nave in the course of the rite at the blessing, "The Lord protect thy coming in and thy going out from this time forth and even for evermore," the baptismal robe; the baptismal candle, subsequently to be lighted annually on the anniversary of baptism; a baptismal certificate suitable for framing and hanging over the child's bed, beside the crucifix that recalls the second, bloody Baptism with which Our Lord was baptized (Mark 10:38). Adequate instruction of parents and sponsors should precede the rite. Afterward a special memento should be made on both the anniversary day of the candidate's natural birth and on the anniversary of the day of his rebirth in God, either at daily matins or at the Holy Eucharist. Parents receiving the Body and Blood of Our Lord in the Holy Communion may well bring their infants to the communion rail to receive the celebrant's blessing: "Defend, O Lord this Thy child in the covenant which Thou hast made with him (or her) in Baptism."

The Holy Eucharist, celebrated with sermon and with the Holy Communion, is the parochial community's great weekly sacramental and sacrificial opportunity. Here in the *sacramentum audibile* of the Word of God as message and in the *verbum visible* of the Word of God as action, the holy community has communicated to it the life and the love of God, and here in Christ it responds by offering itself in total self-oblation to the Giver of Life. The best introduction and initiation into this rhythm of receiving and offering is participation in the church's Eucharistic worship Sunday by Sunday and holyday by holyday. The Eucharist is not an end in itself; it is rather a means to participation in the life of God that we may be better able to share this life with others.

Far less is the Eucharist a wholly individual matter it is tremendously true, of course, that the Holy Communion individualizes the life of God and the grace of God as much as does Holy Baptism or individual Absolution, and that like Baptism and Absolution the Sacrament of the Altar is to the believing recipient a mark of God's election. But as the bond of charity and the sacrament of unity, the Holy Communion is "the family meal of the family of God." For this reason, the presence of all the members of all the families of the parish through the whole service commends itself. Through frequency of celebration and through the good example of regular communion set by the clergy of the parish for the layfolk of the parish, the people can be drawn to greater frequency of reception.

Parish practice will inevitably vary. Nevertheless, certain principles suggest themselves. There should be no celebration of the Holy Communion without an exposition of the Word of God. No Sunday or holyday should go by without at least one celebration of the Holy Eucharist at an hour convenient for the largest number of prospective communicants. Incontestably the ideal is a celebration of the Holy Eucharist at every Sunday and holyday service designed as a parochial service.

The vestments worn, like the rite and the ceremonial employed, should symbolize and attest the unbroken continuity of the church today with the church of the Apostles; thus the alb and the chasuble recommend themselves as the minimum. The historic ideal of a fully choral service should be realized at every service to the fullest possible degree. The ornaments of the church used in the service — whether of fabric or of metal, of wood or of stone — should express in design and material the dignity of the use to which they are being put. The varying moods of the Church Year should find the fullest feasible symbolical and musical expression.

When the life of God is lost through sin, it needs to be restored. When it is imperiled through complacency or sloth, through frailty or fickleness or foible, it needs to be fortified. For these purposes God has given His church the Office of the Keys and the ministry of Holy Absolution. There need be no essential contradiction between the view that sees Holy Absolution comprehended in Holy Baptism as the time-after-time expression of God's faithfulness to His covenant and of Holy Baptism's life-long perduring power and the other view that sees Holy Absolution as the living voice of the Gospel and the essential part of the Sacrament of Repentance. In either view it is vitally important that Holy Absolution be available, not only as it is customarily administered among us *in globo* over a whole congregation of penitents, but individually pronounced as God's reassuring reply to the individual. Thus it should be pronounced not only upon the individual penitent kneeling in individual confession before his confession; it is desirable that it be individually imparted even in the public service in response to the general confession spoken by the individual penitents in common. To do less is to reject not only the clear implication of the Lutheran but also the best traditions of historic Lutheran Christianity.

The life of God does not come from a new program, but through repentance, that is, through contrition and faith. The life of God is not the result of moral instruction and moral living, but of God's gift of a new relationship with Him.

A parish is not required or expected to be "successful" by statistical standards, but to be faithful. There will be those in the parish who do not respond to what seems to them to be novel, and possibly even alien, emphases in parish life. To them the members who have been given a broader and brighter vision must be ready in love to interpret what they have discovered by grace, while refusing to compromise with God for the sake of pleasing men.

The life of God in the Church implies that each parish become more the body of Christ, continuing His ministry in loving and serving the world, that it deepen its corporate commitment and allegiance to God and to His Son as King of Kings and Lord of Lords, that it become more the family of God in which grace for obedience is to be had, in which faith is increased for facing life as it is in the confidence that we are not alone, but are related to God and to one another, and that nothing, not even death, can separate us from this relationship.

The new life in God implies that every parish be a parish of worshippers, that we respond to God's total redemptive action by offering ourselves in our totality — all that we are and all that we have of the gifts of God's creation — back to Him in thanksgiving and praise.

Thus the life of God in a parish implies that the parish takes worship seriously, that it nourish itself at the font, the lectern, the pulpit, the altar. It is here that Christ gives Himself to us so that we may become "other Christs" to others by serving them.

The new life in God implies that each parish be a parish of teachers, "ready always to give an answer to every man who asks us a reason for the hope that is in us" (I Peter 3:15) and searching together in the Spirit to discover and disclose to one another God's will for our individual and corporate existence.

Thus the life of God in a parish implies that the parish will take education seriously, that it realizes that no one is too young or too old to be outside the concern of the teaching church. The opportunity for growth in understanding the life of God should be made available to all and should pervade the life of the parish. This may involve the rethinking and the rescheduling of traditional hours of service and ways of worship, to include opportunities for individualized instruction in the framework of common worship.

The new life in God implies that each parish will be a community of partners, mutually strengthening one another in the awareness that they stand together in a new relationship to one another in Christ and His church, mutually strengthening the faith of one another through reciprocal sharing and witness, mutually confirming one another in the enjoyment of the gifts of God's creation, in living in Christian freedom, and in taking God so seriously that they do not take themselves too seriously.

Thus the life of God in the parish implies that the parish will take prayer seriously. Family prayers in the families of the parish will provide both the extension of and the basis for corporate worship in the greater family of the parish. This may require not only diligent instruction but also careful demonstration. (Tape recordings might be useful.) Daily matins and vespers at hours convenient to the potential worshippers can become the occasion for programmatic intercessions for those desiring such prayers, for those with anniversaries of baptism, birth, marriage, or bereavement falling on these days, with private Absolution and Holy Communion available for those who desire it. The parochial services of Holy Communion will reverse the present trend away from the general use of corporate intercession toward the consistent and more meaningful use of it.

The life of God in the parish implies an end of commercialism in the financial affairs of the parish. If we cook, it will be for the hungry;

if we sew, it will be for the needy; if we collect clothes, it will be for the ill-clad; if we eat, it will be for the joy of being together as children of God and not to raise funds for Him who is the Creator and Owner of the world's wealth. The kingdom of God is not buying one another's pies, but in being faithful stewards of the gifts with which God has bountifully endowed even the poorest. The problem of parish finance is not getting into people's purses, but of getting God into people's hearts.

The new life in God implies that the parish will be a community of servants, recognizing as a parish and as individuals their Christian social responsibility to the world, continuing the ministry of Christ to men by engaging in and supporting ministries to those in need, and in their daily vocations striving to serve God by serving others.

In sum: The life of God in the life of the parish implies that we strive in everything to let God *be* God, that we seek in everything to let the church *be* the church, and that we endeavor in everything to let Christians *be* Christians.

THE LUTHERAN DOCTRINE
OF THE SACRAMENT
OF THE ALTAR,
ECUMENICALLY CONSIDERED

I am grateful for the invitation to participate in this theological conference. For a descendant of Huguenot emigrants from France the very fact that this is St. Bartholomew's Day is a symbol of the assuagement of ancient animosities. Beyond that, I sense the problem that I represent for my Roman Catholic hosts as Father Davis articulates it briefly in his admirable and very recent *The Making of a Christian* (or *Sacraments of Initiation* as the American title designates it). He speaks of the baptized who are "outside of the visible unity" of the Roman Catholic Church as "not enjoy[ing] full membership" in the Church, as not experiencing the "full effect" of "the union with the Church given by their baptism," and as living "in an anomalous situation."[1] On this score I feel that the invitation to me to speak here is a symbol of the conviction that he then proceeds to voice, that "the bond that unites us through our common baptism is deeper and stronger than what divides us" (82-83).

In setting forth the Lutheran doctrine of the Sacrament of the Altar I shall base my presentation primarily upon the Symbolical Books of the Lutheran Church. These documents are contained in the so-called *Book of Concord* (German, 1580; Latin, 1584). In this collection of creedal documents the greatest authority attaches to the so-called Catholic

Creeds — the baptismal creed ascribed to the Holy Apostles, the eucharistic creed popularly called the Nicene, and the pseudonymous Creed of St. Athanasius that begins "Whosoever will be saved, it is necessary above all things that he hold the Catholic Faith." Next in authority for us is the *Augsburg Confession*, the intentionally irenic statement of faith offered by the Lutheran estates of the Holy Roman Empire to the Emperor Charles V in 1530. The remaining documents are regarded as commentaries which establish the true meaning of the *Augsburg Confession* — the two catechisms of Luther from 1528/1529, the *Apology* (or *Defense*) of the *Augsburg Confession* of 1530/1531, the *Smalcald Articles* of 1536 to 1538 drafted for presentation at the projected Council of Mantua, the *Treatise on the Authority and Primacy of the Pope* of 1537, the *Formula of Concord* of 1577, and the Preface to the *Book of Concord* of 1580.

Let me make two observations here. First, the bulk of this material is not from Luther's pen. Second, except where the Symbolical Books make an explicit appeal to another work by Luther, the only pronouncements of his that bind Lutherans symbolically are the three documents in this symbolical corpus, that is, the two Catechisms and the *Smalcald Articles*. To supplement the material in the *Book of Concord* and to illustrate it I shall refer at a few points to the formulations of classic Lutheran orthodoxy, notably to the works of Martin Chemnitz (1522-1586) and of John Gerhard (1582-1637).[2]

I propose to discuss the Lutheran doctrine of the Sacrament of the Altar chiefly from the standpoint of sacrament rather than of sacrifice. I shall discuss it first in positive terms, second with reference to its polemic formulation in opposition to the Swiss and South German Reformers, and third in its polemic formulation in opposition to certain late medieval and Tridentine Roman Catholic developments. I shall conclude with a discussion of three eucharistic problems that are of particular ecumenical interest: (1) The doctrine that historians of dogma call the "ubiquity" of our Lord's human nature; (2) the status of the celebrant; and (3) the sacrificial aspect of the Sacrament of the Altar.

THE LUTHERAN DOCTRINE IN POSITIVE TERMS

Our Lord Himself, on the eve of His Passion, in the night in which He was betrayed, instituted the Sacrament of the Altar as a ceremony and sign which His Church was to continue to celebrate until the *Parousia*. The Lutheran Reformers propose to base their eucharistic doctrine on the four accounts of the words of institution. Even I

Corinthians 10:16-21 is used merely to supplement and support the insights derived from the Synoptics and I Cor. 11:23-25.

2. The Sacrament of the Altar is the Body and Blood of Our Lord Jesus Christ. Almost always the Symbolical Books prefix the adjective "true" to Body and Blood. In this they followed the medieval usage which from the turn of the millennium used "true" to differentiate the Body of Christ in the Holy Communion from the Mystical Body of Christ the Church. When the adverb "truly" replaces the adjective "true" there is a polemic edge to it; it intends to affirm the reality of the Body and the Blood of Our Lord in contrast to a merely symbolical element, the real *parousia*, or presence, of His Body and Blood in contrast to a real *apousia*, or absence. The most explicit and considered formulation is that of the *Smalcald Articles*: "The bread and wine in the Supper are the true Body and Blood of Christ, and ... these are given and received not only by godly but also by wicked Christians" (*S[malcald] A[rticles]*, Part] Three VI 1). "Instituted by Christ himself, [the Sacrament of the Altar] is the true Body and Blood of our Lord Jesus Christ, under the bread and wine, for us Christians to eat and to drink;" (*S[mall] C[atechism]* Sacrament of the Altar 2). "The Sacrament of the Altar ... is the true Body and Blood of the Lord Christ in and under the bread and wine which we Christians are commanded by Christ's word to eat and drink" (*L[arge] C[atechism]* Sacrament of the Altar 8). "[The Sacrament of the Altar is] that bread and wine which are Christ's Body and Blood and with which the words are coupled" (*ibid.*, 28). These statements are all from Luther.

The *Augsburg Confession*, from Melanchthon's pen, declares: "The true Body and Blood of Christ are really present in the Supper of Our Lord under the form of bread and wine and are there distributed and received" (X 1 German).[3]

The *Apology* declared that "in the Lord's Supper the Body and Blood of Christ are truly and substantially present and are truly offered with those things that are seen, the bread and the wine, to those who receive the sacrament" (X 1). The *Formula of Concord* teaches: "In the Holy Supper the Body and Blood of Christ are truly and essentially present and are truly distributed and received with the bread and wine" (Ep[itome] VII 6). In the next paragraph it declares: "The bread ... and the wine ... because of the sacramental union ... are truly the Body and Blood of Christ" (ibid., 7).

3. The Lutheran Symbols are in all this concerned about preserving Catholic doctrine. The Catholic Creeds do not discuss the Holy Eucharist, apart from the reference to *sanctorum communio* in the developed baptismal creed. We know that as early as 388 (the date of the earliest recorded occurrence of the Greek equivalent, *koinonia ton hagion*), the term meant "participation in the holy things," that is, the

Body and the Blood of Our Lord. As I have pointed out elsewhere, we also know that the tradition of interpreting this phrase eucharistically continued in the West at least until as late as about 1325 in France in the case of Francis of Meyronnes; that it survived in England as late as the sixteenth century in the case of a Chester Mystery Play last performed in 1575; and that in a slightly modified form, the *sanctorum* taken as the equivalent of *sacramentorum*, we meet a surviving vestige of this interpretation in 1617 in the fifth volume of John Gerhard's *Theological Commonplaces*.[4] Admittedly this does not say a great deal about the Holy Eucharist. But it affirms the fact. It stresses participation in the Holy Communion. Its occurrence in the Creed asserts the indispensable importance of the Sacrament of the Altar as a means of communicating salvation and redemption to us. It indicates the essentially corporate nature of the Holy Eucharist. The dual number of the genitive *sanctorum* refers to the primitive practice of Communion under both kinds. With all of these emphases the Lutheran position is in full accord.

But there is more to be said. The Lutheran Reformers are concerned about reflecting the belief that the Catholic Church — of which they consciously regard themselves and their communities as a part — held from the beginning as to the "what" of the Sacrament of the Altar. Thus the *Apology* takes cognizance of the fact that the so-called *Imperial Reply* to the *Augsburg Confession*, drafted by the theologians of the party in communion with the Bishop of Rome, had approved the *Augsburg Confession*'s article on the Sacrament of the Altar. In this way the *Apology* could establish its identity of conviction with what it calls the *ecclesia Romana*, that is, the historic Western Church, on "the bodily presence of Christ." It goes on to establish the identity of its conviction with the Eastern Church as well, by quoting the Divine Liturgy as contemporarily used by the Eastern Church, which has the priest pray that the bread might be changed and become the Body of Christ — a formulation with which it does not voice disagreement. Next it quotes the *Commentary on St. Mark* of Theophylact of Ohrid (d. 1108?), known as Vulgarius because he was Primate of Bulgaria, which says that the bread is not the *antítypos* of the Lord's Body — "the earthly form corresponding to the heavenly reality" — but that it is changed into the Body of Christ. Finally it quotes a long passage from the *Commentary on St. John* of St. Cyril of Alexandria which declares that on the basis of the Sacred Scriptures we must hold that Christ dwells in us bodily through the communication of His flesh and that He is in us by a natural participation as well by the *habitus* of love (X 2-4).

Again, the Lutheran confessors commit themselves to the patristic position without reserve: "Whoever eats this bread eats the Body of Christ. This has also been the unanimous teaching of the leading church fathers, such as Ss. John of the Golden Mouth, Cyprian, Leo the Great, Ambrose, and Augustine" (F[ormula of] C[oncord] EP VII 15).

They also accept the common patristic analogy between the hypostatic union and the Holy Eucharist.

> Many prominent ancient teachers, like Ss. Justin the Martyr, Cyprian, Augustine, Leo the Great, Gelasius, John of the Golden Mouth and others, have cited the hypostatic union as an analogy to the words of Christ's testament, "This is my Body." For as in Christ two distinct and untransformed natures are indivisibly united, so in the Sacrament of the Altar the two essences, the natural bread and the true, natural Body of Christ are present together here on earth in the ordered action of the sacrament, though the union of the Body and Blood of Christ with the bread and wine is not a personal union, like that of the two natures in Christ, but a sacramental union (FC S[olid] D[eclaration] VII 36-37).

In passing, it should be noted that the term "sacramental union" is one coined at the Reformation to describe the relationship between the heavenly and the earthly elements. The mode of the relationship is left deliberately undefined. The Lutheran Reformers observe that St. Paul speaks of the Eucharist as bread in the very moment of its being eaten; they observe that Our Lord categorically calls the Sacrament His Body and His Blood. They content themselves with affirming both — this is the implication of the term "sacramental union" — without resolving the mysterious tension of the paradox.

4. The Lutheran Symbols are concerned that the sacrament be received, or that at least it be available. Part of the price paid for the Nicene solution to the Christological problem was the gradual decrease in the frequency of Communions. In the tenth century St. Ulric of Augsburg (890?-973) had to encourage his diocesan clergy to exhort the faithful to receive the Holy Communion at least four times a year. The Fourth Lateran Council in 1215 had to enforce an annual reception of the Sacrament in *Omnis utriusque*. The Lutheran Reformers insisted that every Mass had to be a community Mass and that at every celebration there ought to be communicants who received from the elements consecrated at that Mass. This represented a radical departure from conventional practice. Its net effect was twofold. It increased the real opportunities for Holy Communion to every Sunday and major holy day and other occasions when there were intending communicants (AC XXIV 34; Ap XV 40; XXIV 1). It decreased radically the number of ferial Masses, since, on principle, solitary Masses and Masses without communicants were abandoned. A daily celebration, the Reformers held, is not an ancient universal tradition (AC XXIV 41; Ap XXIV 8), but the possibility of daily celebrations is clearly contemplated (LC Sacrament of the Altar 39; FC SD VII 77).

Pastors are urged to preach winsomely on the benefits of frequent Communion (SC Pref [ace] 22-25; LC Sacrament of the Altar 39-41).

The faithful are warned to regard a lack of desire for the Sacrament of the Altar as a serious symptom of moribund spirituality (LC Sacrament of the Altar 42-44). The fitness of a communicant to receive the Sacrament of the Altar is described as consisting wholly in his repentance, that is, in his contrition and in his faith in the holy obedience and complete merit of Christ (SC Sacrament of the Altar 10; Ap XXIV 73; SA Three I 9; FC Ep VII 20). The Large Catechism quotes St. Hilary of Poitiers in favor of a reception of Holy Communion by every qualified communicant at every celebration. "Lest [the abstainer] deprive himself of life," Luther adds (Sacrament of the Altar 59). Although the number of communicants was not always great, even the first generation of Reformers could assert both that "every Lord's Day many in our circles use the Holy Communion" (Ap XV 40) and that "most people in our churches use the sacraments — absolution and the Holy Communion — many times in the year" (XI 3).

5. Taking their cue from the Dominical command "This do," and St. Paul's "As often as you eat this bread and drink this cup of the Lord," the Lutheran Reformation stressed the dynamic rather than the static element in the Holy Eucharist. In the interest of reception in preference to veneration they extracted from the words of institution the principle, "Nothing has the character of a sacrament apart from the use of it which Christ instituted" (FC SD VII 85-86).

6. The essentially social and corporate, rather than individualistic, character of the Sacrament of the Altar receives extensive stress. On this basis the right of a priest to celebrate the Holy Eucharist privately even for the laudable purpose of receiving Holy Communion is rejected (AC XXIV 5 Latin; SA Two II 9).

7. The benefit of a fruitful reception of the Sacrament of the Altar is described as "the forgiveness of sins, life, and salvation" (SC Sacrament of the Altar 6; LC Creed 55; Sacrament of the Altar 70; Ap XIII 20; SA Three III 40). In detail this benefit is described in many other ways. Through reception of the Holy Communion we find comfort for our straitened consciences and learn to believe God and to expect and ask of Him all that is good (AC XXIV 7); our faith is strengthened in us (Ap IV 210); we remember what Christ has done for us and receive His benefits by faith so that we are made alive by them (Ap XXIV 72); we receive the assurance that we are incorporated into and joined with Christ and washed with His blood (FC SD VII 16; Ap XXII 10). The Sacrament of the Altar is a remedy against sin, flesh, devil, world, death, danger, and hell and a bestowing of grace, life, paradise, heaven, Christ, God, and everything good (SC Pref 23). It embodies the whole Gospel and the article of the Creed, "I believe in the holy Catholic Church, the forgiveness of sins, the resurrection of the flesh, and the life everlasting;" and it is a safeguard against death and all misfortune,

a food of the soul, nourishing and strengthening the new man, a daily pasture and sustenance, a refreshment of faith in the battle of life, a consolation of overburdened hearts, a treasure from heaven, a precious antidote against the poison of weakness, and a pure, wholesome, soothing medicine which aids and quickens us in both soul and body (LC Sacrament of the Altar 22-24.27.32.66.68.70).

POLEMICAL DEVELOPMENT OF THE LUTHERAN DOCTRINE IN RESPONSE TO THE ENTHUSIASTS AND THE SWISS REFORMERS

The realistic Lutheran doctrine of Holy Communion was attacked at an early date by the spiritualistic enthusiasts, such as the Münzerite "Heavenly Prophets" of Zwickau (1521) and Luther's former academic superior, Andrew Bodenstein von Carlstadt (1524). Huldreich Zwingli, the reformer of Zurich, first published his symbolic interpretation of the Holy Eucharist in 1524. A number of literary exchanges between him and Luther preceded their personal confrontation at Marburg in 1529, where the differences between the two Reformers proved insurmountable. John Oecolampadius, the Reformer of Basel, joined in the attack on the Lutheran position in 1525. The South German Reformers tended to side with Zwingli, although a short-lived agreement was worked out between the Lutherans and the Strasbourg party under Martin Bucer in 1536 (Wittenberg Concord). In 1549 the Zurich Agreement (Consensus Tigurinus) united the Zurich party under Henry Bullinger and the Geneva party under John Calvin.

Although there were significant differences in eucharistic doctrine among all of these theologians, they all agreed that the Body and Blood of Christ are not present upon earth but only in heaven and that neither godly nor wicked communicants receive the Body and Blood of Christ with the mouth of the body. At most, only believing communicants eat Christ's Flesh and drink His Blood in any sense at all, but even they do so only in a spiritual sense by faith. This became the normative doctrine of the Reformed churches in Switzerland, Germany, France, Holland, and Central Eastern Europe, of the Presbyterian and Congregationalist churches of the British Isles and the colonies, and of the Anglican Thirty-Nine Articles of Religion. Efforts at an accomodation between Lutheran and Reformed doctrine have, alas, always failed. The Lutheran position insisted upon the sacramental union, the *manducatio oralis* (eating of Christ's Body with the mouth of the body in the Holy Communion) and the *manducatio indignorum* (reception of the Body of Christ by wicked and unfit communicants).

The Reformed position insisted upon a figurative understanding of the words of institution and upon a distance between Christ's Body and Blood and the elements in the Eucharist "as great as the distance between heaven and earth" (Zurich Agreement, 22 and 25). The most recent effort in Europe, the so-called Arnoldshain Theses of 1957, reiterated past failures. The current discussions between Lutheran theologians and Presbyterian and Reformed theologians in this hemisphere have merely clarified the two sets of positions.[4a]

2. The attack on the Lutheran position evoked a series of four brochures from Luther's pen to which the Lutheran Symbolical Books explicitly appeal: *Against the Heavenly Prophets in the Matter of Images and Sacraments* (1525); *That These Words of Christ, "This Is My Body, and so on," Still Stand Firm against the Fanatics* (1527); *Confession concerning Christ's Supper* (1528); and the *Last Confession Concerning Holy Communion* (1544). In all of them he insists, as the Lutheran Symbolical Books insist after him, that "the words of the testament of Christ are to be understood in no other way than in their literal sense, and not as though the bread symbolized the absent Body and the wine the absent Blood of Christ" (FC Ep VII 7). "There can be no metaphor in the word 'bread.' ...Christ himself precluded a metonymy in the word 'body'" (FC SD VII 48-49). Political considerations made it necessary in the sixteenth century for Reformed Christians in the Holy Roman Empire to subscribe to the *Augsburg Confession* in order to survive, since only the Lutheran and the Roman confessions were legally recognized. As a result, the Reformed theologians of the Holy Roman Empire devoted considerable effort to reformulations of their position that would enable them to subscribe to the *Augsburg Confession* without denying their central conviction about the Supper of the Lord. Since they were able to penetrate some Lutheran churches and theological faculties under the pretense of loyalty to the *Augsburg Confession*, the *Formula of Concord* rejects these reformulations comprehensively and in detail. In turn the Lutherans defended themselves against a series of false charges. One was that they taught eucharistic cannibalism, for which the euphemism "Capernaitic eating and drinking" was used (FC Ep VII 41-42). Another charge was that they taught a local extension of the humanity of Christ throughout the created universe (FC SD VIII 92). A third charge was that they based their eucharistic theology upon a Eutychian Christology (FC Ep VIII 21). Against this last charge they reiterate their assertion that the norm of their eucharistic doctrine is the words of institution alone (Preface to the *Book of Concord, Bekenntnisschriften*, 10, 26-11, 5). In turn they insisted that where "the enemies of the Sacrament" had so perverted the meaning of the words of institution that they no longer communicated Our Lord's original intention implied in the word "is," they had rendered the vowels and consonants of the

words of institution a defective form which could not bring about a valid sacrament (FC SD VII 32).

3. The controversy was carried on from both sides with a vehemence and an acrimony that appears almost scandalous to our ecumenical twentieth century (see for example, the quotations in FC SD VII 67). The Lutherans defended their position with such tenacity because they sensed that more was at stake than eucharistic doctrine. The fact that the Reformed attack on the Lutheran position had argued from Christological premises led the Lutherans to believe that at the bottom of the Reformed view lay a seriously defective Christology and therewith a calamitous soteriology. "This doctrine," they argued, "not only perverts the words of Christ's testament, but it opens a way for the accursed Arian heresy. Hence, unless we refute these errors on the firm basis of the divine Word and our simple Christian Creed, we shall finally have Christ's eternal deity denied and we shall lose Christ altogether along with our salvation" (FC Ep VIII 39).

POLEMICAL DEVELOPMENT OF THE LUTHERAN DOCTRINE IN RESPONSE TO CERTAIN LATE MEDIEVAL AND POST-TRIDENTINE ROMAN CATHOLIC POSITIONS

From the first the Lutheran Reformers insisted on Holy Communion under the species of the consecrated wine as well as under the species of the consecrated host. This usage, they stipulated, has Christ's commandment to support it. In apostolic times the whole congregation received both kinds (I Corinthians 11:26). Only Western custom of quite recent times holds otherwise. The conventional reasons alleged in favor of administering the sacrament to the congregation under the species of the consecrated host only are insufficient to change Christ's directive. (AC XXIII 1-8; Ap XXII 1-5). They do not reject out of hand the doctrine of concomitance, but they label it "specious learning" and argue that "even if it were true that as much is included under one form as under both, yet administration in one form is not the whole order and institution as it was established and commanded by Christ" (SA Three VI 2-4). Administration under one kind deprives the congregation of the Blood of Christ (FC Ep VII 24), they say, even though it does not invalidate the sacrament, so that a person receiving a Communion at a Roman Catholic Mass still receives the Body of Christ.

2. Initially the Lutheran position does not polemicize against the idea of transubstantiation. To the sacramental realism of the Lutheran view transubstantiation was in any case more attractive than the symbolist interpretation of the Enthusiasts and the Swiss Reformers. In two passages in his classic 1528 *Confession concerning Christ's Supper* Luther had asserted:

> I have taught in the past and still teach that this controversy [between Wycliffe and his Scholastic contemporaries about transubstantiation] is unnecessary and that it is of no great consequence whether the bread remains or not. I maintain, however, with Wycliffe that the bread remains; on the other hand, I also maintain with the Scholastics that the Body of Christ is present (W.A., 26, 439; American ed., 37, 296). I have often enough asserted that I do not argue whether the wine remains or not. It is enough for me that Christ's Blood is present; let it be with the wine as God wills. Sooner than have mere wine with the fanatics, I would agree with the pope that there is only Blood (W.A., 26, 462; American ed., 37, 317).

But as the Reformation spread and theological tempers were inflamed, there was a widespread insistence on the part of the opponents that transubstantiation was inseparably bound up with the idea of the Mass as in itself an expiatory sacrifice which was effective *ex opere operato sine bono motu utensis*. This led to the increasingly emphatic and almost routine rejection of transubstantiation on the part of the Lutherans. For the benefit of the prelates that would assemble at Mantua the *Smalcald Articles* declare: "We have no regard for the subtle sophistry of those who teach that bread and wine surrender their natural substance and retain only the appearance and shape of bread without any longer being real bread, for that bread is and remains there agrees better with the Scriptures" (SA Three VI 5). The post-Tridentine *Formula of Concord* is stronger: "We unanimously reject and condemn ... transubstantiation, when it is taught ... that the bread and the wine in the Holy Supper lose their substance and natural essence and are thus annihilated in such a way that they are transmuted into the Body of Christ and that only the exterior appearance remains" (FC Ep VII 22; SD VII 108). It will be noted that the rejection is of a specific metaphysical concept and not primarily of the term.

Again, the formula "in, with and under the bread and wine," which was borrowed from Scholastic terminology to affirm an unspecificable relationship (and which at least some Lutherans are likely to regard as the positive Lutheran formulation of the mystery), is explicitly described as a polemical formula in FC SD VII 35: "We at times ... use the formulas '*under* the bread, *with* the bread, *in* the bread' ... to reject ... transubstantiation and to indicate the sacramental union between the untransformed substance of the bread and the Body of

Christ." Thus the formula "in, with and under" has meaning only in terms of its antithesis.

We have observed that the Symbols do not criticize the verb "change" in Eastern theology. In his *Confession concerning Christ's Supper* Luther had used the verb "become" without inhibition (WA, 26, 445, 462; American ed., 37, 303, 317), and the Formula quotes both St. John Chrysostom and Luther as saying that the words of institution "make" the bread Christ's Body and the wine His Blood (FC SD VII 76-77). In the next century the arch-theologian of Lutheran orthodoxy, John Gerhard, is ready to accept "sacramental mutation" as a designation for the Lutheran position, which stands midway between the symbolist position of Reformed and Enthusiastic theology and Roman Catholic transubstantiation. We may say then that classic Lutheran thought objects to the idea of a substantial "exchange" rather than to an accidental "change." Similarly, the Lutheran resistance to having our position described either as "impanation" or "consubstantiation" is a rejection of connotations that these terms have historically acquired and not a rejection of the idea that in the Sacrament of the Altar the bread and wine are the Body and the Blood of Christ.

3. The third area under this head is the cult of the reserved Sacrament. The Lutheran sense of the dynamic character of the Holy Eucharist and the conviction that Our Lord instituted the Sacrament of the Altar for us Christians to eat and to drink combined to militate against the cult of the reserved Sacrament. The external visible elements of bread and wine are not to be adored in the Holy Sacrament, the Lutherans say, although they make the point that only "an Arian heretic can and will deny that Christ Himself, true God and man, who is truly and essentially present in the Supper, should be adored in spirit and in truth in the valid celebration of the [Sacrament of the Altar]" (FC SD VII 126). For this reason the Lutheran rite retains the *Benedictus qui venit* after the *Sanctus* and the *Agnus Dei* after the *Pax Domini*. For this reason too John Gerhard can conclude his commonplace on the Holy Communion with St. Thomas Aquinas' *Adoro te devote* and the anonymous twelfth- (?) century sequence *O panis dulcissime*. Although the Lutherans discountenanced reservation even for the sick as inconsistent with the divine institution and the corporate nature of the Holy Communion, it was not wholly rejected. The church order of Joachim II of Brandenburg (1540), which Luther himself reviewed and approved, provides for taking the Sacrament to the sick after it had been consecrated at the altar. In his *Weighing of the Canons and Decrees of the Council of Trent* Martin Chemnitz disavows for his own time such early church practices as the Communion of the sick at home and of the prisoners in prison by deacons, the sending of the *fermentum* from the altar of the bishop of Rome to the Eucharist celebrated by a visiting celebrant, and the daily communication of the faithful from a portion

of the consecrated elements that they had taken home from the congregational Eucharist in a napkin; but he concedes that the sacramental union did not cease until the consecrated elements had achieved the end for which they were consecrated, that is, reception by the faithful (Pars II, locus V, sectio iii, para. 12; ed. Preuss, 310). It is noteworthy that the *Augsburg Confession* disapproves of the *Corpus Christi* procession on the ground that the division of the Sacrament does not agree with the divine institution (XXII 12).

4. A fourth area is the matter of private and solitary Masses without communicants other than the celebrant. Here two principles combined to determine the Lutheran position. The first is the essentially corporate nature of the Eucharist, which is violated when there are no communicants other than the celebrant. The second is the reaction against the "traffic in Masses," born of the medieval conviction that the Mass is in itself a meritorious and expiatory sacrifice which avails before God on behalf of the living and particularly of the dead *ex opere operato sine bono motu utentis*. Here the Lutheran position was that a Mass celebrated not for the people but only to obtain a favor from God is at least invalid and at worst a sacrilegious and blasphemous perversion of our Lord's intention. Around this point some of the most vehement polemics of the Reformation era were waged. Of the Lutheran view of the sacrificial character of the celebration of the Sacrament of the Altar I shall speak presently.

A FEW PROBLEMS IN LUTHERAN EUCHARISTIC THEOLOGY WITH ECUMENICAL IMPLICATIONS

The first is the question of the omnipresence of the human nature of Christ, which historians of dogma and of Christian thought, following the lead of the Reformed opponents of the Lutheran position, call the question of ubiquity. The issue is of significance before this assembly because sixteenth- and seventeenth-century Roman Catholic (and particularly Jesuit) polemics charged the Lutherans with heresy on this point.

First, the Lutherans never intended to say anything more than that in the Incarnation there is an exchange of properties (*communicatio idiomatum*) between the divine and human natures personally united in Our Lord. As a result of this exchange of properties the human nature in Christ participates mysteriously in the majesty, glory, and might of the divine nature. But this participation does not make these qualities of the divine nature essential properties of the human nature.

Second, the Lutherans never intended to go beyond the teaching of the Fathers that whatever the Scriptures testify that Christ received in time He did not receive according to His divine nature but that the person of Christ received this according to the human nature that He had assumed. They produce a long catena of patristic witnesses to illustrate their point. (*Catalogues Testimoniorum, Bekenntnisschriften,* pp. 1101-1135.)

Third, the Lutherans never taught a local extension of the body of Christ or of His human nature throughout the universe, as they were charged with doing.

Fourth, the idea of the communicated omnipresence of Christ's human nature within the personal union was never the basis for the Lutheran doctrine of the Holy Communion. The basis was the words of institution.

Fifth, the idea of the omnipresence of Christ's human nature played a minor role even as a subsidiary theological support designed to establish the rational credibility of the sacramental union. We do not find it in Luther's writings before 1526 and he does not appeal to it after 1529. Later polemicists revived the issue, but the theologians who wrote the *Formula of Concord* did not regard this position as inconsistent with the alternative formulation that our Lord is able to be present in any manner that He chooses anywhere that He wishes.

Sixth, the debate was as much metaphysical as theological. The Lutherans took the position that in the Holy Scriptures "God's right hand" at which Our Lord had sat down is a verbal symbol of the might and majesty of God. For that reason, they concluded, "God's right hand" is everywhere (FC SD VII 95). Obviously this was not acceptable philosophical doctrine in a century in which the conventional view of the universe was still that of a three-storied structure, with Christ enthroned above the empyrean. In a sense, the Lutheran formula was about four centuries ahead of its time.

In essence, the Lutherans held: Christ as God is present everywhere. Because of the hypostatic union of the two natures His human nature, to which in the view of the Fathers all power in heaven and earth has been given, participates in the presence that He promises when He says, "Lo, I am with you always, even to the close of the age." Accordingly, they say, we must not imagine that it is difficult for Him to give us His Body and His Blood when the Holy Eucharist is celebrated.

The second problem is the role of the celebrant. From the sixteenth century and especially from the seventeenth century on, part of the traditional Roman Catholic polemics has been a denial of the validity of Lutheran Eucharists on the ground that Lutheran clergymen do not have valid orders and thus are unable to confect a valid sacrament.

First, the celebrant at Lutheran Eucharists is a clergyman. If violations of this principle have occurred, they must be put into the same class of abuses that have attended the history of the Eucharist at various times in the past, as when, for instance, in the primitive church ordained confessors who had not met martyrdom were allowed in some places to celebrate on the basis of their confessorhood.

Second, the Lutheran clergyman-celebrant functions before the altar by virtue of his authority of order (*potestas ordinis*; Ap XXVII 13); which he received when he was ordained by another ordained clergyman (*Treatise on the Authority and Primacy of the Pope 72; adhibitis suis pastoribus*). (The role of the total Church in the selection and "calling" of the candidate is of course taken for granted.)

Third, the Lutheran clergyman-celebrant acts both as Christ's agent (Ap VII 47) and as the president of the celebrating congregation, to use St. Justin the Martyr's designation. In line with the Western theological position, a valid sacrament requires in addition to valid matter the recitation of the words of institution as a consecration of the elements to be the Body and Blood of Christ (FC Ep VII 9; SD VII 79-82, 121). (The other requirements for validity, such as the presence of intending communicants, are taken for granted.) "Christ Himself is still active through the spoken words by virtue of the first institution, which He wants repeated. St. John of the Golden Mouth says: 'No human being, but only Christ who was crucified for us, can make of the bread and wine set before us the Body and Blood of Christ. The words are spoken by the mouth of the priest, but by God's power and grace through the words that he speaks, 'This is My Body,' the elements set before us in the Supper are blessed.' ... It is the command and ordinance of Christ that ... make the bread the Body and the wine the Blood that are daily distributed through our ministry and office ... He has bound His own command and deed to our speaking" (FC SD VII 32).

Fifth, the existence of eucharistic devotion in the Lutheran Communion must, it would seem to me, be accounted for by Roman Catholics in one of four ways:

1. It is a blasphemous, idolatrous sham and a diabolic deception.

2. Or, it is a response to an exceptional and uncovenanted grace which a superabundantly compassionate God gives to people who would like to have a valid Eucharist but cannot because their clergymen are not able to confect valid Eucharists. (One might think of St. Augustine's *Crede et manducasti*.)

3. Or, it is the result of valid Eucharists which a superabundantly compassionate God validates in an exceptional and uncovenanted manner in spite of the intrinsic incompetence of the celebrants to confect valid Eucharists.

4. Or, Lutheran Eucharists are valid because Lutheran clergymen possess the authority of order through presumptively valid orders. That Lutherans choose the fourth option is obvious. There may even be a basis in Roman Catholic theology for this explanation. It ill becomes me to speak on this point, I know, but it seems to me that if I were a Roman Catholic I might be moved to ask if, on the basis (a) of I Timothy 4:14, (b) of St. Jerome's *Commentary on the Letter to Titus*, I, v, 9-13, (c) of the bulls *Sacrae religionis* (Feb. 1, 1400) and *Apostolicae Sedis providentia* (Feb. 6, 1403) of Boniface IX, (d) of the bull *Gerentes ad vos* (Nov. 16, 1427) of Martin V, (e) of the bull *Exposit* (April 9, 1489) of Innocent VIII, (f) of the stipulations of Canon 951 of the 1917 Code of Canon Law, and (g) of the analogy with confirmation, it may not be true that at his ordination a priest receives the power to confer holy orders, and if it may not be remotely conceivable that Lutherans possess through an irregular presbyteral succession the power to confer orders and to confect valid sacraments. I am not, however, a Roman Catholic and I know of no Roman Catholic who has seriously pursued this line of argument.

Our final problem area has to do with the sacrifice of the Mass. The Lutheran Symbols, as we have seen, reject the idea that the Mass is a meritorious and in itself expiatory sacrifice which can be applied on behalf of the living and the dead in such a way that by the mere performance of the rite it confers grace and merits for them the remission of venial and mortal sins, of guilt and punishment (Ap XXIV 11:89-93; SA Two II 12-15).

But they do affirm that sacrifice is one of the ends and purposes of eucharistic worship (Ap XXIV 74).

They do not object to the designation "unbloody sacrifice" as applied to the total eucharistic worship of the Church in the canon of Eastern Orthodoxy (Ap XXIV 88-93), where "unbloody" is correlated with "reasonable" or "intellectual" (*logike*; Romans 12:1; cf. also I Peter 2:5).

They are prepared to concede that the Mass, that is the ceremony, with the preaching of the Gospel, the worshipers' response of faith, invocation, thanksgiving, and the reception of the Body and Blood of the Lord is a sacrifice of praise and thanksgiving, a Eucharist in the etymological sense of the word, and the antitype of which the daily sacrifice of the Old Testament (Exodus 29:38f.; Numbers 28:4f; Daniel 8:11f.; 12:11; Malachi 1:11; 3:3) was the type (Ap XXIV 27-40).

The fact that Christ is acting as the eternal Priest through the members of His body the Church in their offering of praise and subsequently in their living out of the Mass in their vocations — in the spirit, say of St. Augustine's *De civitate Dei*, X, 6 — is not brought out in connection with a discussion of the Mass as such, but the Symbols identify Christ as the chief actor in the offerings made by the Christian community in Corinth for the relief of the poor, in the confession of the Christian teaching, in deeds of charity, and in the individual good works that Christians perform even in the most unpublicized occupations, just as it calls these activities sacrifices on the part of those who engage in them (Ap IV 189-193).

I should finally like to adduce three pieces of non-symbolical theological evidence, all the more significant because they occur in frankly polemical contexts.

In his *Weighing of the Canons and Decrees of the Council of Trent*, Chemnitz lists seven senses in which the Mass can be called a sacrifice. The last four are of special interest.

(1) In the Mass the death of Christ is proclaimed in the reading and explication of the prophetic and apostolic Scriptures and a consideration of the causes and benefits of the Passion of Christ is set forth out of the Word of God (Romans 15:16; Phillipians 2:17; I Peter 2:5);

(2) In the celebration of the Holy Eucharist the praises of God are spoken and sung (Hebrews 13:15; Psalm 50:14);

(3) The liturgical action includes public prayers and common acts of thanksgiving;

(4) The celebration is the occasion of offering alms for the relief of the poor and hence the whole action can be called a sacrifice;

(5) In the Mass we consecrate our whole selves to God so that we may cleave to God in a holy association; we engage in exercises of repentance and faith; and our love for God and the neighbor is kindled;

(6) The consecration or blessing of the elements, as part of the sacred ministry of the Gospel, can be called a sacrifice (Romans 15:16);

(7) The distribution and reception of the Holy Communion can be called a sacrifice because it takes place as a memorial of the unique sacrifice of Christ and because the same Victim who was once offered for our sins on the cross is there distributed and received (Part Two, *locus VI, sectio i, articulus ii;* ed. Preuss, 383-384).

In the next century, Gerhard's *Confessio catholica* sees the Mass as a re-representation (*repraesentatio*) in the sense of a making the sacrifice of God's Son present again before God through our prayers, so that we come before the Father not as the *aestimator meriti* but as the *veniae largitor per Christum Dominum nostrum.* In the New Testament sense of the term "to offer sacrifice" (Romans 12:1; Philippians 2:17; 4:18; 1 Peter 2:5) we can think of the Mass as a sacrifice in two ways:

(1) "In the celebration of the Eucharist 'we proclaim the Lord's death' (I Cor. 11:26) and pray that God would be merciful to us on account of that holy and immaculate sacrifice completed on the cross and on account of that holy Victim which is certainly present in the Eucharist;" and

(2) "That he would in kindness receive and grant a place to the rational and spiritual oblation of our prayer."[5]

Gerhard sees the sacrifice of the Mass as "a memorial and a re-presentation of the sacrifice already completed on the cross," in the spirit of the canon prayer *Supplices*: "Command that these things may by the hands of Your holy angel be borne aloft to Your altar on high in the sight of Your divine majesty." He goes on:

> It is clear that the sacrifice takes place in heaven, not on earth, inasmuch as the death and passion of God's beloved Son is offered to God the Father by way of commemoration.... In the Christian sacrifice there is no victim except the real and sub-stantial body of Christ, and in the same way there is no true priest except Christ Himself. Hence this sacrifice once offered on the cross takes place continually in an unseen fashion in heaven by way of commemoration, when Christ offers to His Father on our behalf His sufferings of the past, *especially when we are applying ourselves to the sacred mysteries*, and this is the "unbloody sacrifice" which is carried out in heaven (*ibid.*, p. 1204; emphasis added).

At the end of the era of classic Lutheran orthodoxy stands the last of the great Lutheran systematicians, David Hollatius (Hollaz) (1648-1713). In his *Examen theologicum acroamaticum* he denies of course that the Mass is a sacrifice in the sense that Christ is literally slain and destroyed by death. He declares, however, that:

> If we view the matter from the material standpoint, the sacrifice in the Eucharist is numerically the same as the sacrifice that took place on the cross; put otherwise, one can say that the thing itself and the substance is the same in each case, the victim or oblation is the same. If we view the matter formally, from the standpoint of the act of sacrifice, then even though the victim is numerically the same, the action is not; that is, the immolation in the Eucharist is different from the immolation carried out on the cross. For on the cross an offering was made by means of the passion and death of an immolated living thing, without which there can be no sacrifice in the narrow sense, but in the Eucharist the oblation takes place through the prayers and through the commemoration of the death or sacrifice offered on the cross.[6]

In what I have said, I have tried to be only reportorial, neither contentious or censorious, neither dissuasive or persuasive. At the same time, wherever I have adduced the Lutheran Symbolical Books on behalf of a doctrinal tenet, I have been saying what I myself believe.

I would close by saying for all of us and for all of Christ's one holy catholic and apostolic Church from end to end of the earth two prayers.

One is the Collect for Maundy Thursday from the Lutheran rite, a Collect that emphasized our common debt to the Angelic Doctor:

> O God, who hast left unto us in a wonderful sacrament a memorial of Thy passion, grant, we beseech Thee, that we may so use this sacrament of Thy Body and Blood, that the fruits of our redemption may continually be manifest in us, Thou who livest and reignest with the Father and the Holy Ghost, ever one God world without end. Amen.

The other is the theologian's *suspirium* with which Hollatius ends his chapter on the Eucharist:

> Almighty Lord Jesus Christ, source of life and immortality, I pray and implore You as devoutly as I can to enlighten my mind, full of native shadows as it is, with Your most holy Spirit, so that I shall not think, believe, say or write anything about the sublime mystery of Your holy communion which would be our of harmony with Your majesty or which is contrary to the truth or which veers away from the words of Your convenant. And as often as I shall come to Your holy table to refresh my spirit, I pray You to make me, unworthy as I am, worthy through Your grace; impure as I am to make me clean; naked as I am to clothe me, so that Your Body, so full of divine power, and Your most precious Blood may not become for me, Your servant, the occasion for judgment or punishment, but a memorial of the death which You underwent for me, a strengthening of my faith, a proof of the taking away of my sins, a bond of closer union with You, an increase of holiness, the basis of a glad resurrection, and a pledge of everlasting life. Amen (*ibid.*, 622).

ENDNOTES

1. Clark Davis, *Sacraments of Initiation: Baptism and Confirmation* (New York: Sheed and Ward, 1964) 82.
2. Two recent analyses that concentrate on Luther's eucharistic doctrine in English are (a) an article by the distinguished Danish Lutheran systematician, Regin Prenter of the University of Aarhus, "Eucharistic Sacrifice according to the Lutheran Tradition," in the British monthly *Theology*, Vol. 67, No. 529 [July, 1964], 286-295, and a book by the eminent Norwegian Lutheran church historian, Carl F. Wisløf, of the Menighetsfakultet in Oslo. The Norwegian original came out under the title *Nattverd og Messe: En Studie i Luthers Theologi* (Oslo: Lutherstiftelsen, 1957); in May of this year it was published in a translation by Joseph P. Shaw as *The Gift of Commu-*

nion: *Luther's Controversy with Rome on Eucharistic Sacrifice* (Minneapolis: Augsburg Publishing House, 1964).

3. The significant parallelism of expression with the first constitution of the Fourth Lateran Council, "[*Jesu Christi*] *corpus et sanguis in sacramento altaris sub speciebus panis et vini veraciter continentur*" [*Conciliorum oecumenicorum decreta*], ed., Josephus Alberigus et al. (Basel: Herder, 1962) 206, 35-36 will not go unnoticed.

4. "What the Lutheran Symbols Have to Say about the Sacraments," in Richard Sommerfeld, ed., *Second Annual Institute on Church and Society* (Fort Wayne, IN: Concordia Senior College, 1964) 93.

4a. Paul C. Empie and James I. McCord, eds., *A Re-examination of Lutheran and Reformed Traditions*, Part II: *Christology, the Lord's Supper and Its Observance in the Church* (New York: National Lutheran Council, 1964).

5. Vol. II, pars II, *articulus* xiv, *cap.* I, *ekthesis* 6 [Frankfurt-am-Main: Christianus Genschius (Johannes Andreae), 1679] 1200-1201.

6. 4th ed. by John Henry Hollaz (Stockholm: Johannes Henricus Russwormius, 1725), II, 620.

CHRIST TODAY: HIS PRESENCE
IN THE SACRAMENTS

Three considerations complicate the discussion of our subject. The first is the lack in the sacred Scriptures of a simple concept corresponding to our philosophical abstraction "presence." The second is the lack in the sacred Scriptures of a category corresponding to the theological term "sacrament." The third is the perennial problem of the relation of the Godhead and the humanity in the single person of Jesus Christ.

I

The sacred Scriptures of both the Old and the New Testament have a considerable number of terms which imply presence and absence, going and coming, drawing near and withdrawing. As long as the record refers to human beings who are within or beyond sight or earshot of one another, no problem is presented. As soon as God is spoken of, the matter becomes more complex. Without attempting to describe the unfolding of the concepts involved or to determine the concrete frame of historical reference that underlies each symbolic description, we can distinguish a number of patterns of thinking about the "presence" of God.

The words most commonly used to denote God's "presence" are the very concrete Hebrew and Greek words for "face," *panim* and *prosopon.* God is thought of as present in the sense that he sees and that he — or at least his work — is seen.

Before Yahweh's face is fulness of joy, at his right hand are pleasures for ever more (Ps. 16:11). He hides those who take refuge with him in the covert of his face (Ps. 31:20). The upright shall dwell before his face (Ps. 140:13).

Cain counts it as part of his punishment that he shall be hidden from Yahweh's face (Gen. 4:14); he receives the "mark of Cain" as a kind of substitute and goes away from Yahweh's face to dwell in the land of Nod east of Eden (Gen. 4:16). In the book of Job Satan stands before God's face (Job. 1:12; 2:7).

Liturgical offences, such as a priest's approach to the holy things while he has an uncleanness, cut him off from Yahweh's face (Lev. 22:3). The worshipping congregation is to come before his face with thanksgiving (Ps. 95:2). Of considerable theological interest is Jeremiah 52:3: "Because of the anger of Yahweh things came to such a pass in Jerusalem and Judah that he cast them out from before his face."

God's face can be terrible as well as benign. While the righteous exult joyfully before God, the wicked perish before his face (Ps. 68:2,3). Isaiah prays that God would rend the heavens and come down that the mountains and the nations might tremble at his face (Is. 64:1-3). The earth trembles at Yahweh's face (Ps. 68:8; 114:7). Adam and Eve hide themselves from God's face (Gen. 3:8). Job is terrified at his face (Job 23:15). Israel's enemies are to perish at the rebuke of his face (Ps. 80:16). The fruitful land was a desert, and all its cities were laid in ruins before Yahweh's face (Jer. 4:26; see Nah. 1:5). The idols of Egypt tremble at Yahweh's face and the hearts of the Egyptians melt within them (Is. 19:1). Jacob regards it as a marvel that at Peniel he has seen God face to face and yet his life has been preserved (Gen. 32:30). Yahweh speaks to Moses face to face (Exodus 33:11), yet Moses cannot see God's face and live (vv. 20,23).

Prosopon has a similar force in the New Testament. Those who do not know God and who do not obey the gospel of our Lord Jesus will suffer the punishment of eternal destruction and exclusion from the face of God and the glory of his might (II Thess. 1:9). Christ has entered into heaven itself, now to appear before the face of God on our behalf (Heb. 9:24). (In both passages the Revised Standard Version renders *prosopon* with "presence.")

Whether God shows his "face" in grace or in judgment, his "face" or his "presence" is spoken of as something active, rather than as merely statically "present."

There are other ways of putting it. The heavens are glad, the earth rejoices, the sea roars, the floods clap their hands, the fields exult, the hills and the trees of the wood sing for joy before God as he comes to judge the earth (Ps. 96:11-13; 98:7-9; I Chron. 16:32-33). Israel is to call upon Yahweh while he is near (Is. 55:6). The psalmist looks forward to going to God, his exceeding joy (Ps. 43:4). Yahweh is with Joseph in the house of Potiphar (Gen. 39:2) and in the royal prison (vv. 21, 23). By dwelling in the midst of his people, Yahweh dwells in the land where his people dwell (Num. 35:34; see I Kings 6:13, Ezek. 37:27). He dwells on Mount Zion and Jerusalem (Ps. 74:2; 135:21; Is. 8:18; Joel 3:17, 21). Yahweh's enthronement on the cherubim must be thought of as locating his effective presence in the ark of the covenant (I Sam.4:4; II Sam. 6:2; 7:5,6; Ps. 80:1). Saul laments that God has turned away from him and answers him no more (I Samuel 28:15). The Psalmist's adversaries taunt him: "Where is your God?" (Ps. 42:10).

God is thought of as present when he intervenes and conversely his absence is synonymous with a refusal to intervene. The psalmist asks: "Why dost thou stand afar off, O Lord? Why dost thou hide thyself in time of trouble?" (Ps. 10:1). This insight may help toward a better understand of Psalm 22 and of the implications of our Lord's quotation of the first verse of this psalm on the cross. "Why has thou forsaken me?" says the same thing as "Why art thou so far from helping me?" (Ps. 22:1; see also vv. 11,19; Ps. 38:21; 71:12). Conversely, the wicked do not desire God's presence and say to him: "Depart from us!" (Job 22:17).

Yahweh moves with Israel in its wanderings; this fact distinguishes Israel from all other nations (Ex. 33:14-16; Lev. 26:12; Deut. 4:7; see II Sam. 7:7; I Chron. 17:5,6; Ps. 68:7,8,17,18).

But Yahweh's presence can be perilous. If Yahweh were to go with his rebellious people for even a single moment, he would consume them (Ex. 33:3,5). He goes out before the armies of Israel to smite their enemies (I Chron. 14:15). On the day of Yahweh's wrath safety lies in being hidden from him (Zeph. 2:3; see Luke 23:30).

There is a tendency to locate God's presence in the skies — Yahweh "dwells on high" (Is. 33:5) — although (as in Ps. 121) the mountains may also be thought of as God's dwelling place. Yahweh looks down from the seat above the heavens where his glory dwells upon the heavens and the earth beneath (Ps. 113:4-6; 123:1; see 14:2). Yahweh is represented as going down to inspect the tower of Babel (Gen. 11:5) and to secure first-hand information about the sins of Sodom and Gomorrha (Gen. 18:21); yet in both cases he knows what has happened. He is depicted as resenting identification with the hills. In the war of Ahab with Benhadad the Syrians attribute their defeat to the fact that Yahweh is a hill diety; in an oracle this blasphemous limitation is made precisely the reason why the Israelite army, comparable to nothing more than two little flocks of goats, could defeat a Syrian host that filled the country in the battle at Aphek (I Kings 20:23-28).

God cannot be circumscribed. Special interest attaches to passages which within the frame of a few verses or even of a single verse imply both a specific presence and omnipresence.

Thus the Jerusalemites boast that the exiles have gone far from Yahweh and that the city is now theirs; Yahweh counters with the declaration that while he removed the exiles far off and scattered them he has been a sanctuary to them in the countries where they have gone (Ezek. 11:15-16). The watchpost at Galeed is a witness that Yahweh watches the behavior of both Laban and Jacob while they are absent from each other (Gen. 31:49). "Am I a God at hand," Yahweh asks rhetorically, "and not a God afar off? Can a man hide himself in a secret place so that I cannot see him? Do I not fill heaven and earth?" (Jer. 23:23; see Is. 66:1 and Acts 7:49-50). This theme recurs in the prayer at the dedication of the first temple (I Kings 8: 12, 27, 29, 30) and in the prayer of Hezekiah (II Kings 19:15; Is. 37:16). It is expanded in Psalm 139 to put Yahweh even in She'ol, at the limits of the world girdling sea, and in the darkness of night (vv. 1-12). A theme of the book of Jonah is the impossibility of fleeing from Yahweh (Jonah 1:3, 10); he hears the prayers of the sailors on the Tarshish-bound ship (1:14), answers the cry of Jonah "from the belly of She'ol" (2:2-6), speaks to the great fish in the sea (2:10), observes the repentance of the Ninevites (3:10), and speaks to Jonah in his retreat east of the metropolis (4:5,6). The difficult 68th psalm has God dwelling in Zion for ever and riding in the heavens, the ancient heavens (vv. 16,33). The difference between God's absence and his presence is a matter of morality not of geography in Proverbs 15:29: "Yahweh is far from the wicked, but he hears the prayers of the righteous" (see Ps. 34:18; 85:9; 145:18). In Isaiah 57:15 the high and lofty one who inhabits eternity says: "I dwell in the high and holy place, and also with him who is of a contrite and humble spirit."

In place of the face of God, we may have 1) his glory (Ex. 24:15); 2) his spirit (Ezek. 36:27; note the parallelism in Psalm 51:11 and see I Sam. 16:14, where the Spirit of Yahweh is replaced by an evil spirit from Yahweh); 3) the angel of his face (Is. 63:9; compare the "man" who vanishes before sun-up in Genesis 32:24-30, the very ancient Peniel account); 4) the name of God acting both benignly (Ps. 75:1 Hebrew) and destructively (Is. 30:27).

The New Testament on this point reflects the Old Testament. We have already referred to the use of *prosopon* as a word for "presence."

In a passage of considerable importance for the theology of both holy baptism and the sacrament of the altar, I Cor. 10:1-5, Christ by a kind of appropriation is defined as the spiritual rock that accompanied the Israelites on their wilderness wanderings.

As members of the body of Christ we are in Christ, the New Testament reminds us again and again. By the same token, he is in us (John 17:23; Rom. 8:10), as the hope of glory (Col. 1:27). He dwells in our hearts by faith (Eph. 3:17). He lives in us (Gal. 2:20). Where two or three are gathered together in his name, he is in the midst of them (Matt. 18:20). He will come in to eat with the man that opens the door to his knocking (Rev. 3:20). He will be with his disciples until the close of the age (Matt. 28:20). Where he is, we shall be (John 12:26; 14:3; 17:24). He and the Father will come to us and make their home with us (John 14:23).

God abides in us and we in him (I John 3:24; 4:13-15). We are the temples of the living God; God lives in us and moves among us (II Cor. 6:16; see Lev. 26:11,12; Ezek. 37:27; I Cor. 3:16). The Spirit dwells in us (John 14:17; Rom. 8:9,11; II Tim. 1:14). Yet God also dwells in the unapproachable light, which no man has ever seen or can see (I Tim. 6:16). The creator and Lord of heaven and earth does not dwell in shrines made by man (Acts 17:24).

Our Lord abides in the Father[1] and the Father in him, yet he comes from the Father and goes to the Father. His disciples cannot follow him now, but they will follow him hereafter. They will see him no more, but he will not leave his disciples orphaned; he will come to them. They will know that he is in the Father and they in him and he in them. (John 8:14; 13:3, 33, 36; 14:4, 10-12, 18-20; 15:5-7; 16:5,10, 16). It is to their advantage that he goes away, because otherwise the Paraclete will not come (John 16:7); thus the Spirit becomes the surrogate of Christ.

Our Lord is taken up from his disciples into heaven (Acts 1:11) where he was before (John 6:62; see 20:17; Eph. 4:8-9), and will come again the same way (II Thess. 4:16); he is at God's right hand (Luke 22:69; Eph. 1:20; I Peter 3:22) and pleads for us there as our high priest (Heb. 4:14). Yet St. Paul hears and sees him on earth (Acts 9:4; I Cor. 15:8).

While we are at home in the body we are away from the Lord (II Cor. 5:6,8,9). Our Lord promises the dying thief that they will be together in paradise (Luke 23:42). For St. Paul to live is Christ, yet he has a desire to depart and be with Christ (Phil. 1:21,23).

Parousia, with its eschatological thrust toward both the present and the future, preserves the idea of Christ's advent in messianic glory. Noteworthy in this connection is the fact that *apokalypsis* (I Peter 1:7, 13 see also vs. 5) and *epiphaneia* (in the Pastorals: I Timothy 6:14; II Timothy 4:1,8; Titus 2:13; but not II Timothy 1:10; see Titus 2:11; 3:4) are synonyms for *parousia* and that II Thessalonians 2:8 speaks of the *epiphaneia* of Christ's *parousia*.

Late scholastic theology, followed by Luther (WA 26, 326-336), can speak of circumscriptive, diffinitive and repletive modes of presence. The technical designations can be dropped and Luther and the Symbols can speak of a bodily, a spiritual, and a heavenly mode of presence (FC SD VII 93-103), not, however, without some confusion of terms (para. 105). Classic Lutheran orthodoxy can furnish even more elaborate analyses.[2] However congenial this vocabulary may appear to some, we are here far from the concreteness of the biblical language.

In summary we must say: simply because God is God, in his working in his world he is always mysteriously both present to and absent from us. Put differently, the divine presence is always something that is opaque to the eye of the wayfaring Christian. We must account for his presence analogously. It is always for us a presence *secundum quid*.

II

A s theology uses the word, "sacrament" does not occur in the sacred Scriptures. The ancient fathers differed among themselves on the definition and scope of the term. In the sixteenth century, the fixing of the number of sacraments in the West at seven was still relatively recent, and the scholastic debates about the matter and the form of some of the sacraments and about their direct institution by our Lord had not been wholly resolved. Under the circumstances, the differences of definition and enumeration even within the Lutheran Symbols — with those from Luther's pen inclining formally toward two and those from Melanchthon's pen counting three, four and even five — are not astonishing. The differences at least with reference to holy absolution are not as grave as they are sometimes made out to be. Luther uses the term "third sacrament" for holy absolution but prefers to consider it implied in holy baptism (LC Baptism 74). Melanchthon prefers to consider the "sacrament of repentance" separately from holy baptism and the holy communion (Ap XIII 4). The subsequent rigid Lutheran restriction of the number of sacraments to two is determined as much by anti-Roman-Catholic polemics as by any systematic reflection.

It is significant that Lutheran Symbols proceed inductively from the separate consideration of baptism, the holy communion and holy absolution to the synthetic concept of sacrament, rather than deductively from an *a priori* definition of "sacrament" to an identification of the signs or rites that properly belong as particulars to the species. The numbering and definition of the sacraments is regarded as ultimately unimportant. The important thing is that "the matters and ceremonies instituted in the Scriptures, whatever the number, be not neglected ... We do not believe it to be of any consequence if in teaching different persons count [the number of sacraments] differently ... No prudent man will strive greatly about the number or the term if only those things be retained which have God's command and promise" (Ap XIII 2 and 17).

III

When we come to speak about the presence not merely of God but also of the incarnate word, we have an added complication. We are speaking not only of a divine essence, but also of a humanity that has been inseparably united with the Godhead. The problem of maintaining the difficult and precarious balance which the creed of Chalcedon prescribes is perennial. As a result of sixteenth and seventeenth century polemics we tend to think of the theological problem as centering chiefly around the "real presence" of our Lord in the sacrament of the altar, but we need to remind ourselves that it goes far beyond this.

Various ages and various traditions have translated the biblical descriptions of the ascension and session of our Lord in different ways theologically. Whenever Lutheran theology was most true to its most characteristic insights, however, it rejected the idea that the exaltation of our Lord had resulted in his imprisonment in a 68-by-18-by-9-inch hole in space above the empyrean. On the contrary, it insisted that the exaltation was precisely the decisive self-liberation of our Lord from the circumscribing confines of a state in which his body normally occupied and vacated space as he moved about. As God's right hand is everywhere, Christ's exaltation enabled him to be in a very real sense with his disciples (and they in him) among all nations and until the close of the age, individually and wherever two or three or more gather in his name. This presence includes all space but it transcends all spatial limitations. This presence is that of his true humanity, but it depends upon the omnipresence that is his in the personal union as the second hypostasis of the holy and undivided Trinity (FC Ep VIII 17).

Of his Godhead we can say with Luther: "Nothing is so small, but that God is still smaller; nothing is so big, but that God is still bigger; nothing is so short, but that God is still shorter; nothing is so long, but that God is still longer; nothing is so broad, but that God is still broader; nothing is so narrow, but that God is still narrower; and so on" (*Vom Abendmahl Christi Bekenntnis*, 1528, WA 26, 339, 39 to 340, 1). But because God became man in Christ Jesus, this series of statements has implications for christology and the sacraments as well.

This presence of the Godhead and of the exalted Christ is not something that we can manipulate. "There is a difference between his presence and your taking," Luther observes in *Dass diese Worte Christi, "Das ist mein Leib," noch fest stehen* (1527). "[God] is free and unbound wherever he is and does not have to stand there like a scoundrel locked in the stocks or wearing an iron collar ... The same thing is true of Christ. Even though he is present everywhere, he does not let you take hold of him or catch him. He can divest himself of his shell, so that you get the shell and do not take hold of the kernel. Why? Because it is one thing when God is there and another when he is there for you. But he is there for you when he adds his word, binds himself with it, and says: 'Here you shall find me.' Now when you have the word, you can with assurance take hold of him and have him and say: 'here I have you, just as you say'" (WA 23, 151, 3-17).

We are thus brought back to the biblical insight that an omnipresent God can be absent as far as the apprehension of his activity is concerned. Luther makes this point with specific reference to the sacrament of the altar, but the insight can be generalized: "Both can be true, that Christ is at the same time present and not present, according to different forms ... God can very easily keep Christ's body in heaven in one particular way, and in another way in the bread. If there are two different modes of presence in the two instances, no contradiction is involved, just as it is no contradiction that Christ sat with his disciples after his resurrection, Luke 24[44], and yet at the same time was not with them, as he himself says, 'These things I spoke to you, while I was still with you.' Here we find 'with you' and 'not with you,' and yet there is no contradiction, for dialectics teaches children that contradictories must refer to the same thing, in the same terms, in the same context" (*Vom Abendmahl Christi Bekenntnis*, WA 26, 413, 20-21 and 414, 22-30).

In this connection James Andreae (1528-1590), coauthor of the *Formula of Concord*, can assert: "Here you have only one Christ and not two Christs, in such a way that the one is the son of God the other the son of man, one born of God the other of Mary, the one having suffered, the other not having suffered, the one in majesty, the other not, but there is a single Christ, the son of God and the son of Mary."[3]

We cannot of course describe our creaturely experience in the terms in which God sees it. But it is also obvious that we must not attempt to impose our creaturely category of space upon God, or even upon the humanity of the incarnate word. This carries with it the corollary that we cannot impose upon God or upon the humanity of the incarnate word our creaturely category of time. If his presence measured on one coordinate of creaturely existence, space, both includes and transcends space, his presence measured on the other coordinate of creaturely existence, time, includes time, so that it is completely historical, but nevertheless transcends time. This is true with reference both to the time of our Lord's life upon earth in the days of his flesh and our present time and all time in between and in the future.

Hermann Sasse's words are apposite: "In the Word of the Gospel, Christ, the Word Incarnate, speaks to us. In the Sacrament He gives us the same as He gave to the Twelve at the Last Supper. He gives us His true Body which was sacrificed on Calvary and raised from the dead on Easter. This makes us not only contemporaneous with Him, but unites us with Him in a way that transcends everything that we otherwise call 'remembrance.' The centuries that separate us from His earthly days and from the time of His death disappear."[4]

IV

On the ancient principle that the works of God that go outside of his being are undivided[5] and can be appropriated to any of the divine hypostases, the Symbols speak generally of *God's* operation in the sacraments (for example, Ap XIII 5), or they may speak of the *Father* using the sacraments to draw men to his Son (for example FC SD XI 76), or they may speak of the *Holy Ghost* working through the sacraments (AC V 1-3; Ap XXIV 70; FC Ep II 1, 18; SD II 48,65; III 16; XI 71). Because of the close link between the incarnation and the body and blood of Christ distributed and received in the sacrament of the altar, the *Formula of Concord* asserts that he imparts his true[6] body and blood in the holy communion as one who is present (Ep VIII 17). Because of the relationship of the incarnate word to the Father and the Holy Ghost, he is thought of as present in his Godhead and in his humanity wherever the Father and the Holy Ghost are present.

The presence of the contemporaneous Christ in the sacraments is intimately bound up with his presence in the church, to which God has entrusted the sacraments, and in the sacred ministry, the incumbents of which normally administer the sacraments. The church as the body of Christ and as the new Israel is a particular vehicle of his presence in the world.

"The church is not a purely mundane institution. Her words and her actions are not purely human words and actions. On the contrary, Jesus Christ is in a real sense in the midst of her through his word and sacrament as the second person of the Godhead. When the church is handing on his word and is administering his sacrament, God is acting through her. In the visible church and through the visible church the invisible God is also at work."[7]

The sacred ministry, instituted by our Lord to proclaim his word and to administer his sacraments, is also significant as a vehicle of the contemporaneous Christ's presence. The called and ordained minister of the word and sacraments functions *vice Christi;* Christ has not merely empowered his ordained representatives to act, but he acts through them. As the head of the church he governs and sanctifies the church through the Holy Spirit (Ap VII 5).[8] This double *potestas,* namely, to sanctify (*potestas ordinis*) through the word and sacraments and to govern (*potestas jurisdictionis*) by excommunicating the scandalous sinners and absolving penitents, is precisely the *potestas* of the sacred ministry (Ap XXVIII 13). In a sacrament God is acting mediately in the present to give us in the moment in which the sacrament is received that which the promise annexed to the ceremony offers (Ap XXIV 18).

V

The real minister of holy baptism at every admnistration of the sacrament is our Lord, even though he makes use of human hands to pour or immerse and of human lips to repeat the sacramental formula. He inserts us as members of his body into the fellowship of his church. He cleanses us through the washing of water-in-the-word that he might make us holy (Eph. 5:26). He clothes us with himself (Gal. 3:27). He buries us with himself in the vault that could not hold him. He raises us with himself in his own bursting from the tomb. He makes us alive to God in himself. We say that the officiant baptizes the candidate, or that the church baptizes (SA Three V 4). By this we mean that those to whom God has given the *potestas ordinis* through the vocation of the church (Ap VII 28) represent not their own persons in administering sacraments but the person of Christ.

The name of the holy Trinity in which holy baptism is imparted is not the label of an absent Diety but the manifestation at the font of a God who is present and who acts in the sacrament. "To be baptized in the name of God is to be baptized not by men, but by God himself" (LC Baptism 10). John Gerhard's gloss on Matthew 28:19 is worth recalling. After stipulating that the name of God is God himself, he concludes that "the whole most holy Trinity is present in baptism with its grace and through the water of Baptism is efficaciously active for the salvation of men." Consequently the sense of the words of institution, 'Baptize in the name of the Father and of the Son and of the Holy Spirit,' is this: 'When in the power of this institution and command you administer baptism according to the prescribed form, this is not some bare external ceremony, some kind of exterior washing, but God the Father is present, God the Son is present, God the Holy Spirit is present at this action with a presence of grace. Nor is this a sterile presence, but God the Father through baptism receives the person baptized into grace on account of me, whom he has appointed the mediator and redeemer of humanity. I the Son myself wash the sins of the person away with my blood and I give him my righteousness, I make him a participant of my benefits and all the rest. The Holy Spirit gives him a new birth and impresses the seal of the promise of his heavenly inheritance on his heart.'"[9]

The word in holy baptism is Christ's word, not only in the sense that he commands baptism, but that in baptism he speaks the word of rebirth and of new life. By virtue of the combination of the plain water with the divine word, that water of baptism, even though it remains a coarse external mask (LC Baptism 19), is a divine water, a heavenly water, a holy water, a blessed water, a fruitful water, a gracious water (LC Baptism 14, 17, 27).

The result of Baptism is that even in this life, simultaneously with the act of baptism we enter into the Kingdom of Christ and begin a life with him that lasts for ever. For this is what it means to be saved — negatively to be freed from sin, death and the devil, and positively to enter into the kingdom of Christ and to live with him for ever (LC Baptism 24-25; see also Ap IX 2; SC Baptism 6).

The association with Christ is not something that occurs only while the heavenly washing is being applied. Every Christian has enough to learn and to carry into practice in connection with baptism to last him a lifetime, for he constantly has need to insure that he believes confidently in everything that baptism promises to convey — conquest of satan and death, forgiveness of sins, the grace of God, the whole Christ, and the Holy Spirit and all his gifts (LC Baptism 41).

Similarly the "new man," the dark old Adam's resplendent adversary, who lives "in the presence of God" (*für Gott, coram Deo*) comes forth and arises daily, that is, uninterruptedly.

The linking of the baptized person with the name of the holy Trinity creates a relationship so intimate and permanent that it survives even the relapse of the Christian into the sin that destroys the life of faith in the heart. For when by God's grace he returns to repentance and to a better mind, he has no need of a new baptism. Indeed, it would be blasphemy and sacrilegious profanation to attempt it (FC SD II 69; LC Baptism 55 and 78). The penitent finds that his Lord has been awaiting his return all along, that indeed he was never far from his erring human brother.

VI

Because holy absolution is an effective means of imparting the grace of God, we must regard it as a vehicle whereby the presence of Christ, working through the Holy Spirit, through the church, and through the church's ministry, is effectively accomplished.

The section of the *Small Catechism* entitled "How the Unlearned Should be Taught to Confess" is instructive for our purpose. The penitent asks the confessor to "declare the forgiveness of sins to [him] for God's sake" (21). He confesses his sins both generally in the presence of God (*für Gott*) and in detail before the confessor (*für Euch*) or, more precisely, "under the eyes of the confessor" (*gegen dem Beichtiger*)

(22,23,25). The confessor elicits from the penitent the confession that the latter believes that the confessor's forgiveness is God's forgiveness (27). The confessor pronounces absolution "at the command of our Lord Jesus Christ" and in the name of the holy Trinity (28).

Whether or not we accord holy absolution the specific title of the sacrament, it is the Lutheran position that holy absolution is not the voice or the word of the human being who is present, but the word of the God who forgives sins. For it is spoken in God's stead and by his command. God truly gives life through the word of absolution; the keys truly forgive sins in God's sight in accordance with the passage: "He that hears you hears me." Hence the voice of the absolving confessor is to be believed in no other way than as a voice sounding from heaven (Ap XII 40; see AC XXV 3-4 German). We are forgiven not on account of our contrition but because of the word of Christ, "Whatever you will bind on earth shall be bound in heaven, and whatever you loose on earth shall be loosed in heaven" (Ap IV 397). Absolution is the word of God which the power of the keys proclaims to individuals by divine authority (XII 99). The significance of the close nexus between this authorization and the logion about Christ's presence in the midst of two or three gathered in his name should not be lost on us.

It was precisely in connection with holy absolution that Luther added to the *Smalcald Articles* between their signing and their publication that devastating attack upon enthusiasm in which he asserts with unqualified intransigence the thesis that "God gives his grace and his Spirit to no one except through or with the preceding external word" (Three VIII 3).

When God forgives, the church cannot refuse to absolve. But "when those who have sinned after baptism come at any time to repentance, they obtain forgiveness of sins, and the church should not withhold absolution from them" (AC XII 1-2). This implies both the necessity of reconciliation with the empirical church for the sake of the spiritual health of the returning penitents, because their faith needs the nourishment that they cannot ordinarily obtain apart from the church's ministry; it also implies a necessary coincidence of the church's action with God's.

The church, Christ's body, administers holy absolution in the name of her head, Christ. Hence, though absolution is ordinarily to be administered by the ordained priests of the church, in a case of imperative life-or-death necessity any baptized member of the church can act for the whole body and for the Christ who is the body's head. To illustrate the principle, the *Tractate on the Authority and Primacy of the Pope* appeals to the alleged letter of St. Augustine to Fortunatus that can be found in no collection of the great church father's correspondence but only in the Decree of Gratian. In this letter the author (whoever he was) tells about the two passengers aboard a ship that seemed certain to be wrecked. One was a Christian under discipline, the other an unbaptized catechumen. The Christian under discipline, as the only baptized representative of the church present, baptized the catechumen, whereupon he, as the only member of the church not under discipline present, absolved the penitent from his sins and censures (67).

VII

The almost exclusive reference of the term "real presence" to the holy communion illustrates that fact that in the case of the sacrament of the altar the link with the everpresent Christ is even more direct and concrete than it is in the case of holy baptism. Together with the Catholic church of every age, Lutherans have always taken literally the words, "This is my body, which is for you," and "This is my blood of the Covenant."

The fact that in the holy eucharist the body and the blood of Christ are truly present and are distributed to all that eat therein is one that Lutheran theology is bound to assert with unrestricted vigor. The mode of the sacramental union it refuses, with equal vigor, to define. It rejects certain explanations that it regards as biblically or metaphysically untenable — transubstantiation in the sense of an exchange of the heavenly and the earthly substances with only the appearances of the earthly substances remaining, consubstantiation, impanation, local inclusion, permixture of natures (*naturalis permixtio*), affixture (*affixio*).[10] It cites the canon of the Divine Liturgy of the Eastern Orthodox communion (Ap X 2) to prove that Lutherans share with the Catholic East no less than with the Catholic West a common conviction about the "what" of the sacrament.[11]

Luther found theological support, as we have pointed out, for his doctrine of the holy communion by positing the omnipresence of the human nature of our Lord; the "second Martin" — Martin Chemnitz — contented himself with affirming that "Christ could be according to his human nature wherever he wanted to be." The authors of the *Formula of Concord* regarded these two views as sufficiently congruent to be able to cite them both less than a page apart.[12]

Lutheran theology denies that the human nature of Christ — or, for that matter, his divine nature — is locally extended to all places in heaven and earth (FC Ep VIII 29), but it affirmed that "it is possible and very easy for Christ to impart as one who is present, his true body and blood in the holy communion, not according to the mode or property of the human nature, but according to the mode and property of God's right hand ... This presence is not earthly or Capernaitic, but it is true and essential nevertheless, as the words of his testament read: 'This is, is, is my body'" (FC Ep VIII 17).

Lutheran theology denies the propriety of adoring the visible forms of bread and wine, but it also affirms that "no one except an Arian heretic can and will deny that Christ himself, true God and man, who is truly and essentially present in the holy communion when it is rightly celebrated, ought to be worshipped in the Spirit and in truth" (FC SD VII 126). With SS. Justin Martyr, Cyprian, Augustine, Leo the Great, Gelasius, John Chrysostom and others, Lutheran theology sees the hypostatic union of the Godhead and the manhood in the incarnation paralleled by the sacramental union of the natural bread and the true natural body of Christ in the appointed administration of the sacrament (FC SD VII 37-38). The "rightly celebrated" and the "appointed administration" are directed against "the papistic expiatory sacrifice of the sacrificial mass," as the marginal comment to the final quotation of the *Catalog of Testimonies* puts it, a passage from St. John Chrysostom's seventeenth *Homily* on the Letter to the Hebrews: "Since then sacrifices are offered in so many places, are there many Christs? By no means. But a single Christ is everywhere, complete here and complete there, a single body. Therefore just as he who is offered everywhere is one body and not many bodies, so also there is one offering. He is our high priest, who offered the sacrifice that cleanses us. We offer that sacrifice now, which was brought then, which is never used up. This [we do] as a memorial of what took place then. 'Do this,' he said, 'as a memorial of me.' We do not bring another sacrifice, like the high priest, but always that one; or rather we make a memorial of [that] sacrifice."[13]

The basic insight upon which the Lutheran church rightly insists is that what Christ has promised to give to the communicants in the sacrament of the altar is his body and his blood. This is not to be sacrificed in favor of a vague "real presence" of Christ either in the eucharist or in the celebrating congregation. Such a concession, it is rightly felt, would reopen the door to the Sacramentarian distortion which was quite willing to concede the presence of Christ to faith while it intransigently and sometimes obscenely rejected the objective presence of his body and his blood under the earthly forms of the consecrated bread and wine (see for example, FC SD VII 67). In the final analysis this is all that the *manducatio oralis*, the *manducatio indignorum*, and the *unio sacramentalis* were intended to secure.

That the communication of the body and the blood of our Lord to the communicants involves a personal encounter of the communicant with the incarnate word was cheerfully granted. No depreciation of the personal element in the heavenly gifts of the holy communion is involved in the Lutheran understanding of the words of institution, with their reference both to Christ's body and to his blood, as being more than a mere paraphrase of "this is I." The Symbols speak on occasion "of the presence of the living Christ" (Ap X 4) in the holy eucharist, but with consistently greater frequency they infer from the words of institution the more biblical insight that "in the holy communion the bread and the wine are the body and the blood of Christ" (so SA Three VI 1).[14]

On this basis John Gerhard can repeat in this *Loci* the *Adoro [Te] devote* of St. Thomas Aquinas.[15] Martin Chemnitz can find peculiar comfort in the fact that "Christ himself is present for us in the celebration of the holy communion both in his Godhead and in his flesh, that he comes to us, and that he lays hold on us (Phil. 3:12), and connects us with himself in the most intimate fashion possible. This is the sweetest kind of consolation. For the laying hold on us by the Christ who is both God and man is necessary in order to bring about a mutual joining of Christ and ourselves. But we are weighed down with the load of our sins and oppressed by the burden of our weakness; we cannot enter into the possession of the secrets of the heavens (Col. 2:18), and penetrate to him in glory. And because our frailty cannot bear the glory of his majesty in this life (Matt. 17:6; Acts 9:4), he therefore is present under the bread and wine and his body and his blood are offered and received... There [in the holy communion] we may safely seek him and certainly find him, for there through the sacred ministry he gives his body and his blood to the communicants."[16]

In the sense of that presence, the *Small Cathechism* speaks of the sacrament of the altar as the bestowing of Christ upon the communicant (Preface 23). In the sense of that presence, the congregation addresses the *Agnus Dei* to the Lamb of God slain for the sins of the world and present in his body and blood in the holy eucharist. In the sense of that presence, Luther's *Deutsche Messe* could defend the elevation of the sacred species after the consecration: "It signifies that Christ has commanded us to remember him. For as the sacrament is elevated bodily and yet Christ's body and blood are not seen in it, so he is remembered and elevated through the word of the sermon and is also confessed and highly honored through the reception of the sacrament. Yet it is all apprehended by faith, for we do not see how Christ has given his body and blood for us and even now daily shows and offers it in the presence of God to obtain grace for us" (WA 19, 99, 18 to 100, 3). For Lutheran theology the bodily presence of our Lord in the sacrament of the altar is by definition quite independent of the personal faith or the personal sanctity of either the celebrant or the communicant (LC Holy Communion 5; FC SD VII 32).

More important than the "how" of the eucharist is the "why." The sacrament of the altar confers forgiveness of sins, we say glibly. But the forgiveness of sins is itself only a symbol of much more. "Where there is forgiveness of sins there is also life and salvation." The sacrament of the altar comforts straitened consciences (AC XXIV 7), strengthens our faith (Ap IV 210), assures us that we are incorporated into Christ and washed with his blood (FC SD VII 16). It is a remedy against sin, flesh, devil, world, death, danger, and hell, and a bestowing of grace, life, paradise, heaven, Christ, God and everything good (SC Pref 23). It is a safeguard against death and all misfortune, a food of the soul that nourishes and strengthens the inner man, a daily pasture and sustenance, a refreshment of our faith in the battle of life, a consolation of overburdened hearts, a treasure from heaven, a precious antidote against the poison of weakness, a communication of the entire gospel, and an altogether wholesome, comforting medicine that helps us and gives life to both soul and body (LC Holy Communion 22-24, 27, 32, 66, 68, 70).[17]

VIII

In the light of the interconfessional dialog, the presence of the contemporaneous Christ in the sacrament of the altar needs illumination from another aspect — the question of the nature of the eucharistic sacrifice. Obviously, to suggest that the sacrifice that takes place in the celebration of the holy eucharist supplements by some independent contribution the sacrifice on Golgotha, or that it is instrinsically an expiatory sacrifice, or that the offering of the eucharist sacrifice (apart from or even in connection with the reception of our Lord's body and blood) is meritorious on our own behalf or on behalf of others living or dead, is to advance ideas that are sub-Christian and intolerable (Ap XXIV 11, 89; SA Two II 12-15; FC Ep VII 23; SD VII 109).

At the same time, the Lutheran church has always recognized not only inferentially by its use of the term eucharist but also explicitly in Article XXIV of the *Apology* that the celebration of the holy communion is a sacrifice of praise and thanksgiving (16-43, 74, 87, 88, 93), an act in which we do honor to almighty God by way of response to his great gift to us (18). It sees the incense and the pure oblation foretold in Malachi 1:11 as including the holy eucharist as a ceremony — as long as it is not understood as being efficacious by the mere performance of the rite — together with the proclamation of the gospel and the reception of the holy communion (*ipsa sumptio coenae Domini*) (31-33).[18]

There are other sacrificial aspects to the holy eucharist, but certain historical developments tend to occlude these aspects for many contemporary Lutherans. One of these developments is the limited number of opportunities that many congregations furnish their membership to receive the blessed sacrament — monthly or quarterly communion Sundays in place of the early Lutheran tradition of communion every Sunday and holy day. Another is the elevation of the sermon in some parts of the church to a place of almost exclusive dominance in the Sunday parochial service, with the celebration of the holy communion considered as an optional appendix for the few who insist on receiving it. The ideal, of course, is the recovery as far as feasible of the primitive practice where every communicant in the congregation received the holy communion with his fellow-Christians every Sunday. The *Large Catechism* repeats approvingly the advice of St. Hilary of Poitiers that only they should absent themselves from the altar who had committed a sin for which they could be excommunicated and had not repented of it, lest — Luther adds — the absentees deprive themselves of life (LC Holy Communion 59). The reception of the Lord's body and blood — whatever else it is — is a renewed challenge to, and a renewed act of, commitment to him who through his body and blood that we eat and drink confirms and fortifies our union with him.

Again, we remember that in the primitive Christian community, each communicant would bring to the celebration of the holy eucharist a small loaf of bread and a small flask of wine. These were the symbols of his self-dedication to the Lord of the church. From these offerings enough loaves and wine were set aside for the requirements of the holy communion, and the rest was used for the relief of the poor. Later on these offerings were supplemented with other offerings in kind, and finally for the sake of convenience they were commuted into gifts of money. Here is the ultimate origin of the offertory procession and its modern replacement, the taking up of the offerings. One Lutheran rite includes in the great intercession after the offertory this prayer: "Receive, O God, our bodies and souls and all our talents, together with the offerings we bring before thee, for thou hast purchased us to be thine own that we may live unto thee."[19] Thus our offerings are still symbols of our self-dedication to almighty God, the pledge that all that we have received from him will be used in conformity with his will as he reveals it to us in response to our prayer.

A further aspect of our sacrifice lies in the fact that it is as baptized members of the Christian community that we receive the holy communion, and it is precisely the sacrificial giving up of ourselves for the sake of Christ's bride the Church that our reception of the holy communion implies. We receive it not only — in the words of the familiar Lutheran post-communion collect — that through it God might strengthen us individually in faith toward him, but also that he might by it increase our fervent love toward one another.[20]

Furthermore, there is in the celebration of the holy communion a "representation," in the sense of making present again in the presence of God, of the sacrifice of his Son, so that we come before the Father not as *aestimator meriti* but only as *veniae largitor per Christum Dominum nostrum* ("not waying our merites but pardoning our offences, through Christe our Lorde," as the strongly Lutheran English *Book of Common Prayer* of 1549 rendered the closing words of the medieval canon). In this connection, we may recall that John Gerhard insists that the question at issue between Roman Catholics and Lutherans is not "if the mass has to do with something which is a true sacrifice or if something is offered in the mass." While rejecting the idea of sacrifice in the mass in the strict sense of an immolation, he grants that sacrifice can also mean to "represent" (*repraesentare*) to God the passion of his son — the passion which was a sacrifice in the past — through our prayers. The issue would then be if in the mass or eucharist something that is a sacrifice is offered to God. "Here and there the apostles use the term 'to offer sacrifice' in [this] metaphorical sense, Rom.12:1; Philippians 2:17; 4:18; I Peter 2:5." In this latter sense the Lutherans grant a sacrifice of the mass in two ways, first "that in the celebration of the eucharist 'we proclaim the Lord's death' (I Corinthians 11:26), and pray that God, on account of that holy and spotless (*immaculatum*) sacrifice completed on the cross and on account of that holy victim (*hostia*) which is certainly present in the eucharist he would be merciful to us," and second, "that he would in kindness receive and grant a place to the rational and spiritual oblation of our prayer."[21] A little farther on Gerhard insists that even the canon of the Roman mass does not imply a "true sacrifice," that is, an immolation, "but at most a memorial and a representation (*memoria et repraesentatio*) of a sacrifice already completed," in that the prayer Supplices of the canon reads: "Command that these things may by the hands of your holy angel be borne aloft to your altar on high in the sight of your divine majesty." Gerhard goes on: "It is clear that the sacrifice takes place in heaven, not on earth, inasmuch as there is offered to God the Father the death and passion of his beloved Son by way of commemoration (*per commemorationem*)." Against St. Robert Bellarmine Gerhard makes the point: "As in the Christian sacrifice there is no other victim except the real and substantial body of Christ, so there is no other true priest except Christ himself. Hence this sacrifice once offered on the cross thereafter takes place continually (*jugiter*) in an unseen fashion in heaven by way of commemoration, when Christ offers to the Father on our behalf his sufferings of the past, especially when we are applying ourselves to the sacred mysteries, and this is the 'unbloody sacrifice' which is carried out in heaven."[22]

Gerhard's reference to I Corinthians 11:26 is apposite. In our eating of the Lord's body and in our drinking of his blood of the covenant we proclaim his death until he comes. This proclamation is of course a witness to one another who participate in the sacred mysteries. In a sense it is also a proclamation in the presence of the world, for which Christ died and which he seeks to restore to himself in spite of its rejection of him. The world is aware that we make this memorial of him; the world may even see us make it when those who are still "in the world" visit our churches or when they look at telecasts of our services, or they may hear us make it when our services are broadcast by radio. But it must be remembered that observation by the world is essentially an accident, that basically the Christian eucharist is and under all circumstances must remain essentially private, the restricted meal of a fellowship of people who have been baptized into the same Christ and who recognize one another and are recognized by one another as confessors of the same faith and sharers of the same life. But in addition to our mutual witness, and in addition to whatever witness our eucharistic action may be to the world, our proclamation takes place in the presence of God. It affirms to him as much as it does to one another or to the world our utter dependence upon the life and death and resurrection of his Son for our life.

To whatever extent that we can speak of a sacrifice in the holy Eucharist at all — and we remember that its primary thrust is sacramental, the impartation of the "forgiveness of sins" — the priest who offers that sacrifice is ultimately Christ, and it is at this point that the presence of the contemporaneous Christ becomes important for our present purpose.

When in Christ we plead his merits before God on our behalf it is Christ acting through us, the incarnate word, the son of God and the son of Mary. He is making present for us in our place in the universe and in our moment of time his once-for-all act that he constantly makes present in the sight of God by his intercession. Thus he is still the priest and although the essential historical moment of the sacrifice is for us chronologically in the past, he is still the victim. We in turn are saying in effect: "No offering that we could bring by ourselves could possibly reconcile us to you, our God, and you to us. All that we can plead is the work of your Son, his perfect obedience in all that he did and all that he suffered, his body nailed to the cross for us, his blood of the covenant poured out for the forgiveness of sins. As by the mystery of the sacramental union, you have made this hallowed bread and cup his true body and blood, for us Christians to eat and to drink, let it be present in your sight as the price of our redemption as well. Let it remind you that you have forgiven mankind in the reconciliation which you have wrought in your Son. Before your eyes we appeal to no virtue, no righteousness, no merit of our own, but only to the alien righteousness of your suffering servant and Son, our true Easter lamb, who was offered for us and has taken away the sins of the world, who by his death has destroyed death and by his rising to life again has restored to us everlasting life."

Relevant in this connection is the occurrence of the term *zikkâron* in an active sense in various Old Testament passages — the paschal anniversary to be kept as a feast "to the Lord" (Ex. 12:14), the stones of remembrance that Aaron was to bear before the Lord to bring the children of Israel to continual remembrance before him (Ex. 28:12, 29; see 39:7), the atonement money that was to bring the people of Israel to remembrance before the Lord (30:16), the blowing of the trumpets over the burnt offerings and peace offerings to serve the Israelites for remembrance before their God (Num. 10:10), the Midianite war booty that Moses and Eleazar brought into the tent of meeting as a memorial for the people of Israel before the Lord (31:54). "The *zikkâron*," says a recent writer, "stimulates God's memory and his acts of memory are synonymous with his acts of intervention. The *zikkâron* also stimulates Israel's memory, which produces participation in the sacred order."[23]

Again, in the sense that we offer ourselves to the service of God and of our fellow members of the body of Christ, it is Christ who is acting through us. The *Apology* calls the perils, the labors, and the sermons of Paul, Athanasius and Augustine and of others like them who taught the churches, authentic sacrifices accepted by God. It also calls them contests of Christ by which he trounced the devil and drove him away from the believers. Shortly thereafter it goes on: "We believe the same thing with reference to the individual good works that Christians perform in the most unpublicized occupations. Through these works Christ is trouncing the devil, so that when the Corinthians were making contributions for the relief of the poor, it was a holy work and a sacrifice and a contest of Christ against the devil, who labors constantly to prevent anything being done to the praise of God. To denounce such works, the confession of Christian teaching, the bearing of afflictions, deeds of charity, and mortifications of the flesh is without doubt a denunciation of the external rule of the kingdom of Christ among men" (Ap IV 189-193).

IX

We look briefly at the other rites that the Western tradition (followed in a limited way by the Lutheran Symbols) calls sacraments.

The *Apology* is willing to concede the status of a sacrament to holy orders as such, provided priesthood be understood as the ministry of teaching the gospel and administering the sacraments to others. (The "to others" is addressed against the late medieval doctrine which regarded the priesthood as an order of individuals set aside to offer masses as expiatory sacrifices for the sins of the living and the dead. In these circumstances a priest might offer many times as many private masses where he was the only worshipper and communicant as he would celebrate masses *pro populo*.) The *Apology* is also willing to concede the status of a sacrament to the imposition of hands, that is, to holy ordination as a rite. It argues that Christ instituted the ministry and that "the church has the command to appoint clergymen, which ought to be most gratifying to us, because we know that God approves this ministry and is present in the ministry." The ministry, the *Apology* observes, needs to be accorded every kind of praise because of the anticlericalism of the Anabaptists (Ap XIII 7-13).

Holy matrimony is conceded sacramental status by the *Apology* only with some qualifications. It antedates the new covenant and its promises pertain to the bodily life of this aeon. It ought to be differentiated from the other sacraments, which are sacraments of the New Testament and have testimonies of grace of the forgiveness of sins attached to them. Yet, we might observe, even in this sacrament of the Old Testament and, as it were, of the First Article, the presence of the cosmic Christ, through whom all things came into being, in whom all things hang together, and for whom all things ultimately exist, can still be predicated. If marriage is called a sacrament, the *Apology* points out, other divinely ordained states and offices, such as civil government, might also claim sacramental status. And, one is compelled to add, indeed they might, for they, like marriage are masks behind which the omnipresent God and his Christ are accomplishing ends for which the universe was called into being.

In the case of holy confirmation and of extreme unction, we must regard as justifiable the failure of the *Apology* to concede the term "sacrament" to these rites as the sixteenth century Western church knew and practiced them. The substitution of an anointing with chrism for the apostolic imposition of hands in confirmation underlined the uncertainty with which the medieval church had debated the matter and the form of this "sacrament" and the issue of its institution by Christ. Similarly the medieval Western restriction of unction to the dying as part of their preparation for departure from this life was difficult to reconcile with St. James' injunction that obviously regarded the restoration of the patient to health as one of the purposes of the anointing (XIII 6).

But these two rites are not simply to be brushed aside as having no relevance for the presence of Christ in his church. Our rite has retained the essential formula of confirmation in the post-baptismal blessing which accompanied the vesting with the chrisom or baptismal robe: "The almighty God and Father of our Lord Jesus Christ, who has begotten you anew through the water and the Holy Spirit and has forgiven you all your sins, strengthen (*starke, confirmet*) you with his grace to everlasting life. Amen." (SC *Taufbüchlein* 30; *Bekenntnisschriften*, p. 541.) This blessing involves an invocation of a God who is regarded as present and active, although the activity is appropriated to the first rather than to the second hypostasis of the holy Trinity.

In the same way, it must be conceded that the only mark of a sacrament (even by the developed definition of classic Lutheran orthodoxy) which is lacking in the rite of unction as enjoined by St. James is explicit dominical institution (and, as far as the church is concerned, a demonstrable consensus of the fathers attesting its unbroken use between the writing of St. James' letter and about 400 A.D.). Certainly the anointing with oil in the name of the Lord, that is, in the name of Jesus Christ, involves confidence in the presence and activity of the Saviour whom the priests of the church invoked as they anointed the patient.

ENDNOTES

1. The "who is in heaven" of John 3: 13 is textually dubious but theologically sound (John 1:18).
2. Heinrich Schmid, *The Doctirinal Theology of the Evangelical Lutheran Church*, 3d. ed. tr. Charles A. Hay and Henry E. Jacobs (Minneapolis: Augsburg Publishing House [1961]), pp. 125-126.
3. Jacob Andree, *Von den Sapltungen, so sich zwischen den Theologen Augspurgischer Confession von Anno 1548 biss auff diss 1573, Jar nach und noch erhaben* (Tübingen: Georg Gruppenbach, 1573), p. 84f.
4. Herman Sasse, *This Is My Body* (Minneapolis: Augsburg Publishing House. c. 1959), p. 380. See also Werner Elert, *The Structure of Lutheranism*, tr. Walter Hansen (St. Louis: Concordia Publishing House, 1963), p. 238.
5. So also Luther, *Von den letzten Worten Davids* (1543), WA 54, 57, 35.
6. Since the ninth century at least the "true body" had identified the historical and sacramental Body of Christ in distinction to the "mystical body," the church.
7. Fritz Viering, *Christus und die kirche in römisch-katholischer Sicht* (Göttingen: Vandenhoeck und Ruprecht, c. 1962), pp. 94-95.
8. This ideas is reflected in the collects of our rite which describe the Holy Spirit as governing and sanctifying the church (Second Litany Collect: second collect of the Bidding Prayer) (*Service Book and Hymnal*, pp. 161, 240; *The Lutheran Hymnal*, pp. 112, 116).
9. Johannes Gerhard, *Loci theologici, Locus* XX, para. 82 [ed. Preuss, IV, 298]. See Ap XXIV 18.
10. Lutherans should be careful not to let these rejections take them too far. In disavowing consubstanitation (which almost invariably non-Lutheran writers attribute to Lutherans), they should be careful not to create the impression that they deny that the substantial body of Christ is present and is distributed and received *with* the consecrated bread. Luther defends *"Einbrödtung"* or impanation (although, of course, not in a circumscriptive sense) in his *Bekenntnis* of 1528 (WA. 26. 434). Similarly, while the *Formula of Concord* correctly rejects a "Capernaitic" tearing of the flesh of Christ by the teeth of the comunicants (FC Ep VII 42), in another antithesis Luther can say with reference to the demand of Nicholas II on Berengar of Tours in 1059 to agree that "the true body of Christ is crushed and ground with the teeth" by the communicants: "Would to God that all popes had acted in so Christian fashion in all other matters as this pope did with Berengar

in forcing this confession, for this is undoubtedly the meaning that he who eats and chews this bread eats and chews that which is the genuine, true body of Christ" (WA 26, 443, 1-4).

11. It may be noted that the Symbols do not critcize the Eastern docrine of *metabole*, and that the archtheologian of the Lutheran Church sees a third possibility between Roman Catholic transubstantiation and the metaphorical view of Calvism, "namely that the bread has been changed sacramentally" (*quod videlicet panis mutatus fuerit sacramentaliter*) and that he uses the term "sacramental change" (*mutatio sacramentalis*) as a synonym (although not one to be preferred) for "sacramental union," the term that Luther had devised to express the biblical view. (Gerhard, *Loci theologici, Locus XXI,* cap. xii. paras. 135-136 [ed. Preuss, V. 135]: WA 26, 441; see FC SD VII 38.)

12. FC SD VIII 78 (see also 92), 81 (see also FC Ep VIII 16). John Hülsemann (1602-1661) speaks for Lutheranism when he says: "To what extent and how Christ is present in the sacrament of holy communion is something to be drawn wholly from the words of insitution, which describes the entire nature of the sacrament... Whatever does not depend from Christ's institution does not pertain to the eucharist and is not to be attributed to it" (*Manuale Confessionis Augustanae,* disp. VIII, qu. 1, 2d ed. [Wittenberg: *Haeredes Johannis Bergeri* (Johannes Röhnerus), 1653], p. 314).

13. *Catalog of Testimonies,* 10; Migne, *Patrologia Graeca,* 63, 131.

14. "The Lutheran conception requires us to say both: presence of body and blood of Christ and presence of Christ himself, hence, presence of Christ himself in his body and in his blood. But in any case we must forestall a 'naked' personal presence. It is the living Christ in person who is actively and self-givingly present, but in this way that he gives us himself in his body really given for us and in his blood really poured out." (Ernst Kinder, in Paul Jacobs, Ernst Kinder, and Fritz Viering, *Gegenwart Christi* 2d. ed. [Göttingen: Vandenhoeck und Ruprecht, 1960], p. 42).

15. Gerhard, *Loci theologici, Locus* XXI, cap. xxvi, para. 265 [ed. Preuss, V, 252].

16. Martin Chemnitz, *Fundamenta sanae doctrinae de vera et substantiali praesentia, exhibitione et sumptione Corporis et Sanguinis Domini in coena,* cap. xi. ed. nova (Wittenberg: Clemens Bergerus et Zacharias Schürerus [Johannes Gormannus], 1610), p. 71.

17. "Luther fought the reduction of the real presence of Christ to the forgiveness of sins as the decisive mistake of the Antinomians" (Albrecht Peters, *Realpräsenz: Luthers Zeugnis von Christi Gegenwart im Abendmahl* [Berlin: Lutherisches Verlagshaus, 1960], p. 147).

18. To a large degree the corruption of medieval eucharistic theology arose from the decline in the number of communions at which the congregation received — until finally the constitution *omnis utriusque sexus* in 1215 had to enforce an annual communion as a minimum performance for a professing Christian to retain his status in the community. The concomitant of this was the transfer of the benefits that previously had been associacted with the reception of the blessed sacrament — for example, the *"omnis benedictio caelestis et gratia"* which the prayer Supplices in the canon sought for *"quotquot ex hac altaris participatione sacrosanctum Filii tui corpus et sanguinem sumpserimus"* — to a noncommunicating congregation of worshippers whose sole connection with the eucharist was exhausted in the designation *"circumstantes."* If the heavenly blessing and grace was to be had merely by being a bystander, particularly when this standing by was regarded as meritorious, the old understanding of the eucharist had been superseded by a totally different interpretation of its significance and value.

19. *The Lutheran Hymnal,* p. 24.

20. "The dominant concern of Paul is ultimately this: Christ's bodily communication of himself imposes on us the obligation of concrete bodily obedience in the body of Christ... In that Christ sacramentally obligates our bodies to service in his body, he demonstrates that he is the World-Ruler (*Kosmokrator*), who in our bodies is tearing the world under his rule and through his body is establishing the new world" (Ernst Käsemann, *Exegetische Versuche und Besinnungen*, I [Göttingen: Vandenhoeck und Ruprecht, c. 1960], 34).

21. John Gerhard, *Confessio catholica*, II pars II. article xv. cap. 1 *ekthesis* 6 (Frankfurt-am-Main: Christianus Genschius [Johannes Andreae], 1679), 1200-1201. On some problems created by the term *"repraesentatio"* in the contemporary interconfessional dialog, see Sasse, *This Is My Body*, p. 380, n. 85, and Vilmos Vajta, *Die Theologie des Gottesdienstes bei Luther* (Stockholm: Svenska Kyrkans Diakonistyrelses Bokförlas [1952], pp. 101-103.

22. Gerhard, *Confessio catholica*, p. 1204.

23. Brevard S. Childs, *Memory and Tradition in Israel* (Naperville, IL: Alec R. Allenson, 1962) p. 68.

THE ONE EUCHARIST
FOR THE ONE WORLD

If I were a Scholastic, which I am not, I should begin this presentation by posing the question, *Utrum eucharistia pro mundo sit?* ("Whether or not the Eucharist is for the world"). And I should have to proceed in good Scholastic style, *Videtur aucharistiam pro mundo non esse* ("It appears that the Eucharist is not for the world").

In this way we should have arrived at the paradox that all branches of the Catholic tradition have tended to forget in the Constantinian era, namely, that in its essence the Eucharist is always a private and not a public action.

There have been times when this might have seemed to be so because of external stress. In the era before the peace of the church — and in parallel epochs of persecution into the 20th century — mere participation in a eucharistic assembly was *prima facie* evidence of criminal activity. Under such circumstances it behooved every participant to be sure that every other person present was an authentic and properly certified member of the Christian community.

In the period that followed the peace of the church, when the influx of self-seeking professors of Christianity threatened to undermine the church's integrity, a secret discipline that stressed the principle behind the formula *Ta hagia tois hagiois* ("The holy things to the holy people") highly recommended itself.

But the private nature of the eucharistic assembly is not only a response to an external demand; it is also a datum of the eucharistic situation. In principle, the eucharistic assembly is always the company of those who have been made members of the body of Christ upon earth by Holy Baptism and who are gathered together in this capacity alone to commemorate His triumph in His death and resurrection, to realize anew their oneness in Him, and to share in His act of reconciliation, His divine life, and His deliverance from the demonic powers that hold the world in thrall.

It follows that one may have real misgivings about a public celebration of the Holy Eucharist. I am not suggesting that clandestinity is necessary. I am not suggesting that the church has anything to hide in her celebration of the Eucharist.

But I am suggesting that it is wrong to admit individuals to the Holy Eucharist indiscriminately merely because they are physically present, with no effort to determine if they have been baptized, with no effort to determine their continuing status as members of the church, and with no assurance that they have the requisite dispositions of sorrow for their wrong-doing and faith in the atoning work of our Lord that is made present again in this mystery.

I submit that it is misguided — regardless of the good faith of those who do so — to use the celebration of the Holy Eucharist as such as an evangelistic device and to impose on the celebration of the Holy Eucharist a burden that it was never intended to bear, that is, to serve as the means of communicating the basics of the Gospel to people to whom the Gospel has never been communicated. There are other vehicles for this task.

I submit that it is wrong to use the celebration of the Holy Eucharist as a spectacle. I think of military field masses with 6-inch howitzers replacing tower bells and sacring bells at the elevation. I think of the elaborate climactic celebrations of the Holy Eucharist at international eucharistic congresses and of a bishop of Rome celebrating the Holy Eucharist in Yankee Stadium in New York in the presence of scores of thousands of people and administering Holy Communion to a bare dozen selected school children. Again, I am not passing judgment on the good faith of those who devise these spectacles. I know that such litugical extravaganzas are part of a powerful tradition from which it is difficult even for modern persons to liberate themselves. I know too that the intention behind these spectacles is to do public honor to the Son of God before whom every knee must finally bow and whose lordship every tongue must finally confess. But this is not one of the purposes for which our Lord instituted the Sacrament of the Altar.

Nevertheless, even after affirming the intrinsically private character of the celebration of the Eucharist, after rejecting the propriety of indiscriminate admission to it, of regarding it as an evangelistic device, and of treating it as a spectacle, I am still compelled to affirm that the Eucharist is for the world.

I

What is the Sacrament of the Altar? The Church of the *Augsburg Confession* answers: "It is the true body and blood of our Lord Jesus Christ, for us Christians to eat and to drink." If we take seriously the concern of the Church of the *Augsburg Confession* to derive its eucharistic doctrine wholly from the institution narratives, this is the only definition that has Biblical warrant. At the moment this formulation is not everywhere in good repute. It stresses too much, we are told, the ontological at the expense of the dynamic. It stresses the material at the expense of the personal. It seems to deny the spiritual and verges on magic. Other formulations stress the presence of Christ (rather than of His body and blood) in the sacrament and define the sacramental experience as a personal encounter with our Lord. I shall not impugn this formulation, the validity of which I must concede, as long as it does not intend to evade or to deny that our Lord's body and blood are communicated to those who eat and drink in the sacramental meal and as long as it does not intend to evade or deny the fact of the presence of the incarnate Christ. It would be quite wrong to imagine or to teach that in the celebration of the Eucharist only His Godhead is somehow benignly present at our jejune and ritual meal of rejoicing, in which each communicant receives an average of 140 milligrams (or 1/200 of an ounce) of unleavened bread, with 3/10 of one calorie of food value, and 3.5 grams (or 1/8 of an ounce) of wine. Apart from such a misunderstanding, it is quite true that the Sacrament of the Altar, celebrated as a mystery of sacramental *anamnesis*, is the arena of personal encounter with the incarnate Word of God, with the second hypostasis of the Godhead concealed in the body-and-blood humanity that He assumed.

The stress falls on the fact that He is incarnate. In assuming our common humanity He united Himself with all of humankind, so that there are no human limits to the identification of the Christ of the Eucharist with the one world of human beings. He is linked inseparably with every person, without reference to any person's intelligence, health, sophistication, learning, experience, age, race, color, culture, or epoch. Whatever it was that made the first *homo sapiens* a human being, whatever it is that makes any of us a human being, that Christ assumed and in that humanity He is present in the Holy Eucharist for us Christians to eat and to drink.

This is true for the future also. Whatever it is that will make any of our children's children human beings down to the last human generation at the time of our Lord's final self-disclosure, that is what He assumed. This is so whether they will be living on earth or will have populated the moon and the habitable planets or even — in some way that we are not yet scientifically able to imagine — will have penetrated to earthlike planets of another solar system. Christ will be linked even with them through the body that He took from the mother of God when He was born of the substance of His mother in the world and that He gives and will give in the Eucharist to all who eat and drink in it.

If the Eucharist is truly to be for the one world, this stress on His human, bodily presence in it is vital. I know that it is customary to smile indulgently at the statement of the *Catechism* and other Symbolical Books that the Sacrament of the Altar is the true body and blood of Christ and to omit the adjective from modern translations. But the adjective is still useful, even if the particular connotation that it has in this context has a history that needs first to be understood. It is the church's laudable way of reminding us that the body and blood of our Lord in the Eucharist are not some kind of metaphor, specifically that the body of Christ in this context is not simply the church, but that in the sacramental mystery it is the body and the blood that, as the Creed puts it, was born out of the Holy Spirit and Mary the virgin, the most praiseworthy bearer of the eternal Word. It is the body and the blood that appeared to men in Palestine when Augustus and Tiberius ruled in Rome; the blood that first began to flow at His namegiving on the eighth day of His life; the body that was nailed to the cross and the blood that was the very life of the obedient Servant of Yahweh; the body which God raised from the dead and over which death no longer has dominion and the blood that pleads for the pardon and reconciliation of a world of sinners.

This Christ, bodily and, if you will, bloodily present in the Sacrament of the Altar, is not merely a human being. He is the human being, the model, the standard, the blueprint, the die that determines what authentic humanity is, from the first human being to the last. We human beings — all of us — have not only our salvation but our very humanity from Christ. He stands both as the initial and as the ultimate man, the exemplar of human virtue in its most eminent perfection and the one whose irrefragable integrity stands as the judgment upon all our lapses from genuine humanity. And not the least aspect of this virtue is the unselfishness that He exhibits in the act that the Eucharist primarily makes present again, His sacrificial death on the cross for our benefit that is the climax and the epitome of His total redemptive work, of His unswerving obedience to His heavenly Father, and of His generous readiness to accept at His enemies' hands the consequences of His radical goodness.

The sacrifice that is here made present before God and before the eucharistic assembly is a sacrifice for the whole world. Let it be clearly emphasized that a sacrifice is here present. Indeed a twofold sacrifice is present. Looked at from the standpoint of what the church as a congregation of faithful people does in response to God's act in Christ for the reconciliation of the world, it is a sacrifice of praise and thanksgiving, spiritual (as a translation of *logike*) and therefore unbloody. In this sacrifice people reborn in Baptism (and reconciled again to the holy community if they have denied their part in it by great sin) hear and accept the Word of God applied to themselves, sing their praises to the Paschal Victim, offer their adoring worship to God, entreat Him in intercession, remember before Him in gratitude the saints of both covenants and the faithful departed that are near and dear to them, receive the body and blood of Christ, and commit themselves in anticipation to carry their faith into action in the world around them beyond the four walls of the church. They celebrate the victory of Christ, a victory that He and God accomplished in Him both in His death and resurrection. He is the true Easter Lamb that has taken away the sins of the world and by His rising to life again has restored to the world of human beings everlasting life. This, in essence, is the argument of the 24th article of the *Apology of the Augsburg Confession*. But there is more to it than that. We have already stressed that the Sacrament of the Altar is a making present again of God's act in Christ, His nativity, His baptism, fasting, and temptations, His perfect life of obedience, His rejection, His last supper, His agony and bloody sweat, His betrayal, His arrest, His cross and execution, His precious death and burial, His glorious resurrection and ascension, and in anticipation and in vivid hope His self-disclosure to vindicate and liberate His church and His creation at the great *palingemesia*. All this is made present before God and before us. This sacrifice, this oblation, this offering is for the whole world. It is retroactive to the first human being, and it thrusts forward in its saving effect to the end of the age. Although the essential historical moment of His once-and-for-all sacrifice is chronologically in the past, the one priest is Christ and the one victim is Christ.

We have a part in it only because we are members of His body the church. When we offer our praise and thanksgiving, we do it at the impulse of His Holy Spirit. When we offer ourselves — the real "sacrifice of the mass," according to the Reformers — He is offering Himself and us in Him. We can sing:

> And now, O Father, mindful of the love
> That bought us once for all on Calvary's tree.
> And having with us him that pleads above,
> We here present, we here spread forth to thee
> That only offering perfect in thine eyes,
> The one, true, pure, immortal Sacrifice.

> Look, Father, look on his anointed face
> And only look on us as found in him,
> Look not on our misusings of thy grace,
> Our prayer so languid, and our faith so dim,
> For lo, between our sins and their reward
> We set the passion of thy Son, our Lord.
> *(William Bright)*

Let me in this connection recall to you part of the statement which the official national Consultation of Roman Catholic and Lutheran Theologians in the United States produced in 1967. The members of the Consultation stated:

> The [Roman] Catholic affirmation that the church 'offers Christ' in the mass has in the course of the last half century been increasingly explained in terms which answer Lutheran fears that this detracts from the full sufficiency of Christ's sacrifice. The members of the body of Christ are united through Christ with God and with one another in such a way that they become participants in his worship, his self-offering, his sacrifice to the Father. Through this union between Christ and Christians, the eucharistic assembly 'offers Christ' by consenting in the power of the Holy Spirit to be offered by him to the Father. Apart from Christ we have no gifts, no worship, no sacrifice of our own to offer God. All we can plead is Christ, the sacrificial lamb and victim whom the Father himself has given us (*Lutherans and Catholics in Dialogue*, III, 189-90).

Not without its interest is the documentation that a note appended to this paragraph provides:

> Luther says: 'Not that we offer Christ as a sacrifice, but that Christ offers us;' but he also holds that this involves a sense in which 'we offer Christ:' 'Through it [faith], in connection with the sacrament, we offer ourselves, our need, our prayer, praise and thanksgiving in Christ, and thereby we offer Christ.... I also offer Christ in that I desire and believe that he accepts me and my prayer and praise and presents it to God in his own person' (*A Treatise on the New Testament*, in *Luther's Works*, 35 [Philadelphia: Fortress Press, 1961], 98-101).

This agrees with the testimony of the Second Vatican Council, which, quoting St. Augustine, says that the 'aim' of the sacrifice offered in the eucharist is that

> the entire commonwealth of the redeemed, that is, the community and the society of the saints, be offered as a universal sacrifice to God through the High Priest who in his passion offered his very self for us that we might be the body of so exalted a head (*Decree on the Ministry and Life of Priests*, no. 2; tr. W.M. Abbott and J. Gallagher, eds., *The Documents of Vatican II* [New York: Guild Press, 1966], pp. 535-36; quotation from Augustine's *City of God*, 10,6).

The continuation of this quotation is paraphrased in the 1947 encyclical *Mediator Dei*, no. 125: "In the sacrament of the altar which she [the church] offers, she herself is also offered." The contemporary [Roman] Catholic theologian Karl Rahner explains this point by saying that the eucharistic offering of Christ inseparably involves "the believing, inner 'yes' of men to the movement of loving obedience of Christ to the Father." He goes on to speak directly to the fears which [non-Roman-Catholic Christians] have expressed regarding the notion of the 'sacrifice of the mass:' The sacrifice of the mass creates no new gracious and saving will in God *vis-a-vis* the world which did not already exist through the cross (and only through the cross!). "We can speak of 'moving' God to forgiveness, reconciliation, mercy and assistance through the sacrifice of the mass only in the sense that the gracious will of God, founded exclusively on the reconciliation of the cross, becomes visible in the sacrifice of the mass, comes to man ... and takes hold of him" — producing, Rahner goes on to suggest, manifold effects in the worshipers and, through their actions and prayers, in the world (*'Die vielen Messen und das eine Opfer,'* Zeitschrift für katholische Theologie, 71 [1949], 267 and 288).

II

The Christ who gives us His body and His blood in the Holy Eucharist and makes us all one body with Him and with all His holy church through the one loaf and the one cup is the one through whom all things were made, for whom all things were made, and in whom all things hang together. The intimate Christological link between the "first article" of the creed and the "second" and "third articles" of the creed is something that the Western Christian community has had difficulty in phasing into its theology and sometimes has conveniently forgotten. The Church of the *Augsburg Confession* has not been wholly immune to this charge. But this linkage is inescapably Biblical and thoroughly Pauline. If we of the Church of the *Augsburg Confession* are going to derive our doctrine of justification from the Pauline correspondence, we have to make him at the least as normative for the linkage of creation and redemption and new creation. Precisely why we should have this difficulty is in itself not easy to determine. It may be a kind of lurking distaste for matter and an excessive spirituality. It may be that we have taken the eucharistic creed of Constantinople I (381) with its declaration, "through whom [Jesus Christ] all things were made," less seriously than the Apostolic Creed of the West, which dispenses with this assertion. But the link is there, and the link is precisely the Christ whose person and work are the core and center of the second article and of the whole Christian faith. The Word of God, the true light that enlightens every man, the divine *hypostasis* that became man in order that human beings might be partakers of the divine nature and so "divinized," is precisely the focal point of creation. Through Him the Father made all things, *ta panta,* the universe, the space and the time that are the coordinates of our creaturely existence and everything that fills them, with the one world of human beings as the visible apex and climax. Without him was not anything made. The *world*, the prolog to the fourth gospel repeats, was made through Him (John 1:1,3,10).

But the Father did not only make everything *through* His Son, but also *in* Him and *for* Him. The Son of God, in whom we have redemption, the forgiveness of sins, St. Paul says, is the image of the invisible God, the firstborn of all creation, for in Him all things were created, in heaven and on earth, visible and invisible — all things were created through Him and for Him, so that He is the goal toward which creation is moving. He is before all things and in Him all things hold together (Col. 1:14-17). Christ Himself is the great hoop that circles the universe, the great parenthesis and bracket that unifies the diversity of things. The scope of these words is dizzying. It goes back beyond all history, all paleontology, all cosmogony, to the beginning of all beginnings, no matter how inconceivably remote in time that moment may have been. It spans the entire universe, beyond all solar systems, all galaxies, all quasars, and all the truth that there is in the still unverified and possibly unverifiable speculations of astronomers and physicists and mathematicians. It thrusts forward into time unimaginable, into a possible future where our extrapolations are meaningless and our very attempt at prophecy is ludicrous, a world possibly a hundred times more different from ours than the worlds of Mesillim of Kish or of Narmer of Abydos, the first genuinely historical monarchs of Akkad and Egypt, are different from the world of Richard Nixon and Heinrich Lübke and Gustaf VI Adolf. But in Him and through Him and to Him who gives us His body and His blood in the Eucharist this vast universe has its being and its meaning.

There is even more to it. When I quoted the first chapter of Colossians before, you noted that I omitted one clause. When St. Paul speaks of the created universe, he speaks not only of the things visible but also of the things invisible, and goes on: "whether thrones or dominions or principalities or authorities." He thinks here not only of the minions of malice but also of the unseen messengers of God. I do not pretend to know who or what the seraphim and the cherubim, the thrones, the dominations, the principalities, the authorities, the powers, the archangels, and the angels are. I know that conventional ideas about them are compounded at least as much of the speculations of Pseudo-St. Dionysius the Areopagite and St. Thomas Aquinas — and, in the English-speaking world, of John Milton — and of the desperate efforts of painters and sculptors to make the unseen visible, as they are of the sometimes restrained and sometimes apocalyptically exuberant imagery of the Sacred Scriptures. But whoever and whatever these invisible powers are, they are. The church has been particularly aware of them as she gathers about the altar of the Eucharist ever since the Holy, Holy, Holy became a part of the canon. This chant evoked the image of the heavenly temple with the angels and archangels and all the seven other ranks of celestial militia ("the company of heaven"), adoring the Lord of the angelic armies with theologies that will never cease (*asigetais theologiais*).

In our era and in our culture where we are so uncomfortably aware of a drift toward the demonic, a list toward nonbeing, a flight from integrity toward disintegration and a centrifugal thrust toward undisguised nihilism, we need as the church to be able to affirm that our whole universe hangs together in Christ. Human beings need the assurance that their world is not a gigantic accident or worse, or that their environment is not dominated by a cacodaemon, but that in spite of the malice of the world rulers of this present darkness (Eph. 6:12), as the New Testament personifies the forces of evil, this is our Father's world, which He made through and for His son. The same Word through whom He made the universe, sitting not only as God but also as a human being at the right hand of the divine power (to use the Biblical metaphor), is holding it together and is making ultimate sense of its terrifying absurdities. "Nothing," blessed Martin Luther reminds the readers of his *Vom Abendmahl Christi Bekenntnis* (1528) (and it is not immaterial that he is moved to say so in a discussion of the Eucharist), "is so small but God is still smaller, nothing so large but God is still larger; nothing is so short but God is still shorter, nothing so long but God is still longer; nothing is so broad but God is still broader, nothing so narrow but God is still narrower; and so on. He is an inexpressible being, above and beyond all that can be described or imagined" (*Weimarer Ausgabe*, 23, 339, 39-340, 2; *Luther's Works*, 37 [Philadelphia: Muhlenberg Press, 1961], 228). Because the Christ of the Eucharist is God as well as one of us, this can be affirmed with equal propriety of Him.

III

Because we eat the body and drink the blood of this cosmic Christ, we are bound in Him to His concerns. Because He is preeminently the man who is the model of all men, nothing human is alien to Him. Everything in history, everything in the present, and everything in the future is part of the experience of Him who is the same yesterday, today, and forever. There is no achievement of the human spirit that is not His triumph; there is no disaster that involves human beings that is not His grief. By the same token there is no achievement of the human spirit that is not our triumph, and there is no disaster that involves human beings that is not our grief. The difference is that our time-frame is our short life, our scope the limited personal universes of which we are a part.

There is likewise a prominent element of vocation and opportunity and resources in all of this. Our Lord reminded His hearers on one occasion that there were many widows in Israel in the days of Elijah, but Elijah was sent only to Zarephath, in the land of Sidon, and that there were many lepers in Israel in the time of the prophet Elisha and none of them was cleansed but only Naaman the Syrian. While His immediate point was different, we may observe that even in His own incarnate ministry He did not heal all the sick in Israel or give sight to all the blind or raise all the dead. But we cannot let our limitations paralyze our concern. Granted that we do not all have the same vocational responsibility, the same financial resources, the same opportunities, the same information, the same experience, the same capacity for accurate evaluation, the same ability to foresee the results of various courses of action. A president of the United States can order the mobilization of resources that puts two men on the moon in a decade. A high court can enforce a policy of integration designed to end an epoch of separate and unequal systems of education. Another head of state can stand stubbornly in the way of peace even though it costs his country half a million dead. Or he can command the musicians, the poets, the dramatists, and the artists of his land to conform to a prescribed line, with confinement in a labor camp or a psychiatric ward as the alternatives. The head of a giant research organization can bring about the discovery of a vaccine that ends the threat of poliomyelitis to the children of the world. A charismatic leader can mount a literacy program that liberates millions from the bondage of ignorance. A politically influential corporation can pollute the air with poisonous fumes with impunity and another can clog a waterway with noxious wastes. You and I lack this kind of power individually. Yet, I could repeat, we cannot allow our relative impotence to paralyze such activity on behalf of positive goals as we can muster.

Everyone who eats the body and drinks the blood of the Christ through whom and in whom and for whom all things were made can, according to his vocation and influence and resources, conscientiously seek to redeem the area of his own influence for the Christ whose advent into the world had as its aim the destruction of the works of the adversary. The Christ who in His lifetime manifested Himself as the sworn enemy of injustice, of disease, of prejudice, of discrimination, and of exploitation is calling us to an imitation of Himself in these areas also. He calls upon us to use His gifts of creation with reverence and with the awareness that we have no moral right to exploit them at the expense either of our contemporaries or of the generations that will follow us. He calls us to a concern for minorities, the underprivileged, the disenfranchised, the handicapped, the ill, the lawbreaker as well as the administrator of the law, the perpetrator as well as the victim of violence, the people who rank as our political foes as well as those who rank as our political allies, and for have-not nations as well as for have-not individuals. He calls us to a concern for good government, for peace, for public decency and order, for integrity. He does so because He whose body we eat and whose blood we drink and whose slaves we are has a proprietary interest in these things.

The Eucharist is a symbol of the renewal of all things by Christ and in Christ. This is part of Christ's total sacramental design. By His own baptism He hallows Jordan and all waters to be a saving flood and an abundant washing away of sin. By His own union with His bride the church He reflects this great mystery in the union of every Christian husband with every Christian wife and, in a fainter refraction of the mystery, in every human union where every act of unselfish giving of oneself in authentic love, no matter how fleeting, mirrors His love for the world that He has reconciled to God. By His separation to His service of a man upon whom the Spirit's charism of priesthood is bestowed in the laying on of hands, Christ affirms His will that no potential harvest anywhere in the world be lost because of a lack of laborers — a point that the earliest Lutheran ordinals made very strongly. Through the reconciliation of the penitent in holy absolution He affirms that the door of hope and of rescue that the Holy Spirit opened in Baptism is never closed as long as life lasts.

Without invoking any improper kind of natural theology, the event of the Eucharist goes beyond any of these. For here our Lord takes bread, the product of seed mysteriously produced by the parent grain, scattered upon fields prepared by human labor, harvested and threshed by human toil (or at least through human ingenuity), gathered together and made one, ground up and baked and offered as the symbol of the total consecration of everything that the worshipers are and do and have (at least ideally and intentionally). Again He takes wine from who knows how many grapes, tended by careful hands as they grew on who knows how many vines, pressed and stored by the vintner, and offered as a symbol of the will to obey the Father after the pattern of the Savior whose perfect obedience compensates for our imperfect obedience and our disobediences. What our Lord thus takes is not merely the work of God's creation but the work of human hands and the application of human skills and human knowledge. The bread and wine of the Eucharist stand as it were as symbols of the whole sweep of human activity, from that frustratingly transitory labor that leaves no monument at all — trash and litter removed, floors swept and scrubbed, children's faces and hands washed and wiped in endless repetition, temperatures taken in a clinic, blood transfused, operations performed, and every other necessary but uneventful occupation — to those other human callings that create enduring monuments — structures built, sculptures fashioned, paintings limned, law codes constructed, machines manufactured, music composed, constitutions framed, empires established. Our Lord takes this God-given and man-made bread and wine and by His mighty Word makes it His body and His blood. In so doing He affirms His right by creation and conquest to all the creatures of God's hand, to all the fruits of human labor, and to all the orders and institutions of the universe. But He does more. In taking a particular loaf and a particular chalice of wine as the vehicles of His body and His blood, at random, as it were, He anticipates the time when all of the groaning and travailing creation will have achieved that freedom that is its destiny, when the power of futility and of sin over it will be broken and it will possess the transfiguring glory for which it now waits in hope with such eager longing.

IV

The Eucharist is the occasion for the church's intercession on behalf of all the world. It is at the Eucharist that historically the church has offered her most fervent "supplications, prayers, intercessions, and thanksgivings for all men, for kings and all who are in high positions, that we may lead a quiet and peaceable life, godly and respectful in every way" (1 Tim. 2:1-2). Consider the text of the liturgy itself. Take first the *Kyrie eleison*. In its present abbreviated ninefold or threefold form it is explicitly nothing more than the church's acclamation of the Christ who conquers, who reigns, and who rules. For its implicit significance we need not, however, go back to the divine liturgy of Eastern Christendom, of whose diaconic *ektene* ("fervent prayer") the *Kyrie* is the counterpart and the remnant. In the *Deprecatio Gelasii*, the "Entreaty of St. Gelasius," the late fifth-century bishop of Rome, we have an excellent example of a Western litany of intercession. It brings before God His holy church, His holy servants, those who minister about the altar, all the nations that worship the true God, those who rightly handle the Word of truth, those who discipline themselves in mind and body for the sake of the kingdom of heaven, godly princes and Christian armies, catechumens, those who engage in works of pious devotion, all who enter the holy precincts of the Lord's house, and all those who at a given Eucharist invoke God's compassion for themselves and their needs. But it also pleads for pleasant sunshine and timely rainfall, for gentle winds, and for the regular course of season upon season. It implores God on behalf of those whom human weakness, the enmity of spiritual evil, or the manifold errors of this present world have ensnared; on behalf of those who face dangers in their travels, the oppression of an unjust government, and the burdensome occupation of their land by the enemy; and on behalf of the Jews, the heretics, and the pagans.

While the ancient collects are commonly petitions of Christians for Christians, they remember that God governs all things in heaven and earth (Epiphany II), that in the Easter solemnity God has bestowed restoration upon the world (Easter Monday), that in the humiliation of His Son God raised up the falling world (Easter II), that God can be called upon to order the course of the world peaceably by His governance (Trinity IV), and that His providence never fails as it works itself out (Trinity VII). (The English Lutheran rite correctly sees the implications of this when it paraphrases the clause: "whose never-failing providence orders all things both in heaven and earth.") The collects ask for the grace to imitate St. Stephen, the first martyr, in praying for his murderers (St. Stephen's Day), and they recall that in the preaching of Blessed Paul the Apostle God was teaching the entire world (Conversion of St. Paul).

In the great intercession anciently appointed for Good Friday the congregation is invited to invoke God to deliver the world from all error, take away disease, ward off famine, open the prisons, set free those in bondage, grant a safe return to the wayfarers, health to the sick, and to mariners a harbor of security. The petition that corresponds to this bidding commends to God the prayers of them that in any tribulation or distress cry to Him, that in all their necessities they may mark and receive His manifold help and comfort. The prayer also pleads for schismatics, the Jews, and the heathen. In the admirable extension that the Good Friday Bidding Prayer received in the Lutheran community in the 16th century, the prayer for peace called upon the Lord of heaven and earth, by whose Spirit all things are governed, by whose providence all things are ordered, the God of Peace and the author of all concord. It pleaded explicitly for the enemies of the church, for the fruit of the womb — God's own creatures — and for the fruits of the earth. This last petition recalls that through His Word the Father has created and blesses and upholds all things, and on that basis demands the grace that makes possible His blessing on all the fruits of the earth.

We remember that Luther revived the litany in the Lutheran community in 1529 because of the threat from the East to the Holy Roman Empire as symbolized by the siege of Vienna. He saw it not only as a threat to the religious values and institutions of the West, but as a threat to all the institutions and all the values that the West cherished. We remember too that the scope of this intercession included all kings and princes and the emperor, all those in affliction and peril, mothers-to-be, children, those who are ill, captives, widows, and orphans, the church's enemies, persecutors, and slanderers, the fruits of the earth, and in an unlimited sweep, the mercy of God upon all men.

Our vernacular translations occlude what was intended to be another occasion in the liturgy for praying for more than the church. From the tenth century on the final *miserere nobis* of the *Agnus* had increasingly given place to the plea: *Dona nobis pacem.* We spiritualize it and render it: "Grant us your peace." But it is worth noting that there is impressive evidence that while the initial impetus for this change may have originated in the *Pax Domini* and the kiss of peace that preceded the *Agnus,* it was the political situation that led to the retention of this plea for peace in all its forms.

V

The Eucharist is part of our preparation for service to the whole world. In giving us His body and His blood, our Lord is uniting us with Himself. In a real sense He is reconciling us to God. He is imparting to His God's own divine life. He is saving us, that is, He is rescuing us from our fallenness, our lostness, our isolation, and our alienation, and giving us in this age a part of that independence and power and wholeness that will be ours totally when He once more manifests Himself at the great epiphany. This is ultimately what we mean when we say that "forgiveness of sins, life, and salvation" are there for us in the Sacrament of the Altar. The Holy Eucharist is not the only channel of the Holy Spirit, but it is a unique one from which we cannot dispense ourselves. Here, even though not here alone, we receive the strength that we need in order to convert merely making a living into a Christian vocation. Here, even though not here alone, God gives us the encouragement that we need in order to look beyond the shrunken horizons into which we perenially slip. Here the eating of our Lord's body and the drinking of His blood are a part of our sacrifice of praise and thanksgiving. Here we have the divine remedy against sin, flesh, devil, world, death, danger, and hell, and a bestowing of grace, life, paradise, heaven, Christ, and God, the *Small Catechism* (Preface 23) affirms. Here — to cite the *Large Catechism* — we have a safeguard against death and all misfortune, a food of the soul, nourishing and strengthening the new man; a daily pasture and sustenance, a refreshment of our faith in the battle of life; a consolation of overburdened hearts; a treasure from heaven; a precious antidote against the poison of weakness; and a pure, wholesome, soothing medicine that aids and quickens us in both soul and body (Sacrament of the Altar 22-24.27.66.68.70). Here we receive the bread and the flesh that the Son of God gave for the life of the world. In our participation in his holy sacrament He makes present again for us His saving death and His life-giving resurrection. That death on a cross, He Himself tells us, was to be the means by which He would draw the whole world to Himself. In the power of that death in our lives we too can rise above the fears and the apprehensions and the selfishness that threaten to paralyze our witness in word and in work and can become the agents of Christ in our own individual universes of influence that Christ calls us to be. It is not an accident that eucharistic renewal and a renewal of the church's awareness of her servant role in the world outside the walls of her buildings have always tended to go hand in hand, and that liturgy and a sense of awareness of the Christian responsibility for society have so often accompanied one another. It was a profound sense of the way things are that moved the third-century church in Africa to modify its rigorist refusal to communicate penitent apostates and *libellatici* and in the face of a new wave of persecution to seek to give its probable victims all the resources of courage and strength and fortitude that the church had in her hands. The power of the Eucharist to strengthen and fortify 20th-century Christians for their witness has not diminished.

VI

The fellowship that the Eucharist creates is universal. The church in which and by which the Eucharist is celebrated is not the totality of those whom Christ by His atoning death has reconciled to the Father, but neither is it something that exists in isolation from the total community in which it witnesses to the presence of Christ. The church may include a large percentage or a very small percentage of a nation or a tribe or a territory or a culture, but the entire culture and the entire territory and the entire tribe and the entire nation is present in the church. Because the fellowship that the Eucharist creates binds in one all those who ever ate and drank in it, who eat and drink in it, and who will ever eat and drink in it, *donec veniat* ("until [Christ] comes"), it is a universal fellowship and community. There is no race outside it, just as there is no racial difference within it. There is no nationality that is not represented in the people of God. There is no language in which the words "Take, eat, this is My body.... All of you drink of it, this cup is the new covenant in My blood" are not spoken. There is no culture whose art has not been drawn on to glorify the King that comes in the name of the Lord. There is no ideology that has not had to yield to Christ in its total demand upon persons whom this sacrament has nourished. There are no divisions that it has not transcended — the unnatural barriers that the Tower of Babel account attributes to the divine judgment upon human *hybris;* the hatreds that have been generated and diligently perpetuated for generations and for centuries; the walls, sometimes of brick and mortar and barbed wire and sometimes of more tenuous stuff, that have been built to divide nations and cities and families; the bitterness created by the conqueror's oppression of the vanquished; the wars that have been fought, sometimes for literally no better reason than the War of Jenkins'

Ear, that had England declaring war against Spain in 1739 and involved the British in the War for the Austrian Succession until 1748; the national guilt felt by countries that in periods of crucial challenge remained neutral or even supported a less just side out of considerations of craven fear or greedy avarice.

The fellowship of the Eucharist, the fellowship of the one body that Christ creates through the one loaf, transcends them all. I am not suggesting that a Christian does not share in the feelings of the larger society of which he is a part. He is always a child of his age, influenced by his own environment, diverted by the biases and prejudices that pervade his world, propagandized by mass media that are never wholly neutral, solicited to make moral decisions in terms of selfish advantage. But these do not have the final word in the Christian's commitment. The Eucharist transcends these and makes us in our dividedness and separation one body in Christ. Its thrust toward unity is more powerful than the divisive elements that fragment our world and our lives. The God who is one is finally stronger than the demons that are legion. And ultimately even those who build the fences of race and nationality and language and ideology and denomination around the altar of Christ must, whether they will or not, suffer themselves to be united with those whom they seek to exclude. For the altar of the Eucharist is one and its fellowship is one and its communion is one and the body that it creates is one.

VII

Because the sacrifice that is made present again in the Eucharist avails for the reconciliation of the entire world with God, our own task is clear. We need to communicate the good news of God's act in Christ to those whom it affects, that is, to all men. Communication calls for more than speaking. We do not necessarily communicate when we use the jargon into which we as theologians or as pastors fall quite naturally. We do not even communicate when we use the alien vocabulary and the alien repertoire of metaphors even of the Sacred Scriptures, precious as this vocabulary and these metaphors invariably become to a Christian. Somehow we need to say in a plain and intelligible way that every individual whom we meet in existential contact is a redeemed and forgiven child of God. We need to make it clear that he is not one who is still to be saved (except in the exclusively subjective sense of the term), but one who is saved. Somehow we need to say exactly what St. Paul sensed as his message: "Be reconciled to God. Know that He reconciled you to Himself as part of the one world. Become what you are."

In all this we must not think of ourselves as in any sense bringing Christ where He is not already. It is His all pervading Holy Spirit that we hail as Creator and Recreator. We know, in the words of the Augustana, that in His exaltation Christ sits at the right hand of the Father forever to reign and be Lord over all creatures (3,4). We know that He calls all men to brotherhood and that He is latently present wherever, even at a "secular" or "profane" level, the ideal of brother-hood is anywhere or at any time achieved. (By the same token, the existence of the denial of brotherhood is a mark of the active presence of the demonic forces that our Lord came to destroy.) We know that He who is the truth and the faithfulness of God is at least latently present wherever there is any kind of truth and any kind of faithfulness. And we know that He through whom God made all good things for human beings to use and to enjoy and to share is latently present wherever there is any unselfish sharing, just as He who will judge the world in justice at the end of time is present wherever there is justice, that He who is God's Word of pardon to the world is present latently wherever there is any forgiveness, and that He who gave Himself as a sacrifice for the sins of all the world is latently present in every act of generous self-sacrifice.

It is our task in humility, in holy reverence for His world, in the kind of love for our fellow human beings that echoes the love with which He loved us, and with the joy that is His special gift to His own, to take seriously what He is, what He has done, what He does, what He will do, and what He gives us when He lets us, His frail brothers and sisters, eat His body and drink His blood and makes us thereby one with Him and with one another and with all those whom He has reconciled to God.

LIGHT AND GLORY:
Devotional Reflections On
The Holy Gospel For February 2

The Gospel account of the presentation of our Lord Jesus Christ and the Purification of the Blessed Virgin Mary sets four people before us. We shall look at them in turn: first at our Lord Himself; then at the Blessed Virgin Mary; next at St. Simeon the Seer; finally at St. Anna the Prophetess.

I
St. Luke 2:22-32

Our Lord's role is passive, inevitably. Yet this is first and foremost *His* day, *His* feast. He is the Cause and Center of everything that happens, the Focus of universal attention. We are so used to the King James Version's account that we forget that the Holy Gospel begins in the original, "When the time came for *their* purification, according to the Law of Moses, they brought Jesus up to Jerusalem to present Him to the Lord." Thus the evangelist conceives the occasion as the purification not only of the Mother of God but also of our Lord, in the sense that it was His birth that occasioned the carrying out of the ancient rituals which the Pentateuch (Ex. 13:2 and parallels; Lev. 12) traces back to the decades of Israel's desert wanderings. It is our Lord who as the firstborn male child of His mother is holy to the Lord and whose release from His obligation must be bought for five shekels of temple silver. It is He whom St. Simeon takes up in his arms and hails God's Salvation and all mankind's Light. He for whom Saint Anna is to give thanks and about whom she is to speak to all who were looking for Jerusalem's redemption.

We may well be mystified that God let the event be recounted or even let it happen, because the purification and the presentation and the poor man's sacrifice of a brace of turtledoves were all so unnecessary. This was the one birth that called for neither a burnt offering nor a sin offering to restore the mother who offered it to her place in Israel's worshiping congregation, for in connection with this virgin conception and this virgin birth there was no impurity to be purged away. No presentation of the heavenly Boy was needed to acknowledge the obligation and the dedication and the consecration of this Child to God, for this was God's eternally chosen Servant, God's appointed Worshiper par excellence, no less the Incarnate Word because He wore the form of a slave. We have no record that either the Mother of God or St. Joseph paid the five-silver-shekel fee to secure our Lord's formal release from the priest's hand. But all the silver and all the gold and all the wealth of the world could not have bought His release from the priestly ministry that was the whole purpose and end of His mission — a lifetime of sacrificing His will to the Father's and an expiatory death on the cross as simultaneous Priest and Victim.

The Holy Spirit has left it to us to infer why the presentation and the purification took place. It obviously witnesses to our Lord's complete solidarity with our human kind. He had not merely assumed human nature and become *a* human individual in the world of men, to wit, the Son of Mary, or as He appeared to the world, the son of Joseph the artisan. He did more. Through His own people He identified Himself fully with mankind in sin, in alienation, under wrath, under the Law. "When the time had fully come, God sent forth His Son, born of woman, born under the Law" (Gal. 4:4). The apostolic proclamation had affirmed it. Now the evangelical record was illustrating it in its Spirit-stimulated recollection of what had happened in His holy infancy. He is our Brother all the way, not merely in the big aspects of shared human flesh and shared human blood but also, more subtly, in the homely aspects of religious and social ritual that in God's providence are the outward and visible signs of the inward and invisible bonds that tie men together.

But there is more to it, just as there is more to the Incarnation that a desperate demonstration on God's part that He feels sorry for our human plight. Whatever theologians may have to say about the absolute place of the Incarnation in God's design, in historic fact God used the Incarnation as a means to an end of redeeming us who were under the Law that we might receive adoption as children. At the very beginning, God lets His Son be publicly marked for His vicarious, representative ministry of expiation and reconciliation and liberation, and of that ministry we in our generation are still the beneficiaries. The presentation, like His circumcision and His Baptism, equally unnecessary by the canons of strict logic, are a part of His total obedience, part of all that He did and suffered for our salvation.

And when we go to God's temple to seek our purification and to make our offering, He is the only one whom we can set before our eyes and God's eyes. There is no other sacrifice that we can bring, just as even the pair of turtledoves or five shekels of temple silver were only tokens and types of His real offering. There is no sacrifice that we can plead except the one that He has brought. And when we present the symbols of our self-offering, our adoration, our prayers, our money, our good intentions, as our response to His generous gift, the only value these oblations have is what they derive from *our* union with Him. Our works are acceptable in any degree only because God has made us acceptable in His beloved Son. But in Him the same God who was pleased to note and to recall that at His Son's presentation He received a pair of turtledoves or two young pigeons is still pleased with our 20th century equivalents — as long as we really bring them through His Son and in His Son and with His Son.

II
St. Luke 2:22, 24,25,27, 28, 33-35

The first impression of St. Mary in the account before us is that of a thoroughly self-effacing person. If the ancient tradition is right and the first two chapters of the Gospel According to St. Luke ultimately go back to the lips of the Blessed Virgin herself, the significance of this appears all the greater. In the three sentences in which she is a subject of the verb she does not appear once by herself. "They" brought the holy Child up to Jerusalem, and the plural subject of the verb, unexpressd by a pronoun in the Greek original, is clearly St. Joseph and the Blessed Virgin. "The parents" bring the child Jesus into the temple to do for Him according to the custom of the Law. "His father and His mother" marvel at what St. Simeon says about the holy Child. She shares with her husband and her Son in Simeon's blessing, and she is singled out only as an object when St. Simeon, led by the Spirit, foretells the ministry and destiny of our Lord and predicts her own passion in connection with it. In brief, she exemplifies in her behavior the words that she takes on her lips: "My soul magnifies the Lord, and my spirit rejoices in God, my Savior, for He has regarded the low estate of His handmaiden; for behold, henceforth all generations will call me blessed" (St. Luke 1:46-48). She means what she sings. Do *we*?

The second characteristic that impresses us in this account is the determined earnestness of her piety. We have already reflected on the fact that the whole procedure here recounted was ultimately unnecessary. Whatever her insight into the mystery of salvation in which she was so vital a participant may have been, the temptation to dispense herself from these ceremonies must have been very real. After all, neither Law nor custom required her attendance in the temple. The redemption of the Son could be made before any priest. Even the mother's purification did not require her presence. That chore could easily be delegated to the ministering laymen who represented in the worship of the temple all the people who came from their district. Again, the ceremony was not particularly edifying. Liturgical efficiency experts had been at work, and a brisk commercialism pervaded the whole procedure. The price of the sacrificial turtledoves was calculated and announced once a month. The proletarian worshiper dropped the specified amount in chest number three in the court of the women. Once a day the chest was emptied, and half the contents was applied to sin offerings, half to burnt offerings. At the hour when incense was kindled on the golden altar, those who were present and the substitutes for those who were absent took their places, the sacrificial birds, were dispatched with practiced skill, and the congregation departed, their liturgical defilements removed. Whatever prayer and praise did come out of genuinely grateful hearts remained unspoken. The significant fact in this connection is that the Blessed Virgin did *not* dispense herself, and her insistence on personal participation even under the circumstances described says something about the way *her* heart was fixed. It is something that *we* can take to heart.

The third impressive fact about her in the narrative is her amazement at St. Simeon's *Nunc Dimittis.* As we have already suggested, the Sacred Scriptures do not satisfy the curiosity of theologians about the extent of the Blessed Virgin's insight into the divine plan for the world's salvation. Apart from unrecorded revelations which she may have had, St. Gabriel's words at the Annunciation, St. Elizabeth's words at the Visitation, and angelic revelations to St. Joseph, and the staggering events of Christmas Night had given her enough to ponder. That is not to say that there were no gaps in her knowledge, or to suggest that she might have formulated the Decree of Nicaea or have anticipated by 15 centuries Martin Chemnitz' *On the Two Natures.* David Chytraeus is giving way to historical hyperbole when in his *Onomasticum* he describes the first church council in the New Testament as the one attended by St. Mary, St. Joseph, St. Elizabeth, St. Zechariah and their intimates, which defined the mystery of the virgin conception of our Lord on the basis of divine interpretation of the events in which they have been participants.[1] Still, by any criterion, the Blessed Virgin Mother must have known very, very much. But with all that she knew, the marvel is that she could still marvel at what was said about her Son. And yet in secret of this holy wonderment is no secret; it is disclosed every time that the Gospel of the infancy tells us that she *kept* all these things *pondering* them in her heart (St. Luke 2:19,51). Here is the antidote to that spiritual disease from which we all suffer — that acedia, that spiritual torpor and apathy and sloth and laziness and coldness of heart — which lets our little knowledge grow weary so promptly and after so little time spent in reflection, and which makes so sated and so satisfied so soon. If we too should learn the secret of keeping and pondering in our hearts the mighty acts and words of God, we too might marvel more.

So much for the Blessed Virgin as subject. She has one important thing to teach us as object. The lesson is hid in the parenthesis that St. Simeon inserts into his mysterious oracle. After describing her Son as being set for the fall and rising of many and for a sign that is spoken against, he adds: "A sword will pierce through your own soul also." Therewith he enunciates a fact in the case of the Blessed Virgin Mary that 19 centuries of Christian experience allows us to generalize into a principle: To be close to Christ involves getting hurt. St. Simeon is not talking about the pain of martyrdom, acute, brief, and glorious. No tradition of martyrdom surrounds the Virgin's falling asleep as the ward of St. John the Beloved either in Ephesus or in Jerusalem, and we do not read that a hand of violence was ever raised against her. The sword Saint Simeon foretells is not the efficient blade of the Roman legionary, but the barbarous, brutal, bloody, messy scimitar of the uncivilized Thracian. Hers was the slow sorrow, the protracted pain of seeing Him who was both her Son and her Savior misunderstood, misrepresented, deserted, hated, hounded, nailed to a cross as a common criminal, and mocked and blasphemed in the very hour in which He died to save His persecutors. The scimitar that pierced the Virgin's soul is still the occupational hazard of all those who walk in the company of her Son. If you belong to Him, it will be alternately poised over you and pressed into your soul as long as you live. It has no saving value in itself; our salvation, like that of the Blessed Virgin Mary, rests wholly on the atonement wrought by her Son. But when you feel the pain of the scimitar's piercing, rejoice, for this is one of the ways in which God is telling you that you are His.

III
Isaiah 25: 7-9; 46:13; 49:6, 52:7-10

The third of the four figures to whom the account of our Lord's presentation and the purification of the Blessed Virgin Mary directs us is St. Simeon the Seer. It would be asking too much of flesh and blood to expect that the devout reflection of succeeding generations of Christians would leave this austerely mysterious figure, who appears here and here alone in the sacred Record, unembroidered by pious fancy.

Thus the fabricators of apologetic but apocryphal gospels, like that ascribed to St. Nicodemus, gave him two sons, Charinus and

Leucius, who allegedly were raised from the dead, were summoned before the Sanhedrin, described before Israel's high court their experiences in the underworld at the death of our Lord, and eventually saw their narrative ordered and incorporated into the official register of the acts of the procuratorship of Pontius Pilate.

When a few centuries later the veneration of the saints began to find expression in the cult of their relics, the body of St. Simeon was conveniently discovered, translated to Constantinople, and ultimately shared with the Western Roman Emperor Charles the Great. At Aix-la-Chapelle, in consequence, the arm was exhibited against which the holy Child nestled while St. Simeon recited the *Nunc Dimittis*. Rival relics came into being, a whole body at Zara in Yugoslavia, another whole body in Bavaria, a head in Brussels, and in the words of a distinguished hagiologist of the last century, "numerous other relics, mostly arms, elsewhere."[2]

A somewhat more sophisticated and scholarly version of the same spirit has ransacked the history of Jewry in the beginning of the Christian era and identified him with the eminent Rabban Simeon, who appears in the Talmudic tractate Shabbath as the president of the Sanhedrin between the administrations of Hillel and Gamaliel, an identification that several commentators justly describe as "precarious."

The fact that the person of Simeon remains an enigma, possibly as a providential reminder that the prophecy is more important than the prophet, the message more important than the messenger, and the Word of God more important than the preacher.

Let St. Simeon be remembered for what the sacred page tells us about him. One thing it does not say, and that is that he was old although he may have been. It does characterize him by adjectives that express the ideal of Old Testament piety — devout, righteous, looking for the consolation of Israel. In an exceptional degree he was endowed with and responsive to divine inspiration. Within the span of 29 words in the Greek text of St. Luke 2: 25-27 the Holy Spirit is mentioned three times — "the Holy Spirit was upon him," we are told; "it had been revealed to him by the Holy Spirit that he should not see death before he had seen the Lord's Christ;" in the Spirit {RSV margin} he came into the temple" at precisely the moment when the Blessed Virgin Mary and St. Joseph brought in Our Lord. To complete the portrait, we have his own self-image in the opening words of the *Nunc Dimittis*. The term he uses of himself is *doulos*, slave; the term he uses of God is not *kyrios*, the usual word that we render with "lord," but *despota*, "slave owner," and the indicative verb is *apolueis*, that is, "*manumit*, emancipate, set free." The picture is strikingly that of the petition in the collect for Christmas Day: "Grant that the new birth of Thine only-begotten Son in the flesh may set us free, who are held in the old bondage under the yoke of sin."

St. Simeon's credo finds expression in the hymn that he recites and the oracle that he utters. His God is a God who saves, and the salvation that the Seer affirms is one that God has prepared in the presence of all people as a witness that His plan embraces the whole wide world. The Christ of his faith is one in whom there is no East or West, no North or South. He is the Redeemer not merely of a chosen race but a Redeemer in whom all races become chosen peoples, a light both for the tearing away of the veil that kept non-Jewish world in dark ignorance of God's will and for the restoration to Israel of the blue radiance of the vanished cloud of glory that once dwelt behind the curtain of God's sanctuary.

Furthermore, St. Simeon's faith is tempered by a sober and holy realism. The Messiah is set forth for the fall and rising of many in Israel, a stone of stumbling and a rock of offense, a prodigy and a phenomenon of such dimensions that Israel could not ignore it, but of such a character that it would scandalize the Messiah's compatriots before imparting to them the power to rise and take their stand upon it. The Messiah is to unfurl a standard that will be a rallying point in the war between God and the prince of evil. But it will also be an ensign which attracts enmity both to itself and, as we have reflected, to those who would stand in its shadow. The Messiah is to be the Touchstone that will reveal the secrets of men's most intimate and ultimate loyalties.

Thus St. Simeon's credo becomes a literally improbable faith. A sensitive personality like his could not be unaware either of the general disillusionment and disappointment and secularization that marked the masses of Israel at the beginning of our era or of the tragedy of the proliferating sects that were draining off so much of what enthusiasm and moral earnestness there still remained. He would not have disagreed with the analysis of the situation three decades later that the fourth Gospel was to furnish retrospectively in two damning sentences at the end of the century: "The true Light that enlightens every man was coming into the world ... He came to His own home, and His own people refused to receive Him" (St. John 1:9,11). This was part of the unpromising picture. The other just as unpromising part lay in the fact that the divinely identified salvation was a six-week old Baby whose parents were a have-not artisan and his equally poor bride. The only assurance St. Simeon had was a word of God and enough contact with God to be sure of Him.

We have been told often enough by the social diagnosticians of our time that the confused second half of the 20th century is part of the post-Christian era. Precisely what the post-Christian era will bring is something that not even their prognoses make wholly clear. But whatever it is, it is not a roseate era of reassurance for the church.

These diagnosticians may be right. In any case it would be folly for us blandly to assume that they are wrong because we do not like the idea. But even if they are right, the prognosis is relatively unimportant. What is important is that the faith be carried forward by men and women like Saint Simeon, men and women who have the Word of God and enough contact with God to be sure of Him.

IV
St. Luke 2:36-38

L ike St. Simeon, St. Anna is something of a mystery. As far as the bare biographical facts are concerned we know just enough about her to whet our curiosity. What is this descendant of the so-called lost tribe of Asher doing in Jerusalem? Was it the prominence of her father Phanuel that makes the evangelist remember his name in describing her while forgetting her late husband's? Had she carried on in her person the tradition of the women of her tribe, uniquely remembered in Israel for their beauty as proverbially fit brides for monarch or high priest?

In a period that acknowledged no male prophet in Jewry and in a culture that tended to minimize the role of women in public, she was revered as a prophetess in the tradition of a Miriam, a Deborah, and a Huldah.

In an era when longevity was a much rarer phenomenon than it has become among us in recent years, she had achieved the venerable age of at least 84, and it may be the intention of the text to tell us that she had passed 100. Thus her lifetime spanned the entire sad epoch of the Roman occupation of Israel, and old Abbot John Bengel of Alpirsbach calculates that she was 24 when Pompey's armies took the Holy City.

In a religious tradition that generally discouraged asceticism, she is remembered for her fasting and prayers in the temple night and day. In a social environment that brought strong pressure on young widows to remarry she had chosen at a relatively youthful age — at most in her twenties — to defy the pressure and to live in holy widowhood. At the time when the worship of the temple was becoming to a notorious degree self-righteous, self-satisfied, coldly mechanical, and crassly commercialized, she pinned her faith and her hope, and she addressed her worship, to a God who would presently act to accomplish the redemption of Jerusalem by His intervention.

It is this astonishing woman who suddenly appears in the temple at the very hour that St. Simeon takes the holy Child from the arms of the Mother of God. The closing words of St. Simeon's blessing on the Holy family merge into the anthem of praise with which St. Anna the Seeress gives thanks to God for the coming of the promised Christ. The verb implies no single paean. Instead it indicates that she kept on doing it, just as she kept on speaking of the holy Child to the company of those who were not merely hopeful but expectant about the early advent of Jerusalem's redemption. How great the circle of these waiting and watchful worshippers was we do not know; to justify the word "all" the number must have been considerable. In any case it was a circle whose faith in the God who saves was kept alive — as our faith is — by mutual witness and by common worship.

Besides the necessity of this mutual worship and witness, St. Anna has one other thing to teach us. Christianity is by nature and by divine design a conservative faith, carefully concerned about transmitting unchanged from one generation to another the unalterable Gospel of a Redeemer who died and rose again for all of humanity in every generation. As long as it does not make our witness irrelevant, this conservatism is not to be confused with conventionalism, that professional disease of the vocationally religious which refuses to recognize the validity of any mode of serving God for which it has no carefully labeled pigeonhole. Conventionalism has no place for St. Annas.

Happily, an unconventional church, with nothing but St. Luke's account to go on, reserved a place for her in the *Martyrology* — the church's chronicle of her witnessing members — for Sept. 1: "At Jerusalem, Blessed Anna, prophetess, whose sanctity is revealed in the Gospel." With the church, not only on Sept. 1 or on Feb. 2, but at all times and in all places, we give thanks to God for St. Anna and for all who, conventional or not, are bound to the service of our Lord by the ties of the same faith and the same hope and the same love that bind *us* to Him.

ENDNOTES

1. *"Prima Synodus Novi Testamenti fuit congressus Mariae, Elizabeth, Zachariae et aliorum, in quo promulgatus est Articulus de concepto et iuxta promissiones patribus datas exhibito Messia Redemptore, Luc. 1."* From the *"Catalogus Conciliorum"* appended to David Chytraeus, *Onomasticum theologicum recens recognitum* (Wittenburg: [Clemens Scheidt et Antonius Schön], 1578 [1577]) p. 895.
2. Sabine Baring-Gould, *The Lives of the Saints*, 3d ed., XI (Edinburgh: John Grant, 1914) p. 165.

SACRAMENT, SACRIFICE AND STEWARDSHIP

The thesis of this paper is four-fold: 1) Whenever God through the Church imparts His grace to human beings in the Sacraments of Holy Baptism and Holy Communion, He empowers in and expects from each recipient of His grace a response in the form of sacrifice, understood in the broad sense of "an action (*ceremonia*) or work which we give to God to do Him honor" (*Apology of the Augsburg Confession* XXIV, 18). 2) This sacramental gift of God and our sacrificial response stand in the relation of cause and effect, even though there need be no interval between the two. 3) This rhythm of sacrament and sacrifice finds expression in the historic rites in which the Church — and specifically the Churches of the *Augsburg Confession* — administers these Sacraments. 4) This double movement of sacrament and sacrifice deserves serious attention in our stewardship training efforts.

There is a widespread impression among Lutherans that "sacrament" and "sacrifice" are mutually exclusive concepts, that if a rite or an action is a "sacrament" it cannot be a "sacrifice" and vice versa.

In Lutheran theology this is not necessarily the case. At this point let me illustrate with a single example. The preaching of the Gospel in a sermon is by common consent a "sacramental" action, the effective offer and communication of the divine forgiveness to men by one of God's responsible ambassadors. Yet in Lutheran theology sermons are called sacrifices. *The Apology of the Augsburg Confession* (IV 190) declares in so many words: "The sermons ... of St. Paul the Apostle, of St.

Athanasius, of St. Augustine and of others who like them taught the Churches are ... authentic sacrifices that God accepted."

This is not merely Lutheran doctrine. It is Biblical doctrine as well. In Romans 15:16, St. Paul asserts that grace was given to him by God "in order that I might be the priest of Jesus Christ to the nations, ministering the Gospel of God in priestly fashion, so that the sacrifice of the nations might be acceptable, being made holy by the Holy Spirit." The word rendered "priest" in this passage is *leitourgos*, from the same root that occurs in our word "liturgy." It designates the officiating priest at a public sacrifice. The word rendered "ministering in priestly fashion" is *hierourgon*, "one who performs sacred rites, one who sacrifices." The word rendered "sacrifice" is *prosphora*, "the presenting or sacrificing of something." When the *Apology of the Augsburg Confession* quotes this passage (XXIV 34) it renders it: "I sacrifice the Gospel of God, that the oblation of the nations might become acceptable, sanctified by the Holy Spirit, that is, that the nations might be sacrificial victims acceptable to God through faith, etc."

We can make parallel statements in connection with the administration of Holy Baptism and the celebration of the Sacrament of the Altar, and if we want to understand the fulness of meaning that Holy Baptism and the Sacrament of the Altar have in the Lutheran Church's theology and practice, we need to consider not only the so-called "sacramental" but also the so-called "sacrificial" aspects involved in the administration of these Sacraments.

If this does not appear immediately, part of the difficulty may be terminological. Some definitions are accordingly in order.

Of the three words in our title, "Sacrament, Sacrifice and Stewardship," the latter two occur in the Sacred Scriptures.

Starting with the last, "stewardship," we have here a concept that occurs frequently in narrative portions of both the Old and the New Testament (for example, Genesis 43:19; 44:4; St. Matthew 20:8; St. Luke 12:42; 16:1-4,8). The "steward" is the estate owner's business manager. The term is used four times in the New Testament in a figurative sense. In three places (1 Corinthians 4:1,2; Titus 1:7) it is applied to the clergy, to stress the point that their relation to God on the one hand and to the Christian community on the other is that of the owner's business manager. In the First Epistle of St. Peter all the readers are urged to "minister to one another the charismatic gift as each has received it as good managers of the varied grace of God" (4:10). This is as close as we come in the Sacred Scriptures to the conception that we habitually attach to the term "stewardship" when we use it in our circles today. Our stress on money and on resources of time and native ability is thus somewhat alien to the literal sense of this one passage in which Christians in general are explicitly compared to "stewards" or "office managers," although something of this stress is implied in Our Lord's application of the parable of the unjust steward.

A somewhat similar fate has befallen the concept "sacrifice." Strictly speaking, it is simply a gift given to a deity. For a variety of reasons, however, we have come to attach to the term the suggestion of a selfishly interested motive.

Actually, of course, this idea is not necessarily implied in the Biblical concept of sacrifice. The Biblical concept is not a simple one to analyze, and any brief statement about so complicated a subject is bound to be something of an over-simplification. Nevertheless, looking at the idea of sacrifice in both covenants, the Old and the New, from the historical and theological vantage point of the New Testament, we can note a number of facts about sacrifice.

1) The most important point is that sacrifice is a *divine* institution. The sacrificial system as portrayed in the Old Testament was a legitimate part of the public worship of God because He Himself prescribed it. Sacrifice is a gift of God to His people through which He wills to pardon them. Sacrifice is particularly efficacious for violations of the covenant legislation, since it can restore the offender to the status of which his breach of the law deprived him. Again, sacrifices, notably the so-called "sin-offering," are thought of as covering over the offender's sins of ignorance, frailty and fickleness. We may also note that the so-called "guilt-offering" (called 'asham in Hebrew) furnishes the term to describe the sacrifice of the Suffering Servant: "When thou shalt make his soul" — that is, "His life or Himself" — "a guilt-offering, he will see his seed, he will prolong his days, and the purpose of the Lord shall prosper in his hand" (Isaiah 53:10). It is this ideal which Our Lord Himself picks up and combines with the picture of a ransom when He says that the Son of Man came "to give his soul" — that is, again, "His life, Himself" — "as a ransom for many" (St. Mark 10:45). And while some of the external forms of sacrifice have been abolished, the sacrificial principle persists in the New Testament. The New Testament knows not only the sacrifice of Christ, but also the sacrifices of God's people — precisely, St. Peter argues, because the Christian community is the New Testament Israel of God.

2) Specific sacrifices are gifts to God by which men acknowledge their dependence upon Him for everything. They are not given, at least not always and not wholly, with the purpose of receiving something from God in return. The motive of giving in order to receive is admittedly not entirely absent in the Old Testament, and even the New Testament exhibits some traces of it, but this motive is never dominant. Vow-fulfilment — to which the Old Testament so frequently exhorts its readers — is essentially a sacrifice of thanksgiving.

3) Sacrifice is a legitimate way of communicating with God. Sacrifice is worship, and in a sense genuine worship is always sacrificial. Sacrifice is always a *response* to God's initiative, but it is a legitimate and acceptable response. It is, we can say, the human answer in the dialog that God begins with man.

4) The external act of sacrifice is always symbolic of an inner disposition. In a sense the inner disposition is the real sacrifice, of which the external act is only an outward and visible sign, and so necessary is a right interior disposition that without it the external sacrifice is worse than valueless.

5) Sacrifice frequently involves the death or destruction of the thing offered, the killing of the animal victim, the burning of the incense, the pouring out of the libation. The idea is not that of presenting something dead to God, but of recognizing His absolute claim upon everything.

6) Sacrifices are holy, not in the sense that they possess the moral quality of sinlessness, but, by being offered and consecrated to the God Who as creator is separated from mortal man, they share in His "separate differentness" that is at the root of the word that we translate "holiness."

7) There is a prophetic quality about the Old Testamental sacrificial system. It points to a reality that is to come, that is to say, to Our Lord. Sacrifice is one of the pictures, although of course not the only one, that the New Testament uses in order to explain the "how" of Our Lord's atoning work. Thus it ultimately sees in every sacrifice of the Old Testament an antitype, a prophetic parallel, an anticipatory analogy of the great, decisive, once-for-all Sacrifice that took place on Golgotha. (St. John 1:28,36; 1 Corinthians 5:7; Ephesians 5:2; Romans 3:25 with its allusion to Exodus 25.) The whole Letter to the Hebrews, especially chapters 9 and 10, so interprets Our Saviour's atoning ministry. The picture of sacrifice is combined with the picture of ransom not only by Our Lord, as we have seen, but also in 1 Peter 1:18,19, "You were redeemed with the Precious Blood of Christ, like that of an unblemished and spotless lamb," and in Revelation 5, with its hymn to the mystic Lamb that was, as it were, slain from the foundation of the world, and that had bought His followers with His own blood.

The New Testament affirms the ultimate inadequacy of the Old Testament kind of sacrifice in two directions. First, it confirms the insight of the Old Testament which saw the various kinds of sacrifice as limited remedies availing only for sins of ignorance, frailty and fickleness, and inefficacious for the deliberate, "presumptuous" sins committed with "a high hand." Second, it recognizes that "it is not possible that the blood of bulls and goats should take away sins" (Hebrews 10:4).

We now come to the term "sacrament." This is really an exclusively ecclesiastical term, which theologians from time to time have defined in different ways. This is one of the reasons why the number of Sacraments varies from period to period and from denomination to denomination. Medieval Latin theologians defined the term "sacrament" in one way and came up with seven sacraments. The Lutheran Symbols used different definitions and came up with three (Holy Baptism, Holy Communion and Holy Absolution) or four (by adding Holy Ordination) or five (by adding Holy Matrimony as a sacrament that God ordained in the Old Testament) (*Ap[ology]* XIII 3.4.9-14). Again, when our Synodical Catechism adopts the definition of seventeenth century Lutheran Orthodoxy (Q. 242), it comes up with two. Clearly, these are not things to quarrel about, as the *Apology of the Augsburg Confession* (XIII 2) reminds us.

The classic Lutheran definition of "sacrament" and "sacrifice" in their relation to one another you will find in the *Apology* (XXIV 18): "A sacrament is a ceremony or work in which God conveys to us what the promise attached to the ceremony offers ... A sacrifice on the other hand is an action (*ceremonia*) or work which we give to God to do Him honor."

Thus in our title "sacrament" reminds us of God's gift, "sacrifice" of our response, and "stewardship" of the practical expression of our sense of sacrament and sacrifice.

I

We turn now specifically to Baptism.

St. Matthew 28:19 describes Holy Baptism as part of the process whereby the Apostles and after them the Church were to make disciples of all nations. In this passage Baptism in the Name of the Father and of the Son and of the Holy Ghost implies the benefits and privileges which this Sacrament confers (the sacramental side), while the human response of observing all that Christ has commanded the Eleven connotes the responsibilities (the sacrificial side) that discipleship carries with it.

From ancient times the Church has understood St. John 3:5,6 as a reference to Holy Baptism: "Truly, truly I say to you that if a person is not born out of water and Spirit, he cannot enter the Kingdom of God," with the clear inference that one who has the new birth out of water and Spirit can and does enter the Kingdom of God.

"Let everyone of you repent and be baptized upon the Name of Jesus Christ for the forgiveness of your sins, and you shall receive the gift of the Holy Spirit," St. Peter told his audience on the first Pentecost (Acts 2:38). "Let yourself be baptized and wash away your sins," St. Paul remembered that St. Ananias had told him in Damascus (Acts 22:16). Elsewhere in the Book of Acts, Holy Baptism is the inevitable way in which people enter the Christian community - the treasurer of Queen Candace of Ethiopia (Acts 8:38), Simon the Magician and his followers in Samaria (Acts 8:12,13), Cornelius the Centurion of Caesarea and his household (Acts 10:48), Lydia of Thyatira and her household (Acts 16:15), the jailer of Philippi and his household (Acts 16:33), the first members of the Corinthian Christian community — SS. Crispus and Gaius and the household of Stephanas (Acts 18:8; 1 Corinthians 1:14,16; 16:15; cf. Romans 16:5) — and the disciples of St. John the Forerunner in Ephesus (Acts 19:5).

Cf. also Romans 6:3-11; 1 Corinthians 6:11; 12:13; Galatians 3:27; Ephesians 5:26; Colossians 2:12,13; Titus 3:5; Hebrews 10:19; 1 Peter 3:21.

There are many other passages in the New Testament that probably refer to Baptism, such as the repeated references to being born out of God in the Fourth Gospel and in the First Epistle of St. John, the white clothing promised to the victorious remnant in Sardis (Rev. 3:5) and the robes that the martyrs of the Apocalypse have washed white in the blood of the Lamb (Rev. 7:14), and the passages that speak of the Holy Spirit Whom God has given us as a pledge (2 Cor. 1:22; 5:5; Eph. 1:14), but we can justifiably limit ourselves to the explicit passages that we have already cited.

These passages the Lutheran Symbols synthesize when they say that by virtue of its combination with the divine word of Our Lord's institution the water of Baptism is correctly described as divine water, heavenly water, holy water, blessed water, fruitful water, and water of grace (L[arge] C[atechism] Baptism 14.17.27).

The Symbols echo the Biblical assertion that Baptism saves by declaring that "Baptism is necessary to salvation," and that "we must be baptized or we cannot be saved" (A[ugsburg] C[onfession] IX 1; LC Baptism 6) Baptism is "not a mere empty sign (LC Baptism 63). "The power, work, profit, fruit and end of baptism is this — to save ... To be saved, we know, is nothing else than to be freed from sin, death and the devil, and to enter into the Kingdom of Christ and to live with Him for ever" (LC Baptism 24-25). "Salvation is offered with Baptism," says the Apology (IX 2).

All this intends to affirm that through Baptism the atoning work of Our Lord Jesus Christ is made a present reality for us. The events of nineteen hundred years ago, His birth, His passion, His death on the cross, His rising to life again, become accessible to us. The once-for-all, objective reconciliation whereby God in Christ broke down the wall that separated men from Him by not counting their sins against them becomes our subjective possession.

According to the *Small Catechism*, "Baptism works forgiveness of sins, delivers from death and the devil and gives eternal salvation to all who believe this." Elsewhere the Lutheran Symbols tell us that Baptism gives us the grace of God (AC IX 2; LC Baptism 41). It brings about the rebirth without which all men propagated in the natural way since the Fall of Adam are condemned under the eternal wrath of God (AC II 2). It imparts the very life of God, because the Name and the Word of God are in Baptism (LC Baptism 27). Through Baptism we are initially received into the Christian Church (LC Baptism 2).

Baptism communicates the Holy Ghost with all His gifts to the person baptized (Ap IX 3). It is this fact which furnished both the *Large Catechism* and the *Apology of the Augsburg Confession* with one of their most potent arguments in favor of infant Baptism. The argument runs like this. To understand Sacred Scriptures the assistance of the Holy Ghost is absolutely essential. But the Holy Ghost is given in Holy Baptism. Now we observe that there are in the sixteenth century and there have been in previous centuries theologians who have understood the Sacred Scriptures. Blessed Martin Luther points to himself as a case in point; he sees as other cases in point the Czech martyr John Hus, the learned and pious Jean Charlier de Gerson, and St. Bernard of Clairvaux, the great Cistercian monk. Since the Church has not ceased to exist in the West, but on the contrary has continued to have theologians baptized in infancy whose understanding of the truth of the divine Word shows they had the Holy Spirit, infant Baptism must be both effective and pleasing to God (LC Baptism 49-50; Ap IX 3).

Holy Baptism, say the Symbols, gives us the entire Christ, God and man and makes us partakers of Christ's victory over death and the devil (LC Baptism 41). It snatches us out of the very maw of Satan (LC Baptism 83). It makes us God's own again; it takes away the guilt of sin and reduces its might over us (Ap II 35-36; LC Baptism 68-71; 75-77).

Baptism makes a mighty difference among men, the *Formula of Concord* (*S[olid] D[eclaration]* II 67) points out. "Since, according to what St. Paul teaches, all those who are baptized have put on Christ and are accordingly reborn, they now have an *arbitrium liberatum*, a freed will, that is, as Christ puts it, they have been made free again, because they not only hear the Word, but also can assent to and embrace it, even though very weakly."

"Through Baptism and the Holy Spirit [God] regenerate[s] and illumine[s] us ... [and] kindle[s] and effect[s] a beginning of the true knowledge of God and faith," says the same article (15.16).

"In Baptism there is brought free to every man's door such a treasure and medicine as utterly destroys death" — Luther is thinking of Isaiah 25:8 — "and preserves all men alive ... If I am baptized ... I shall be saved and have everlasting life both in soul and body" (LC Baptism 43).

So much for Holy Baptism as a sacrament in the Symbols.

But are we justified in talking about a sacrificial aspect in connection with Baptism? If we regard sacrifice as the human response to sacrament, as man's answer to God's grace, we unquestionably are, even though the primary thrust in Baptism is not sacrificial (cf. LC Baptism 35 and Ap XXIV 18).

Here a significant Biblical datum is the fact that in the schematic parallel which the New Testament draws between the Old and the New Israel, Baptism is the counterpart of circumcision. Baptism is obviously what St. Paul has in mind when in his letter to the Colossians (2:11-12) he talks about the circumcision not made with hands. While the whole thrust of this passage in its context is indubitably sacramental, circumcision in the *Old* Testament can be regarded as a kind of sacrifice, a symbolic offering to the God of the Covenant of part of the member by which human life is transmitted from one generation to another, as the acknowledgement of God's total claim upon the person so marked and upon all his powers. It is an ineradicable symbol of total dedication to the God Who wholly on His own initiative had offered his covenant to men. Similarly the persons who are baptized are forever dedicated to God by the circumcision not made with hands. In the words of 2 Corinthians 1:22, "God has sealed us." This underlies the consistent Christian conviction that a valid Baptism cannot be repeated. Repetition of a valid Baptism "would mean blaspheming and profaning the Sacrament to the highest degree," the *Large Catechism* (Baptism 55; cf. 78) affirms.

It is further worth noting that Our Lord Himself used the term "baptism" to describe His atoning passion and death for the sins of the whole world, the priestly ministry upon which He entered through His own baptism "to fulfill all righteousness." It is His Baptism — as the quotation of Isaiah 42:1 in St. Mark 1:11 shows — that identifies Him as the One in Whom the hymns of the Suffering Servant of the Lord find their ultimate fulfillment. It is His Baptism that identifies Him to St. John the Forerunner as the Lamb of God that takes away the sins of the world (St. John 1:29-34). Yet that Baptism, begun in Jordan, would not cease until all God's waves and billows had gone over Him on

Golgotha. "I have a baptism to be baptized with," the Gospel according to St. Luke (12:50) record Our Lord as saying, "and how I am distressed until it is over." What is more, he used the term "baptism" of the experiences that await the members of the Apostolic company (St. Mark 10:38-40).

Again, the term "firstfruits," with which St. Paul designates the early Corinthian converts, the household of Stephanas (1 Corinthians 16:15; cf. 1:16) and Epaenetus (Romans 16:5), is a sacrificial term, borrowed from the Old Testament. In the spirit of Romans 15:16, we can say that Baptism becomes for the minister of the Sacrament a means of offering a sacrifice to God, in that he consecrates and dedicates to Him those who are no longer to live for themselves but for Him Who for their sake died and was raised.

In the Lutheran Symbols, the idea that the administration of Holy Baptism involves sacrificial aspects is suggested by the Latin text of Article IX of the *Augsburg Confession*. Here we are told that "after children have been brought (*oblati*) to God through Baptism they are accepted into God's grace." The parallel passage in the German version reads: "(The children) through Baptism are surrendered to God and become acceptable (to Him)."

The question arises: Who is the subject of this action? We are not told. We have a clue in the *Taufbüchlein* of 1526, traditionally a part of Blessed Martin Luther's *Small Catechism* from 1529 on, where we are told that "the Christian Church carries in the little child and then confesses in consistent, indubitable language that the child is possessed by the devil and is a child of sin and disgrace, whereupon the Church pleads diligently for help and grace through the baptism that the child may become a child of God" (2).

Following this clue, we can say that the subjects of the action are the baptizing clergyman as the representative of the whole Church and the sponsors as the representatives of the local Christian community who are offering the child to God.

There are other elements in the *Taufbüchlein* rite that have a sacrificial ring about them. We think of the two exorcisms (11.15), regrettably absent from our own rite. These are designed to establish God's claim upon the candidate, and by the ordering out of Satan to affirm that the candidate is being set apart by Baptism from the common uncleanness that is the state of natural man. The sign of the Holy Cross upon the forehead and the breast (12) is the traditional Christian symbolic action of consecration, a setting apart for the service of God. "Receive him," the celebrant prays in the first (13) of the two prayers that follow the signing with the Holy Cross. The idea of separation finds expression again in the so-called "Deluge-prayer," where we still pray "that through this holy Deluge everything about him that he has inherited from Adam and that he himself has added thereto may be drowned and destroyed and that, separated from the number of those who do not believe, he may be preserved dry and safe in the holy ark of Christendom" (14). At the font, the officiant asks the child if he renounces the devil and all his works and all his being (18-22). After an affirmative answer through the sponsors to the interestingly formulated creed questions (23-25) and the further question, "Do you want to be baptized?" (26), the officiant is directed to take the child and immerse it in the font (27). Being immersed is a symbolic being put to death. After the Baptism the sponsors are directed to hold the child in the font, while the officiating priest puts on the child the white hooded cape that the Germans call *Westerhemd* and that is called "chrisom" in English, as a symbol of the fact that everyone baptized into Christ has put on Christ and His robe of perfection (29).

Granted that the *Augsburg Confession* probably thinks of the Church as the subject of the action of bringing children to God in infant Baptism, when we consider the sacrificial aspect of the baptismal rite we cannot overlook the sacrificial response that the candidate is called upon to make. Where the candidate is a child, the sacrificial response is not an act of his conscious will. The requirement is still there, however. We recognize this in our rite of Confirmation, when the officiant interprets the significance of what the candidates for Confirmation are doing in these words: "When you were little children, you were received into God's covenant of grace in Holy Baptism. And now ... you are gathered here before God and this Christian congregation publicly ... to confirm your covenant with Him, *to dedicate yourselves* body and soul for time and eternity to your God and Lord." (*The Lutheran Agenda*, p. 23.)

Part of this sacrificial response is the act of faith, the act of committing oneself wholly and absolutely to God's grace in Christ Jesus, the giving up of any dependence upon the works of righteousness that we have done or that we can do, the determination to cleave to Him in weal and woe and to regard everything that befalls us as a manifestation of His good and gracious will. Admittedly faith is the gift of God, not of works, lest any man should have something to boast about (Eph. 2:9). But even though faith is God's gift and utterly impossible without the Holy Spirit, it remains man's necessary response to God's grace, man's indispensable commitment of himself in freedom to the divine mercy. This highest worship of all, the worship of faith and hope, the desire to receive God's benefits, forgiveness of sins, grace and righteousness, is authentic worship, and in common with all worship in the New Testament, a genuine, if paradoxical, sacrifice (Ap IV 49.310; XXIV 25. 26. 29. 30). This is solidly Biblical doctrine. In Philippians 2:17 St. Paul speaks of the faith of the Philippians as an offering and a sacrificially rendered service, and of himself as the drink-offering poured out as a libation upon it.

Another aspect of the sacrificial response in connection with Baptism is related to the self's symbolic being put to death. Baptism, we repeat, is a mystical death of the person being baptized. The candidate is united to Christ in death, and as surely as Christ died on the cross the candidate dies with Christ to sin. And as certainly as Christ rose again from the dead on the third day, so certainly the baptized person rises to a new God-ward life that he did not know before, the life of God Himself. This is the clear teaching of Romans 6. It is also implied in Colossians 3:3: "You died and your life is hid with Christ in God." The dying and the rising to life again is not a mere picture; it is as real as the death and the resurrection of the Lord Jesus Christ. But what Baptism initiated must go on. "The old Adam in us must by daily contrition and repentance be drowned and die with all sins and evil lusts, and the new man must daily come forth and arise to live before God in righteousness and holiness forever." We all know the words; but we forget that the force of the German word that we usually translate "daily" does not mean "once a day," but "constantly, continually." The old man must die all the time. He does not die by himself. St. Paul has a number of words for the process. Two of them the *King James Version* translates "mortify" (Romans 8:13; Colossians 3:5). (The *Revised Standard Version* is more blunt with "put to death.") In Galatians 5:24, he speaks of "crucifying." The killing of the old self thus becomes the constant occupation of the Christian, until his death in this world ends the process. Let it be stressed that he cannot do it by his own powers in any degree, that he cannot do it without the Holy Ghost, but the fact remains that he must do it, by constant contrition and repentance. This constant slaying of the Old Adam in us is part of our sacrifice (cf. *Large Catechism;* Baptism 65-67).

A third aspect of the sacrificial response in connection with Baptism is the offering of our good works to God. This is an aspect on which Lutheran theology has often maintained an unwarranted silence. But there is a memorable passage in the *Apology of the Augsburg Confession* to which we do well to take heed. Very significantly, it occurs almost exactly in the middle of the great fourth article on the subject of the sinner's justification before God by grace for Christ's sake through faith. "On account of faith [the works which Christians do because they want to exercise their faith, because they want to confess their Christianity before the world, and because they want to show their gratitude to God] are holy works, divine works, sacrifices, and the ruling activity of Christ as He displays His kingdom before this world. We believe the same thing with reference to the individual good works that Christians perform in the humblest and most unpublicized occupations. Through these works Christ is trouncing the devil, so that when the Corinthians were making contributions for the relief of the poor it was a holy work and a sacrifice and a contest of Christ against the devil, who labors continually to prevent anything being done to the praise of God. And here we also add what we have to say about rewards and about merit. We teach that rewards are offered and promised to the works of the believers. We teach that good works are meritorius — not that they merit forgiveness of sins, grace and justification, for these things we obtain by faith alone, but that they merit other bodily and spiritual rewards in this life and in the life to come, because St. Paul says, 'Each one will receive a reward in proportion to his labor'" (IV 189-194).

We repeat, no one can do good works by his own innate powers, without the Holy Spirit; no one can do authentically good works acceptable to God until he himself has become acceptable by faith. But the Christian *must* do good works (AC VI 1; cf. F[ormula of] C[oncord], SD IV 14-18), and these good works are sacrifices acceptable to God, they are part of the constant coming forth and arising of the new man of which Baptism is the beginning. This too is solidly Biblical doctrine. We hear St. Paul tell the Philippians (4:18) that the gifts which they have sent him for his support at the hand of St. Epaphroditus are a sweet savor, an acceptable sacrifice, pleasing to God. We hear him implore the Christians at Rome to present their bodies through deliberate conformity to the will of God as a living sacrifice, holy, acceptable to God, their intellectual worship of Him (Romans 12:1). The First Epistle of St. Peter in the same vein calls upon its readers, because they corporately constitute a sacred priestly college, to offer spiritual sacrifices which are acceptable to God through Christ Jesus (2:5).

We are thus confronted with the paradox, the mysterious seeming contradiction that runs through all of Christianity, the fact that on the one hand God does everything and the equally indisputable fact that just as soon as the Holy Spirit has begun His work of rebirth and renewal in us, He requires us, in the might that the Holy Spirit supplies, to participate totally, with all our faculties, qualities and parts, in and at every stage of the process by which His Holy Spirit transforms us from sinners into holy people (FC SD II 65; XI 21).

What has all this to do with stewardship? Taking the term in the way in which we ordinarily use it, simply this. The people to whom we come with our appeals for the stewardship — the good management — of time and money and talents on God's behalf are baptized individuals. The handful of water that they have had poured on them (LC Baptism 15.36; but cf. 65) was divine water, heavenly water, holy water, a laver of rebirth. By it they have been united to the dying and rising Christ Who has offered Himself as a sacrifice for the sins of all men. Thereby they have been saved, they are being saved, and they will be saved. United by Baptism to the community of God they have received at God's hand the forgiveness of sins, the grace of God, everlasting life, God's pledge in the form of the Holy Ghost with all His gifts, the entire Christ, victory over eternal death, deliverance from the jaws of Satan, a new freedom of the will, the cancellation of the guilt of their native sinfulness, the faith that lays hold on God's gift. These things are theirs through Baptism as long as they live. They are the recipients of a divine sacrament.

At the same time, at their Baptism the Church — acting through the officiating minister and through the sponsors, and possibly through an entire worshipping congregation gathered as in the primitive Church about the Holy Eucharist — has brought them to God, dedicated and consecrated them to God for this world and for the world to come to be His own. God has selected them to be separated from the lost world of "Not-God's-People," and to become a part of His New Testament Israel, like Israel of old a chosen generation, a royal priesthood, a holy nation, a people purchased with an awful price.

Likewise, according to the teaching of the New Testament, the gift of faith communicated to them through the Holy Spirit, as they appropriate it and make it their own, becomes a sacrifice which they bring.

The good works which they perform through the power of the Holy Spirit Who has been given to them in Holy Baptism — the virtues that are the contraries of the vices that they are putting off continually with the Old Adam — these too are part of the continual sacrifice which they offer in Christ: the generosity, the gentleness, concern for others, the love for Christ and His Holy Church practically expressed, the willingness to forgive, patience in suffering, the deliberate mortification of the flesh through the exercise of self-control, the corporal and spiritual works of mercy, the life of witness and prayer and praise and intercession.

A major part of our task in stewardship thus becomes to make ourselves and one another realize the full meaning of God's sacramental gift in Holy Baptism and of our sacrificial response to it.

II

Now we turn our attention to the Sacrament of the Altar.

That the Sacrament of the Altar — or the Holy Communion, or the Holy Supper, or the Holy Eucharist, or the Mass, to use some of the other names that our Lutheran symbols give it — is a Sacrament needs no demonstration.

The term "sacrament," we remember, is a Church-word and not a Bible-word. It receives its definition not from the Sacred Scriptures but from theology. In Lutheran theology as determined by the Lutheran symbols, we have seen that a sacrament is a rite which God has commanded and to which He has attached a promise of grace (Ap XIII 15-17). Let us see how this definition works out in the case of the Holy Eucharist.

We Lutherans take it for granted that God, or more specifically, Our Lord Jesus Christ, instituted the Sacrament of the Altar on the first Maundy Thursday, and when St. Paul affirms, "as often therefore as you eat this Bread and drink the Cup you are proclaiming the Lord's death until He comes," we believe that he is by divine inspiration giving perpetual force to the injunction of the Savior, "this do in remembrance of Me."

The Words of Institution remain for us the basis of our doctrine of the Holy Communion precisely because they are the words of "our Lord and Saviour," of "our only Teacher," of "the eternal Truth and Wisdom itself," of "Almighty God," of our "Creator and Redeemer, when He is just beginning His bitter suffering and death for our sins," as the *Formula of Concord* (SD, VII, 43-45) puts it. For that reason, "we unanimously reject and condemn ... the doctrine that the words of the Testament of Christ must not be understood or believed simply as they read, but that they are obscure expressions, whose meaning must be sought first in other passages of Scripture" (FC Ep VII 21.25).

The first thing that God gives us in the Sacrament is His Son's Body and Blood. Usually we say that He gives us His Son's true Body and Blood, the word "true" being a kind of traditional theological shorthand symbol designed to say that the Body which we receive in the Holy Communion is the same Body to which the Most Blessed Mother of God gave birth in Bethlehem, which hung on the cross, which rose again on Easter Day, and which was taken from our physical sight in His glorious Ascension.

Like Baptism, the Holy Communion is one of the links that spans the centuries and that in 1961 makes the events of the first Maundy Thursday and the first Good Friday and the first Easter Day contemporary happenings. The Holy Communion is a means by which in the Church we appropriate to our individual persons the objective and universal pardon that is the pre-eminent benefit of Christ's Passion.

The Lutheran Symbols assert the identity of the Holy Communion at our altars with the Body and Blood of the Crucified and Risen Lord most emphatically and baldly and succinctly in Blessed Martin Luther's *Smalcald Articles* (Part Three VI 1) of 1536. Here, after he had made some deliberate changes in his original draft, Luther asserts: "The bread and wine in the Holy Communion is the true Body and Blood of Christ and is distributed and received not only by pious but also by wicked Christians." In the Sacrament the bread and wine is "such bread and wine as is the Body and Blood of Christ," says the *Large Catechism* (V 28). On account of the sacramental union, the bread and wine are truly the Body and Blood of Christ, says the *Formula of Concord* (FC Ep VII 7; SD VII 14). The "Lord's bread in the Supper is His true natural Body," says Blessed Martin Luther in his *Last Confession concerning the Sacrament of the Altar* (1544), a statement which the *Formula of Concord* (SD VII 33) appropriates.

If at times we Lutherans, in our Symbols and otherwise, use such non-biblical terms and phrases as "Real Presence," "sacramental union," "sacramental mutation" (John Gerhard), "in," "with," or "under," or any combination of these prepositions, of "substantially and essentially present," these are simply efforts on our part to ward off some misconception that has developed about the Biblical doctrine. We never intend thereby to give these more or less philosophical paraphrases primacy and priority over the Biblically based assertion, "The Sacrament of the Altar is the true Body and Blood of Christ."

Nor are we Lutherans satisfied with the simple statement that Christ is present in the Sacrament of the Altar — even if some adverb like "substantially" or "truly" is added. It is of course, not wrong to say that Christ is present in the Holy Communion. Our Symbols, for instance, say, "We speak of the presence of the living Christ, for we know that death no longer has dominion over Him" (Ap X 4; cf. FC Ep VII 17; VIII 17; SD VII 100). Again they say that "no one except an Arian heretic" — who rejects the Trinity and the true Godhead of our Lord — "will deny that Christ Himself, true God and man, Who is truly and essentially present in the Supper, should be adored in spirit and in truth in a legitimate celebration of the same" (FC SD VII 126). But side by side with this assertion that Christ is present in the Holy Communion must come the equally unqualified declaration that in the Holy Eucharist the bread and wine are His Body and His Blood. The *Formula of Concord* furnishes us with a simple test: "Do you believe that in the Holy Communion the Body and Blood of Christ are distributed with the bread and wine?" "Do you believe that in the Holy Communion all the communicants receive the Body and the Blood of Christ with their mouths, regardless of whether they are worthy or unworthy, pious or impious, believers or unbelievers?" If you can answer these questions with Yes, you are a Lutheran; if you cannot, you are not (FC Ep VII 2).

This Body and this Blood, says the *Large Catechism* (Holy Communion, 28-30), is the treasure that the Sacrament of the Altar imparts to us, for it is only through the Body and the Blood of Christ that forgiveness of sins has been achieved for us. This Body of Christ, it goes on to say, can never be an unfruitful and vain thing, static and useless, but a dynamic and powerful force in our lives, that communicates to us the forgiveness of sins in the most comprehensive sense possible (cf. Ap XIII 20).

If we understand the "forgiveness of sins" entirely in terms of the cancellation of the guilt of past transgressions, our conception of it is much too small. It is always much more. Let me recall to you the familiar words of the *Small Catechism*, "In the Sacrament forgiveness of sins, life and salvation are given us through these words, 'Given and shed for you for the remission of sins.' For where there is forgiveness of sins, there is also life and salvation." The *Large Catechism* (V 70) puts it this way, "In the Sacrament you receive from Christ's mouth forgiveness of sins, which contains and brings with it the grace of God and the Spirit with all His gifts, protection, shelter, and power against death and the devil and all misfortune."

Hence the Symbols describe the effect of the Sacrament of the Altar in many other ways. Through the Sacrament of the Altar we find comfort for our tortured consciences and learn to believe God and to expect and ask of Him all that is good (AC XXIV 7). The Sacrament of the Altar confirms our faith within us and enables us publicly to confess our convictions and proclaim the benefits of Christ (Ap IV 210). It calls to our mind the benefits of Christ in such a way that we receive His benefits and are made spiritually alive by them (Ap XXIV 72). It gives us the assurance that we are incorporated into and joined with Christ and washed with His Blood (FC SD VII 16; cf. Ap XXII 10). The Sacrament of the Altar is a remedy against sin, flesh, devil, world, death, danger and hell, and a communication of grace, life, paradise, heaven, Christ, God and everything good, says the *Small Catechism* (Preface 23). The *Large Catechism* (Holy Communion 22-24.27.66.70) calls the Sacrament of the Altar a safeguard against death and all misfortune, a food of the soul which nourishes and strengthens the new man in us, our continual pasture and sustenance, a refreshment of our faith in the battle of life, a consolation of overburdened hearts, and a precious antidote against the poison of weakness. In this Sacrament, the same document declares elsewhere (Holy Communion 32), the Word embodies and presents to us the entire Gospel and the article of the Creed that says, I believe one holy Christian Church, the forgiveness of sins and so forth. In yet another context, the *Large Catechism* (Holy Communion 68) asserts: "The Sacrament of the Altar is an altogether wholesome, comforting medicine, which helps you and gives you life both in soul and body." The official Latin translation expands the idea in these words: "It is a pure, salutary and useful medicine which heals your diseases and gives you life of soul and body." "For where the soul is healed," Blessed Martin Luther observes, "relief is afforded the body also."

"The Mass," says the *Augsburg Confession* (XXIV 30-33), "was instituted that the faith of those who use the Sacrament should remember what benefits it receives through Christ and cheer and comfort the anxious conscience. For to remember Christ is to remember His benefits and to realize that they are truly conveyed to us .... The Mass is to be used to this end that there the Sacrament may be administered to them that have need of consolation, as St. Ambrose says, 'Because I always sin, I am always bound to take the medicine that avails against it.'"

All this — and there is nothing more to give — God gives us in the Sacrament of the Altar.

The question to which we next turn is this: Is the celebration of the Holy Communion a sacrifice?

Admittedly, many of us, thinking in terms of vulgar Roman Catholic description and practice, would answer with a prompt "No."

It is well that we start out, therefore, by rejecting as energetically as our Symbols do the idea that the celebration of the Holy Eucharist is an expiatory sacrifice that can be applied for the sins of the living and the dead. The celebration of the Holy Communion does not confer grace by the mere performance of the rite (*ex opere operato*, in the sense in which this term was widely understood in the sixteenth century). When applied on behalf of others, alive or dead, it does not merit for them by the mere performance of the rite remission of venial and mortal sins, of guilt and punishment. "To apply the Holy Communion, which was instituted for commemoration and proclamation among the living, on behalf of the dead ... is to violate the Second Commandment by abusing God's Name" (Ap XXIV 11.93).

It should be noted, however, that this assertion does not completely rule out the idea of sacrifice. It says that no ceremony in the Church, even the celebration of the Holy Communion, is able by the mere performance of it to propitiate the divine anger or to expiate human sin. That is, no celebration of Holy Communion by the mere performance of the rite avails before God to compel or to cajole Him into looking favorably upon the desires of someone who is living or into shortening the pains of purgatory for someone who has already departed this present life.

But it does not reject the idea of sacrifice altogether. On the contrary, the section of our Symbols in which the sacrificial character of the Mass is most extensively discussed is precisely this same Article XXIV of the *Apology of the Augsburg Confession*.

After an introduction in which it affirms, among other things, that the Lutherans religiously retain and defend the Mass (1), the article proceeds to analyze the concept of sacrifice. We remember its basic definition: "A sacrifice is an action (*ceremonia*) or work which we give to God to do Him honor" (18). Basically, it goes on, there are only two kinds of sacrifices. The first is a propitiatory or expiatory sacrifice, offered to reconcile God, to placate His wrath, or to merit forgiveness of sins for others. The other kind of sacrifice is a eucharistic sacrifice, which does not merit remission of sins or reconciliation, but which is offered by those who have already been reconciled as a thank-offering for the forgiveness of sins that they have received or for other benefits that they have from God's hand (19).

Actually, the article asserts, there has been only one really expiatory or propitiatory sacrifice in all history, the death of Christ, the once-and-for-all sacrifice by which the sins of all mankind were atoned for and all mankind was reconciled to God. Ultimately all other acceptable sacrifices are exclusively eucharistic, that is, sacrifices of thanksgiving — the preaching of the Gospel, faith, calling upon God, thanksgiving, confessing one's convictions, the bearing of the cross by God's holy people, in a sense all the good works of God's faithful people. The proof for this Melanchthon sees in 1 Peter 2:5: "You make up a sacred college of priests, to offer up spiritual sacrifices," that is, spiritual in the sense that the Holy Spirit supplies the motive, in contrast to the animal sacrifices of the Old Testament as well as in contrast to a purely external kind of mechanical worship. He understands the word "rational" or "intellectual" in Romans 12:1 the same way: "Offer up your bodies as a living and holy sacrifice, a rational or intellectual worship," that understands and lays hold on God with the resources of the mind and understanding. Hebrew 13:15 seems to him to be decisively explicit, "Through Christ we offer the sacrifice of praise to God continually, that is, the fruit of our lips confessing His Name," specifically such things as calling upon God, giving Him thanks, and confessing our faith (22-26).

In sum, he says, the worship of the New Testament is spiritual, the righteousness of faith and the fruits of faith. While many passages in the Old Testament teach us that God cannot be mollified by the mere performance of ceremonies, there are passages which forecast the coming of a day when the sacrifice of praise will be offered throughout the world. One of these is Malachi 1:11: "From the rising of the sun in the East to its going down in the West, my Name shall be great among the nations, and everywhere incense and a pure oblation shall be offered to my Name." The Name of God becomes great through the preaching of the Gospel, which creates faith in those who accept it. These call upon God's Name, give thanks to Him, bear the afflictions that confession of their convictions involves, and do good works to Christ's glory. The Levitical sacrifices of the Old Covenant have their counterpart in the New Testament in the ministry of the New Testament Levites, the clergymen who preach the Gospel. Consequently the sacrifices of righteousness that the purged sons of Levi (Malachi 3:3) are to bring in the New Covenant are the preaching of the Gospel and its fruits, in the spirit of St. Paul's words that we have already quoted, "I sacrifice the Gospel of God so that the oblation of the nations might become acceptable, sanctified by the Holy Spirit." As part of the New Testament sacrifice of praise the *Apology* is prepared to include the celebration of the Holy Eucharist as spiritual worship, with the proclamation of the Gospel, the response of faith, the invocation and praise of God, and the reception of the Holy Communion (*ipsa sumptio coenae Domini*, 33). It is the memorial of the death of Christ that is the continual sacrifice of the New Testament, the proclamation of the Gospel and the faith that believes that through Christ's death God has been reconciled to us (27-40).

The *Apology* brings out a basic antithesis between the practice of the Lutheran community and the practice of the adversaries of the Papalist party. In contrast to a celebration of the Mass that is nothing more than the carrying out of a prescribed rite, without instruction or Communion, the Lutheran celebration of the Mass preserves the essence of the continual sacrifice through the incorporation of the preaching of the Gospel and the actual use of the Sacraments of Our Lord's Body and Blood. The Lutherans can claim better Church attendance and greater devotion than among the adversaries (41-51).

The *Apology* readily grants that the Fathers of the ancient Church described the Mass as a sacrifice. It has no quarrel with them, since they did not regard it as a propitiatory or expiatory or meritorius sacrifice, but as a sacrifice of praise and thanksgiving. The proof for this is the very name that they gave to the celebration of the Holy Communion, Eucharist, which comes from a Greek word meaning thanksgiving. The *Apology* insists that what the Lutherans say about the use of the Holy Communion in this connection is in full agreement with the Fathers and the Scriptures (66-67).

There are two things in a sacrament, the sign and the Word. The word is the promise of the forgiveness of sins. The sign is the eating and the drinking of Christ's Body and of the chalice of the New Covenant. Through both the Holy Spirit works to create faith, to put to death the old man, and to revive terrified consciences. This is the principal use of the sacrament (69-73).

But now the element of sacrifice enters in. Sacrifice and sacrament are not mutually exclusive. The same action can have several ends or purposes. The Holy Communion can free the conscience from its fears and create faith, its sacramental purpose, and then the celebration can be used for the praise of God, obediently to express gratitude and to witness that it magnifies the gifts of God. Thus the ceremony becomes a sacrifice of praise (74).

The *Apology* finds nothing offensive therefore in the statements of the Eucharistic prayer of the Eastern Orthodox Liturgy of St. John Chrysostom: "And make us to become worthy to offer to Thee prayers and supplications and unbloody sacrifices for the whole people ... Moreover we offer unto Thee this rational and unbloody worship" (88).

So far our analysis of *Apology* XXIV. The celebration of the Holy Eucharist is thus not without its sacrificial aspects.

Nor is this all we can say about it. Fully to appreciate some of the other sacrificial aspects of the celebration of the Holy Communion we need to call to mind the fact that in the primitive Church, as in the Lutheran Church for roughly two hundred years after the Reformation, the normal Sunday and festival act of worship of the Christian community was the celebration of the Holy Eucharist. Originally every communicant in the congregation received the Holy Communion with his fellow-Christians and if he were absent because of illness or because he had been imprisoned for his Faith, the deacons of the Christian community took the Holy Communion to him. We need to remind ourselves that the *Large Catechism* approvingly repeats the advice of St. Hilary of Poitiers to the effect that only they should absent themselves from the altar who had committed a sin for which they could be excommunicated and had not repented of it, lest — Luther adds —the absentees deprive themselves of life (LC Holy Communion 59). Our so-called "Morning Service without Communion" witnesses in its structure to the fact that what we really ought to be celebrating is *the* Service, which includes the Holy Communion.

We cannot afford to make the mistake that is often made, that of imagining that we can somehow separate the Church at work in the world from the Church at worship about the altar of the Holy Communion. The whole work of the Church is eucharistic worship as long as Eucharistic worship remains an integral part of the work of the Church. By the same token the whole life of individual Christians in the world remains a continual *eucharistia*, or thanksgiving, as long as they have constant recourse, in the company of their fellow-members of the mystical Body of their Lord, to His Eucharistic Body and Blood. There is no dispensation from Our Lord's words: "Do this in remembrance of me!"

As a symbol of this insight, each communicant would anciently bring to the celebration of the Holy Eucharist a small loaf of bread and a small flask of wine. These were symbols of his self-dedication to the Lord of the Church. From these offerings enough loaves and wine would be set aside for the requirements of the Holy Communion, and the rest would be used for the relief of the poor. Later on these offerings were supplemented with other offerings, and finally, for the sake of convenience, they were commuted into gifts of money. Here is the ultimate origin of the custom that our rite still recognizes, the gathering of the offerings just before the Eucharistic action proper begins. It is these offerings which our present Eucharistic rite has in mind when it bids the celebrant say in the name of the congregation, "Receive, O God, our bodies and souls and all our talents, together with the offerings we bring before Thee, for Thou hast purchased us to be Thine own, that we may live unto Thee" (*The Lutheran Liturgy*, p. 19). These offerings still are symbols of our self-dedication to Almighty God, the pledge that all that we have will be used in conformity with His will as He reveals it to us in response to our prayer.

The aspect of sacrifice in connection with the celebration of the Holy Eucharist finds further expression when we think of the essentially social character of this sacrament.

The Holy Communion is the national meal of the New Israel, as the Passover was of the Old Israel. "We being many are one Body, because we all participate in the one loaf," St. Paul asserts (1 Cor. 10:17; Rom. 12:5). The bond of union of the mystical body of Christ is the Eucharistic Body and Blood of the same Redeemer. Hence the eleventh chapter of First Corinthians condemns in particular the sins against the corporate life of Christians in connection with the sacrament that is to be the sign and the instrument of the common incorporation in Christ.

It is as a baptized member of the Christian community that the individual Christian receives the Holy Communion, and it is precisely the sacrificial giving up of oneself for Christ and for the sake of His Bride the Church that our reception of the Holy Communion implies. We receive it not only so that through it God might strengthen us individually in faith toward Him, but also that He might increase our fervent love to one another.

In the *Betbüchlin* which Blessed Martin Luther published in 1529 there is this illuminating passage:

> Love is depicted in these signs and appearances first of all in the bread. For when the grains lie in a heap and are not ground up, each one is a body for itself, and is not mixed with the others. But when they are ground up together they become a single body. The same thing takes place in the wine. If one does not press the grapes, each retains its shape for itself. But when they are pressed out, it all flows together and becomes a single drink. One cannot say any longer, the flour comes from this grain or that little drop comes from this grape, for each has crept into the other's shape and thus it has become one bread and one drink. St. Paul interpreted it the same way in 1 Corinthians 10: 'We, who are many, are one loaf and one body, in that we all participate in one loaf.' We eat the Lord through faith in the word that the soul takes to itself and feeds upon. In the same way my neighbor eats me again. And I give him my possessions, my body, my life, and everything that I have, and let him feed on it and make use of it to the extent that he needs it. Again, I need my neighbor; I am poor and indigent, and I let him help and serve me. Thus we are woven into one another, so that we help one another as Christ has helped us, which is what spiri-

tually eating and drinking one another means (Martin Luther, *Ein Betbüchlin mit eym Calender und Passional hübsch zu gericht* [Wittenberg: (Hans Lufft,) 1529], folio R i verso – folio R ii verso).

It almost goes without saying, of course, that when we speak of our sacrifice in the celebration of the Holy Eucharist we must always remember that in the strict sense of the term we have nothing to offer except what we have received from God. When we celebrate the Holy Eucharist in remembrance of Christ's saving death, we are in effect saying: "No offering that we could bring could possibly reconcile us to Thee, our God. All that we can plead is the work of Thy Son, His perfect obedience in all that He did and all that He suffered, His Body nailed to the Cross for us, His Blood poured out for the forgiveness of our sins. As by the mystery of the sacramental union Thou hast made His true Body and Blood present for us in this Bread and in this Cup, for us Christians to eat and to drink, so, we beseech Thee, let it be present in Thy sight also as the price of our redemption. Let it remind Thee that Thou hast forgiven mankind in the reconciliation which Thou hast wrought in Thy son. Before Thee we appeal to no virtue, no righteousness of our own, but only to the alien righteousness of Thy Suffering Servant and Son, our true Paschal Lamb, which was offered for us and has taken away the sins of the world, Who by His death has destroyed death, and by His rising to life again has restored to us everlasting life."

Ultimately this insight must characterize all our sacrifices, our works and our gifts as well as our faith and our worship. Because God is the Creator and Redeemer and Transformer and because we are always only the recipients of His bounty, whatever we plead before Him, whatever we give Him, whatever we do for His sake is always under the signature, "All things come of Thee, O Lord, and of Thine own have we given Thee."

Thus what we have said in connection with Holy Baptism applies here as well. Whatever we do that is acceptable to God we do "in Christ." What we do by our own native powers is only to resist the impulse and to handicap the operation of His Holy Spirit — to quench the Spirit. Yet the good that we do, even though we do it in Christ, *we* do. It is *our* sacrifice of praise and thanksgiving, *our* oblation of service, *our* offering of faith. But because the impulse and the power comes from Christ, because He works both the will and the deed within us, it is still Christ who is the ultimate Priest, the One Who is really offering the sacrifice of perfect obedience in deed and in suffering to His heavenly Father. To deny this or to minimize this, is to deny the Biblical doctrine of the unity of the Head and the Body, of the Bride and the Bridegroom.

The classically beautiful collect that our own Maundy Thursday rite has adapted from the pen of St. Thomas Aquinas sums it all up beautifully: "O Lord God, Who hast left unto us in a wonderful Sacrament a memorial of Thy Passion, grant, we beseech Thee, that we may so use this Sacrament of Thy Body and Blood that the fruit of our redemption may continually be manifest in us, Thou Who livest and reignest with the Father and the Holy Ghost ever one God, world without end."

What are the implications of all of this for stewardship? What we have said about Holy Baptism and its administration has its parallel in connection with the Sacrament of the Altar and its celebration.

We need to remember that the people to whom we are addressing our pleas for the good management of their talents, their time and their money are communicants of the Church, who receive the true Body and Blood of our Lord Jesus Christ into their mortal bodies as a medicine and pledge of immortality, who have received the forgiveness of sins in the fullest sense of the term, who have been made One with Christ and with one another through the Sacrament of unity, who have already received Christ, God, the Holy Spirit, paradise, and the life of the world to come in the Sacrament of the Altar. They are people who have, like the Macedonians, first given themselves to the Lord (2 Corinthians 8:5). At every offertory they are symbolically giving themselves in the gifts that they bring to the altar. Yet they are profoundly aware that these very sacrifices of theirs ultimately inspired and motivated by the Christ Who is the Head of the Body of which they are members and by the Spirit through Whom that same Christ sanctifies and rules them (AC III 4.5). As they eat the Body that is for them and drink the Blood of the Covenant poured out for the forgiveness of sins they are united with the Christ Who has suffered and died for their salvation and for that of all humankind. Their sympathies for every member of their own Christian community, for every other member of the larger group community of which their own is a part, for every other Christian and for the pagans for whom Christ died no less than for them have been sharpened and broadened and deepened by the fact that they have in Christ entered into one another. Money, time, talents are things which they have already offered to God. What remains is merely the workaday application of an accomplished commitment. That this workaday application is not easy, that it is fraught with many perils, not least that of the hypocrisy that killed Ananias and Sapphira, is something that we all recognize. It is precisely for this reason that we need to support one another and to strengthen one another, to *live* our community in Christ and not merely to *affirm* it.

Thus a large part of the task of stewardship is the interpretation to ourselves and to one another of the meaning of the Sacraments and the encouragement of ourselves and one another to make more extensive, more liberal and more meaningful use of them.

It involves the careful scrutiny of our conventional practice to see if it really accords with God's will as the Church of which we are a part understands it.

It involves inquiring, for instance, if we ought not to try in every way to make Baptism more important in the lives of our people and of our parishes than it now is.

It involves inquiring if we ought not to give individual Absolution, that "third Sacrament" which our Symbols see as implied in Holy Baptism (LC Baptism 74-82; cf. Ap XI 3, XIII 4), the role in our parochial practice that it has in the Symbols (AC XI 1; Ap VI 3.4; SA Part Three VIII 1.2) to which we stand committed.

It involves rethinking the justification for withholding the Holy Communion from our children until they are thirteen and fourteen years old, instead of admitting them at a much younger age as the Church of the Reformation did (LC Holy Communion 87).

It involves inquiring if we ought not to increase the frequency of our celebrations of the Holy Communion until we have achieved the standard of the Lutheran Symbols (AC XXIV 34; Ap XV 40; XXIV 1; LC Holy Communion 47) and of the primitive Church — every Sunday at every parochial service, every major holy day, and as often in addition as the devotion of our people requires.

It involves considering what we can do in order to increase the frequency with which our people receive the Holy Communion.

It involves, in brief, adapting our stewardship appeals to the sacramental realities of Holy Baptism and the Holy Communion and the sacrificial realities of the life to which they summon us and for which they enable us. It involves making the practice of stewardship the practical living out of that which our participation in Holy Baptism and in the Holy Communion already and irrevocably implies.

THE LUTHERAN UNDERSTANDING OF BAPTISM ... A SYSTEMATIC SUMMARY

The "Baptismal Booklet" Appended to the Small Catechism

This essay proposes to answer the questions with which Roman Catholic teaching on baptism confronts Lutherans. As far as possible it will give these answers out of the Lutheran symbolical books, as representing the common conviction of all Lutherans. Where these are silent, any answer that is not clearly given by the sacred Scriptures commands acceptance among Lutherans only on the basis of its plausibility and inherent persuasiveness. The answers of classic Lutheran orthodoxy — the era of the great Lutheran systematicians from about 1580 to 1713 — in such cases may serve as a guide to the direction that Lutheran thinking took. The essay also attempts to take account of current Lutheran theological reflection on its subject.

On the principle *lex orandi lex credendi* the "Baptismal Booklet" (*Taubüchlein*) appended to the *Small Catechism* from 1529 on (and part of every complete edition of the *Book of Concord*) provides important insights into the Lutheran position on holy baptism. The "Baptismal Booklet" — an order for infant baptism — as we have it dates back to

1526. It is a simplification and abbreviation of an earlier reworking (1523) by Martin Luther of the medieval Western baptismal rite.

The 1526 rite begins with the same introduction to the Christian reader that the 1523 rite had had. Among its emphases are the following:

1) Luther laments the carelessness with which the holy and comforting sacrament of baptism had been administered, partly because the participants did not understand the Latin rite. He has begun to baptize in German so that the sponsors and bystanders would be excited to greater faith and serious devotion and the priests compelled to proceed with greater diligence.

2) The traditional ceremonies are not the aspects of baptism that repel the devil. To conquer him the sponsors and bystanders must attend in confident faith. They must listen to the word of God. At the priest's "Let us pray," they must pray with him. Hence the priest must say the prayer plainly and slowly, and the sponsors must really interpose themselves in prayer against the devil on the child's behalf.

3) God himself calls baptism a new birth, which frees us from all tyranny of the devil, from sin, and from death and hell, and turns us into children of life, heirs of all of God's goods, sons of God himself, and brothers of Christ.

A subsequent rubric implies that the rite — identical for both sexes — will begin at the entrance to the church. The priest adjures the devil with a shortened form of the *Exi et recede*. He makes the sign of the holy cross on the infant's forehead and breast. Then he offers a prayer which combines the address of the old petition *Omnipotens sempiterne Deus* with the body of the prayer *Deus immortale praesidium*. This prayer refers to the unbaptized child as "God's servant." Then follows a 169-word prayer for which there is apparently no immediate precedent in the medieval baptismal rite. It recalls the flood and the crossing of the Red Sea as Old Testament types of baptism; it sees in our Lord's baptism the hallowing of Jordan and of all waters to be a blessed flood and an abundant washing away of sin; it calls on God to look graciously on the candidate and to bless him with the gift of right faith in the Spirit, so that this saving flood may drown and destroy in him everything that he has inherited from Adam and what he himself has added to it, to the end that, severed from the number of the unbelievers, he may be preserved dry and safe in the holy ark of Christendom and, aglow with the Spirit and rejoicing in hope, may serve God's name, so that with all believers he may become worthy of God's promise and come to everlasting life.

The priest again adjures the devil in a formula abbreviated from the medieval *Exorciso te* and reads as the holy gospel St. Mark 10:13-16 (a parallel to the medieval gospel, Mt 19:13-15). Then the priest lays his hands on the child and prays the Our Father with the kneeling sponsors.

While saying Psalm 121:8, the priest conducts the child into the church and to the font. The candidate's threefold creedal interrogation reproduce the Latin. The priest asks: "Do you want to be baptized?" The response is "Yes." The priest takes the child and immerses it as he says, "And I baptize you in the name of the Father and of the Son and of the Holy Spirit." The sponsors take the child and the priest vests the child in the white chrisom, saying meanwhile an adaptation of the suffrage formerly associated with the chrismation, *Deus omnipotens, pater domini nostri,* with *ipse te linit chrismate salutis in Christo Jesu domino nostro* replaced by "confirm you with his grace." The formula is of importance both for the use of the verb "confirm" and because it is one of the two passages in the rite which explicitly link baptism with the forgiveness of sins. (The other is the "Flood" prayer, referred to above.)

It will be noted that the rite of 1526 adheres closely enough to the medieval rite to demonstrate its ancestry but varies sufficiently to suggest that what has been retained reproduces the Latin deliberately.

The retention of the exorcism, the subject of a great deal of interdenominational polemics and of intra-Lutheran debate during the next two centuries, was justified by its Lutheran defenders on the ground that it characterized the spiritual condition of newly-born children, underlined the power of baptism, stressed the splendid powers by which God has destroyed the reign of Satan, and served as an anti-Pelagian witness and a demonstration of Christian liberty in indifferent matters.

The Conception of Baptism in the Lutheran Systematic Tradition

The Lutheran discussions of baptism through the last four centuries reflect the philosophical fashions of the time. The era of the Reformation itself tends to be strongly biblical, but with the revival of scholastic patterns in the age of classic orthodoxy, the vocabulary in which the theologians treat baptism is reminiscent of the high middle ages. Recent discussions in turn are likely to avail themselves of more existential and personalist concepts to describe baptism as an encounter with the God of grace himself as he works through the sacramental masks of water and people to incorporate men and women and children into his holy community.

1. Baptism as a Sacrament

Fundamental to the Lutheran understanding of baptism is the sacramental character. As one of the Dominically instituted sacraments, it is held, baptism participates in the characteristics of sacraments generally. But it does so without losing its particularity. Against the Swiss Reformed view, Lutherans maintain that God did not institute the scaraments "merely to be marks of profession among men, but especially to be signs and testimonies of the will of God toward us, intended to awaken and confirm faith in those who use them."[1] Sacraments moreover are "signs of the forgiveness of sins."[2] The words of Bishop Aulén are apposite here: "If we speak of baptism as a sign, it is a sign in the same sense as the works of Christ during his earthly ministry were 'signs.' Baptism is in other words really a divine 'act of power.'"[3]

The Lutheran symbolical books define sacraments as "rites which have the command of God and to which the promise of grace has been added,"[4] or as ceremonies or acts "in which God offers us the content of the promise joined to the ceremony."[5] Specifically, the Holy Spirit offers us the righteousness of the "entire obedience which, by doing and suffering, in life and in death, Christ rendered for us to his heavenly Father ... through the Gospel and in the sacraments."[6]

The purpose of the sacraments is to constitute and identify the church, to establish the church's oneness, to offer the remission of sins, to impart the Holy Spirit, to beget and confirm faith, and to make Christians.[7]

As a sacrament, baptism is an enacted form of the word of God, *verbum actuale*. We must here think of the word of God chiefly as "gospel." That is, baptism is a demonstration of what God has done and still does for our salvation in and through Christ, and God's application to the individual in the church of the objective reconciliation and atonement that he accomplished in Christ. At the same time, baptism is also "law," in that it increases the condemnation of those who receive it with contempt. Similarly, as a sacrament, baptism is part of the manward initiative of a gracious God. A classic passage in the Lutheran symbolical books in this connection reads:

> The gospel ... offers counsel and help against sin in more than one way, for God is surprisingly rich in his grace: First, through the spoken word, by which the forgiveness of sins (the peculiar office of the gospel) is preached to the whole world; second, through baptism; third, through the holy sacrament of the altar; fourth, through the power of the keys; and finally, through the mutual conversation and consultation of brethren.[8]

But baptism also involves sacrifice, our human Godward response to the divine initiative.

As an enacted form of the word of God, the sacraments are coordinated with the oral proclamation of the word of God. The fundamental difference between the communication of the divine grace in the word (*sacramenium audibile*) and in sacrament (*verbum visibile*) is the concrete character of the sacramental action and the individualized nature of the divine address to one particular person.

> To obtain (justifying) faith God instituted the office of the ministry, provided the gospel and the sacraments. Through these, as through means, he gives the Holy Spirit.[9]
> When we are baptized, when we eat the Lord's Body, when we are absolved, our hearts should firmly believe that God really forgives us for Christ's sake. Through the word and the rite of God simultaneously moves the heart to believe and to conceive faith, as Paul says: 'Faith comes from what is heard.' As the word enters through the ears to strike the heart, so the rite itself enters through the eyes to move the heart. The word and the rite have the same effect, as St. Augustine said so well when he called a sacrament 'a visible word,' for the rite is received by the eyes and is a sort of picture of the word, signifying the same thing as the word. Therefore both have the same effect.[10]

The Göttingen theologian Eduard Lohse has recently summarized the coordination of the proclaimed word and the sacraments in this way:

> Word and sacrament stand in a real mutual relationship. The sacrament secures the right understanding of the proclamation of the word and preserves it from an impermissible spiritualization. Conversely the preaching of the Word protects the sacrament against a materialistic or enthusiastic misunderstanding and precludes in this way a magical conception .... The sacrament demonstrates in a way which cannot be overlooked that God's saving act in Christ strikes us in a historical fashion, that the body that is subjected to sin is put to death with in a bodily way, that the body that is subjected to sin is put to death and that our body from now on has been committed to the *Kyrios* to obey him. Just as the event of the cross and the resurrection of Jesus Christ contains reconciliation and salvation for the whole world, so at the point where a man begins to be a Christian there is the event of baptism, in which the old man is crucified with Christ, the new man is subjected to the dominion of the risen Lord, and the person baptized in being made a member of the body of Christ is incorporated into God's holy people of the end-time. As Christ died and rose again once and therewith once and for all, so baptism is administered to a human being only once. But the proclamation of justification — needing constant repetition as it does — reminds the baptized Christian again and again of the foundation for his being a Christian that God has laid, and it calls upon him to let himself be determined by this foundation that has been laid in baptism and constantly to appropriate it anew in confident faith and in a life of obedience.[11]

Thus in contrast to the classic Reformed doctrine of the sacraments, Lutheran theology stresses their effective, rather than a primarily cognitive word (plus, at most, the written word) exhaust the idea of the word of God has strongly marked Lutheran theology and practice for over 250 years. Notably in Europe this tendency has been reinforced by the twentieth century neo-orthodox "theology of the word" with its strongly cognitive emphasis and its basically anti-sacramental thrust. It is difficult to evaluate the final effect of this impact. That is has jeopardized the role of baptism is obvious. At the same time strong reactions that stress the importance of the sacraments in general and baptism in particular have made themselves felt in the European Lutheran community.

2. Baptism as Water-and-Word-of-God (or word-of-God-with-water)

The fact that both formulations, "baptism is water-and-word-of-god" and "baptism is word-of-God-and-water," occur illustrates the insep- arable conjunction of the two. "Both, water and the word, are one baptism."[12] "Baptism is nothing else than the word of God in water commanded by the institution of Christ."[13] On the other hand, the Large Catechism declares: "Baptism is simply water and God's word in and with each other."[14]

A contemporary commentator on the Lutheran symbolical books, Edmund Schlink, warns:

> The definition of baptism which begins with water must not be weakened ... Rather, beginning with water in defining the essence of baptism must be regarded as a highly pregnant theological antithesis against the Enthusiasts. Nor is the revers- ing of terms in the definition of baptism an accidental way of speaking, but it presents a kind of analogy to the relation of the divine and human natures in Christ.[15]

The Lutheran Reformation perpetuated the inherited distinction of matter and form in the analysis of the sacraments, although the Lu- theran symbolical books do not explicitly use these terms. Instead they operated with the Augustinian equivalents "element" and "word." This substitution is not unprecedented. We have an interesting medieval example of the substitution of *"elementum"* for *"materia"* in connection with baptism (together with a citation of Mk 16:15 as the "word") in the letter *Non ut apponeres* of Innocent III to Archbishop Thorias of Nidaros, dated March 1, 1206.[16] The epigrammatic assertion of St. Augustine *"Tolle aquam, non est baptismus; tolle verbum, non est sacramentum,"* ac- cords exactly with the position of the Lutheran symbolical books.

The Lutheran symbolical books reject both the theory that "for- gets the word, God's institution, and says that God has joined to the water a spiritual power which through the water washes away sin" and the theory that "baptism washes away sin through the assistance of the divine will, as if the washing takes place only through God's will and not at all through the word or the water."[17] The Dominicans, the latter to Duns Scotus and the Franciscans. The debatable justice of these ascriptions is not the question. The important thing is that the Lutherans are concerned about keeping the water and the word of command and promise inseparably together. Schlink notes on this point:

> In the definition of the sacrament either the word or the water can be the predicate-noun. Faith can cling both to the word and to the water. Whoever does not receive the water of baptism does not receive the promise of the word of baptism. God effects salvation not only through the word but through word and water, through the word in the water and the water in the word. Water and word are now in one another. The word is visible in the water of baptism. Therefore one may and should believe that he may 'receive in the water the promised salvation.'[18]

By virtue of its combination with the divine word, the symbolical books variously describe the water applied in holy baptism as divine water, heavenly water, holy water, blessed water, fruitful water, and gracious water, and as the laver of rebirth, even though it is a coarse external mask.[19]

3. The "Matter" of Baptism

The "sign" or the "element" in holy baptism is the washing with water. The "sign" is also called the water, but with the implication of the water in its actual application, even when the symbolical books do not so specifically state. Of and by itself and to all appearances, the water is not worth a straw.[20] In an analogous sense, it is a *larva* or mask for the divine gift, as we see the shell of a nut.[21] "Because the word embraces the water, the water embraces the word; because the word is in the water, the water is in the word," says Schlink. "The word is monergistically the agent in creating the sacrament."[22] There is no "natural theology" here, no dependence on the symbolic qualities or possibilities of water as such, nor on the symbolic-indicative significance which immersion as such could have by itself.

Such symbolism as the early Lutherans recognize thinks in terms of the water as an agent that washes, cleanses, surrounds, covers on all sides, preserves, delivers, or even kills the old man. They do not maintain any of these points of comparison with any degree of consistency. The symbolism of water as slaking thirst and of being life giving in this sense is absent. Contemporary Lutheran theology finds it necessary to antagonize a tendency to overstress the "spiritual" aspects of baptism to the point where the fact is forgotten that God is working through a material element which he has created and over which he still retains a Pantocrator's authority and power.

Because of their conception of baptism as a dynamic action and of the "matter" of baptism as being primarily a washing with water, the Lutherans criticized the use of water specially prepared and blessed on Easter Eve and Whitsuneve for use in baptism throughout the year.[23] This possibly too great fear of superstition resulted in the abolition of the services of Easter Eve and Whitsuneve among the Lutheran churches and the ultimate elimination of the blessing of the font from the Lutheran baptismal rites. But the fear of superstition was not altogether ill-founded. As late as 1580 the Church Order of the Duke August of Saxony had to stipulate that pastors must warn their sacristans not to sell the baptismal water for magical purposes and must assure them that future violations of this injunction would meet with dire punishment.[24]

The mode of baptism may be either immersion or pouring.[25] The *Large Catechism* refers both to "a handful of water" and "allowing the water to be poured over you."[26] At the beginning of the Reformation immersion was normal; by the end of the sixteenth century affusion had generally replaced it. The Lutheran symbolical books nowhere countenance aspersion. As late as 1708 a Lutheran pastor's failure to use a sufficient quantity of water was punishable with suspension or ecclesiastical censure.

Early Lutheran practice reveals differences of opinion and procedure as far as baptizing in the public service is concerned, but the insistence upon the church as the normal place for the administration of baptism is unanimous. When at a later date the practice of baptism in the parents' home becomes frequent in many places, this is due largely to the concern of the lesser nobility and the *bourgeoisie* for social position.

4. The *"Formale"* of Baptism

The *"formale"* of baptism is the word of God. On this the Lutheran Reformers were agreed. The content of this word they differentiated into the baptismal command to baptize in the Triune name and the baptismal promise, with the promise in a sense already implied in the fact that candidates are baptized into divine name.

Since the word of God in baptism is the baptismal command and promise,[27] the *Small Catechism* has two initial sections: "What is baptism?" which appeals to Mt 28:19, and "What does baptism give or profit?" which appeals to the textually dubious passage Mk 16:16. For the same reason the *Large Catechism* cites both texts in its opening section of the discussion of baptism. In the analysis of baptism the reader is reminded that we need to be careful not to think of water alone or to tamper "with God's ordinance and tear from it the precious jeweled clasp with which God has fastened and enclosed it and from which he does not wish his ordinance to be separated."[28]

The Lutheran Reformers demanded a clear Dominical institution for a sacrament strictly so called to guarantee the sacramental promise. Because more is involved than obedience to an ordinance, the divine institution of baptism receives a considerable amount of explicit stress. Replying, for example, to the spiritualizers' charge that "baptism is an external thing and that external things are of no use," the *Large Catechism* counters: "No matter how external it may be, here stand God's word and command which have instituted, established, and confirmed baptism."[29]

The possibility that the Trinitarian formula of St. Matthew 28:19 does not exactly reproduce the expressed command of our Lord, but that it is either the baptismal formula of the particular community within which the first Gospel emerged or a theological specification and interpretation of the baptismal act is, of course, a relative novelty. Lutheran theological opinion, as far as it is ascertainable, is divided on the issue.

The charge is sometimes made that Lutheran theology operates with the doctrine of justification through faith as a material principle. But in spite of the intimate and obvious link between baptism and the forgiveness of sins (of which "justification" in the Lutheran understanding of the term, is a synonym), the Lutheran doctrine of baptism is derived not by inference from and explication of justification as a principle, but directly from the divine institution that the sacred Scriptures record.

5. *"Materia Coelestis"*

The idea of a *materia coelestis* in baptism is generally absent in the oldest Lutheran theologians. In the early 17th century Leonard Hütter in his *Loci* makes the Holy Spirit or the blood of Christ or both the heavenly *pars substantialis*. Later in the century Abraham Calovius says:

> Correctly defined, the *materia coelestis* of baptism is the most Holy Trinity, God the Father, God's Son Christ the God-Man to whose entirety there pertains not only his divine nature, but also his human nature, whereto his blood, of which he became a partaker of our account, also belongs, and the Holy Spirit. This *res coelestis* in one word is called the word and name of God, that is the Triune God himself, Father, Son and Holy Spirit.[30]

At the end of the era of orthodoxy David Hollaz defines the *materia coelestis baptismi analogice dicta* as "the entire most Holy Trinity, *peculialiter et terminative* the Holy Spirit."[31]

6. The Effect of Baptism

The primary and basic effect of this purifying and sanctifying sacrament is the forgiveness of sins in the broadest and most comprehensive sense, as the *Nicaenoconstantinopolitanum* affirms:

> The power, effect, benefit, fruit and purpose of baptism is to save ... To be saved, we know, is nothing else than to be delivered from sin, death and the devil and to enter into the kingdom of God and live with him forever.[32]

Baptism "works forgiveness of sins, delivers from death and the devil, and gives everlasting bliss to all those who believe that it does this."[33] Baptism applies to the individual the reconciliation and pardon that God in Christ achieved for the whole world of mankind. This forgiveness includes the remission of original sin, understood as the removal of the guilt, but not of the "matter" of original sin.[34]

While Lutherans hold that the effect of baptism is not so to be understood as if it took away sin the sense that no vestiges of sin remain in the person baptized, they do assert that it takes away the culpability and liability of sin by forgiveness. Beyond that they stipulate that baptism initiates a renewal that lasts through the individual's whole lifetime as he continually puts to death the actions of the flesh through the might of the Holy Spirit and that this renewal will find its consummation in the life of the world to come. They insist that the viciousness, the disorderliness, and the lawlessness of sin is broken, diminished, and restrained by the Holy Spirit, and that he helps the baptized Christian to resist and conquer its dominion. "Sins are not only covered and remitted in baptism, but they are put to death (*mortificari*)," Gerhard declares.[35] While there is no chronological separation between the forgiveness of sins and the beginning of the new life of holiness, in the order of causality the renewal is consequent upon the pardon. "As soon as the Holy Spirit has initiated his work of regeneration and renewal in us through the word and the holy sacraments, it is certain that we can and must cooperate by the power of the Holy Spirit, even though we do so in great weakness."[36]

Intimately and inseparably associated with the effect of forgiveness are the gifts of new life through rebirth and salvation.[37] "Where there is forgiveness of sins, there is also life and salvation."[38] Baptism is the sacrament of regeneration, recreation, and renewal. The rebirth of baptism involves no change in identity but a transformation of the person. The rejection of baptismal regeneration by Samuel Simon Schmucker in the "American recension" of the *Augsburg Confession* in the mid-19th century — never very widely endorsed — has been universally transcended in the Lutheran community in America.

Another way of saying that baptism bestows life is the affirmation that baptism liberates the candidate from and gives him victory over death.[39] Thus baptism has eshcatological implications for the person baptized. "One is baptized in order ... to be saved. To be saved, we know, is nothing else than to be delivered from sin, death, and the devil, and to enter into the kingdom of Christ and live with him for ever."[40] As the sacrament of *palingennesia* baptism points forward to the great cosmic *palingennesia to come* (Mt 19:28).[41]

In this spirit Schlink can call baptism "already the eschatological event of the resurrection from the dead which it promises. For this reason alone the invitation to a daily return to baptism makes sense. Baptism as *promissio salutis* is not only a promise but also the bestowal of what is promised, just as the gospel a *promissio* is both promise and assurance."[42]

Baptism bestows the grace of God,[43] and it imparts illumination and a perfecting of the knowledge of God and of his gracious disposition toward us.[44] In addition it confers on the person baptized a "liberated will" (*arbitrium liberatum*). His relation to the law has been changed from one of servile subjugation to willing obedience in freedom, an authentic *imitatio Christi*.[45]

Since baptism is an indication of God's providential predestination to life, the baptized person is to invoke its comfort when the author of all evil tempts him even as a believer to despair of the divine mercy and to embrace the ensuing great shame and vice. "To appreciate and use baptism aright, we must draw strength and comfort from it when our sins or conscience oppress us, and we must retort, 'But I am baptized! And if I am baptized, I have the promise that I shall be saved and have eternal life, both in soul and body.'"[46]

Baptism imparts to the candidate the entire Christ in his entire life and death and rising again.[47] It is not a mere symbol of the death and resurrection of Christ; it is the mystical and sacramental participation of the candidate in those events. The link of baptism specifically with the death of Christ is underlined by the parallel language of the Second Article of the Creed and secondly of Baptism. The early versions of the *Small Catechism* (prior to 1540) read *"im Tode"* rather than, by accommodation to the vernacular bible translation, *"in den Tod."* Johannes Meyer sees the original form as implying not the death of the old man, but the death of Our Lord, in which we experience the burial of our sins.[48] The candidate's sharing of the death and resurrection of Christ is not to be thought of as if these events had some kind of transtemporal existence so that they can be communicated in baptism under a sacramental mask. Rather the process is to be conceived in such a way as to make Christ's death and resurrection virtually present, or, even more precisely, as an incorporation into Christ who in his incarnation has died and risen and will come again. The *Nicaenoconstantinopolitanum* itself suggests this with its accusative participles: *"kai ies hena kyrion Iesoun Christon ... staurothenta te hyper hemon ... kai pathonta kai taphenta kai anastanta."* This incorporation implies that we become God's children by adoption and grace, like the Christ into whom we have been incorporated, not *kata physin* but *kata thesin*. Today the Lutheran conception of baptism as incorporation into the whole saving act of God in Christ is being enriched as Lutheran systematic theology in general increasingly stressed the significance of Our Lord's exaltation for the salvation of the world, in contrast to its previous sometimes one-sided overemphasis upon His death.

Baptism also imparts Christ's victory over the tyrannical evil powers and delivers the candidate from the jaws of the devil.[49] The vocabulary of the sixteenth century is less sophisticated than that of our own day when it comes to talk about the demonic. Where we tend to use the neuter gender, the *Catechisms* exhibit no reluctance to talk in the terms of a personal masculine. "Baptism effects forgiveness of sins, delivers from death and the devil and grants eternal salvation to all who believe."[50] Baptism thus becomes a means of applying subjectively the objective reconciliation which Our Lord achieved by his incarnation, his life, his death, and his exaltation. The explicit citation of Romans 6 in this connection reinforces this point.[51]

Baptism imparts to the candidate the Holy Spirit with his gifts.[52] This effect is one that endures throughout the lifetime of the person baptized, even if he falls into grievous sin. Lutheran theology would concur with St. Basil's assertion that the Holy Spirit remains present to the soul of the baptized person who lapses after baptism, if necessary awaiting his conversion from sin.[53] "The power and effect of baptism ... is simply the slaying of the old and the resurrection of the new man, both of which actions must continue in us our whole life long. Thus a Christian life is nothing else than a daily baptism, once begun and ever continued."[54]

On this basis, the symbolical books from Luther's pen subsume the *sacramentum poenitentiae* under baptism. "Baptism, both by its power and by its signification, comprehends also the third sacrament, formerly called penance."[55] In explicating this position Luther declares:

> Baptism remains continually. Even though we fall from it and sin, nevertheless we always have access to it so that we may again subdue the old man. But we need not again have the water poured over us. Even if we were immersed in water a hundred times, it would nevertheless be but one baptism, and the effect and signification of baptism would continue and remain. Penance, therefore, is nothing else than a return to baptism, to resume and practice what had earlier been begun but abandoned. I say this to correct the opinion, which has long prevailed among us, that our baptism is something past which we can no longer use after falling again into sin. Indeed, St. Jerome is responsible for this view, for he wrote, "Repentance is the second plank on which we embarked when we entered into the Christian church." This interpretation deprives baptism of its value, making it of no further use to us. Therefore the statement is incorrect. The ship does not flounder since, as we said it is God's ordinance and not a work of ours. But it does happen that we slip and fall out of the ship. If anybody does fall out, he should immediately head for the ship and cling to it until he can climb aboard again and sail on it as he had done before ... [Baptism] tears us out of the very gorge of the devil, makes us God's own, suppresses and takes away sin, and thereafter continually strengthens the new man, remains con-

stantly efficacious and abides as long as we are in our present misery until we finally come to everlasting glory. For that reason everyone ought to regard baptism as his everyday garb, in which he is continually to walk around, that he may always let himself be found in the faith and in its fruits, that he may suppress the old man and grow up in the new man. If we want to be Christians, we have to engage in the activity from which our being derives. If anybody falls away from [his baptism], let him return to it. As Christ, the mercy-seat [Romans 3, 25; Heb. 4, 16] does not recede from us or forbid us to return to him even though we sin, so all his treasures and gifts remain. As we have once obtained forgiveness of sins in baptism, so forgiveness remains day by day as long as we live, that is, as long as we carry the old Adam about our necks.[56]

As an instrument of the Holy Spirit, baptism aids the Christian in the conquest of the cardinal sins that disfigure his life — anger, hatred, envy, impurity, greed, sloth, pride, and infidelity (gluttony is the only one omitted) — and in the development of the contrary virtues, like gentleness, patience and meekness.[57] Since through baptism the Holy Spirit imparts forgiveness of sins, through it he must also foster the fruits of the Spirit. In this sense, *theopoiesis* (divinization) is an effect of baptism.[58]

Lutherans do not feel themselves hit by Trent's Canon 10 on baptism: "*Si quis dixerit, peccata omnia, quae post baptismum fiunt sola recordatione et fide susepti baptismi vel dimitti vel venalia fieri, an. s.*"[59] They do not hold that persons who fall into grave sins after baptism and persevere in them without true and earnest repentance receive forgiveness of sins merely by recalling in a perfunctory and purely historical way that they were once baptized, so that they have no need of genuine repentance and the ministry of the keys. They do hold that the power, efficacy and operation of the cleansing and hallowing that takes place through baptism perdures and avails throughout the whole life of the Christian. When he falls into grave sin after baptism, they hold that in serious and earnest repentance he can and ought to renew and reestablish the cleansed and hallowed condition by means of the recollection of the covenant into which baptism does not extend to future but only to past sins, they hold, is unduly limiting the scope of the sacrament. "Baptism," Bishop Aulén observes, "must not be understood simply as an act of initiation. Baptism does not look toward the past but to the future, both in regard to life in the church of Christ and in regard to the eschatological consummation."[60]

What has been said about the effect of baptism on the individual needs to be complemented by indicating the ecclesiastical dimension of baptism. In the prefatory summary of his discussion of baptism Bishop Aulén writes:

Baptism is the act of the prevenient grace of God through which man is received into fellowship with the body of Christ, the church. Herein lie both the gift and the obligation of baptism. The validity of infant baptism rests on the fact that the grace of

God is a prevenient grace. Infant baptism imposes upon the church an obligation and a responsibility toward baptized children. The Christian view of baptism must be distinguished from a mechanizing interpretation which nullify the primacy of grace.[61]

In baptism God makes the candidate a member of the church.[62] But from a human standpoint the church, as the body and the bride of Christ on earth, applies in baptism the universal and objective reconciliation of the whole world of mankind to the individual in such a way that he is, in and through the church, united with Christ. Through baptism the church as the nation and the people of God perpetuates herself in time. It is precisely because the church baptizes that she is our mother and the font is her womb. The Holy Spirit "has a special community in the world, the mother that conceives and bears every Christian through the word of God which the Spirit reveals and makes use of and which enlightens and sets on fire the hearts of men so that they may embrace it, receive it, cling to it and remain with it."[63] In this way baptism is not merely a means of salvation for the individual, but the church's own act of creating spiritual offspring. Baptism is the act of the whole church, even when the church is represented only by priest and sponsors. Baptism lays stress on the fact that God calls us into the church. It is a line of demarcation between Christian and non-Christian, but also in the case of each individual a line of demarcation between the pre-Christian and the Christian segments of his life. By being incorporated into the holy community the person baptized participates in the circulation of Christ's own life that flows through all of the body of Christ. This involves more than a juridical reception into membership in a denomination or church-body; it is a sacred incorporation into the church as Christ's body.

In the era between the decline of orthodoxy and the 19th century confessional revival Rationalist and Pietist influences on the Lutheran Church tended to be more concerned with the subjective aspects of baptism that about its objective significance. Even the confessional revival did not wholly redress the balance and the influence of Pietism is still strong in many sectors of the Lutheran Church. Contemporary Lutheran systematic theology has been exploring more extensively the implications of baptism as a basis for ecumenical effort and therewith as a basis for the Christian's moral and ethical activity in both the church and the world.

Because baptism is the first and fundamental sacrament, "the first door to grace, the sacrament of initiation" and incorporation into the church,[64] it is a kind of *janua sacramentorum,* a necessary prerequisite for the reception of the other sacraments.[65] The sacrament of the altar, for example, is in a sense the complement of baptism and Lutherans hold that "only those who have been baptized in the name of the Lord" may receive it.[66] Similarly holy absolution in the sacrament of penance is the restoration into baptismal grace and status,[67] and only a baptized person can be ordained.

Even though the marriage is a sacrament of the old covenant,[68] holy matrimony is a sign of the mysterious relation between Christ and His bride the church,[69] but only where the contracting parties are themselves parts of the heavenly bride. Lutheran theology does not understand the Pauline privilege (1 Cor 7:15) as permitting a convert to the Christian faith to leave a pagan spouse and to marry another Christian, an interpretation that has played an official role in Roman Catholic pastoral practice since the response of the Holy Office to the Bishop of Kochchiband (*Episcopus Coccinensis*) in 1759.[70] Lutherans would instead concur with the statement of Innocent III to the Bishop of Tiberias in *Gaudemus in Domino* (1201): *"Per sacramentum baptismi non solvantur conjugia, sed crimina dimittantur."*[71]

7. The Role of Faith in Baptism

The requirement of faith as a condition for an effective reception of baptism is as old as the first written reflection of the church on baptism. This requirement underlies both the demand for catechetical instruction before baptism and the practice of reciting a declaratory creed before the actual rite. Similarly, repentance has been the classic pre-condition of baptism. But repentance in the Lutheran analysis is contrition and a special faith in the redemption achieved by our Lord, with amendment of life following as the fruit of repentance.[72]

Two general Lutheran sacramental principles create a problem if they are too literally applied to baptism. The first principle is that the sacraments create faith. That in a given case an adult candidate for baptism may possess faith in the sense of *fiducia* prior to baptism is probable. But there is no explicit statement in the sacred Scriptures which affirms that baptism creates faith. And it is not experimentally demonstable that in the case of an infant holy baptism creates anything that can be called faith in any of the usual senses of that word. The second principle that creates a problem if applied too literally is the principle that for their fruitful use sacraments require faith. Again, in the case of the infant candidate, Lutherans affirm the *saving value* of baptism, even though the presence of faith in the ordinary sense of the term is not demonstrable. Part of the difficulty arises from a too rigid synonymity of conversion, rebirth, creation of faith, and incorporation into the church in the conventional Lutheran theological vocabulary.

Nevertheless the stress of the Lutheran symbolical books is on faith as a prerequisite for the *profitable and fruitful use* of the baptism. "Faith alone makes the person worthy to receive the salutary, divine water profitably ... Just by allowing the water to be poured over you, you do not receive baptism in such a manner that it does you any good."[73]

We have a clue to the way in which the Lutheran symbolical books conceive of the faith that baptism creates in infants in the parenthesis interpolated into the declaration of the *Large Catechism:* "Even if infants did believe — which, however, is not the case, as we have proved — still their baptism would be valid and no one should rebaptize them."[74] There is no explicit cross-reference for the "as we have proved," but the only passage that can come onto consideration if this statement: "That the baptism of infants is pleasing to Christ is proved from his own work. God has sanctified many who have been thus baptized and given them the Holy Spirit. Even today there are not a few whose doctrine and life attest that they have the Holy Spirit. Similarly by God's grace we have been given the power to interpret the Scriptures and to know Christ, which is impossible without the Holy Spirit."[75] "To have faith" in the context of infant baptism thus means to have become a person in whom God has initiated his work of sanctification and to whom he has given the Holy Spirit. As the individual matures, the Holy Spirit enables him so to see in the divine word God's revelation of his gracious self and of his saving purpose in Christ that the individual comes to know, trust in, and worship Christ in the sense of *beneficia Christi cognoscere*.[76]

From this point of view, at least some Lutherans hold that in the case of infants baptism effects its ends of adoption into sonship, the forgiveness of sins, and participation in the life of God not immediately but through faith, although they are reluctant to pronounce on the nature of that faith or on its mode. They do not affirm that infants understand the movements of faith, but they do assert that the Holy Spirit is imparted in baptism and that the Holy Spirit is actively at work in them so that they can enter the kingdom of heaven, that is, receive the divine grace and the forgiveness of sins. They regard as unbiblical the view that baptized infants do not have actual faith or any new interior movements or inclinations similar to the acts of faith and love. They further hold that to concede that they have saving and justifying faith is to grant that this faith is living and efficacious. Heinrich Schmidt summarizes the reflections of classic Lutheran theology on this point:

> Since both the word and baptism are intended to confer saving grace, baptism is intended to produce this result only in those cases in which it applies to an earlier period than the word; this is the case with infants who are not yet capable of understanding the preaching of the gospel. In adults who have a developed reason and can understand the preaching of the gospel, the word has precedence and produces its results before baptism. In such cases, baptism serves to seal and establish the gracious result already accomplished by the word.[77]

A modern Lutheran theologian, Ernst Sommerlath, puts it this way:

> Baptism cannot be withheld from children, since the believing church acts vicariously on the child's behalf and since baptism derives its objective validity and power from its divine institution, even though the faith of the child may lay hold on baptism only at a later date.[78]

On the other hand, some contemporary Lutherans like Bishop Aulén minimize the role of faith in the baptized infants.[79] Even in the case of the adult, however, his faith is not the prerequisite for baptism but the organ that lays hold on that which God offers objectively in the sacrament.

In essence the problem of faith in the candidate for baptism is part of the larger polarity which asserts the monergism of divine grace in the entire process of salvation on the one hand and on the other the completeness of the individual's involvement in the process. In the beginning of his conversion he is a *subjectum patiens;* after his conversion has begun the Lutheran symbolical books call for a synergy between the Holy Spirit and the human being acting by means of the powers that the Holy Spirit has communicated to him. It is essential to recognize that in any case the faith which for the Lutheran is a prerequisite of a fruitful use of the sacrament of holy baptism is in no sense to be thought of as an intrinsically meritorious work. Beyond these considerations any attempted resolution of the problem must be regarded as a theory of a theologian rather than as a clear teaching of the symbols. Likewise, the *fiducia* that faith must exhibit to be saving faith cannot in the New Testament be merely a kind of faith in faith, as extremer types of existentialist theology seem to suggest, or a general faith of the *credere Deum* type, but a special faith that clings to the Savior as the sacred Scriptures describe him and his work and that regards his saving work as including the believer personally within its scope. It must be faith in a Christ who acted and acts *pro me.*

Ultimately the problem is linked with the Lutheran rejection of the idea that the sacraments — notably the holy Eucharist offered as an expiatory sacrifice for the sins of the living; and the dead — are effective *ex opere operato sine bono motu utentis.* This vulgar misunderstanding of the *opus operatum* principle was apparently widespread enough in the 16th century to justify the vehement polemics of the Reformers against it.[80] The Lutheran symbolical books are not denying the objective validity of the sacraments. A properly administered sacrament is always and unfailingly a divinely valid offer of grace. This fact is utterly independent of the faith of the recipient. But the offer becomes effective, the communication of grace actually takes place, the sacrament is used fruitfully, only when there is a right *motus,* that is faith in the proffer of grace, in the user's heart. The Lutheran Reformers felt that they could appeal to St. Augustine's opinion on this point: *"Ait Augustinus ut fides sacramenti non sacramentum justificet."*[81] The cited words with are an epigrammatical reformulation of St. Augustine's words with specific reference to baptism: *"Unde ista tanta virtus aquae, ut corpus tangat et cor abluat, nisi faciente verbo, non quia dicitur, sed quia creditur?"*[82]

At the same time, with specific reference to infant baptism, a Lutheran can hardly refuse to deny what appears to be the theological intent of the scholastic assertion that the sacraments achieve their purpose *ex opere operato sine bono motu utentis* as long as the recipient does not interpose an obstacle (*obicem non ponet*). It is noteworthy that the Lutheran symbolical books do not discuss the scholastic principle in question with specific reference to baptism, but only in connection with its application to Eucharist as an expiatory sacrifice for the sins of the living and dead. Strictly speaking, the technical terms *ex opere operato, sine bono motu utentis, und obicem non ponere* had aquired a vulgar meaning that their original authors did not intend them to have. In essence, the declarations of the *Large Catechism* that baptism is not our work but God's and that this sacrament is not a work of ours, but a treasure which God gives and which faith only appropriates, assert implicitly what the medieval schoolmen sought to affirm by their teaching on the *opus operatum*.[83]

Two factors are directing Lutheran systematic theology to a new consideration of faith in connection with baptism. One factor is the size of the gainsaying community before which the Lutheran Church must defend its practice of infant baptism. In the European homelands of the Lutheran Church the groups that insist on "believer's baptism" constitute in the main relatively small sectarian minorities. On this continent the bodies that insist on believer's baptism constitute an impressive fraction of organized Christianity and one denominational family of this group — the Baptist community — is the second largest denomination in the United States. The second factor is the increasing number of adult converts who enter the Lutheran Church through baptism. These factors are demanding a view of faith that takes into account not only the effect of baptism upon an infant recipient of the sacrament, but also the nature of faith as a mature commitment to Christ created by the Holy Spirit through the witness of the corporate church to the gospel prior to the reception of baptism.

8. Stress on Certainty

The basic question of the Lutheran Reformation, as conventionally formulated, is "How can I find a gracious God?" This question underlies the concern for the "thoroughly terrified conscience" in the *Augsburg Confession* and the *Apology* and the concern for deliverance from the demonic tyrants of sin, death, hell, flesh, world, and devil. The calculated theological stress of the late middle ages lay on these elements of the Christian revelation that contribute to the individual's subjective uncertainty of salvation. The unabashed emphasis of the Lutheran symbolical books is on those elements in Christianity that establish the objective certainty of salvation for all who lay hold on the divine promise of pardon through faith. Both emphases involve elements of authentic truth that must be held in tension. When the paradox is relieved either by an exclusive nomistic stress on the divine wrath and the divine judgment or by an antinomian stress on a purely cognitive and intellectual conception of faith, spiritual tragedy results. The concern of the Lutheran symbolical books is advanced by their stress on baptism as evidence of the divine concern for the individual. The fact of baptism serves the person who stands in a state of faith and of grace as evidence that God will provide him with all the means necessary to assure him a happy death and a resurrection to everlasting life.

Nevertheless, it is possible to receive baptism, but not the benefit of baptism, without faith. From this follows not only that the fruit of baptism may be received later than the baptism itself but also that the benefit received in baptism can be lost if the person baptized rejects his faith and no longer makes use of his baptism.

9. Necessity of Baptism

The Lutheran symbolical books categorically affirm that "baptism is necessary for salvation."[84] Put negatively, original sin, understood as the condition in which human beings are natively full of evil desires and inclinations and are by themselves unable to have genuine reverence for and faith in God, "is truly sin, which even now damns and brings eternal death on those who are not born again through baptism and the Holy Spirit."[85] This necessity of baptism, however, as the theologians have always stressed, is not absolute but ordinate.

10. Infant Baptism

An inference both from the divine command to baptize and from the conviction of the necessity of baptism for salvation is the baptism of infants. "Children are to be baptized."[86] The Lutherans aver that they cannot tolerate in the church the article "that in the sight of God unbaptized children are not sinners but are righteous and innocent, and that as long as they have not achieved the use of reason they will be saved in this innocence without baptism (which according to this view they do not need),"[87] or the article "that without and prior to baptism the children of Christian parents are holy and the children of God by virtue of their birth from Christian and pious parents."[88]

In infant baptism we see the monergism of divine grace operating most explicitly and most dramatically. Here God, on the basis of his predestination and vocation, makes a child of wrath, who has been able to do nothing toward his own salvation, his own child and imparts to him by sheer grace the sonship that the eternally begotten Son possesses by nature. As the child is carried to the font, it is incapable of meeting any precondition. It does not have contrition; it does not have faith; it does not have the intention of receiving a sacrament; it cannot comprehend or respond to a proclamation of the gospel. What is more, the minister of the sacrament may be immoral and unrepentant. The sponsors that represent the church may be members of the holy community *nomine tantum non re*. Whatever happens in baptism must be God's work. Thus infant baptism becomes a paradigm of God's dealing with man.

The Lutheran symbolical books explicitly reject the logic that concludes from the absence of faith in the infant candidate to the invalidity of infant baptism. On the contrary, they argue *ad hominem* that "precisely because baptism has [in some cases] been wrongly received it has existence and value."[89] The baptism of infants is regarded as a prime example of the proper use of tradition in early Lutheran theology.[90]

The Lutheran apologetic for infant baptism has always conceded the absence of a direct Dominical (or even apostolic) command to baptize infants on the sacred Scriptures. But it is now taking into account increasingly the fact that the patristic evidence is not as absolutely decisive as it had once appeared to be, and is making its appeal to the biblical theology of baptism a stronger component in its defense of infant baptism.

The necessity for baptism is a witness to the role of the institutional necessity of the church and her ministry for the salvation of those whom God calls into fellowship with himself. It is through the witness of the church and the activity of the sacred ministry that the Holy Spirit confers the new birth on men and women and preserves them in the faith. Outside the regular ministrations of religion within the holy community of the church the new life would die very soon. Since infants are *extra ecclesiam* as they come into the world, they can enter the family of God only through baptism. Infant baptism is essential to apply to small children the promise of salvation according to Christ's command, and the nurture of the church is no less necessary to preserve them in the faith.[91]

The Lutheran community has not remained wholly unaffected by contemporary controversies about infant baptism. The awareness of living in a "post-Constantinian" era has caused some Lutheran clergymen in Germany to revolt against the idea of an "automatic baptism." They have proposed that even their religiously committed parishioners postpone the baptism of their children until the latter can make a decision for themselves. (In a few cases they have reportedly set their parishioners an example.) This line of thought, although nowhere very influential, seems to be more seriously pursued in the German Democratic Republic, where the possibility of apostasy is a clear and present peril.

Because baptism is a divine gift of which man stands in dire need, it is not something which the church has in her competence to administer or withhold but which she must administer and to which the Christian has a right for himself and for his children. However, pastoral prudence normally requires baptism to be withheld from the minor children of non-Christians, unless one of the parents is a Christian, and of heretics, unless one parent is orthodox. Exceptions are to be made in the case of children in imminent danger of death and in such cases where there is reasonable hope that the other part of the baptismal commission, "to teach them to observe everything that I have commended," will be carried out.

In view of the ordinate necessity of baptism, Lutheran theology traditionally teaches that, while "baptism is the ordinary sacrament of initiation and means rebirth for all men, necessary for the rebirth and salvation even of the children of believing parents, at the same time, we say that in the case of deprivation or of impossibility, the children of Christians can be saved through an extraordinary and special divine dispensation .... We are bound to baptism; an extraordinary action of God is not, however to be denied."[92]

Also in the case of the death of unbaptized children, born or unborn, of Christian parents the theologians argued from the ordinate necessity of baptism and from the thesis that "we are bound to baptism, God is not." They invoked St. Bernard's principle *"Contemtus sacramenti damnat, non privatio."* In the case of the unbaptized children of non-Christians they generally refuse to pronounce and commit such children to the mercy of God.

11. Surrogates for Water Baptism

The Lutheran symbolical books have nothing to say explicitly about "baptism of desire" or "baptism of blood," tacitly recognizing the metaphorical use of "baptism" in these designations. "Baptism" in their vocabulary is always water baptism.

12. Adult Baptism

Adult baptisms were so rare that most of the 16th century Lutheran church orders make no formal provision at all for them. Where they did take place, they usually involved Jewish or Moslem converts among prisoners of war. In such cases pastors invariably instructed the candidates in the Christian faith and the significance of Trinitarian baptism and adapted the rite for the baptism of infants.

The *Smalcald Articles* contemplate a delayed action of the preaching of the gospel in the case of previously unbaptized adults. "Adults who have attained the age of reason must first have heard, 'He who believes and is baptized will be saved' (Mk 16:16), even if they did not at once believe and did not receive the Spirit and Baptism until ten years later."[93] Noteworthy is the implication that they will receive baptism, indeed that they must receive baptism.

Adult baptisms underline the fact that baptism has more than an exclusively cognitive significance, although this aspect must not be depreciated. Again they stress that baptism is more than an act of confession, although it has this too as a secondary aspect.

In reflecting on the date of Christian history, contemporary Lutheran theology is impressed by the fact that it is precisely in the era of the New Testament and of the primitive church, when the bulk of the church's new accessions came through adult baptisms, that baptism is credited with saving power, with communicating the Holy Spirit, with imparting forgiveness of sins, with banishing demons from the heart, with equipping Christians with weapons for spiritual warfare, with effecting rebirth, with bestowing illumination and the knowledge of God, with making men "no longer the sons of mortal men only, but also the children of the immortal and indefectible God," and with supplying them with an earnest of the resurrection.

13. Who Baptizes?

The first answer is: God. "To be baptized in God's name is to be baptized not by men but by God himself."[94] "Baptism is primarily an *action* of God," Bishop Aulén declares, "with respect to which the church's act is a *re-actio*."[95]

From another point of view, the Church baptizes.[96] Immediately, the ordinary minister of the baptism is the priest, to whom God has given the authority of orders (*potestas ordinis*) through the vocation of the church.[97] While it is desirable that the ordained ministers of baptism be believers and personally pious, this is not a condition of a valid or an efficacious baptism. "It is allowable to use the sacraments even when they are administered by evil men .... Both the sacraments and the word are effectual by reason of the institution and commandment of Christ even if they are administered by evil men."[98]

Because baptism is necessary for salvation, the Lutheran Church approves and enjoins emergency baptism. The Lutheran symbolical books hark back to medieval canon law to exemplify the principle that a layman may baptize validly in a life-and-death emergency.[99]

It is nowhere specifically asserted that a baptized laywoman can be the extraordinary minister of the sacrament of baptism, but it is not stated that she cannot be. In the polemics against the Reformed rejection of emergency lay baptism the competence of a midwife or other laywoman is specifically emphasized as a Lutheran practice.

The Lutheran symbolical books do not speak of the question of the validity of baptism administered by a heretic or an unbaptized person. The dogmatic tradition reflects the divided opinion of the pre-Reformation church and is not without inconsistencies. Baptism in a Trinitarian Christian denomination like the Roman Church or the Reformed community is presumed to be valid, but baptism administered by a "Photinian," or a "Sabellian," that is to say, by a Socinian, was held invalid by the classic orthodox theologians. Baptism by an unbaptized person was held valid by Gerhard, on the analogy of the effective proclamation of the word by an unreborn and not truly converted preacher. But he notes that St. Gregory II regarded such a baptism as invalid, that St. Augustine was undecided, and that St. Nicholas I and St. Thomas regarded it as valid.

Sponsors, as representatives of the church, are to be communicants.[100] The number of sponsors was fixed at one, for the divine unity, or two, for the duality of parenthood, or three, for the divine Trinity. Where there were three sponsors, custom directed that two be of the candidate's sex. No spiritual affinity is created by sponsorship, and the traditions that it does so are branded as unjust.[101]

14. Symbolism and Ceremonies

The catechisms try to steer a course between a reduction of baptism to a merely symbolical action and a rejection of the obvious symbolism of baptism. Its concern is with God's word and activity. Baptism is not "an empty sign,"[102] it saves. Yet the symbolism is undeniably there in the sacred Scriptures themselves. "What does such baptizing with water signify?" asks the *Small Catechism*. "It signifies that the old Adam in us is to be drowned through continual contrition and repentance and die with all sins and evil desires and again a new man who lives everlastingly in God's presence in righteousness and purity is continually to emerge and rise."[103]

In the view of the *Large Catechism* the immersion in or the generous affusion with water and the candidate's emergence from the font similarly symbolize the continuing slaying of the Old Adam and the resurrection of the new man.[104]

Subsequent Lutheran liturgiology distinguishes between the *ceremoniae essentiales* in baptism and the *ceremoniae accidentales*. The latter are the prayers, reading of the sacred Scripture, the admonitions and warnings, the use of sponsors, the annunciation, the giving of a name, the exorcism, the signing of the Holy cross, and the use of the chrisom.

One of the most prominent of these ceremonies is the renunciation of the devil and all his works and all his pomps. As Hans Kirsten sees it, this is not merely one more ceremony but a key to the understanding of the whole rite, possibly *the* key to such an understanding. Historically a part of the most primitive level of surviving customs and antecedent both to the exorcisms and to the blessing of the water, it is closely linked with the idea of putting off the old man and being clothed with Christ, and it is the negative human side of the baptismal compact, as the confession of faith is the positive human side of it.

15. Baptismal "Character" and the Unrepeatability of Baptism

The Lutheran symbolical books nowhere explicitly reject the idea of an indelible sacramental character. They do not, however, operate with this construct, in part because of its late origin in Western theology, in part because of the lack of a biblical basis, in part because of the obviously metaphorical nature of the term, and in part probably because of a vague uneasiness about the Hellenistic rather than biblical doctrine *de anima* which underlay it. Their insistence on the unrepeatability of baptism, which is all that the teaching of an indelible character seems to have intended to say, in a sense makes this construct unnecessary. The repetition of a valid baptism "would be to blaspheme and desecrate the sacrament in the worst way."[105] Thus, when we lapse after baptism and repent "we need not again have the water poured over us."[106] These passages accord with the convictions that the grace of baptism is amissable, but not the baptism itself; that the unrepeatability of baptism is implied by the one-and-for-all act of Our Lord; and that precisely because baptism is a new birth it is unrepeatable.

Pastoral practice in the Lutheran Church in cases where the baptismal status of a prospective member of the church is uncertain generally reflects the pastor's theological presuppositions. The obligation devolving on him to exercise due diligence to establish the facts surrounding the reported baptism is universally recognized, and he ought to have credible documentary evidence of the prospective member's baptism. When he holds that it is sufficient that the baptizer understood his act as the administration of Christian baptism and that he applied a sufficient quantity of water that it ran while saying "I baptize you in the name of the Father and of the Son and of the Holy Spirit," the pastor will accept a credible previous baptism regardless of the baptizer's affiliation with the Christian community. Where he holds that only a baptized Christian may validly baptize, he will not accept the administration of the sacrament by an unbaptized person. Where he has not been able to establish decisively the fact of a previous baptism he will normally baptize absolutely. The number of pastoral theologians who have endorsed baptism *sub conditione* in dubious cases is small, and the tradition of the Lutheran Church which discountenances conditional baptism goes back to Luther himself.

A problem is presented by baptisms administered in the liberal churches, where the form and matter may technically be acceptable but where the understanding of the nature of the Godhead is so defective as to be sub-Christian at best. Conventionally in the cases of Unitarian-Universalist baptisms a Lutheran pastor baptized a convert. The case of baptisms administered in denominations without a specific and universally asserted Trinitarian confession — such as the United Church of Christ and the Disciples of Christ — creates particular casuistic problems.

16. Vulgar Misconceptions Related to Baptism

Lutherans objected to the "baptism" of inanimate objects, such as altar-stones and bells, coupled as they were with characteristic features of authentic baptism, such as a name-giving and the presence of sponsors who were expected to make contributions.[107] The belief that the bells thereby received special power to repel diabolical attacks, to ward off thunder and lightning, and to help the poor souls was looked upon as a compounded superstition.

The Lutheran symbolical books energetically reprehend the notion that the monastic profession has the same saving effect that baptism confers.[108] It must be conceded that the proofs which the symbolical books submit as evidence that the followers of the pope held this view are too general for examination or they are inaccurate in their specification. That the view was held, not only at the vulgar level, but that it enjoyed rather respectable traditional and official support among influential theologians is also true.

In the 16th century both popular piety and liturgical practice linked baptism and holy water. The Reformers regarded holy water — despite its 1000-year-long history in the church — in the form and understanding of this sacramental that the 16th century had inherited as inextricably bound up with vulgar superstition and misleading opinions to a point where, along with some other traditional ceremonies that had suffered a similar fate, it could no longer be rescued and rehabilitated.[109]

17. Some Questions for
Roman Catholic Theologians to Answer

The impression that a Lutheran is likely to take from Roman Catholic discussions of grace in connection with baptism is that grace is conceived of as something quantifiable. If this impression is correct, does this adequately communicate the idea that this kind of language must be understood metaphorically and that the grace which the sacraments really convey is primarily the divine love and pardon?

May not the insistence on water ritually prepared on Easter Eve and Whitsuneve be conducive to superstition?

On the basis of the word of God, is the designation of implicit desire for baptism or of death by martyrdom as species of baptism defensible as anything more than a figure of speech? Can one conclude with theological certainty that these "baptisms" meet the requirement of the absolute necessity of baptism for salvation? Is it the "baptism" of desire that saves or the "perfect contrition" that is demanded in conjunction with it?

Does a limbus of unbaptized infants have any basis in the word of God?

Does the common opinion which denies the beatific vision to children who die without baptism take full account of God's universal love and Christ's universal redemption?

Does the Roman Catholic attitude toward the sacrament of penance take adequate account of the perduring effect of baptism and its efficacy with reference to sins committed after baptism?

How can the existence of an internal intention (as distinguished, say, from a merely external or a habitual intention) in the minister of baptism be adequately certified to the recipient of baptism?

How can one determine the existence of the habitual desire requisite for a valid reception of baptism by an adult with a sufficient degree of certainty to satisfy the doubt that baptism was actually received?

Is the idea of an indelible character imparted in baptism in actuality anything more than a metaphorical assertion of the unrepeatability of baptism? Is the character as *signum distinctivum* certainly known to anyone except God?

What basis in the word of God is there for the doctrine that baptism needs completion by means of an anointing of the forehead with chrism?

ENDNOTES

1. AC XIII 1-2. See also Ap XIII 1; XXIV 69.
2. Ap XII 42.
3. *The Faith of the Christian Church*, trans. Eric H. Wahlstrom (2nd ed., Philadelphia: Fortress Press, 1960), p. 337.
4. Ap XIII 3.
5. Ap XXIV 18.
6. FC, SD III 15-17.
7. Ap VII 3; 10; 30-31; also SA Two IV 9.
8. SA Three IV.
9. AC V 1; see also Ap XXIV 70.
10. Ap XIII 4-5. Cf. FC, Ep. II 2, "The grace of God [is] offered in the Word and the Holy Sacraments." See also 13; 18; 50; III 16; XI 72; 76.
11. "*Taufe und Rechtfertigung bei Paulus*," *Kerygma und Dogma*, II (1965), p. 325.
12. LC Baptism 45.
13. SC Three V 1.

14. LC Baptism 53.
15. *Theology of the Lutheran Confessions*, trans. Paul F. Kohneke and Herbert J. A. Bouman (Philadelphia: Muhlenberg Press, 1961), p. 145, n. 2.
16. DB 787.
17. SA Three V 2-3.
18. Schlink, *op. cit.*, p. 148.
19. LC Baptism 14; 17; 19; 27.
20. LC Baptism 8; see also 22.
21. LC Baptism 19.
22. Schlink, *op. cit.*, p. 147.
23. Cf. John Gerhard, *Loci theologici, locus de baptismo*, 74.
24. Emil Sehling, et. al., ed., *Die evangelische Kirchenordnungen des 16. Jahrhunderts* (Leipzig: Reisland, 1902-1913; Tübingen: J. C. B. Mohr, [Paul Siebeck] 1955-), I, 426.
25. LC Baptism 65.
26. LC Baptism 15; 36.
27. SC Baptism 4.
28. LC Baptism 16.
29. LC Baptism ; see also *ibid.*, 4; 6 and 29.
30. *Systema*, X, p. 166.
31. *Examen theologicum acroamaticum*, II, p. 554.
32. LC Baptism 24.
33. SC Baptism 6; see also LC Baptism 41.
34. Ap II 35-36.
35. *Confessio catholica*, p. 1128.
36. FC SD II 65.
37. LC Baptism 27; AC II; LC Sacrament of the Altar 23.
38. SC Sacrament of the Altar 6.
39. SC Baptism 6; LC Baptism 41; 43-46.
40. LC Baptism 24-25.
41. Cf. Titus 3:5; SC Baptism 10; LC Baptism 26-27; LC Creed 54-58.
42. Schlink, *op. cit.*, p. 151.
43. AC IX 2; LC Baptism 41.
44. FC, SD II 15-16. The "enlightened me with his gifts" of the *Small Catechism* explanation of the Creed may also echo the old designation of baptism as *photismos*.
45. FC, SD II 67; FC, SD IV-V.
46. LC Baptism 44.
47. LC Baptism 41.
48. *Historischer Kommentar zu Luthers Kleinem Katechismus* (Gütersloh: C. Bertelsmann, 1929), p 457.
49. LC Baptism 6. Cf. LC Baptism 41; 83.
50. *Ibid.* Cf. LC Baptism 41; 43.
51. SC Baptism 13-14.
52. Ap IX 9; LC Baptism 41.
53. *On the Holy Spirit*, 40.
54. LC Baptism 65.
55. LC Baptism 74.
56. LC Baptism 77-86.
57. LC Baptism 66.
58. FC, SD II 16.
59. DB 1623.
60. Aulén, *op. cit.*, p. 337.
61. *Ibid.*, pp. 335-36.

62. LC Baptism 2.
63. LC Creed 42.
64. Gerhard, *Loci theologici*, IX, 67.
65. LC Our Father 37. Cf. LC Sacrament of the Altar 23-24.
66. LC Sacrament of the Altar 87.
67. AC XII 1-2.
68. Ap XIII 14-15.
69. Marriage Booklet 16.
70. DB 2580-2585.
71. DB 777.
72. AC XII 3-6.
73. LC Baptism 33; 36.
74. LC Baptism 55.
75. LC Baptism 50.
76. Cf. Ap IV 46; 154; 228; 310.
77. *The Doctrinal Theology of the Evangelical Lutheran Church*, trans. Charles A. Hay and Henry E. Jacobs (Minneapolis: Augsburg Publishing House, 1961), p. 537.
78. *Die Religion in Geschichte und Gegenwart*, Vol. VI (6 vols.; 3rd ed.; Tübingen: J. C. B. Mohr [Paul Siebeck], 1962), p. 647.
79. Aulén, *op. cit.*, p. 341.
80. Ap XIII 2-3; 18-19.
81. Ap XIII 23.
82. *In Joannis evangelium* 15, 3, Tract 80. Migne's *Patrologia latina*, vol. 35.
83. LC Baptism 36.
84. AC IX 1.
85. AC II 3.
86. AC IX 2. Cf. Ap IX 2, "The promise of baptism applies also to little children...," and LC Baptism 49-50.
87. FC Ep XII 6.
88. *Ibid.*, para. 8.
89. LC Baptism 59.
90. Cf. Martin Chemnitz, *Examen concilii tridentini, locus de traditionibus*, sec. V, paras. 2-3.
91. Cf. Aulén, *op. cit.*, pp. 339-40.
92. John Gerhard, *Loci theologici, locus* XX, 236.
93. SA Three VIII 7.
94. LC Baptism 10.
95. Aulén, *op. cit.*, p. 336.
96. SA Three V 4.
97. Ap XXVII 13 and AC XIV.
98. AC VIII 1-3. Cf. Ap VII 28; 47.
99. Treatise 67.
100. SC Preface 11,
101. Treatise 78.
102. LC Baptism 63.
103. SC Baptism 11-12.
104. LC Baptism 64-65.
105. LC Baptism 55.
106. LC Baptism 78.
107. SA Three XV 4; cf. FC SD VII 87.
108. AC XXVII 11; Ap XXVII 9, 20.
109. Ap IV 282; XV 44 (Sermon).

THE MOMENT AT WHICH THE SACRAMENTAL UNION BEGINS

The question at issue, which continues to engage the interest of Lutherans,[1] is really twofold: 1) When does the sacramental union of the Body and Blood of Christ with the bread and wine of the Holy Eucharist begin? 2) Did the early Lutheran theologians hold that the sacramental union of the Body and the Blood of Christ with the bread and wine is achieved prior to the distribution?

The only source that the Lutheran Symbols admit for their doctrine of the sacramental union of the Body and the Blood of Christ with the bread and wine of the Holy Eucharist is the fourfold account of the institution of the Sacrament of the Altar in the Synoptic Gospels (Matthew 26:26-28; Mark 14:22-24; Luke 22:19-20) and in St. Paul (I Corinthians 11:23-25).[2] The tenses of the verbs used and the sequence of elements are such that it is not possible to argue from these data to a conclusive answer to the question: When does the sacramental union begin? Nor does the tradition of the Church help us to interpret the biblical data; the primitive Church that might have had Dominical or Apostolic instructions was apparently unconcerned about the question.

That no dogmatic answer to this question can be given is the expressed conviction of two weighty doctors of the church of the *Augsburg Confession*. John Gerhard (1582-1637) asserts: "[Christian simplicity] is not gravely concerned about the moment in which the Body of Christ begins or ceases to be present, but just as the mode of the presence defies research, so also it declares that these questions about the moment of the presence are unanswerable."[3] Similarly, John William Baier (1647-1695) declares: "[It is] not necessary to define the moment of time in which the Body and the Blood of Christ begin to be sacramentally united with the bread and the wine."[4]

Historically the question became an issue only with the growing theological separation between the East and the West after the fourth century. The West stressed the sufficiency of the words of institution to confect the Sacrament. The East insisted that the Words of Institution needed at least to be supplemented with an invocation (*epiklesis*) of the Holy Ghost upon the elements.

The theological development that followed in the wake of the controversies with the spiritualizers of Eucharistic doctrine, with the dissidents within the Church, and with the antisacramentalist heretics outside the Church made the issue more acute for the West than for the East. Also influential in keeping the issue in the foreground were the West's efforts at reunion with at least parts of the Eastern and the Far Eastern Churches down to within a century before the Reformation.[5] The issue continues to be an acknowledged point of difference between the Roman Catholic Church and the Churches of the East and the Far East.[6]

Bl. Martin Luther and his supporters — inclined as they were to feel themselves at this point to closer to the Papalist party than to the innovating Sacramentarians[7] — consistently held that the sacramental union is accomplished in close temporal as well as causal connection with the recitation of the words of institution of the Holy Eucharist. At the same time they insisted on the integrity of the total sacramental action and denied sacramental reality as much to the private masses of the Latin clerics[8] as to the communions of the "enemies of the Sacrament."[9]

In *De capitivate Babylonica ecclesiae praeludium* (1520), Luther affirmed that the Body and Blood of Christ were present at the time of the elevation;[10] he takes the same position in the *Deudsche Messe und ordnung Gottis diensts* (1526)[11] and in his *Kurzes Bekenntnis vom heiligen Sakrament* (1544).[12] In the *Formula Missae et Communionis* (1523) he approved the use of the prayer, *Domine Jesu Christe*, with its reference to "this Thy Most Holy Body and Blood," prior to the celebrant's self-communion during the *Agnus Dei*.[13] In *Ein brieff an die zu Franckfort am Meyn* (1523), he reduces the issue for doubting parishioners to "what the hand [of the minister] and the and the mouth [of the communicant] here encloses."[14] The notes of George Rörer (1492-1557) on one of Luther's catechism sermons on the Holy Eucharist (September 25, 1528) describe the Body of Christ as clothing itself with the bread when the word is added to the elements.[15] Luther's *Vermanung zum Sacrament des leibs und bluts unsers Herrn* (1530) records the counsel that he gave to a curate to consign to the fire a host which had been put into the mouth of a patient who expired before he could swallow it;[16] he repeated the counsel to George Spalatin (1484-1545) of Altenburg on December 10, 1543.[17]

Article X of the *Augsburg Confession* asserts that the Body and Blood of Christ are truly present in the Holy Communion under the form of the bread and the wine and that they are distributed to and received by all the communicants.[18]

The travel diary of Wolfgang Musculus (1497-1563) of Bern describes the service in St. Mary's Church, Wittenberg, on the morning of Cantate Sunday, 1536; he notes that celebrant diligently drained the chalice and thereupon cleansed it with wine that he poured in, "that no Blood might remain." He also records that during the negotiations leading to the Wittenberg "Concord" of 1536, John Bugenhagen (1485-1558) whispered into Luther's ear concerning the bread and wine left over after the celebration of the Holy Eucharist, and added that in some (presumably South German) churches the remaining bread was mixed with "profane" (that is, unconsecrated) pieces of bread, as if it were itself "profane." Both Luther and Bugenhagen then explained that to avoid having hosts left over they counted out the hosts to match the number of communicants at each service.[19]

The 1540 Lutheran Church Order of the Electorate of Brandenburg provided that when the parish priest had to administer Holy Communion to a dying person in the village he was to consecrate the elements on the altar in the presence of the parishioners who had notified him of the emergency and then, vested in surplice and preceded by the sacristan carrying a bell and a lighted lantern, to take the most venerable Sacrament under both kinds to the sick person, to whom the priest was to administer the Sacrament without repeating the words of institution.[20] Luther was familiar with these provision of the Church Order and did not condemn them, as long as they were carried out "without superstition."[21]

John Hachenburg of Erfurt reports that about 1542 a woman communicant at St. Mary's Church, Wittenberg, bumped against the chalice as she was kneeling down so that some of its contents spilled upon her clothing. Luther and Bugenhagen, who were present, assisted the curate in wiping off the woman's jacket. After the celebration Luther had the affected portion of the lining of the jacket cut out and burned, along with the wood that he had had shaved from the part of the choir stall upon which the contents of the chalice had likewise been splashed.[22]

When Bugenhagen, apparently without consulting Luther, abolished the elevation of the host and chalice in St. Mary's Church, Wittenberg, in 1542, Luther is reported as defending the practice to the princes of Anhalt (who were wondering if they should follow in Bugenhagen's train) on the ground that "since Christ is truly present in the bread, why should it not be handled and adored with the greatest reverence?"[23]

In 1543, when a controversy broke out between Simon Wolferinus (Wolfrum), the rector of St. Andrew's Church, Eisleben and Fredrick Rauber of St. Peter's Church in the same city, Luther sent the former a letter — in which Bugenhagen concurred — condemning his practice of mixing the consecrated elements remaining after the celebration with unconsecrated elements as a scandalous Zwinglian insanity.[24] In a subsequent letter Luther defined the sacramental action as starting at the beginning of the Our Father (that is, immediately after the recitation of the Words of Institution) and continuing until all had been communicated, the chalice had been drained, the hosts consumed, and the communicants had left the altar.[25]

In the *cause célèbre* of Adam Besserer, curate at Friessnitz in the Voigtland — who had dropped a consecrated host with the unconsecrated ones after the service (over the protest of a lay worshipper), and had been put into prison for his malfeasance — a Wittenberg theological faculty opinion (1546) by Luther and Bugenhagen condemned the offender as a despiser of God and man who ought to be ejected from the Lutheran community and go to his fellow-Zwinglians because he dared in public to treat consecrated and unconsecrated hosts alike.[26]

In an equally famed and frequently misrepresented case of John Saliger (Beatus) of Rostock, John Wigand (1523-1587) of the Jena theological faculty presented an opinion in which he stated that the bread which had been blessed in the name of the Lord was the true Body of Christ even before the eating and that parallel statements could be made about the chalice.[27] In October, 1569, the "Wismar Opinion," probably the work of David Chyträus (1531-1600), one of the authors of the *Formula of Concord,* was promulgated in an effort to end the controversy; this opinion *condemned* the views — which it asserts that no Lutheran holds — that the Body and Blood of Christ are not present in the Holy Communion until the communicant's lips touches the consecrated bread and wine or his mouth encloses them and that the Body of Christ is not in the bread but in the eating.[28]

Martin Chemnitz (1522-1586), also an author of the *Formula of Concord,* disavows the opinion that the consecrated bread which is distributed, which is imparted, and which the Apostles received from Christ's hand, is not the Body of Christ, but only becomes the Body of Christ when the communicants begin to eat it.[29] Without approving the practices for the sixteenth century, he likewise holds that when in the days of St. Justin Martyr (130?-165?) a deacon customarily took the Holy Communion from the altar before which the congregation was worshipping to the sick, or in the days of St. Irenaeus of Lyons (c.130-c.202) the Holy Eucharist was sent as a symbol of intercommunion by the bishop of the place to other bishops visiting in his community, or in the days of Clement of Alexandria (c.150-c.214), St. Cyprian of

Carthage (died 258), or St. Augustine (354-430), communicants took a part of the consecrated elements home with them, the sacramental use or action continued until the elements had been consumed.[30]

The *Formula of Concord* itself asserts that Lutherans teach that Christ's truly and essentially present Body and Blood are distributed in the Holy Eucharist and that the Sacramentarians unmask themselves by denying it;[31] declares that the recitation of the words of institution is the "blessing" to which St. Paul refers in I Corinthians 10;[32] quotes with approval the statement of St. John Chrysostom that the crucified Christ makes the elements offered on the altar His Body and Blood;[33] and while it stipulates that the recitation of the words of institution consecrate a sacrament only in a situation where the remainder of the divinely prescribed action follows, it also makes clear that the *actio* or *usus* are not restricted to the reception.[34]

In the next century, John Gerhard describes the recitation of the words of institution as effecting a sacramental change of the bread (*sacramentalis panis mutatio*);[35] asserts that "in the order of nature" we could not eat the Body of Christ sacramentally unless it were present in the bread before being eaten; and defends Martin Chemnitz' assertion "that the Body of the Lord is present on the altar before the eating" against the criticism of the Italian Jesuit Robert Bellarmine (1542-1621).[36]

In summary: As Lutherans we cannot assert less than that the true Body and Blood of Christ are truly and essentially present in the Holy Communion and that with the consecrated bread and wine they are distributed to and orally received by all who use the Sacrament, whether they are worthy or unworthy, pious or impious, believers or unbelievers.[37]

If any one joins us in saying this much, we cannot compel him to say more.

Hence, any attempt at defining the precise moment at which the sacramental union begins — at the consecration, at the beginning of the distribution, or at any point in between — must remain in the domain of theological opinion. Whatever opinion we may hold on this point, we must be careful on the one hand not to elevate it to the status of a doctrine and on the other not to charge with heresy or error a fellow-Lutheran who holds a different opinion.

In any discussion of the issues involved, a careful distinction must be made between the *mode* of the sacramental union (under which head the Lutheran Symbols obligate us to reject transubstantiation as taught by the Roman Catholic Church)[38] and the *time* of the sacramental union.

Finally, the Lutheran stress must always be on the total action and we must resist every tendency which would atomistically attach unwarranted, unhistorical and unbiblical importance to one phase of that Dominically directed "action outside of which nothing has the character of a sacrament."

ENDNOTES

1. For instance, Hermann Sasse, *This Is My Body* (Minneapolis: Augsburg Publishing House, 1959) 164-176; "The Moment of the Real Presence in the Lord's Supper," *Concordia Theological Monthly,* Vol. XXX, No. 7 (July 1959), 530-531.
2. Preface to the *Book of Concord,* in Hans Lietzmann, ed., *Die Bekenntnisschriften der evangelisch-lutherischen Kirche herausgegben im Gedenkjahr der Augsburgischen Konfession* 1930, 3rd ed. (Göttingen: Vandenhoeck und Ruprecht, 1956), 753, lines 6-18. I Corinthians 10:16 does not decide the matter for us either.
3. John Gerhard, *Loci theologici,* Locus XXI, cap. xvii, para. 195, ed. Edward Preuss, V (Berlin: Gustav Schlawitz, 1867), 188.
4. John William Baier, *Compendium theologiae positivae secundum editionem anni 1694,* Part three, cap. XI, para. viii-e ed. Edward Preuss (Berlin: Gustav Schlawitz, 1864), 551 Carl Ferdinand William Walther, ed. (St. Louis: *Officina Synodi Missouriensis Lutheranae,* 1879), III, 504.
5. The situation at the end of the Middle Ages is illustrated by the letter of Innocent III, *Eius exemplo* (1208), in J.-P. Migne, *Patrologia Latina* 215, 1511; the letter of Innocent IV, *Sub catholicae* (1243), in John Dominic Mansi, *Sacrorum conciliorum collectio,* XXIII, 580; the libel of Benedict XII, *Cum dudum* (1341), in Caesar Baronius, *Annales ecclesiastici,* ed. Augustine Theiner, XXV, (Bar-le-Duc: Louis Guerin, 1872) 259; the letter *Super quibusdam* of Clement VI (1351), in Baronius-Theiner, *op. cit.,* XXV, 506; the bull of Eugene IV, *Exsulate Deo,* the so-called *Decretum ad Armenos* (1439), in Mansi, *op. cit.,* XXXI, 1057, Cf. also the decree of the 13th session (1551) of the Council of Trent and its Canon 4 on the Holy Eucharist, in H. J. Schroeder, ed., *Canons and Decrees of the Council of Trent* (St. Louis: B. Herder Book Co., c. 1941), 351-352, 356.
6. R. Janin, *Les Eglises Orientales et les Rites Orienteaux* (Paris: Letouzey et Ané, 1955) 87; cf. 48-49. For the Roman Catholic position, see Ludwig Ott, *Fundamentals of Catholic Dogma,* tr. by Patrick Lynch, ed. by James Bastible (St. Louis: B. Herder Book Co. [1954]) 384-385. Representative of the position of European Eastern Orthodoxy is (Metropolitan) Seraphim, *Die Ostkirche* (Stuttgart: W. Spemann Verlag, 1950) 192. For the position of American Eastern Orthodoxy, see Leonid Soroka, (Dean) Umw and Stan W. Carlson, *Faith of our Fathers* (Minneapolis: Olympic Press, 1954), 58-59 and Constantine N. Callinicos, *The Greek Orthodox Catechism* (New York: Greek Archdiocese of North and South America, 1953), 118. A recent attempt at bridging the gap from the Roman Catholic side is that of G.C. Smit, *"Epiclèse et théologie des sacrements,"* in *Mélanges de science religieuse,* XV (1958), 95-136, in which the author follows the theory of the Dominican theologian Heinrich Schillebeeckx; the article is summarized under the title, "The Moment of Transubstantiation," in *Theology Digest,* VIII (1960), 37-41.
7. For instance, *Von Abendmal Christi Bekendnis* (1528), WA, 26, 313, 26-28; 462, 4-5.
8. *Smalcald Articles,* Part Two, II, 7-9.
9. *Von Abendmal Christi Bekendnis,* WA, 26, 506, quoted in F[ormula of] C[oncord], S[olid] D[eclaration], VII, 32.
10. WA, 6, 524.
11. WA, 18, 99-100.
12. WA, 54, 163.
13. WA, 12, 213.

14. WA, 30/III, 561.
15. WA, 30/I, 53; compare also *Von Abendmal Christi Bekendnis* WA, 26, 442, 29-443, 7; 445, 8-15;462, 4-8, and the Sermon on the Eucharist preached on December 19 of the same year, WA, 30/I, 117, 34-35.
16. WA, 30/II, 624.
17. WA, *Briefwechsel*, X, 462 (No. 3944).
18. Equally emphatic are the *Apology* (X); the *Small Catechism* (VI, 1-2); the *Large Catechism* (V, 8-10), and the *Smalcald Articles* (Part Three, VI,1). The assertion that Article X of the *Augsburg Confession* implies that the Body and Blood of Christ are present "in the hands of the administrant as well in the mouth of the communicant" was endorsed by the 22 Missouri participants (including C. F. Walther) in the second assembly of the Free Evangelical Lutheran Conference, Pittsburgh, PA, Oct. 28 to Nov. 4, 1857 (*Der Lutheraner*, XIV, No. 11 [Jan. 12, 1858], 84).
19. Theodore Kolde, *Analecta Lutherana* (Gotha: Fredrick Andreas Perthes, 1883), 217, 223.
20. "*Kircken-ordnung im churfürstenthum der marcken zu Brandenburg, wie man sich beide mit der leer und ceremonien halten sol,*" in Emil Sehling, ed., *Die evangelischen Kirchenordnungen des XVI, Jahrhunderts,* III (Leibzig: O. R. Reisland, 1909), 77-79. The practice of taking the Sacrament to the sick in the manner prescribed seems to have persisted — in Berlin at least — until some time after the Augsburg Interim of 1548 (Nicholas Muller, *Der Dom zu Berlin,* I [1906] 399, in WA, *Briefwechsel,* VIII, 624, n.9).
21. WA, *Briefwechsel,* VIII, 623 (No. 3420); WA, *Tischreden,* V, 55 (No. 5314). The disputation in connection with the promotion of John of Scotland (Johannes Scotus Macchabaeus) to licentiate of sacred theology in the Wittenberg Theological Faculty on February 3, 1542, for which Melanchton drew up the theses and at which Luther was present, is obviously relevant to the whole question under discussion, but the poorly taken, badly transmitted and sometimes ambiguous notes do not admit of any certain interpretation (WA, 3/II, 146-184).
22. John Hachenburg, *Wider den jrrthumb der newen Zwinglianer nötige unterrichtung* (Erfurt: Merten von Dolgen, 1557), discussed in detail in George Kawerau, "*ein Beitrag zur Geschichte der lutherischen Lehre von der Konsekration im 16. Jarhhundert,*" in *Zeitschrift für Pastoral Theologie,* XXV (Berlin: Reuther und Reichard, 1902), 293-294. See also Hachenburg, *Vom anbeten des Sakraments, Dazu vom vbriegen vnnd niderfallen Sacrament im Abendmal des HERREN Christi, Declaration* (No place of publication: 1561); Kawerau, *art. cit.,* 294, n. 1. The event was assigned to 1544 by an alleged eye-witness (WA, *Briefwechsel,* X, 337 [ad No. 3888]). Related to this account is an undatable item of table-talk in WA, *Tischreden,* V, 416 (No. 5984).
23. WA, *Tischreden,* V, 308 (No. 5665). It is admittedly difficult to reconcile the satements on *adoratio* in this item with the view ascribed to Luther on *adoratio* in No. 5589, *ibid.,* 265-266 (probably to be dated, if correctly transmitted, in the spring of 1543) and No. 6360, *ibid.,* 621 (undateable). The latter mentions elevation only in the title, not the text; furthermore, synonymous with the practices associated with reservation in the sacrament-house or with theophoric processions.
24. WA, *Briefwechsel,* X, 340-341 (No. 3888).
25. WA, *Briefwechsel,* X, 348-349 (No. 3894).
26. Rudolf Herrmann's article in *Beiträge zur Thuringer Kirchengeschichte,* III, 350-351, summarized in WA, *Briefwechsel,* XI, 258, gives a fairly complete account of the case. The faculty opinion referred to is reproduced in WA,

Briefwechsel, XI, 259 (No.4186). See also *ibid.*, 298-299 (No. 4206), and WA, *Tischreden*, VI, 179 (No. 6771).

27. Quoted in Julius Wiggers, *"Der Saliger'sche Abendmahlsstreit,"* in *Zeischrift für die historische Theologie*, new series, XII (Leipzig: F.A. Brockhaus, 1848), 632-635.

28. Wiggers, *op. cit.*, 640.

29. Martin Chemnitz, *Examen Concilii Tridentini*, part two, locus IV, sect. III, para. 9, ed. Edward Preuss (Berlin: Gustav Schlawitz, 1861), 309.

30. *Ibid.*, Sect. III, para. 13 (ed. Preuss, 310); Sect. VII, paras. 12, 14, 17, 19 (ed. Preuss, 329-331).

31. FC, Ep[itome], VII, 2. The German agenda of The Lutheran Church-Missouri Synod explicitly directs the celebrant at a bed-side celebration of the Holy Eucharist to give the sick person the Body and the Blood of the Lord (*Kirchen-Agenda fur Evangelische-Lutherische Germeinden ungeänderter Augsburgischer Confession* [St. Louis: Concordia Publishing House, 1902] 36).

32. FC, Ep, VII.9.

33. FC, SD, VII, 76.

34. FC, SD, 83-87. A large part of this section is taken almost verbatim from the "Wismar Opinion" of 1569, probably from the pen of Chyrtäus, in the Saliger controversy. A point has been made that in FC, SC, VII, 15, the "Wittenberg Concord" of 1536 is quoted as denying the Real Presence of Christ's Body *"ausser der Niessung."* It should be noted that this document is not in form or content a "formula of concord," but a memorandum of record, in which the Lutherans are not setting forth their own opinion, but are merely setting down their understanding of the position of Martin Bucer and his associates; the Strasbourgers signed it to attest the correctness of the Lutheran understanding. Furthermore, the sense of the German *Niessung* is fixed by the Latin translation with *usus;* the document is cited as evidence of the concession that the Strasbourgers were willing to make; and the Strasbourgers, unable to win general support among the Swiss and the South Germans, receded from the "agreement" in less than a year. The very brief study of the joint faculties of Concordia Theological Seminary, Springfield, Illinois, and Concordia Seminary, St. Louis, Missouri (see fn. 1 above), obviously leans on Sasse's *This Is My Body*. Both the joint faculties opinion and Sasse (p. 176) perpetuate the typographical error of the *Bekenntnisschriften* (p. 1016, fn.4) which assigns the *Kurtz Bekentnis und Artickel vom heiligen Abendmal des Leibes und Bluts Christi* (the so-called "Torgau Articles," which are, however, not to be confused with Melanchthon's [Wittenberg-] "Torgau Articles" of 1530) to 1571. The correct date is 1574, after the exposure of the Cryptocalvinist conspiracy in Electoral Saxony. E. Wolf calls these articles "antiubiquitistic" (*Bekenntnisschriften*, xxxvi), that is, opposed to Luther's position on the presence of the human nature everywhere as a result of the personal union with the divine nature. Leonard Hutter (1563-1616) says of the articles that "they are not altogether orthodox" (*Concordia concors: de origine et progressu Formulae Concordiae* [Frankfurt-am-Main: Johann Christoph Föllginer, 1690] 204). Their actual influence on the *Formula of Concord* is debatable; it was very limited in any case. Hence to say, as the joint faculties' opinion does, that this document is a "forerunner of the *Formula of Concord"* is true only in a chronological sense; Lutheran theologians have consistently rejected as a mistake the thesis of the Swiss Calvinist Rudolf Hopinian (1547-1626) that "the *Book of Concord* was born out of these articles." SD, VII, 127, which is presumed to have the questions of the *Kurtz Bekentnis* — only a few of which are cited in the *Bekenntnisschriften* footnote (for a complete list see Hütter, *op. cit.*, 200-202) — in mind, does not refer to the

Kurtz Bekentnis. The "condemnatory statement" of this paragraph addresses itself against "all presumptuous, scoffing and blasphemous questions and expressions which are advanced *in a coarse, fleshy, Capernaitic* way about the supernatural and heavenly mysteries of this Supper," that is the kind of question that the Sacramentarian Protestants had been using to ridicule the Lutheran position. The opinion of the joint faculties is gratifyingly explicit in insisting upon the consecration of the elements as a condition of a valid sacrament.

35. Cf. *Apology*, X, 2.
36. John Gerhard, *Loci theologici,* Locus XXI, cap. xii. paras. 136, 149, 153 (ed. Preuss, V. 135, 151, 153). and cap. xvii. para. 195 (ed. Preuss, V. 187-188). Cf. also David Hollaz, *Examen theologicum acroamaticum,* Part three, sec. II, cap. V. qu. xi, obs. 2 (ed. Albert Joachim de Krakevitz [Stockholm: Gottfried Kiesewetter, 1741], 1113).
37. FC, Ep, VII, 2.
38. FC, SD, VII, 108.

PART III:
MARY, ARCHETYPE OF
THE CHURCH

CHAPEL ADDRESS ON THE FEAST OF THE ANNUNCIATION OF THE BLESSED VIRGIN MARY

The church's calendar calls this day the Annunciation of the Blessed Virgin Mary, carefully calculated back nine months from the date that the church finally selected to keep as the birthday of our Lord. Thus it is the day of the revelation of the divine motherhood of the woman that God chose to bear His son.

We have something else to celebrate today. This is the day that commemorates the "fulness of the time" of which St. Paul speaks in Galatians 4:4-5: "When the fulness of the time had come, God sent forth His Son, born of woman, born under the Law to redeem those who were under the Law, so that we might receive adoption as sons." Today commemorates that crucial moment in history when God's purpose of redemption would brook no further delay, when God's plan of reconciliation of the world with Himself that He had formulated before time began entered the phase where the divine "must (*dei*)" asserted itself, when the love of God for you and for me and for every other human being refused to wait for another dawn. On this day God sent forth His Son as the great apostle of His purpose — to become a human being, to be born of a mother like every other human being, to be born under the limitations and the restrictions and the requirements and the demands that burden every other human being, to be born under what St. Paul calls

"Law." The purpose of this apostolate was to buy us back like slaves in the marketplace so that for our servitude we might receive sonship.

This is accordingly a day to celebrate the Gospel — the Gospel of our redemption, to put it explicitly. The Gospel of our redemption is the Gospel in its most abrasive and scandalous and uncomfortable and offensive form. It is the Gospel of the incarnation, of God becoming a human being. It is the Gospel of deliverance, with its disconcerting reminder of something that we pridefully prefer not to ponder — that we were natively slaves, human animals in the thrall of the demonic powers, unable to free ourselves, needing to be freed by someone else, and actually freed by his death, the death that ended the life that began this day and by the victory that conquered that death.

I am deeply moved by the account of the annunciation of the Blessed Virgin Mary in the third gospel every time I reflect on it. I also confess that sometimes I am inclined to prefer the unembroidered businesslike directness and brevity of the first gospel: "When Christ's mother Mary had been betrothed to Joseph, before they came together, she was found to be with child of the Holy Spirit."

My problem, of course, is conceptualizing the account in the third gospel. It is all highly instructive, which is what it was intended to be. But I do not live in the environment in which the Holy Spirit moved the early Christian community to remember what had happened on the day when the fullness of the time had come about in precisely the way that the third gospel sets it down.

How am I to think of the encounter of the Mother of God with St. Gabriel? I have no experience by which I can reconstruct what the third gospel is trying to tell me. I have worshiped with angels and archangels — indeed, I do it at every celebration of the Sacrament of the Altar. I also try hard — but not very successfully — to do so with the constant awareness of my companions in worship that the word "evermore" in the Preface implies. But I have never seen an angel, and when I meditate on this pericope I have a problem. I am reasonably sure that St. Gabriel did not look to the Blessed Virgin Mary like the winged and brocaded heavenly visitant of the 1969 Christmas postage stamp. The part of the picture that I reconstruct in my mind where St. Gabriel stands is accordingly very often a bit blurred. It comes into focus only as I remember that St. Gabriel has turned up before in the biblical narrative — at the annunciation of skeptical St. Zechariah standing beside the altar of incense in the temple, and, possibly even more importantly, in the apocalyptic visions of Daniel 8 and 9. Here, I remember, the prophet saw Saint Gabriel as having the appearance of a man (Dan.8:15) and the prophet quite flatly says that the same man Gabriel came to him "in swift flight at the time of the evening sacrifice" (9:21).

Then I recall that the appearance of Saint Gabriel is less important than the message that he brings. The message is the same in the third gospel and in the Book of Daniel. It is the assurance of God's final and ultimate victory. This tells me why it is Gabriel that is the bearer of the messages to Saint Zechariah and to the Blessed Virgin Mary. Just to underline the point, the third gospel not very slyly introduces the seventy weeks of Daniel's vision (9:24-27) in the form of the 490 days — seven times seventy — between St. Gabriel's annunciation to Saint Zechariah with which the third gospel's infancy narrative begins and the presentation of our Lord in the temple with which the same narrative ends. This warns me to attend to the fact that Gabriel has come to the Blessed Virgin Mary with another message of divine victory. This child will accomplish the saving purpose for which He came into the world, "to destroy the works of the devil" (1 John 3:8) or, if you prefer the language of Daniel 9, to insure that "the decreed end is poured out on the desolator" par excellence (Dan.9:27). Just as God's victory in Daniel 8 and 9 is final and decisive, so is His victory in Christ. He will be great and will be called the Son of the Most High. The Lord God will give Him the throne of His father David. He will reign over the house of Jacob forever. Of His kingdom — a phrase that the church carefully worked into the Creed of the 150 Fathers that we say before the altar — there shall be no end! (Luke 1:32-33)

But there is one other item. It turns up in the words of the Blessed Virgin Mary: "Behold, I am the handmaid of the Lord; let it be to me according to your word" (Luke 1:38). She has to say it before the celestial messenger can leave. It is of course past our imagination that she would have said "no" to God. But it is she that must say "yes." Obviously this is not the synergism that imagines that an unreborn person can contribute to his conversion. The Blessed Virgin Mary is in St. Gabriel's words of greeting, *kecharitômenê* — that is, one in whom the action of divine grace has been going on for along time, long enough to justify a past perfect participle. God's grace had been preparing her for this hour — and for the many years ahead when she would have to be the one who after giving the Son of God birth would have to provide the nurture that would see Him increase in wisdom and in stature and in favor with God and human beings. And so she said her "yes." How much she really understood of the ultimate meaning of the chain of Old Testament assurances that the third gospel puts on Saint Gabriel's lips we cannot know. There are significant indications in the gospels that her understanding was limited and that the magnificent implications of the words of St. Gabriel unfolded only as the church reflected on them year after long year. But she understood enough to say her "yes" to God.

And that's the way it is today, on March 25, 1971. God comes with His plan to each of us whom He has called by the Gospel, enlightened in baptism, hallowed and kept His holy Christendom. It is a plan that has a place for us, individually. We too are *kecharitômenoi*, in whom the grace of God has been working ever since our baptism. We may not understand all the implications of God's plan for us. Our theological grasp of it may well turn out to have been defective in spots. But when we become aware that God is calling us concretely to be co-workers with Him, as St. Paul puts it in a passage (2 Cor. 6:1) that the *Formula of Concord* (Solid Declaration, 2,66) applies in just this kind of context, we have to respond. We can do so in the assurance that with God no thing (*rhêma*) is impossible; we stand within the scope of His power if we say: "Let it be to me according to Your word (*rhêma*)." It is not at all important who plays Gabriel to our Mary. When the Word of God comes to us, the Lord who gave us the grace that has structured our lives in Christ so far is ready to give us the further grace that enables us to say our "yes" to Him: "Let it be to me according to Your word." You almost have to say it in Greek to catch the parallel with another formula: *Genoito moi kata to rhêma sou.* The other formula is the one that our Lord has put on our lips whenever we pray, the formula that puts us at His disposal when we say: *Genêthêto to thelêma sou,* "Let Your will be done!"

MARY'S PLACE WITHIN
THE PEOPLE OF GOD
According To Non-Roman Catholics

Mariology *is the point at which the totality of the doctrinal differences between evangelical Christianity and the [Roman] Catholic Church discloses itself,* declares Karl Rahner.[1] What he says is not much different from what the Lutheran theologian Kristen Ejner Skydsgaard asserts: "There is probably no place where the difference between two understandings of Christianity becomes so plain as in their different conceptions of the Virgin Mary."[2]

Writing in *America* for January 3, 1959 Titus Cranny observed: "The desire for unity on the part of our separated brethren has brought them to a closer study of the [Roman] Catholic position. It has made them aware of [Roman] Catholic teaching ... especially of the Blessed Virgin Mary. But they view our Lady, not as the great means of effecting unity, but as an obstacle of staggering proportions."[3]

In 1950 Pierre Maury of Paris affirmed that "the doctrine of Mary and the cult of the Virgin seem to pose with increasing precision — and with an unmistakable clarity at the present time — the real problem of our relations with the Roman Church."[4]

Max Thurian, of the French Reformed community at Taizé, writing in the symposium prepared in advance of the 1952 Lund Conference on Faith and Order, *Ways of Worship,* made this provocative charge in his paper on Mariology (one of four contributed respectively by the Dominican priest Conrad Pepler, the Orthodox lay theologian Vladimir Lossky, the Anglican scholar T. M. Parker, and Frére Max): "The doctrine and the veneration of Mary in the Roman Church create extreme difficulties" — in another place he calls it "the most agonizing problem" — "for ecumenical thought ... One can see no way through the problem posed by Mariology and the veneration of the Blessed Virgin in the [Roman Catholic] Church."[5]

This paper travels over a road rather solidly packed down by the feet of predecessors. Other recent surveys of non-Roman-Catholic thought about Mary — all, incidentally, by Roman Catholics — are: chapters 3, 4, 5, and 7 of Thomas A. O'Meara, *Mary in Protestant and Catholic Theology;*[6] William J. Cole, *The* Role of Scripture in the Current Understanding of Our Lady among Our Separated Brethren (Especially United States Protestants);[7] and Albert Brandenburg's *Maria in der evangelischen Theologie der Gegenwart.* All three have impressive bibliographies that illustrate the formidable volume of material on the subject in English, French, German, and Latin.[8]

Three stipulations are in order. First, there is no single conception of the place of the Blessed Virgin Mary within the people of God among non-Roman-Catholic Christians. The x and *non-x* type of dichotomy (Jew and non-Jew, or Jew and goy; Greek and non-Greek, or Greek and barbarian; Americans and non-Americans, or Americans and foreigners) tends to occlude for the x element the possibility that *non-x* may be a very complex aggregation of incommensurable and heterogeneous entities without any antecedent principle of inherent unity. Accordingly you must not expect to be able to generalize from any observation that I make. It may seem inconsiderate of non-Roman-Catholics not to agree with one another in their views on the Blessed Virgin Mary, but in the premises there is really no reason to expect them to do so.

The second stipulation is that when the word "church" occurs in this inquiry I mean by it the one holy catholic and apostolic Church that exists empirically wherever the Gospel of the divine grace in Jesus Christ is proclaimed and the sacraments are administered and the Holy Spirit imparts the new birth and the life of God Himself to men and women. In the view of your reporter this one holy catholic and apostolic Church subsists in every church and ecclesial community to the extent that it meets these criteria, but in his view *the* Church does not subsist only or even pre-eminently in one Church or ecclesial community.

The third stipulation is that this is a report, not an arraignment, a survey, not a tract. As a Lutheran, that is to say, an ecumenically oriented Evangelical Catholic, I have been influenced by my own convictions in the selection both of the material and of the words in which I introduce the material, but I have tried to operate with an awareness of my biases and prejudices and to keep them from affecting my objectivity. Where I have failed, I can only ask the pardon of those whom I have inadvertently misrepresented and of you whom, to that extent, I shall have inadvertently misled.

I

For the theologian for whom God is really dead and for his followers it would seem obvious that the Blessed Virgin Mary can have no religiously exceptional significance within the people of God.

The same is true of the theologian for whom "God" is merely a verbal symbol for something else. It may be the verbal symbol of the totality of the integrating forces of the universe. It may be the verbal symbol of the sum of all the positive values in our environment. It may be the verbal symbol of the claim that my fellow-men place upon my love and that I place on their love and of our several responses to these claims.

Nor can the Blessed Virgin Mary have a religiously exceptional place among the people of God in the case of these theologians for whom it is difficult, if not impossible, honestly to affirm that Jesus Christ is the unique Son of God, begotten of His Father before all ages, God out of God, Light out of Light, true God from true God, begotten not made, possessed of the same being as the Father, and the One through whom everything was made. If our Lord only *became* God in some sense in the course of His life, say at His baptism, or at His crucifixion, or at His rising to life again, no religiously exceptional significance would seem logically to attach to His human mother.

Again, if the Biblical affirmations about Our Lord's preexistence are simply a part of a redeemer-myth, Gnostic or otherwise, that needs to be demythologized before it can be proclaimed to contemporary scientistic man, or if the special virtue of the Christian Gospel is that it provides "stories" which have an unusually high potency in evoking the intention to practice an agapeistic mode of life, the mother of this mythical person obviously cannot really hold a religiously exceptional place in the community of Christians.

To the extent that theologians who hold such views may accord the accounts of the life of the historical Jesus in the Sacred Scriptures any credibility, they may praise the pedagogical skill and ability of the mother that was able amid the negative influences of her environment to rear the kind of person who could evoke the faith of so many people in the primitive Christian community, and who could inspire the legends that came to cluster about His name. They may describe with great detail and on the basis of diligent research and reflection how the subsequent image of his mother in the Christian community came into being and what factors entered into its evolution. But on their own premises they cannot accord the real, historical person who bore our Lord anything more than an incidental biological or educative significance.

So far we have been speaking of theologians who, in spite of their desire and determination to be identified with and to instruct the Christian community, are, by the standard of Nicene orthodoxy, sub-Christian. But now we come to a phenomenon that is clear intra-Christian, the crisis of belief in the virgin conception and birth of our Lord.

Questions and doubts about the virgin conception and birth are not new even with Christendom. Schleiermacher voiced them over a century and a half ago. What is new is the extent to which theological scholars assert that they feel compelled to call the Virgin Birth into question, partly, they insist, in order to avoid presuppositions and presumptions that have led to certain later Mariological developments.

There is common agreement that there is probably no area of Christian conviction, in Europe or America, where the difference between the professional theology of university faculties and the faith of the Christian layfolk is so striking.[9]

The late Emil Brunner conceded that the doctrine of the virginal conception and birth of our Lord "has exercised a very wholesome influence and, as the first attempt of primitive Christianity to proclaim the mystery of the Person of Jesus it deserves our utmost respect," but on both biblical and theological ground he vigorously rejects the virgin birth. He implies that a human being conceived without a father is only half a human being, one who lacks the most essential aspect of humanity, that is, to have been born as we all have been born.[10]

Walther von Loewenich, who takes a disapproving view of Roman Catholic Mariology in general, asserts: "The germ of Mariology is to found in the virgin birth, as presented in Matthew 1 and Luke 1 .... The virgin birth has made an essential contribution to the mythologizing of Christianity when once it was raised to the status of a dogma. That the virgin birth has a profound symbolical significance we would not for a moment deny. But it is not suitable for treatment as a dogma. We can understand it as an expression of Christian experience of the person of Christ, but it cannot be used as a jumping ground for an interpretation of his person."[11]

In 1958 the American ecumenical weekly, *The Christian Century*, editorialized: "Those for whom we write do not reject the Virgin Birth because it is 'impossible.' In the discussion of miracles, possibility cannot be an issue. The virgin Birth is rejected because it is so radically out of character with the rest of the manner and the matter of Christian revelation. We doubt the Virgin Birth not because it has not been 'proven;' we doubt it because it does not prove what has to be proven.

To account so materially, so biologically, so cellularly for the uniqueness of Jesus is to land dead center on what is precisely *not* the point.

"The paradox of Jesus' divine humanity is not a physical-spiritual ambiguity. To make it such is an absolute contradiction of biblical anthropology. Yet what else does the Virgin Birth assure except that Jesus was some kind of *tertium quid*, half and half, substantially divine creature? And that is not the central Christian claim. He is not God in his structure, but in that unique relationship to God and his purpose which still identifies Jesus as Christ. He is not half-God-half-man, he is not man-trapped God or God-inflated man — which are the only interpretations the Virgin Birth helps with."[12]

The *Evangelisches Kirchenlexicon* is a distinguished modern German reference work. In the article on the virgin birth, Werner Wiesner of Mayence insists that primitive Christianity had, in addition to what he calls the poorly attested virgin birth tradition, a tradition that Jesus was born by natural generation. He expresses some surprise that Karl Barth retains the virgin birth as an article of faith, not as a fact on which salvation depends but as a sign of the mystery of the Incarnation. For himself he regards the virgin birth as "the inadequate expression of the fact that the birth of Jesus Christ is not to be understood in terms of the natural biological context nor in terms of human action ... but alone in terms of the divine miracle which has made this man Jesus to be a new beginning of humanity."[13]

The third edition of *Die Religion in Geschichte und Gegenwart* is an even more prestigious theological lexicon. In it the late Erlangen theologian, Paul Althaus, argues that the virgin birth is not "a dogmatically necessary and indispensable part of the commitment to Jesus Christ." It could signify that "although Jesus appears in the context of Adamic humanity and participates in its inheritance [Romans 8:3], the Incarnation of God takes place through His conception and a new humanity begins." But the certainty of this divine miracle is not bound to the historicity of the virgin birth and it is not affected by our recognition that the infancy accounts are legendary in character.[14]

The rejection of the virgin birth by the former Protestant Episcopal Bishop of California, the Right Reverend James A. Pike, in spite of the occurrence of the article in both the Apostles' and the Nicene Creeds that his denomination has incorporated in the Chicago-Lambeth Quadrilateral as part of the basis of its ecumenical effort, was one of the factors that led some of his fellow-bishops to demand a few weeks ago that he be tried for heresy. One of his earliest statements on the subject appeared in an article in *The Christian Century,* subsequently republished in a symposium entitled *How My Mind Has Changed*: "I am more liberal in theology than I was ten years ago. When Norman Pittenger [of General Theological Seminary, New York] and I were writing *The*

Faith of the Church (a semi-official Episcopal book on doctrine), he did not find reason to accept the historical virgin birth; I *thought* I did. Our wrestling over the matter — not only a personal wrestling, but a wrestling with both theological professors and bishops of our church — resulted in the book's leaving an opening for people like Dr. Pittenger.[15] *Now I am with him.* While neither he nor I would deny the possibility of the miracle, the biblical evidence and the theological implications seem to be in favor of assuming that Joseph was the human father of Jesus. We certainly do not deny in the least the *doctrine* of the virgin birth, namely the paradox which the image so well presents: Jesus as part of the historical process and also as divine interruption in history — a mighty act of God, indeed the Supreme Mighty Act of God."[16] (It should be stressed that the virgin birth does not lack Protestant Episcopal defenders. In an article in *A Handbook of Christian Theology,* J. V. Langmead Casserly concedes that the reference to Isaiah 7, 14 in the Mattthaean infancy account is "almost certainly due to an exegetical mistake" and that "the New Testament evidence is not as strong in the case of the Virgin Birth as it is in that of the Resurrection." Nevertheless, "there is no evidence at all for any other alternative and those who accept the complete doctrine of the Incarnation would probably contend that the Virgin birth accords perfectly with their belief that the eternal Son of God entered the realm of nature and history by assuming human nature to himself without emerging as a consequence of natural processes. Those who deny the virgin birth usually tend toward some kind of adoptionism or Nestorianism in Christology — which is often called a 'reduced Christology' — and toward some kind of naturalism in philosophy.")[17]

The distinguished Heidelberg church historian, Hans Baron von Campenhausen, in *Die Jungfrauengeburt in der alten Kirch* surveys the historical evidence down to St. Augustine and argues that the primitive Church never knew a Mariology in the strict sense. The infancy accounts of the first and the third Gospels disclose different primitive traditions about the ancestry of our Lord; one stream of tradition sees him as Joseph's natural son, the other as virgin-born. The rest of the New Testament knows nothing about the virgin birth, nor do the Apostolic Fathers, St. Ignatius excepted.[18]

The European Reformed theologian Otto Weber holds that the virgin birth is inconsistent with the doctrine of Christ's preexistence and that the virgin birth represents a later stage of Christian tradition. The doctrine says nothing about the ancestry (*Herkunft*) of Jesus, but speaks only about his origin (*Ursprung*). It is a proclamatory assertion, not a biological one; its meaning derives from the fact that it is an "eschatological" account.[19]

In 1962 John Harwood Hick, professor at Princeton Theological Seminary (United Presbyterian Church in the U.S.A.), was denied membership in the New Brunswick (N.J.) presbytery of his church for refusing to affirm belief in the virgin birth. In defending him, a member of the presbytery, Conrad Henry Massa, is quoted as declaring: "The basic Christian doctrine is the divinity of Jesus Christ, not the virginity of Mary."[20]

Thomas Boslooper, a Reformed theologian in this country, says in his book *The Virgin Birth*: "The story of the virgin birth represents in mythical form two of Christendom's principal logical propositions: that God acted in history and that monogamous marriage is civilization's most important special institution ... This virgin birth is a positive affirmation of the sanctity of marriage ... What is set forth in the record of Jesus' ministry as a bold and provocative moral injunction (Mark 10:6 ff.) is portrayed in the narrative of his origin with poetic beauty and esthetic sensitivity. The couple is betrothed. The marriage bond has been established. Within this relationship God acted. The atmosphere is charged with ethical purity and moral vigor. Those who receive this story with faith accept premarital chastity, heterosexuality, and monogamous marriage as a divinely ordained way of life ... The birth narratives, then, are 'Christian midrashic haggada' which reflect the following Christian convictions based on the teaching of Jesus and the faith of the earliest church: the unity of God and man in Christ, the sanctity of sex, the necessity of monogamy and fidelity in marriage, the superiority of Christianity over astrology, the superiority of Christianity over the Baptist movement, the fulfillment of Judaism in Christianity, the universality of the gospel, and the inevitability of the success of the Christian mission."[21] Paradoxically, although Boslooper denies the historic *fact* of the virgin birth, he ends his book with the hope that the time will soon come when the whole church will confess: "I believe in Jesus Christ, His only Son, our Lord, who was conceived by the Holy Ghost, born of the Virgin Mary."[22]

It would not be difficult to provide additional quotations. Where these views of the virgin birth are seriously held — and this position represents the view of the bulk of modern liberal theological thought — all that is left of Mariology is the thesis that the mother of Jesus of Nazareth was called Mary. But where she is merely the wife of Joseph the artisan and the mother of a considerable number of his children, one of whom bore the name of the successor of Moses and later achieved distinction as the eponym of the Christian community, we cannot speak of a religiously exceptional place of the mother of Jesus in the Christian community and in the people of God.

There is another large group of Christians who deny to the mother of Christ any religiously exceptional place among the people of God.

These are the numerous conservative evangelical Christians who intransigently affirm and defend the virgin conception and birth of our Lord as an often indispensable (biblically and theologically) part of Christian teaching and belief, but for whom His mother is only a biologically necessary means. In this group we should count the very considerable body of conservative Reformed, Presbyterians, Baptists, Methodists, Episcopalians, and Evangelical United Brethren who identify themselves broadly with the theology of the biweekly, *Christianity Today*,[23] together with the Churches of Christ, the major Holiness bodies, the Trinitarian Pentecostals, the Mennonites, and others who belong to conservative groups like the National Association of Evangelicals, the American Council of Christian Churches, and the Associated Gospel Churches.[24]

A case in point is J. Oliver Buswell, Junior, a respected conservative systematician on the faculty of Covenant Theological Seminary (Evangelical Presbyterian Synod), Creve Coeur, St. Louis County, Missouri. He affirms that the importance of the Virgin Birth is such that, if it is not historically true, there is no reason or basis for holding other evangelical doctrines. "We cannot conceive of the eternally preexistent Son of God becoming man by means of ordinary generation without ceasing to be God. In ordinary generation a new person begins to exist."[25]

Similarly Howard A. Hanke, professor of Bible at Asbury College, Wilmore, Kentucky, in his book *The Validity of the Virgin Birth*, sees belief in Christ's deity, His Saviorhood, His bodily resurrection, His second coming, His relationship to God the Father, and the new birth of believers as all dependent on faith in the virgin birth.[26]

When this conservatism is linked with the anti-Roman-Catholicism that is often endemic in these religious subcultures, the result may be an aggressive polemic against any statement about our Lord's mother that cannot be literally documented in the Sacred Scriptures.

One of the most influential journals among American evangelical conservatives is *Eternity*. Its June 1960 issue carried a three-page review of C. X. J. M. Friethoff's *A Complete Mariology* (Westminster, MD.: The Newman Press, 1958) which concluded: "This book, *A Complete Mariology*, should be in everyone's library ... Its a work which is clearly presented and authoritatively documented, with the accompanying frank admission that the doctrine of Mary is not a scriptural doctrine but the product of church tradition and church logic."[27]

J. Dwight Pentecost, professor of Bible exposition at Dallas (Texas) Theological Seminary, has written *Romanism in the Light of Scripture*. It can stand as a sample of the attitudes that a large segment of American Fundamentalism takes toward Roman Catholic Marian teaching and practice: "The steps that have been followed to establish the Mariolatry of the Roman Church are plain: First, they pronounced her the Mother of God; to that they added the doctrine of the perpetual virginity of Mary; from that they built the doctrine of the Immaculate Conception; because she was immaculately conceived she was taken bodily into heaven without her body seeing corruption and was seated at the right hand of the Father, together with her Son, Jesus Christ. There is only one step left, and that is the step of absolute deification. I do not know how long it is going to take Rome to promulgate that doctrine. Some pope, claiming to speak to God, will pronounce that Mary is God."[28]

Opposition to Roman Catholic Marian doctrine and practice is not restricted to the conservative fraction of Christendom.[29] Particularly the definition of the Assumption in 1950 proved to be a potent catalyst in precipitating some of this animus.

The attitudes of such mid-20th-century theological bellwethers as Karl Barth, Paul Tillich, and Reinhold Niebuhr toward Roman Catholic Mariology are commonplaces. "We reject Mariology 1) because it is an arbitrary innovation in the face of Scripture and the early church, and 2) because this innovation consists essentially in a falsification of Christian truth," says the first.[30] "Apollo has no revelatory significance for Christians; the Virgin Mother Mary reveals nothing to Protestantism," says the second.[31] "Another basic religious cause of tension is the increased Mariolatry of modern [Roman] Catholicism. Building on Catholic piety with roots preceding even the medieval period, the church, for some mysterious reason, has chosen to widen the breach between it and modern culture ... It has virtually lifted the Virgin Mary into the Godhead (some say into the Trinity), replacing the less historical Holy Spirit." So says the third.[32]

Following the promulgation of the dogma of bodily Assumption of the Blessed Virgin Mary, Heinrich M. Köster compiled an instructive article for *Marianum* in which he documented the vehemently negative reaction of German Lutheran, Reformed, and United Church circles and their conviction that the definition had seriously impeded interconfessional understanding;[33] an English abridgement appeared in *Theology Digest* in 1957.[34]

Among the most scathing criticisms of the definition of the Assumption is the theological opinion drafted by Edmund Schlink, Peter Brunner, Wilfred Joest, Hans Baron von Campenhausen, and Günther Bornkamm. The fact that these five could unite to produce the opinion, despite the wide range of their individual viewpoints, is in itself significant; only a definition that represented a fundamental threat to a great variety of cherished values could have brought them together as coauthors. The opinion describes the definition as the dogmatization of a myth, sees the danger of an obscuring of the Incarnation and of the entire salvific work of the Son of God, and fears serious consequences for the relation between Rome and evangelical Christianity.[35]

Karl Bernhard Ritter, one of the leaders of the mid-20th-century German Evangelical liturgical revival, also criticized the Roman Catholic Church for defining the Assumption. Thereby, he avers, it has not administered the deposit of the faith but has enlarged it. At the same time he appeals to the Evangelical community seriously and positively to address itself to the creation of an Evangelical Mariology. This must include, as he sees it, the realization that the virgin Mother of God is the link that unites Christ and humanity, and that in her *fiat mihi* the cooperation of all generations since Adam with the divine grace culminates.[36]

Even Max Thurian joined the critics. His long and penetrating analysis voices the outrage of a great many other Christians at the commination which Pius XII attached to *Munificentissmus Deus* when he declared that those who deny the Assumption have completely apostatized from the divine and Catholic faith and have incurred the wrath of Almighty God and of the blessed Apostles Peter and Paul.[37]

The French Reformed theologian Hébert Roux denies the Blessed Virgin any place in Reformed piety, although he sees her as a type of the human creature, as the object of the divine grace and redemption, and as an example of humility, hope and joy in the Lord. He urges that the biblical doctrine of the Blessed Virgin appears precisely to guard against what he calls the fundamental heresy of making this creature, who is the witness of faith in and the devotion to the Savior alone, herself an object of faith and devotion in the Church.[38]

In 1961 Friedrich-Wilhelm Künneth published his major contribution in this area, a patiently and carefully detailed survey of modern German Roman Catholic Mariological reflection. It is of interest because of his categorizations of Mariologies as either unipolar or bipolar. The unipolar type he sees as primitive; it concentrates on the role of the Blessed Virgin Mary in the Incarnation and its iconographic symbol of St. Mary with the Holy Child. The bipolar type Künneth sees as a late development in Western Christianity that perpetuated itself in Roman Catholicism; it concerns itself with the implications of the Mother of God standing under the cross, and seeks to give her, in addition to her maternal role, an active mediatorial role in the redemption and salvation of mankind. Another matter of ecumenical interest in this revises Erlangen doctoral dissertation is Künneth's frank expression of a fear that a number of Roman Catholic theologians themselves have voiced (and that the present writer finds himself unable entirely to banish). It is the fear that the thrust of a great deal of modern Roman Catholic Mariology is in the direction of a 20th century rejection of the real humanity of our Lord, the feat that the increasing emphasis on His deity has pushed Him outside the realm where He is one of us and has thus created a vacuum which Mariological speculation is filling. The representative offering of Christ's resurrection if no longer a sufficient guarantee of our own; His mother must rise from the dead (or even escape death) and be taken up bodily into heaven. Christ's virginal conception and birth are not enough to heal the ravages of the original sin; His mother must be preserved from the taint of original sin from the first moment of her existence as a human being.[39]

Stanley Irving Stuber, one of the most widely-known American observers at Vatican II, is a Baptist. He declares that "Protestantism does not venerate the Virgin Mary, because on scriptural grounds it accepts Mary not as the 'Mother of God,' but as the human mother of Christ ... Protestants are at an absolute loss when it comes to appreciating the Roman Catholic attitude in regard to the Virgin Mary .... Considerate Protestants will say that her alleged appearances, miracles, and special blessings verge on the side of superstition — if they are taken in any literal sense, as they are by many in the Roman Catholic Church."[40]

A propos Mariology Mario Colacci of Augsburg College and Theological Seminary, Minneapolis, sees the real tragedy less in the content of Mariology than in its official sanction. If the Roman Catholic Church had left the Mariological dogmas within the realm of private evaluation and private commitment, the gulf between the Roman Catholic Church and other Christians might perhaps not be as deep and as wide as it is now. As things stand, Mariology seems to have become for other Christians the most obnoxious feature of Roman Catholicism and one of the strongest barriers that keeps them from the Roman Catholic Church. Other Christians feel, he says, that with the increasing emphasis on Mary the Roman Catholic Church has been overshadowing the power of the Cross and pushing into the background the person and redemptive work of Christ.[41]

Cyrus Pangborn sees three possible effects of Mariological development upon both Roman Catholicism and other Christians, none of them exclusive: "The first possibility is that ... the operative doctrine may become one in which Mary displaces Christ in the Trinity ... A second possibility ... is that [Roman] Catholic Christianity may be entering upon a second 'Dark Age' of competition with the gods of the world's remaining polytheisms ... A third possibility is that Mariology ... may seriously hamper communication with non-[Roman]-Catholic Christians and may even isolate the [Roman] Catholic Church from the world of general intellectual discourse."[42]

Richard A. Newman, a Presbyterian minister, asserts: "The promulgation of St. Mary's Immaculate Conception and Assumption, along with the phenomena of the [Roman] Catholic Marian Year and robust popular [Roman] Catholic devotion to the Virgin appear ... at best as an inscrutable riddle to Protestants; at worst as the making authoritative of nonbiblical and nonhistorical materials, or even superstition. The Protestant concern at this point is that the unique, once-for-all intercessory atonement of Christ is being threatened or obscured, the fine points of [Roman] Catholic doctrine notwithstanding."[43]

Even as sympathetic an observer of Roman Catholicism as Jaroslav Pelikan is constrained to make an assertion that represents not only his own view but that of many others: "The real evil is in the elevation of ... naive piety to the status of a system and in the use of advertising tricks to 'merchandise' the cult of Mary. The simple and unreflecting *Ave Maria* of a South American peon is one thing, and a multivolume theological opus on 'the prerogatives of the Blessed Virgin Mary' is quite another thing. The theologians and bishops of the Church, who ought to watch and warn the faithful of the excesses in such piety, are actually the ones who encourage the excesses."[44]

Distinctly exceptional is the quasi-apologia for Mariology in Walter Marshall Horton's *Christian Theology: An Ecumenical Approach*. He wrote this work during a sabbatical leave at the University of Strasbourg, where he had the opportunity to discuss its contents with the members of the Roman Catholic theological faculty:

> What must be understood if this doctrine is not to be unfairly misinterpreted is the Catholic doctrine of the Communion of Saints. The Eastern Orthodox Churches, which take their Mariology more mystically and less logically than Rome, are accustomed to pray for St. Mary and ask her to pray for us, just as they do with all the great saints, but ... on the highest level below Christ. The issue here is not whether Christ's saving Mediatorship is unique, but whether there is a place below Christ for other mediators, who mediate Christ's grace and presence as Christ mediate God's. In Protestant *practice* ... does not each generation of Christian parents and teachers mediate Christ to the next? And is there not a psychological analogue to the cult of the Blessed Mother in that cult of 'Home and Mother' which plays such a role in revivalistic hymn books?

> It is of course unlikely that interpretations and comparisons of this sort will ever bring [Roman] Catholics and Protestants together on this crucially divisive issue. But to confront the other party — perhaps through the Orthodox and Anglo-Catholics who occupy intermediate positions — may be a salutary source of self-knowledge and corrective self-criticism for both parties. If [Roman] Catholics need to be made aware of the dander of idolatry in the veneration of the Virgin and the saints, Protestants need to be made aware of the danger of reverting, through fear of idolatry, to a bare, austere Old Testament piety in which the joyful New Testament sense of 'God *with* us' would be lost.

> Protestants commonly object to Unitarians for losing the distinctive Christian revelation in an abstract devotion to 'mathematical unity;' but they should realize that they seem to [Roman] Catholics to fall short of Unitarianism in their failure to recognize the Communion of Saints and the place of the Virgin Mary at the head of the saints. Vigorous, concrete faith in God thinks of the Deity as *supreme but not solitary*, sur-

rounded by messengers (angels) and mediators, why should Protestantism try to confine itself exclusively to the One Mediator? ... If there is idolatry in [Roman] Catholic Mariology, there is worse idolatry ... at the root of Protestant sectarianism.[45]

II

The judgment of Roland A. Seboldt, the book editor of Concordia Publishing House, St. Louis, is still only slightly exaggerated: "The common position of Protestantism and recent Lutheranism has been to ignore Mary altogether."[46] Yet both before and after Vatican II, some non-Roman-Catholic Christians have been ready to accord the Mother of God a special place in the company of His people.

Their motivation may vary, and it is likely to be complex, with one or the other stand strongest in a given case. One of these strands may be biblicist in the good sense; it rises out of the awareness that along with St. John the Baptist and two or three individual apostles the Blessed Virgin Mary possesses a prominence of her own in the accounts of the evangelists that is not limited to the simple fact of her parturition. Another may be an indispensable commitment to the Catholic tradition; this would be particularly present in the case of Lutherans and Anglo-Catholics but also among tradition-oriented Christians of other denominations. A third may be sober reflection on the lessons which the history of dogma and of Christian thought teaches. A fourth may be an ecumenical awareness which senses that the veneration of the Blessed Virgin Mary by so many Christians, in spite of intolerable excesses from time to time and from place to place, points to an underlying verity of which a genuinely ecumenical approach must be ready to take account. A fifth factor, one that is likely to function chiefly as a reinforcement of others, is the impact of centuries of the art and the poetry that have taken the Blessed Virgin Mary as their theme.

These Christians would be likely to concur in two of Jaroslav Pelikans's observations. In his introduction to the English version of Otto Semmelroth's *Mary, Archetype of the Church*, Pelikan declared: "Neither the doctrine of the church nor the doctrine of Mary ... Christological orthodoxy ... was bound up with the clarification of the role of Mary in the plan of God. Protestant theology must ask itself whether this connection between Christology and Mariology was a historical coincidence or whether there was in fact some ineluctable obligation in the orthodox confession of Jesus Christ that compelled the church to speak as it did of his mother."[47]

The next year he was quoted as asserting that any criticism of Roman doctrine concerning Marian idolatry "must be accompanied by a positive discussion of the Mother of our Lord from a biblical and evangelical perspective." Mary cannot be ignored, because she "is the warrant for the Christian declaration that our Lord was a true man, flesh of our flesh, and bone of our bone." She also has a significance for the church; "the brief description of her career in the New Testament is a summary of the church's life in its elations and in its depressions."[48]

We turn to concrete examples of this approach. Still a notable contribution to the discussion, even after fifteen years, is that of Lutheran provost Hans Asmussen, *Maria die Mutter Gottes*. Herein he observes, for example, that one cannot ask about Jesus Christ without including His mother in the purview of the question. "One does not have Jesus Christ without Mary."[49] He asserts that "the true church of Christ confesses that Jesus was born of the virgin. Apart from this confession there is no true church but only Christian-ism."[50] Mary is the primordial type of the Church and she has a significance that transcends her individual person; her *fiat mihi* was a decision on behalf of all humanity. "To speak of Mary demands that at the same time we speak of the history that begins with Adam, but it also demands that we speak about the church that is committed to the Son of Mary as a spotless virgin so that she too might bear children without a human husband."[51] At the same time he refuses to concede that the Mother of God was conceived without original sin.[52]

The brilliant Presbyterian medievalist, Allen Cabaniss, published a little essay a dozen years ago, in which he defends the completely evangelical character of such Marian titles as mother of the Savior, intercessor with her Son, ever-virgin Mother of God, seat of wisdom, cause of our joy, and mother of sorrows.[53]

The retired bishop of Oldenburg Wilhelm Stählin, has given German Lutheranism a charming biblical Mariology. He sees it as her great role to have been the concrete place where the incarnation takes place; she is the gateway through which God himself entered our world; she is the "representative of humanity."[54]

In the Otto Karrer *Festschrift* the Reformed Dean Werner Meyer of Küsnacht-Zürich sketches a biblical Mariology which depicts the Mother of God as the picture of grace, in whom Christ is glorified.[55] "Her grace consists in this that in her and through her, God accomplishes a prodigy that is rooted neither in her existence nor on her own constitution."[56] Hers is a "grace of such incomprehensible magnitude, that in comparison with all other recipients of the divine grace throughout the history of salvation Mary constitutes a unique exception."[57] Since "God is glorified only by a freely given assent," her *fiat* has resting on it a reflection (*Abglanz*) of the utter odedience of her Son.[58] Mary is also the picture of sanctity; the woman who has been the recipient of grace is at once hallowed and being hallowed through humility, repentance, and suffering. As the creaturely reflector of the divine grace, the Blessed Virgin Mary radiated grace and holiness into the Church as a supremely attractive example.

Probably the most comprehensive biblical Mariology to come from the pen of a Reformed theologian is the one written by the French monk of Taizé-sur-Cluny, Max Thurian.[59] The British edition of the English translation rendered the original title literally: *Mary, the Mother of the Lord, Figure of the Church.*[60] The American edition put out by Herder, however, changed the title to *Mary, the Mother of All Christians,*[61] a designation not once used by Thurian himself and justified in the book itself only by a quotation from Martin Luther. Thurian sees Mary as the poor virgin, whose virginity is not a badge of disgrace but the new sign of the divine nearness. She is the symbol of the presence of God among his people, the one who combines in her person all the expectation of Israel and the entire mystery of the Church. She is the handmaiden of the Lord who lives by faith in him, the first herald of the Gospel in her visitation of St. Elizabeth, when, like the Church, she bears within her the word and the body of the Lord. At Cana she is the believer in the midst of the messianic community. Under the cross she is the suffering daughter of Zion, who brings forth her hope in her Son's resurrection and suffers the birth of the new people of God in her own flesh. The woman clothed with the sun in Revelation 12 has many of the traits of Mary the Mother of God. She has a privileged place in the communion of the saints. In her the Church militant sees a sign of certain victory. On her feasts — the Annunciation, the Visitation, the Purification, and her Falling Asleep (for with all other Christians she still awaits the resurrection) — the Church praises the wonderful works of God and her own example of obedience, perseverance, and faith.[62]

One expects a certain degree of native sympathy for an appreciation of the uniqueness of St. Mary's role within the people of God from Anglicans and Lutherans, although the position of neither tradition is likely to give a great deal of comfort to Marian maximalists.

In 1960 Francis C. Lightbourn, the book editor of the American Anglo-Catholic weekly, *The Living Church*, sent a questionnaire at random to every seventh name on the clergy list of the Protestant Episcopal Church in the U.S.A. He received 539 valid responses. Of these 39 (7%) said "no" to the virgin conception, birth; 346 to St. Mary's perpetual virginity; 382 to her delivery of the Holy Child *clauso utero*, 425 to St. Mary's freedom from actual sin; 445 to the Assumption; 467 to the Immaculate Conception; 476 to a vow of profession of purpose of virginity; 507 to the title Coredemptress; and 522 (97%) to the title Mediatress of All Graces. Lightbourn offers the understated summary: "Most of the [Protestant Episcopal] Church's clergy do not habitually think in Roman Mariological terms."[63]

Lutheran affection for the Blessed Virgin Mary is rooted both in the Lutheran symbolical books as well as in Lutheran history.

Martin Luther's personal devotion to the Mother of God is life-long; not even the casual reader can escape this impression, which every recent study in depth has abundantly established and confirmed.[64] At the same time, Luther's devotion to the Blessed Virgin Mary is basically theological and Christological rather that Marian, and must be read against the background of his own religious evolution. He begins as the docile disciple of John von Paltz, whose magnum opus, the *Coelifodina,* converts the history of our Lord's passion into a history of the compassion of His mother, whose great merits (as von Paltz says in one of his sermons) drew God down from heaven and became the foundation not only of monastic piety but of the entire Christian faith. From this kind of distortion Luther gradually emancipates himself. As early as 1516, the dominant image of the Blessed Virgin has ceased practically for Luther to be that of the Queen of Heaven and has become that of the paradigmatic humble worshipper of God. "She is not puffed up because of the great distinction that has been given to her and the great praise with which she is lauded, because she has recognized therein the Lord, who is far greater, and she acknowledges him, thanks him, loves him and blesses him."[65]

By 1523 Luther no longer invokes the Mother of God, but his devotion to her remains unabated. Hermann Joseph Brosch sees a large area of Mariological doctrine that both Roman Catholicism and Martin Luther hold. After specifying details he summarizes: "It is accordingly a great common heritage that we must watch over together."[66]

The Lutheran love for the Mother of God is tempered, but by no means eliminated, during the era of Lutheran Orthodoxy (1580-1713), with its embittered interconfessional polemics. Indeed, the mid-17th century sees the founding of a Lutheran order of sisters at Mount St. Mary, Helmstedt.[67] It is during the periods of Pietism and Rationalism that Lutheran interest in the Blessed Virgin goes into progressively deeper eclipse, only to come to light again in the age of the 19th century confessional and liturgical revival. In the history of both American and German Lutheranism of the last century one of the preeminent names is that of Wilhelm Löhe of Neuendettelsau, Bavaria. Most Lutherans would agree that if their denomination had a process of canonization, he would certainly have been elevated to the honors of the altar. It is characteristic of his attitude to the Blessed Virgin Mary that in his lovely study *On Womanly Singleness of Heart* he devotes nearly half the book to the Blessed Virgin as a model of feminine modesty, faith and devotion.[68]

For normal Lutheran theology the Blessed Virgin Mary is *theotokos, Deipara. Meter theou, Dei genetrix, mater Dei* are less satisfactory, because they are superficially misleading. The German can create the word *Gottesgebärerin* to stand beside *Gottesmutter* or *Mutter Gottes*. The English has the choice between "Mother of God" or an overly complicated paraphrase, "The woman whose child is God" or "The woman who gave birth to God." Lutherans stand committed to the title by their subscription to the Book of Concord, which twice applies the term to her. "We believe, teach, confess, that Mary did not conceive and bear a mere and ordinary human being, but the true Son of God; for that reason she is rightly called and in truth is the Mother of God."[69] "Because of this hypostatic union and communion of the natures the most praiseworthy (*hochgelobte, laudatissima*) virgin Mary did not bear a merely ordinary human being, but a human being who is truly the Son of God the Most High, as the angel attests. He demonstrated his divine majesty even in his mother's womb, in that he was born our of a virgin without violation of her virgin state. For that reason she is truly the Mother of God and yet remained a virgin."[70] The *Book of Concord* also calls the Blessed Virgin Mary "most worthy of the amplest honors" and grants that "Blessed Mary prays for the church."[71]

The Lutheran *Book of Concord*, on the basis of the Sacred Scriptures and the Catholic Creeds, affirms the virginity of the Mother of God *ante partum* and *im partu*. The official (1584) Latin version of the *Smalcald Articles* (Part One, IV) expands the "pure, holy Virgin Mary" of the original into *"Maria pura, sancta, semper virgo."*[72] But in general, Lutheran theologians feel themselves constrained to urge that the biblical evidence, when subjected to a sober exegesis, appears to provide no basis for demanding acceptance of the perpetual virginity of the Blessed Virgin Mary as an article of faith. Thus, unless an individual found an interpretation of the texts which come into consideration as personally compelling him to hold the perpetual virginity as a biblically-based conviction, for a Lutheran this tenet would be a theologoumenon and a pious opinion, a tenet in harmony with the analogy of the faith rather than an article of the Christian faith, a conviction that recommends itself on account of considerations of propriety and decency and that is entirely consistent with the biblical evidence.[73]

As far as the other privileges that Roman Catholic theology ascribes to the Blessed Virgin Mary are concerned, neither the Immaculate Conception nor the bodily Assumption appear to have commended themselves to contemporary Lutherans even as pious opinions, tolerable as long as no heretical inferences are drawn from them. This is true even though Martin Luther's personal adherence to the Immaculate Conception of the Mother of God (barring two lapses) seems to have been life-long and even though as orthodox a theologian as Valerius Herberger affirmed the bodily Assumption of the Blessed Virgin Mary in a sermon one part of which explained why there in nothing in the Sacred Scriptures about this event.[74] Unquestionably a polemic reaction against the Roman Catholic advocacy of these two tenents has played a part in discouraging any wide-spread acceptance of these opinions as a concomitant of the liturgical and confessional revival.

The ideas that the Blessed Virgin Mary is the Mediatress of All Graces and a Coreredemptress come in for general criticism among Lutherans. This is undoubtedly due in part to misconceptions about the scope of these terms, evoked by their irresponsible popular use on the lips of Roman Catholics in such a way as to suggest that the Blessed Virgin Mary personally contributed to the objective redemption of the human race. In part, however, even Lutherans who fully understand the theological limitations that must be put on these terms still regard them both as misleading and as stressing an aspect of the role of the Blessed Virgin Mary in the subjective redemption of men for which there is no explicit word of God which would differentiate her activity from that of any other saint.

A Lutheran would see the analogy between the Mother of God and the Church as nowhere better typified than in the use of the *Magnificat* as the vespers canticle. In this place the *Magnificat* has become more than a memorial; the words that the Gospel attributes to our Lord's mother have been wholly appropriated as the prayer of His bride. What the mother of the Savior said of herself expresses exactly the faith of the Church that is mother of us all. When we sing the *Magnificat* — every phrase of it profoundly informed by Hannah's Song, *Exsultavit vor meum,* and by the Psalter — we are not imitating someone else's hymn; we find ourselves singing our own. The Ecclesia-Mary parallel that primitive reflections saw in the vision of Revelation 12 thus receives practical liturgical sanction.

Again, on the occasion of her Purification, the Blessed Virgin offered both her Son and the two birds that Leviticus prescribed, in what was of course an intrinsically unnecessary action. There was no need for her to buy back her son from Yahweh, for He was Himself Yahweh. Nor did she stand in need of purification whose body had been the temple of God. Certainly we can speak of a priestly element in the Blessed Virgin's activity as the Sacred Scriptures here depict it. She was part of both old Jewry and of the new Israel, both of the *qahal* and of the *ekklesia,* thus doubly a part of the chosen race, the royal priesthood, the holy nation, God's own people. In offering her own self and her own future to God at the Annunciation and her Son to Him at the time of the Presentation, she was performing acts that are of the very essence of Christian sacrifice, the yielding up of body and mind, of will and intellect and affections, to Him from whom we have everything, and the pleading before God of the sacrifice of Him through whom we have everything that is needful for this life and profitable for our salvation. Herein the Blessed Virgin stands as a symbol of the church.[75]

The Lutheran Liturgy provides propers for the Annunciation, the Visitation, and the Purification/Presentation. The tract for the Annunciation includes the opening verse of the *Angelus:* "The angle of the Lord came in unto Mary and said, 'Hail, thou that art highly favored, the Lord is with thee; blessed art thou among women.'" The Collect for the Annunciation is the same medieval postcommunion for the feast that Roman Catholics use in connection with the *Angelus.* The alleluia verse for the Visitation includes the apostrophe: "Blessed art thou, O Mary, among women, and blessed is the fruit of thy womb."[76] The first one hundred hymns of *The Lutheran Hymnal* also has a metrical version of the Eastern *Theotokion:* "O Higher than the cherubim, more glorious than the seraphim, lead their praises; thou bearer of the eternal Word, most gracious, magnify the Lord!"[77] As a post-communion hymn we often sing the medieval "O Lord, we praise Thee, bless Thee, and adore Thee," with its stress upon the *verum corpus:* "May Thy body, Lord, born of Mary, that our sins and sorrows did carry, and Thy blood for us plead in all trial, fear and need: *Kyrie, eleison!*"[78]

III

Is a fruitful dialogue about the place and the role of Mary within the people of God between Roman Catholics and non-Roman-Catholics possible?[79]

Obviously this is not something for any non-Roman-Catholic to decide, since it takes two to create dialogue.

If Roman Catholics desire such a dialogue, it cannot effectively be carried on with Roman Catholics on the one side and a heterogenous and indiscriminate assembly of non-Roman-Catholics on the other. A non-Roman-Catholic with any kind of Roman Catholic acquaintance soon receives the impression that Roman Catholics are not all completely unanimous in every detail of their Mariological faith and practice. If this be true, the diversity is incalculably greated among non-Roman-Catholics. It would seem doubtful if an effective dialogue could be carried on with a panel of partners divided among themselves, say, on an issue like the virgin conception and birth of our Lord. I am not saying that fruitful separate dialogues could not be carried on; I merely suggest that the disparity of conviction within one part of the panel would largely paralyze effective overall dialogue.

Again, any dialogue would require Roman Catholic partners who realize that an appeal to the authority of the Roman Catholic Church or of the bishop of Rome to define doctrine would carry little weight, and that in consequence the dialogue would have to be on a basis that both partners could accept, the Sacred Scriptures as the primitive

Church understood them. On such a basis, it seems to me, a considerable measure of agreement could be established — a place for Mary in prophecy (although it would probably be somewhat more restricted than a Marian maximalist would rejoice at); the virgin conception at birth; the rightfulness of the title *theotokos;* the Virgin's place in the Church as the first of the redeemed; her role as the *keckaritômene* par excellence, uniquely endowed with God's favor; her paradigmatic piety, patience, humility, and faith; her status as the most blessed of women; her *fiat mihi* as the typical divinely empowered response that God elicits from all those of His children whom He calls to be in freedom workers together with Him; the analogy between the Blessed Virgin Mary and the church[80] that makes is possible for a Lutheran to use the *Magnificat* as the canticle at vespers and to say the first, pre-Counter-reformation part of the *Ave Maria* (as far as "and blessed is the fruit of you womb, Jesus") as memorial of the Incarnation; the probability of her intercession for the Church; the paradoxical parallel between the obedient Virgin Mary and the disobedient Virgin Eve that theologians have noted since the second century (although originally the thrust was Christological rather than Marian); St. Mary's virginity certainly *ante partum* and *in partu* and fittingly *post partum;* the legitimacy of apostrophes to her hymns and in the liturgy; the propriety of celebrating the Annunciation, the Visitation, and the Purification for what they really are, feasts of our Lord, to which some non-Roman-Catholics following the Church's example in the case of St. John the Baptist, would be willing to add their Nativity on September 8 and her falling Asleep on August 15; the devotional value of good, unsentimental representations of her in the arts, especially after the earliest surviving models which always show her with the holy Child; and the legitimacy of naming churches and church institutions after her and after the mysteries of her Annunciation, Visitation, Purification, Birth, and Falling Asleep.[81] As long as distinctions are carefully made among homiletic exuberance, poetic formulation, theological speculation, and binding doctrine, the tolerable nature even of certain other views and practices might be mutually established. Differences certainly would emerge in the area of piety;[82] the invocation of the Mother of God or of any saint, for that matter, in the absence of a clear word of God in its favor, seems to many outside the Roman Catholic Church with whom a large area of agreement might be otherwise established to be based upon unexamined assumptions in the area of theological anthropology and eschatology that it is difficult to reconcile with divine revelation.

It might be well to recognize from the outset that agreement on the revealed character of the definitions of the Immaculate Conception and the bodily Assumption cannot forseeably be reached, fruitful as a critical discussion of the meaning that these dogmas have for the Roman Catholic may be for both participants in the discussion. The one eventuality that a non-Roman-Catholic can contemplate is so unlikely at this moment that a Roman Catholic would be bound to reject it as impossible. This eventuality is that with the maturing of certain insights in the Roman Catholic doctrine of the Church that have found seminal and nascent expression in *Lumen gentium* and *Unitatis redintegratio*, it may some day be realized and recognized that the *whole* Church did not concur in and consent to the definitions, and that whatever degree of canonical validity these definitions have for those who accept the authority of the bishop of Rome, they are still open questions for the *whole* Church did not concur in and consent to these definitions, and that whatever degree of canonical validity these definitions have for those who accept the authority of the bishop of Rome, they are still open questions for the *whole* Church.

But the difficulties, formidable as they are, ought not to be allowed to deter us from this *opus arduum* either in terms of our inquiry or of our mutual conversation. René Lautentin has proposed as an ecumenical Mariological program the rediscovery of the Virgin by Roman Catholics *in* the Bible and the rediscovery of the Virgin by "Protestants" *through* the Bible.[83] I should prefer to paraphrase his proposal and urge that *all* Christians who receive the Sacred Scripture as the written word of God should seek to discover the Virgin both *in* the Bible and *through* the Bible, that we all in our time may meetly join in the chorus of generations that perennially calls the Handmaid of the Lord and the Mother of God blessed.

I cannot end without following the example of two of the Lutheran tradition's archtheologians — Martin Chemnitz and John Gerhard. As each concludes his discussion of the conception of the Blessed Virgin Mary, he disclaims in the foregoing discussion to have detracted in any way from the dignity of the Mother of God that the Sacred Scriptures ascribe to her in the just cited verse of the *Magnificat*. John Gerhard concludes with the observation that even though she was not wholly immune from the contagion of original sin, "it is our pious belief that St. Mary was never guilty of any flames of illicit passions, but that she obtained the perpetual adornment of virginity both in body and in soul and thus was in perfect fashion a virgin."[84] And Chemnitz closes: "But for the same reason, I hold that the Virgin Mary is set forth as blessed when those things are attributed to her which are in harmony with the sacred Scriptures and can be proved out of it, so that the Name of the Lord is Holy. Nor can she herself find any other glorification pleasing."[85]

Ave Maria, gratia plena, Dominus tecum; benedicta tu in mulieribus et benedictus fructus ventri tui, JESUS. Amen.

ENDNOTES

1. Quoted in Albert Brandenburg, *Maria in der evangelischen Theologie der Gegenwart* (Paderborn, 1965) 118.
2. Kristen Ejner Skydsgaard, *One in Christ*, tr. by Alex C. Kildegaard (Philadelphia, 1957) 207.
3. Titus Cranny, *Our Lady and Ecumenism*, in *America*, 100 (1959) 402.
4. Pierre Maury, *La Vierge Marie dans le catholicisme contemporain*, in *Le protestantisme et la Vierge Marie* (Paris, 1950) 25.
5. Max Thurian, *Mariology*, in Pehr Edwall, Eric Hayman, and William D. Maxwell, eds., *Ways of Worship* (London, 1951) 289.
6. Thomas A. O'Meara, *Mary in Protestant and Catholic Theology* (New York, 1966).
7. Fr. Cole has kindly made this available to me in manuscript.
8. Other important surveys are Walter Delius, *Geschichte der Marienverehrung* (Munich, 1963), which devotes pp. 300-320 to *"Der Protestantismus und das marianische Zeitalter,"* and Reintraud Schimmelpfennig, *Die Geschichte der Marienverehrung im deutschen Protestantismus* (Paderborn, 1952), of which chapter 5, pp. 115-145, surveys the first half of the 20th century. See also *Evangelische Marienverehrung*, in *Eine heilige Kirche*, 1955/1965, no. 1. The reportedly very complete survey in Heinrich M. Köster, *Heilige Schrift und Maria*, (Essen, 1963) 166-260, was not accessible to me. Hilda Graef, *Mary: A History of Doctrine and Devotion*, 2 (New York, 1965) devotes two pages to contemporary Anglicanism and "Continental Protestantism" (pp. 133-135).
9. See, for instance, the editorial, *Ex Virgine or Ex-Virgin*, in *Dialog*, 2 (1963) 103-104.
10. Emil Brunner, *The Christian Doctrine of Creation and Redemption*, tr. by Olive Wyon (Philadelphia, 1952) 352-356. The quotation is on page 356.
11. Walter von Loewenich, *Modern Catholicism*, tr. by Reginal H. Fuller (New York, 1959) 237. See also his somewhat more objective article in Julius Bodensieck, ed., *The Encyclopedia of the Lutheran Church*, 2 (Minneapolis, 1965) 1495-1496. Heiko A. Oberman, *The Virgin Mary in Evangelical Perspective*, in *Journal of Ecumenical Studies* 1 (1964) 271, holds that the Virgin Birth is *didache* not *kerygma;* see also pp. 277-280.
12. Editorial, "A Choice of Miracles," *The Christian Century* 75 (1958) 396. See also Paul M. van Buren, *The Secular Meaning of the Gospel based on an Analysis of Its Language* (New York, 1963) 164-165.
13. Werner Wiesner, article *Jungfrauengeburt*, in Heinz Brunotte and Otto Weber, eds., *Evangelisches Kirchenlexikon* 2 (Göttingen, 1958) 498. In the article on *Maria, Marienverehrung*, Kurt Nitzschke of the traditionally anti-Roman-Catholic Konfessionskundliches Institut at Bensheim summaries the place of the Blessed Virgin for an evangelical Christian: "In evangelical thought, Mary is a human being whom God richly endowed with grace in a unique encounter with Him. In evangelical thought this encounter with God stands in the foreground. Thus the Marian question cannot read: What is Mary, what characteristics and prerogatives does she have? Instead it must read: What happens to this human being in this encounter with God and Christ? It is this precisely that the few New Testament passages about Mary record. Mary too must learn to conquer her own maternal will and to submit herself wholly to the will of God. In this way she can be an example to us, but nothing more" (*ibid.*, 2, 1250-1251).
14. Paul Althaus, article *Jungfrauengeburt*, in Kurt Galling, ed., *Die Religion in Geschichte und Gegenwart*, 3rd ed., 3 (Tübingen, 1959) 1069. In the article *Marienverehrung in der evangelischen Kirche der Gegnwart* in the same work,

Wilhelm Jannasch expresses concern that evangelical veneration of the Blessed Virgin, especially when thought of in Hans Asmussen's terms as "the echo of the blessing that God spoke over the mother of the Lord," will become "a new law" and "an attack on the evangelical message of justification and a restriction of the 'Christ alone.'" Precisely in the era of the new Marian dogma, "no evangelical group and no individual evangelical clergyman has the right to proceed practically with the veneration of Mary until the very disparate modern stimuli to the veneration of Mary that come from theologians ... and poets ... have been thoroughly worked over in serious discussion among theologians" (*ibid.*, 4 [1960] 766).

15. See W. Norman Pittenger, *The Word Incarnate: A Study of the Doctrine of the Person of Christ* (New York, 1959) 66-67, 69-72.

16. James A. Pike, in Harold E. Fey, ed., *How My Mind Has Changed* (Cleveland, 1961) 170-171. See also Pike, *A Time for Christian Candor* (New York, 1964) 139-140.

17. J. V. Langmead Casserly, article *The Virgin Birth*, in Marvin Halverson and Arthur A. Cohen, eds., *A Handbook of Christian Theology* (Cleveland, 1958) 369-370. In Alan Richardson, ed., *A Theological Wordbook of the Bible* (New York, 1951) 277, the Scottish Presbyterian theologian J. K. S. Reid sees the virgin birth commended to the credence of Christians by its factual probability, theological propriety, excellent tradition, and spiritual fittingness.

18. Hans von Campenhausen, *The Virgin Birth in the Theology of the Ancient Church* (Naperville, 1964). The German original was published at Heidelberg in 1962. See the review by Robert Wilken in *Una Sancta* 22, No. 2 (Pentecost, 1965) 59-61, which ends: "We must ask ourselves as Lutherans: Can a theology of Mary rely solely on the evidence of primitive Christianity?"

19. Otto Weber, *Grundlagen der Dogmatik* 2 (1962) 120, quoted in Brandenburg, 43.

20. Hick declared: "I distinguished between the central Christian faith in the incarnation and the theologically peripheral stress of the virgin birth, and following St. Paul, St. John, and St. Mark, and most of the other New Testament writers, I do not found my belief upon the virgin birth tradition." Editorial, *Ministers Protest Exclusion of Professor*, in *The Christian Century* 79 (1962) 450. See also the special report, *United Presbyterians in Action, ibid.*, 750-751.

21. Thomas Boslooper, *The Virgin Birth* (Philadelphia, 1963) 234-236.

22. *Ibid.*, 237.

23. See for example, the article by F. F. Bruce, *The Person of Christ: Incarnation and Virgin Birth*, in the symposium edited by the editor of *Christianity Today*, Carl F. H. Henry, *Basic Christian Doctrines* (New York, 1962) 124-130.

24. Typical tributes to the Blessed Virgin from these circles are the appeal not to "neglect to give Mary, the mother of Jesus, the distinguished place which the Holy Scriptures itself accords her," by Samual M. Zwemer, *The Mother of Our Lord*, in *Eternity* (December, 1958) 18-19 and 44 (abbreviated from Zwemer's book *The Glory of the Manger: Studies on the Incarnation* [New York, 1940] 61-70), and Arthur F. Glasser, *Mary in His* (December, 1960) 4-6 and 25-26.

25. J. Oliver Buswell, Jr., article *Virgin Birth of Jesus (The)*, in Everitt F. Harrison, ed., *Baker's Dictionary of Theology* (Grand Rapids, 1960) 545. It may be significant that while this conservative theological lexicon has critical articles on the Assumption, the Immaculate Conception, Mariolatry, and the title Mother of God, it has no article on Mary herself.

26. Howard A. Hanke, *The Validity of the Virgin Birth: The Theological Debate and the Evidence* (Grand Rapids, 1963) 53-63.

27. Ralph L. Keiper, *The Virgin Mary and the Roman Church*, in *Eternity* (June, 1960) 15-17. The quotation is on p. 17.

28. J. Dwight Pentecost, *Romanism in the Light of Scripture* (Chicago, 1962) 26-60. Similiarly vehement polemics are found in E. Harold Henderson, *Romana Dogma versus Bible Doctrine* (Little Rock, 1964) 9-20, published by the North American Baptist Association; Loraine Boettner, *Roman Catholicism* (Philadelphia, 1962) 132-167; F. C. H. Dreyer (formerly of the China Inland Mission), *Roman Catholicism in the Light of Scripture* (Chicago, 1960) 179-196; and C. Anderson Scott, *Romanism and the Gospel* (Philadelphia, 1946) 68-81.

29. The distinguished Dutch theologian, Gerrit C. Berkouwer, deserves special consideration. See his *The Conflict with Rome* (Grand Rapids, 1958) 152-178; his *Recent Developments in Roman Catholic Thought* (Grand Rapids, 1958) 17-25; and especially his *The Second Vatican Council and the New Catholicism*, tr. by Lewis B. Smedes (Grand Rapids, 1965) 221-248.

30. Karl Barth, *Church Dogmatics*, tr. by G. T. Thomson and Harold Knight, edited by Geoffrey W. Bromiley and Thomas F. Torrence, I/2 (Edinburgh, 1956) 143. See also W. Paul Jones, *Mariology: An Unrecognized Entrée to Ecumenical Dialog*, in *Journal of Religion* 44 (1964) 210-222, which is especially useful for its discussion of Barth's attitude toward the Blessed Virgin.

31. Paul Tillich, *Systematic Theology* 1 (Chicago, 1951) 128. See also Thomas A. O'Meara, *Paul Tillich and Ecumenism*, in O'Meara and Celestin E. Weisser, eds., *Paul Tillich in Catholic Thought* (Dubuque, 1964) 278-284.

32. Reinhold Niebuhr, *A Plea for Tolerance*, in *The Atlantic Monthly* 210 (1962) 76. A propos the Marian Year 1954 the General Assembly of the Presbyterian Church in the United States of America "in charity but with candor" criticized the "cult whose chief contemporary emblem is 'Our Lady of Fatima'" for having "widened the breach between the Roman Catholic Church and all other Christian communions." The text of the Assembly's statement is reproduced in *The Christian Century* 72 (1955) 756-758.

33. Heinrich M. Köster, *De novo dogmate mariano quid protestantes Germaniae sentiunt*, in *Marianum*, 17 (1955) 37-75.

34. Köster, *Protestant Reaction to Mary's Assumption*, in *Theology Digest* 5 (1957) 105-108. See also *Das neue Mariendogma im Lichte der Geschichte und im Urteil der Oekumene*, in *Oekumenische Einheit*, edited by Friedrich Heiler and Friedrich Siegmund-Schultze, Vol. 2, No. 2.

35. *Zur Dogmatisierung der Assumptio Mariae: Ein Gutachten evangelischer Theologen*, in *Theologische Literaturzeitung* 75 (1950) 578-586. See also Gehard Ebeling's short survey, *Zur Frage nach dem Sinn des Mariologischen Dogmas*, in *Zeitschrift für Theologie und Kirche* 47 (1950) 383-391. In the conservative Lutheran tradition is Walter Künneth, *Christus oder Maria? Ein evangelisches Wort zum Mariendogma* (Berlin-Spandau, 1950).

36. Karl Bernhard Ritter, *Das römische Mariendogma*, in *Evangelische Jahresbriefe*, edited by Walter Uhsadel, 1951/1952, 8-16, quoted in Brandenburg, *op, cit.*, 57.

37. Max Thurian, *Le dogme de l'Assomption*, in *Verbum caro* 5 (1950) 2-41.

38. Hébert Roux, *Pour une doctrine biblique de la Vierge Marie*, in *Le protestantisme et la Vierge Marie*, 69-89. Another French Reformed voice is that of J.-J. von Allmen, *A Companion to the Bible* (New York, 1958) 292-295. In his article, *Mary, the Mother of our Lord*, written in the best style of modern biblical theology, he says of the Blessed Virgin: "She is not comparable to any other woman and her vocation was ... unique and unrepeatable."

39. Friedrich-Wilhelm Künneth, *Maria, das römisch-katholische Bild vom Menschen: Der Zusammenhang von Anthropologie und Mariologie in der römische-katholischen Kirche im deutschen Sprechaum* (Berlin, 1961) — The closing words of the article by Marc Lods, *Marie, Mère de Dieu, selon le*

concile oecuménique d'Éphèse 431, in *Positions Luthériennes* 13 (1965) 280, are apposite: "Monophysitism did not remain triumphant only in the schismatic churches of the East, the Jacobite Church of Syria, and the Coptic Church of Egypt. The Catholic Church itself, by an unhappy rebound, has known a deviation which little by little has imposed itself on its piety and its theology. Without disavowing the decisions of the Council of Chalcedon, the Catholic Church little by little has come to consider in Jesus Christ nothing beyond his unique nature as incarnate God. Lifted up higher and higher into heaven, adored as He sits on the throne of God His Father, His Godhead has been venerated to the detriment of His manhood. His role as Mediator has been attenuated. And then, more and more, the Virgin Mary has been installed in the place where He was no longer found, as the availing intermediary between God and men. Then this kind of Mariology becomes Mariolatry; the return of Monophysitism to the church explains in a large measure the direction and — let us speak the word — the deviation of Christology after Ephesus."

40. Stanley Irving Stuber, *Primer on Roman Catholicism for Protestants*, revised edition (New York, 1960) 128-129. See also his *How Protestants Differ from Roman Catholics* (New York, 1961), 65-75. For a British Congregationalist view, see E. L. Allen, *Mariology and Christology*, in *Congregational Quarterly* 35 (1957) 33-43.

41. Mario Colacci, *The Doctrinal Conflict between Roman Catholics and Protestant Christianity* (Minneapolis, 1963). A former Roman Catholic priest, Colacci is now a Lutheran. See also Georges A. Barrois' careful evaluation of the significance of Marian developmentss in the Roman Catholic Church in *Roman Catholicism: New Look in Doctrine*, in *Religion in Life* 29 (1960) 167-173, and his earlier *The Rise of Marian Doctrine*, in *Theology Today* (1955-1956) 463-476. Barrois, a former Roman Catholic priest, is now a Presbyterian.

42. Cyrus Pangborn, *Christian Theology and the Dogma of the Assumption*, in *Journal of Bible and Religion* 30 (1962) 98-99. The late Waldensian theologian Giovanni Miegge, *The Virgin Mary: The Roman Catholic Marian Doctrine*, tr. by Waldo Smith (Philadelphia, [1956]) 188-191, takes a similar position. The original Italian edition of Miegge's work work was elicited by the definition of the bodily Assumption of the Blessed Virgin Mary in 1950.

43. Richard A. Newman, *A Protestant Note on St. Mary*, in *The Ecumenist* 2 (1963-1964) 27.

44. Jaroslav Jan Pelikan, *The Riddle of Roman Catholicism* (Nashville, 1959) 140.

45. Walter Marshall Horton, *Christianity Today: An Ecumenical Approach*, revised edition (New York, 1958) 202-203.

46. Roland A. Seboldt, *Christ or Mary* (St. Louis, 1963) 46.

47. Pelikan, in Otto Semmelroth, *Mary, Archetype of the Church* (New York, 1963) xii. For a critical Lutheran reaction to Semmelroth's book, see Bernard Erling, *Recent Roman Studies in Mariology*, in *Lutheran Quarterly* 16 (1964) 322-326.

48. In *What Mary Means to Protestants*, in *Time* (September 11, 1964) 58. See also the statement of Albert C. Outler, *A Response* [to *Lumen Gentium*], in Walter M. Abbott, ed., *The Documents of Vatican II* (New York, 1966) 105: "The identification of the Blessed Virgin (in Chapter VIII) as the foremost of all those who have shared in, and who still enrich, the communion of saints may well have the effect, among other things, of recalling Protestants to an important aspect of Christian faith that they have tended to underestimate in their reaction to what was deemed the excesses of conventional Mariology."

49. Hans Asmussen, *Maria die Mutter Gottes* (Stuttgart, 1950) 13.

50. *Ibid.*, 17. The "Brunswick Theses" of the *Aktionsgemeinschaft för Bibel und Bekenntnis* (Association for Action on Behalf of the Bible and the Symbolic

Books) in Germany strongly repudiates denials of the virgin conception and the birth of Our Lord (*The Braunschweig Theses on the Teaching and Mission of the Church*, translated by Paul M. Bretscher, *Concordia Theological Monthly* 37 [1966] 512). See also Otto Rodenberg, *Der Sohn: Beitrage zum theologischen Gespräch der Gegenwart* (Wuppertal, 1963) 9-61.

51. Asmussen, 26.

52. *Ibid.*, 40.

53. Allen Cabaniss, *Our Lady of the Apocalypse* (Oxford, 1954).

54. Wilhelm Stählin, *Maria die Mutter des Herrn: Ihr biblisches Bild*, in *Symbolon* (Stuttgart, 1958) 226, quoted in Brandenburg, *op. cit.*, 47-48. See also Stählin's earlier but no less charming *Freu dich, Begnadete: Eine Betrachtung über die Verkündigung der Geburt des Herrn* (Kassel, 1950).

55. Werner Meyer, *Maria als Bild der Gnade und Heiligkeit*, in *Begegnung der Christen* (Stuttgart, 1959) 573-592.

56. *Ibid.*, 577.

57. *Ibid.*, 578.

58. *Ibid.*, 579.

59. Thurian, *Marie, mère du Seigneur, figure de l'église* (Taizé, 1963).

60. London, 1963.

61. New York, 1964.

62. While, in general, the Reformed tradition has been less appreciative of the Blessed Virgin Mary than the Lutheran tradition, the survey of John Calvin's mariology by James A. Shuel, *The Virgin Mary in a Reformation Theology*, in *Canadian Journal of Theology* 6 (1960) 275-283, is designed to pose the question, "looking at the Reformed tradition from the outside, whether its essential doctrinal principles necessarily impose the inhibited silence or the automatic rejection of serious Mariology" that Shuel has noted among the spiritual progeny of Calvin.

63. Francis C. Lightbourn, *What About the Virgin Mary?* in *The Living Church* 141, No. 1 (July 3, 1960) 10-12. These data may be compared with the results of a survey reported in by Kenneth F. Dougherty. In 1957 a questionnaire was sent out to the superiors of 52 Anglican religious communities in England. Twenty-five replies were returned. All those replying regarded the Blessed Virgin Mary as the Mother of God, 16 affirmed her Immaculate Conception, 15 her perpetual virginity, 14 her bodily Assumption, 8 held her to be Corredemptress and Dispenser of All Graces, and 7 accorded her the title Queen of Heaven (Kenneth F. Dougherty, *Our Lady and the Protestants*, in Juniper B. Carol, ed., *Mariology* 3 [Milwaukee, 1960] 431).

64. Schimmelpfennig, *op. cit.*, 195-229; Walter Tappolet and Albert Ebneter, *Das Marienlob der Reformatoren* (Tübingen, 1962) 17-160; Théodore Süss, *La Mère de Jésus-Christ dans la pensée de Luther*, in *Positions Luthériennes* 2 (1954) 97-122; Gottfried Voigt, *Die Mutter des Herrn: Gedanken aus Luthers Weihnachtspredigten*, in *Evangelisch-lutherische Kirchenzeitung* (December 15, 1951) 357-361.

65. *D. Martin Luthers Werke* 1 (Weimar, 1883) 61. See the account of Luther's Mariological development through 1520 in Hans Düfel, *Luthers Stellung zur Marienverehrung*, in *Luther* 35 (1966) 122-131.

66. Hermann Joseph Brosch, *Eine katholische Antwort auf die evangelischen Bedenken einer bipolaren Mariologie*, in *Maria im Kult* (1964) 202-203, quoted in Brandenburg, *op. cit.*, 25, n. 18.

67. Marianne Nordström, *Klostertraditionen i Tyskland efter reformationen*, in Wilhelm Harsten, ed., *Kyrkotankar* (Lund, 1958) 44-51.

68. Wilhelm Löhe, *Von der weiblichen Einfalt*, 3d edition (Stuttgart, 1856) 63-111.

69. *Formula of Concord*, Epitome, 8, 12.

70. *Ibid.*, Solid Declaration, 8, 24.
71. *Apology of the Augsburg Confession*, 21, 27.
72. *Smalcald Articles* (Latin), Part One, IV.
73. Some Lutherans explicitly reject the perpetual virginity of the Blessed Virgin; see, for example, Stephen Benko, *The perpetual Virginity of the Blessed Virgin Mary*, in *Lutheran Quarterly* 16 (1964) 147-163. Benko regards this as "the basic problem of Mariology." He holds that "it is a historical fact that Joseph and Mary had severak children after the birth of Jesus," and regards the "theory of the perpetual virginity of Mary as dangerous to the Christian faith."
74. Valerius Herberger, *Evangelische Nertz-Postilla*, Part Two (Leipzig, 1697) 257.
75. See this writer's *Eve Reversed: Intentionally Noncontroversial Reflections on the Woman Who Gave Birth to God*, in *Seminarian* 51, No.2 (February, 1960) 6-19, and his '*Blessed Art Thou Among Women,*' in *Una Sancta* 15, No. 3 (Visitation, 1958) 4-7.
76. *The Lutheran Liturgy* (St. Louis, [1948]) 187-190; *The Lutheran Hymnal*, (St. Louis, 1941) 85-87. *Service Book and Hymnal* (Minneapolis, 1958) the other major American Lutheran rite, has different texts (pp. 108-110).
77. *The Lutheran Hymnal*, No. 475; *Service Book and Hymnal*, No. 437.
78. *The Lutheran Hymnal*, No. 313.
79. See *Dialogs on Mary* in *Mary Today* 56, No. 1 (January-February, 1965). Oberman, *op. cit.*, sees as problems in the biblical area Roman Catholic hermeneutics, form history, and "Protestant hermeneutics." In the historical area he sees problem especially in the early Church and in the medieval and Reformation periods. In a final section he argues against an "independent Mariology" and, inverting the principle to read *lex credendi est lex orandi*, against giving her a place in the worship of the Church.
80. Hans Carl von Haebler, *Maria-Ekklesia*, in *Quatember* 28 (1963-64) 1, refers, in connection with an editorial reflection on the representation of the Blessed Virgin Mary as sheltering her clients beneath her mantle (*Schutzmantelmadonna*), to the vision of St. Birgitta in which she believed that the Blessed Virgin told her: "My wide mantle is my mercy; truly, my daughter, my Son's mercy makes me merciful." He goes on: "I believe that the representation of the Blessed Virgin with the sheltering mantle was prayed out of the picture of the Mother of God which represents her in prayer and which ties her up with the church. The representation belongs together with the picture of Christ's ascension. The Lord ascends to heaven and leaves His church behind Him on earth, so that, filled with the Holy Spirit, she may produce progeny for Him. As Christ was born out of Mary through the Holy Spirit, so Christians are born out of the church through the Holy Spirit. In the figure of the Blessed Virgin of the sheltering mantle, who opens her mantle and discloses her offspring, the church reveals her own mystery."
81. See the excellent statement of Andrew Weyermann, assistant professor of practical theology at Concordia Seminary, St. Louis, *Mary in the Church: A Lutheran Position*, in *American Lutheran* 49 (1966) 126-129, especially the concluding section "Current Relevance," as well as Warren A. Quanbeck, *Problems of Mariology*, in George A. Lindbeck, ed., *Dialogue on the Way* (Minneapolis, 1965) 175-185; Alvin Horst, *Mariology and Ecumenical Discussion*, in *Seminarian* 51, No. 5 (May, 1960) 24-27; Gustav Aulen, *The Faith of the Christian Church*, tr. by Eric H. Wahlstrom (Philadelphia, 1960) 195-196, 311-312; and Skydsgaard's interesting article, *Maria, Herrens moder*, in Ragnar Askmark and others [editors], *Nordisk teologisk uppslagbok* 2 (Lund, 1955) 958-967, in which he affirms the doctrine of the New Testament against postcanonical Mariological developments based on tradition, and

rejects an independent Mariology but stresses the need for recognizing the Blessed Virgin's uniqueness as the divinely chosen *theotokos* as well as the need for interconfessional dialog.

82. See, for instance, the words of Lutheran editor Wilfred Bockelmann in *I'm Hoping to Meet More Catholics*, in *America* (July 18, 1964) 68: "Protestants will undoubtedly continue to believe that Catholics worship Mary. I hope Catholics will be tolerant of us for thinking that. To one not schooled in your rather complex doctrine, it does seem that when a Catholic prays: 'Hail Mary...' he is indeed praying to Mary. I've become convinced Catholic doctrine does not teach this. Nevertheless, I am convinced that many Catholics do just that."

83. René Laurentin, *The Question of Mary*, tr. by I. G. Pidoux (New York, 1965) 119, 157-158.

84. Johannes Gerhardus, *Loci theologici*, II, *locus* IX, cap. vii, para. 121, ed. Eduard Preuss (Berlin, 1864) 179.

85. Martinus Chemnitius, *Examen Concilii Tridentini*, Pars.I, *locus* V, para. 9. ed. Eduard Preuss (Berlin, 1861) 122.

BLESSED ART THOU
AMONG WOMEN

In the Name of the Father and of the Son and of the Holy Ghost. Amen.

The distinguished Roman Catholic publishing house of Friedrich Pustet in Regensburg recently put out the first part of what promises to become a thoroughly formidable reference book. It bears the title *Lexikon de Marienkunde,* or *Mariological Encyclopedia.* It will run to 2,400 double-column pages and just under a million and a half words. It will have in addition to some 2,500 text-illustrations over 200 pages of full-page plates. Subscribers will pay the equivalent of sixty American dollars per copy, unbound. Not the least interesting of its features is the use of a special logograph or type-character which it substitutes for the name of Mary — a medieval Gothic capital "M" with the vertical center member converted into a cross by a horizontal stroke through it. This special logographic abbreviation for the Blessed Virgin's name is used 22 times in the four-page sample that accompanied the announcement. This is one extreme of the Mary-cult.

At the other extreme we have so many modern Protestant theologians rejecting not only the Virgin Birth but also the Virgin Conception of Our Lord that another dogmatic denial of either has ceased to be noteworthy even in religious circles.

Yet both extremes — the extreme of excessive veneration and the extreme of excessive downgrading of the Mother of God — are sources of concern and scandal to Christians who stand committed to the *Book of Concord* and to the Book of God. The reason for their concern in both directions finds a focus in the words of St. Elisabeth in today's Gospel: "And why is this granted me, that the Mother of my Lord should come to me?" That is precisely the point. She is the Mother of *Our Lord,* hence Elisabeth's awed delight. But she is the *Mother* of Our Lord, so that the bright aureole that enfolds her figure is only a reflection of His blazing and unearthly glory.

The function of the Blessed Virgin Mary in the Sacred Scriptures in the history of salvation, and in the faith and worship of the Church, is to point to her Son. The noblest picture that can be painted of her is with her Child in her arms. She is the living and loving proof that when the time had fully come, God sent forth His Son, born of woman, born under the Law, to redeem those that were under the Law, so that we might receive adoption as children.[1] She is the living and loving proof that for us men and for our salvation the only God[2] Who is in the bosom of the Father came down from heaven and was incarnate by the Holy Ghost and was made man; that He who died for us is one of us; that the one Mediator between God and man is the man Christ Jesus,[3] that "there is no other God besides this Man,[4] that the merciful and faithful High Priest Whom we have in the service of God to make expiation for the sins of our fallen kind is made like us His brethren in every respect,[5] that we have an Intercessor Who is able to sympathize with our weaknesses, one Who in every respect has been tempted as we are, yet without sinning,[6] that He partook of our nature of flesh and blood so that through death He might destroy him who has the power of death, that is, the devil, and might deliver all those who through fear of death were subject to lifelong bondage.[7]

As long as the focus of the spotlight is on the Lord Jesus Christ, the richer the radiance that reflects upon His Mother the better. We are not offended that St. Gabriel addressed her, "Hail, O favored one,"[8] or that St. Elisabeth by divine inspiration twice called her blessed,[9] while expressing humble amazement that the favor should be granted her of entertaining in her home the Mother of her Lord; or that by the same inspiration the Holy Virgin herself should say, "All generations will call me blessed."[10]

Nor ought we to feel any particular compulsion to execrate pious opinions long held by Christians. We need not feel obligated to blacken her reputation and to invent transgressions for her to have committed, as if somehow we were saved by the sinfulness of the Blessed Virgin rather than by the sinlessness of her Son.

Here we stand with Blessed Martin Luther. In his exasperated distress at the exaggerations of the medieval Mary cult, he might declare: "I should wish that the veneration of Mary be altogether exterminated solely on account of its abuse."[11] Yet, three years before his death he was still affirming in print the opinion that he had worked out in detail and with considerable theological ingenuity twenty-five years earlier,[12] namely, that through the merits of her Son-to-be the Blessed Virgin was marvelously preserved from the taint of sin from the first moment of her existence as a human being.[13] We who have been reading him at least in English will recall that in the *Exposition of the Magnificat* he calls "Queen of Heaven" a true enough name for her,[14] and that elsewhere He acknowledges her as a gracious Lady exalted above all empresses.[15]

We remember that so doughty an adherent of the *Augsburg Confession* as Blessed John Brenz could say of the bodily taking up of the Blessed Virgin into Heaven: " About this let everyone think as he will."[16] And that the great Lutheran hymn-writer and preacher of the late seventeenth century, Blessed Valerius Herberger, presents a careful justification of this theological opinion in a sermon in his *Evangelische Herzpostille*.[17] It is when these pious opinions are elevated to the status of dogmas which must be believed under pain of eternal condemnation that we declare this kind of constraint — rather than the opinions themselves — to be antichristian and diabolical.

We Lutherans have no reluctance about apostrophizing the Blessed Virgin in our hymns and in our worship. Today's gradual repeats the inspired words of St. Elisabeth: "Blessed art Thou, O Mary, among women, and blessed is the fruit of thy womb; behold there shall be a performance of those things which were told thee from the Lord."[18] In the propers for the Feast of the Annunciation, the tract is the *Angelus*.[19] One hymn in our German hymnal addresses her:

> Mary, God has chosen thee
> To become a mother.[20]

A hymn that we have sung in this summer's series of chapels services paraphrases the Eastern Church's *Theotokion:*

> O higher than the cherubim,
> More glorious than the seraphim,
> Lead their praises!

And it goes on to call for her, as the Bearer of the Eternal Word, to continue to magnify the Lord as she first did in the events that we celebrate today.[21] In one of our most popular Christmas carols we describe her as the prophetically foretold "Branch of loveliest form and grace."[22] while at least two others describe her as "undefiled."[23]

The official editions of our Church's Symbols twice apply to her the title that the Council of Ephesus approved in 431, "The woman who gave birth to God,"[24] or, as we usually translate it into English, "Mother of God."[25] They speak of her perpetual maidenhood and the birth of our Saviour without violation of her virgin estate.[26] They call her "the pure, most holy, and most praiseworthy Virgin."[27] And they cheerfully concede that in the presence of God she is interceding for the entire Church upon earth.[28]

Yet in all of this she is first and always, "the Mother *of Our Lord.*" If in our hymns we call her — as we do — "most gracious" and "full of grace,"[29] it is because God has filled her with the grace of which His Son is the Incarnate expression. And if we call her blessed, it is because we can imagine her bliss in bearing the Lord Jesus beneath her heart by reason of the operation of the same Holy Ghost in our heart. The Blessed Virgin is an integral part of the Second Article of the Creed, but the key word of that article, as the *Large Catechism* reminds us, is "Lord" applied to our Redeemer.[30] It is of Him that we all affirm: "I believe that Jesus Christ, true God, born of the Father in eternity, and also true man, born of the Virgin Mary, is my Lord, Who has redeemed me, a lost and condemned human being, bought me and won me from all sins, from death and from the power of the devil, not with gold or silver, but with His holy, precious Blood and with His innocent Passion and Death, so that I might be His own and live under Him in His Kingdom, and serve Him in everlasting righteousness, innocence and bliss, even as He has risen from the dead and lives and reigns for ever."[31]

That every one of you may today and always add to this confession of the Church your own hearty "This is most certainly true, " is a grace and a blessing which I wish you in the Name of the Father and of the Son and of the Holy Ghost. Amen.

ENDNOTES

1. Galatians 3:4,5.
2. This is the most probable reading of St. John 1:18; see Eberhard Nestle, *Novum Testamentum Graece,* 21st Edition, Erwin Nestle (Stuttgart: *Privilegierte Wurttembergische Bibelanstalt,* 1949), p. 231.
3. 1 Timothy 2:5
4. So B. Martin Luther, *A Commentary on St. Paul's Epistle to the Galatians,* trans. by Erasmus Middleton and edited by Philip S. Watson (Westwood: Fleming H. Revell Co., 1953), p. 43 (*ad* 1,3); Weimar edition, 40/1,78.
5. Hebrews 2:17
6. Hebrews 4:15
7. Hebrews 2:14, 15
8. Luke 1:28
9. St. Luke 1:42,45. St. Luke's quotation of St. Elizabeth employs two different words, *eulogemene,* "blessed," which she also uses of the Fruit of the Virgin's womb, and *makaria,* "happy."
10. Luke 1:48. The Greek has *makariousin.*
11. "*Ego velim quod Mariae dinst werde gar aus gerot solum propter abusum"* (*Sermon on the Ave Maria* [1523], Weimar edition, 10/3, 314).

12. *Sermon on the Gospel for the Feast of the Conception of the B.V.M.* (1517), Weimar edition 17/2, 288.

13. *Vom Schem Hamphoras und vom Geschlecht Christi* (1543) Weimar edition, 53, 640. Compare for the year 1553, 37, 231, where he describes the B.V.M. as *an sund* (i.e. *ohne Sünde*, "without sin").

14. Jaroslav Pelikan, (editor), *Luther's Works,* Volume 21 (St. Louis: Concordia Publishing House, 1956) 327.

15. Weimar edition, 10/3, 325. On the Mariology of B. Martin Luther in general see Reintraud Schimmelpfennig, *Die Geschichte der Marienverehrung im deutschen Protestantismus* (Paderborn: Ferdinand Schöningh, 1952), 9-18; Gottfried Voigt, *"Die Mutter des Herrn: Gedanken aus Luthers Weihnachtspredigten,"* in *Evangelische-Lutherische Kirchenzeitung,* Dec. 15, 1953, 357-361; Théodore Suss, *"La Mère de Jésus Christ dans la pensée de Luther,* in *Positions luthériennes,* II (October, 1954) 97-122.

16. *"De hoc posteriori sentiat quod quisque velit"* (*Sermon on the Feast of the Assumption of the B.V.M.* [1541], in John Brenz, *Pericopae evengeliorum,* 1223, quoted in Schimmelpfennig, *op. cit.,* 26).

17. Valerius Herberger, *Evangelische Herzpostille* (Leipzig: John Frederick Gleditsch, 1740) II, 287f.

18. "The Visitation: Gradual," in *The Lutheran Liturgy* (St. Louis: Concordia Publishing House, 1941) 192.

19. *Ibid.,* 190.

20. *"Maria, du bist auserkorn, dass du Mutter wärest"* (*Kirchengesangbuch für Evangelisch-Lutherische Gemeiden,* 23rd edition [St. Louis: Lutherischer Concordia Verlag, 1886], No. 17).

21. *The Lutheran Hymnal* (St. Louis: Concordia Publishing House, c. 1941), No. 475.

22. *Ibid.,* No. 645. No. 341 calls her by the medieval title, "Mystic Rose."

23. *Ibid.,* Nos. 95, 104.

24. John Dominic Mansi, *Sacrorum Conciliorum nova et amplissma collectio,* IV (Florence: Antonius Latta Venetus, 1760), 887-891, 1137-1169.

25. *Formula of Concord,* VIII, Epitome, 12; Solid Declaration, 24. Compare the Decree of the Council of Chalcedon quoted via Evagrius, *Historia ecclesiastica,* in *Catalogus Testimoniorum,* I.

26. *Smalcald Articles,* Part One, IV (Latin); *Formula of Concord,* VII. Solid Delaration, 100; VIII, Solid Declaration, 24.

27. *Smalcald Articles,* Part One, IV; *Augsburg Confession,* III, 1 (German); *Formula of Concord,* VIII, Solid Declaration, 100 (Latin); VIII, Solid Declaration, 24.

28. *Apology,* XXI, 27.

29. *The Lutheran Hymnal,* Nos. 475 and 98 respectively.

30. *Large Catechism,* Creed, 26, 31.

31. *Small Catechism,* Creed, 4.

Afterword
Richard John Neuhaus
on the occasion of
the first awarding of the
ARTHUR CARL PIEPKORN PRIZE
10 October 1984

I have been asked to address "the abiding theological significance of Arthur Carl Piepkorn," and that is a happy assignment indeed. To speak of Arthur Carl Piepkorn the theologian is to speak also of Arthur Carl Piepkorn the man, and that for theological reasons. With Blessed Martin Luther, he affirmed the indivisibility of the theological vocation from the life and mind surrendered to theology's proper object, God the Father, Son and Holy Spirit. He understood and appreciated other ways of doing theology; he did not scorn second-order theologies of mainly academic interest, but he was a theologian of faith, and of the community of faith that is the Church. I do not mean that he did not engage the general culture in which the Church must pursue its mission; he did that and he did it energetically. But he engaged the culture, both to affirm and to judge it, always from an uncompromised base of devotion to Christ and his Church.

Permit me to say something about the man. We called him "the Pieps," although, to be sure, never to his face. Then he was always

"Father Piepkorn" and we were "Mister," until we were ordained. For those of us who came under his sway at seminary, hardly a day passed without some lively discussion of a new point raised by the Pieps. I could say he was an awesome man, for he was awesome in his achievements, but in his manner he seemed more whimsical than awesome. I intend no disrespect when I say that he was a funny little man. He was short of stature, military in bearing, and he laughed a great deal, a breathy little laugh that, with lips compressed, came out more like a whistle than a laugh. He was ever trotting about campus with great armloads of books, and would stop to share his delight in his latest discovery, the more exotic the discovery the better. Did you know, for example, that an East Prussian Lutheran parish regularly used incense in the 19th century — but only to cover the smell from the horse stables next door? His knowledge was encyclopedic. And he exhibited it. He exhibited it not in pride but as an invitation to join him in wondering at all that there is to be known. In wonder before the truth, he was a child; in conveying the truth, a master.

He was accessible to a fault. Countless were the hours in classroom, study and his home when we students would gather to learn and to challenge and to argue. I do not recall any time when he did not listen with patience and correct with kindness. But now you may say I am reminiscing and wandering from my assignment. Perhaps so, but I think not, for so wedded is the person and the theologian. It is important to say this because many who did not know Piepkorn personally are, quite frankly, a bit puzzled by the fuss that some of us make over him. He did not write as much as we wish he had. That is, he did not write many books. His monographs, articles and reviews, however, number in the many hundreds. The importance of the Arthur Carl Piepkorn Prize [and this volume of his essays] is that a new generation is invited to come to understand the man and his work. I hope that those who accept the invitation will come to know not only Piepkorn but also the Pieps, for he is there to be found also in his writings. In his many and elegant understatements, in his wry delight at paradox, there is to be heard, for those with ears to hear, even his whistling little laugh.

Piepkorn was a rare soul. What he espoused he embodies, what he taught he exemplified. He persuaded not only by his intellect but by his being. Raymond Brown, the noted Roman Catholic biblical scholar, came to know Piepkorn through the years of Lutheran-Catholic dialogue and has remarked that, knowing Piepkorn, it would be as preposterous to doubt the validity of his priestly orders as to doubt the orders of the Cardinal Archbishop of Milan. As Father Brown acknowledges, that is not a decisive theological argument for Lutheran orders, but neither is it merely a personal impression untouched by theological significance.

As is not so rare with rare souls, Piepkorn's ministry was in its beginning and in its ending at the margins of the church body he served with such devotion. At the beginning there were those who, failing to appreciate both his restlessness and capacity, thought his academic career a bit eccentric. He was called to parishes where it was thought little would be put at risk by the oddity of his insistence that Lutherans are evangelical catholics. His writings were welcomed by publications that were less than official, including, I am pleased to note, *Una Sancta* and the predecessor to *Lutheran Forum*. It was the military chaplaincy, not the synod, that first recognized the excellences of this man. When he was finally called to Concordia Seminary, St. Louis, it was by procedural accident and became a cause of consternation to those in charge of synodical affairs. Toward the end their time would come again, when they would remedy the accident and succeed in making clear that such rare souls have no place, as they said, in the church of God.

Over the years I have been in meetings with Lutheran theologians when the name of Piepkorn would come up. These were theologians, only some of whom had been students of Piepkorn, who were deeply engaged in the quest for Christian unity, and deeply concerned about current directions among Lutherans in North America. The question would be raised as to how we should describe the various alignments within American Lutheranism and how, within that context, would we describe ourselves. On more than one occasion the answer agreed to with surprising readiness is that we are "Piepkornians."

What does it mean to be a Piepkornian? (He would have laughed at the funny sounding term.) Speaking personally, and of course not for any party, permit me to try some answers. It means, as I suggested earlier, that the theological task is part of a life surrendered to advancing a "traditioned" truth. We are not our own men or our own women, but people who found liberty in obedience to a task that has elected us. In this respect Piepkorn was different from some ideas about the great teacher. Encomiums to former teachers frequently include President James Garfield's remark on what it means to be a true teacher. "Give me a log hut, with only a simple bench, Mark Hopkins on one end and I on the other, and you may have all the buildings, apparatus and libraries without him." That tribute does not apply in the case of Arthur Carl Piepkorn. No, there was nothing of himself that he would transmit, except in so far as he was the bearer of the tradition, of the sacred story. To learn from Piepkorn you would need the library, for he was the servant of a learned history. And you would need an altar, and you would need a pulpit, for the learning was nothing of real importance apart from the community of faith. Mark Hopkins may have needed only a simple bench to give what he had to give; Piepkorn needed the Church catholic, for he had to give only that to which he was given.

Piepkorn tried to teach us to order our loves and our loyalties. It is critical, he said, to understand who we are. First of all that we are Christ's. That is the first ordering of our love. And our loyalty to Christ's Church is in this order: we are Christians, we are Western Christians, we are Western Christians pledged to the Augustana, and then we are members of a particular church called Lutheran. Piepkorn was a champion of clear thinking and of clear definitions. He understood well a culture that was at war with definition, a culture that had made such devastating inroads in the Church. He knew well the siren arguments that words need not correspond with reality, that it is permitted to take liberty with words, that feeling and authenticity are all that matter. He knew those arguments well and challenged them with courage. Piepkorn was a friend of forms — the forms of ideas, of language, of historical experience, of manners. He was a friend of form because he knew that form is a friend of freedom. Unformed expression, he knew, tends always toward ignorance and gives license to the brutishness in our nature.

It is in this connection that we must understand what some viewed as his obsession with the Lutheran confessional writings. He typically referred to them as the Lutheran symbols, meaning those signs which give form to our distinctive way of being Christian. Piepkornians know that commitment to tradition and confessions is not a heavy burden or a confinement; it is the freedom of having a place to stand, and from which to challenge the lies and illusions by which we are otherwise bound. Within the life of the Church, such symbols demarcate a normative zone of truth, a place of leverage against those forces which respect only that truth which is effective in manipulating feelings and power.

The confessional writings, in the Piepkornian view, are not shackles by which we are restrained, nor are they a foil by which we test our independence. They are more like a friendly house, if you will. Amid the myriad ways of being Christian, here we live out our Lutheran way of being Christian. And when you are really at home in a house, and develop a real affection for it, you can live in it with a degree of relaxed confidence. You can poke about in the attics and explore the cellars and even do a bit of renovating, always of course within the limits of a decent respect for the other people who live in the house, and for the neighbors. In sum, you accept a measure of responsibility for the house; setting things right where they have fallen into disrepair, restoring original points of interest that have been obscured by the ill-conceived renovations of others. And all the while you know that future tenants will do their own renovating, with which you may or may not agree. The important thing is to have left them a clear statement of what you believe is true to the design of the house. And Piepkorn surely did just that.

But of course the image of a confessional house can be pushed only so far, not least of all because no earthly structure is our permanent home. I use the image only to suggest the way in which Piepkorn was on friendly terms with the tradition to which he was pledged. When you are on friendly terms with a tradition that is rich and various, you can play a part in reshaping and redefining that tradition. Indeed you have an obligation to do so, for it is in the nature of a lively tradition that it can only be transmitted as it is always being transformed. It is to be transformed, needless to say, not in obedience to the ephemeral fashions of the day, but in the regeneration of its constituting genius. Its originating vision — its vocation, if you will — is asserted anew in a new time. It is asserted in response to new opportunities and duties, and it is asserted in resistance to the new forms of old deceptions.

Arthur Carl Piepkorn was so confidently at home in the tradition that he could, in fidelity to the tradition, articulate its genius in a new way. His abiding contribution is that he restated the meaning of the Lutheran movement, and, by the grace of God, his restatement will carry the day in our common future. Today many people nod their heads in agreement when we say that Lutheranism is a confessional movement within and for the entire Church of Christ. A growing number assent to the proposition that it is the ecumenical vocation and destiny of Lutheranism to heal the breach of the sixteenth century and to be an agent of the visible unity of all Christians. These ideas are controversial in some circles still today, but forty years ago they were almost unheard of. Piepkorn retrieved these ideas from the constituting confessional vision of Lutheranism, and what he retrieved he refurbished so that this lively tradition might enliven generations to come.

Piepkorn opened our Lutheran self-understanding to the full resources that are rightfully ours. For many Lutherans theirs had been a skeletal tradition, skipping from Paul to Augustine to Luther to whatever was the reigning theological fashion of the day. For them, the medieval aspects of the Lutheran symbols were vestigial, an embarrassment to be burned away by the fire of Reformation truth. Piepkorn, however, saw that the Reformation was not against the Church catholic but to make the Church more catholic. Ambrose and Abelard and Teresa and Bonaventure and Thomas, he contended, must be doctors of our church if our church is part of the only Church that Christ has. The Lutheran symbols, he insisted, are not a door shutting us off but the cord that binds us to the fullness of the mystical body of Christ in time.

Piepkorn's legacy should be seen as part of an ongoing contestation within American Lutheranism. In the 19th century Samuel Schmucker had a particular vision of the Lutheran future in America. It was a Lutheranism shed of its medieval burden and merged into the Americanized Christianity of pan-Protestant optimism. Against

Schmucker stood C. F. W. Walther with his frequently brilliant, sometimes cantankerous, but always adamant insistence that Lutheranism is defined by its confession. Piepkorn, I believe it should be argued, is the heir of Walther in that he adapted this confessional movement to the ecumenical opportunities, and therefore theological imperatives, of our day.

Twenty years ago it seemed beyond doubt that the confessional party had prevailed in American Lutheranism. Today, however, we are engaged in renewed contest over the identity, even of the soul, of the Lutheran movement. That contest is focused in the deliberations of the current process of merger. I cannot guess at all that Father Piepkorn would say in our present situation, but I am sure of this: He would remind us most forcefully that this so-called new church is not ours to do with as we wish, that it is bound by confessional commitment and ecumenical destiny, that it is previously pledged, and to that pledge we will be held accountable before the judgment throne of God.

Piepkorn was, then, a theologian of the Church. And the Church, he insisted, is the community at worship. Of course the Church does many things, but worship is the source and the summit of its life. We do not worship in order to assist, to facilitate, to serve any other end, no matter how honorable or urgent that end may be. We worship God because God is to be worshiped. Worship is as close as we come here on earth to discovering an end in itself, for it is our end eternally. Piepkorn repeatedly invoked the words of the Athanasian Creed (which he would remind us is properly titled the "*Quicunque Vult*"): "The Catholic *Faith* is this that we *worship* one God in Trinity and Trinity in Unity." All of our believing and all of our obeying, including all of our theology, is brought to the altar. It is liturgy or it is nothing.

Arthur Carl Piepkorn is himself now part of the lively tradition that is transmitted to our care. I really do not think he is embarrassed to hear us call ourselves Piepkornians, for he was always keenly aware of the earthenness of the vessels whom God's grace turned into saints. We can now join the Pieps in agreeing with the *Apology* of the Augustana that "Just as when the saints are alive they pray for the Church in general, so in the heavens they pray for the Church in general." I would only add that the Pieps did not care much for generalizations, so I expect his prayers are a good deal more specific. I am confident that he joins us tonight in praying that this Arthur Carl Piepkorn Prize will enliven the confessional tradition that was his way, and is our way, of ordering our loves and loyalties.

About the Author...
The Rev. Dr.
ARTHUR CARL PIEPKORN

1907-1973

Born on June 21, 1907 in Milwaukee, Wisconsin the son of John Albert and Betha Taenzer Piepkorn, Arthur Carl Piepkorn would graduate from Concordia College, Milwaukee in 1925 and begin his service to the Church as a student at Concordia Seminary, St. Louis, Missouri. From here he graduated in 1928 and was ordained to the Holy Ministry of Word and Sacrament in 1930. Piepkorn continued his studies at the University of Chicago, earning a doctorate in 1932 with a specialty in Babylonian archeology.

In 1936 he married Miriam Agatha Södergren, daughter of Carl and Agatha Chester Södergren of Minneapolis. They had four daughters, Mary, Faith, Felicity, and Angela. He was not only a scholar but also a parish pastor and military chaplain in the United States Army. He served pastorates in St. Louis, Missouri; Chisholm, Minnesota; and Cleveland, Ohio. He served with great distinction as a chaplain from 1940-1953 and was senior chaplain of the U.S. occupational forces in Germany (1945), the commandant of the Chaplain School in Pennsylvania (1948-1950), and president of the Chaplain Board (1950-1951). When he retired from his military service in 1967, he had received thirteen medals and decorations.

He returned to Concordia Seminary, St. Louis, Missouri, in 1951 to teach as a professor of systematic theology. Among his varied interests, as well as, a specialized interest in medieval and Reformation paleology, were the symbolic books of the Lutheran Church, liturgical studies and practices. He was an original and faithful participant in the Lutheran-Roman Catholic dialogues for many years. Piepkorn was a voluminous writer, essayist, and co-author of the Tappert edition of the *Book of Concord*. His death in 1973 interrupted the completion of *Profiles in Belief: The Religious Bodies of the United States and Canada.*, which subsequently was undertaken by John Tietjen and a former student, David Truemper. The first volume was published by Harper and Row, in 1977.

During the mid-seventies amidst the storm of the Lutheran Church-Missouri Synod controversy, Piepkorn was among those of the faculty majority at Concordia Seminary, St. Louis, cited as teaching false doctrine by the 1973 New Orleans Convention resolution 3-09. Piepkorn was a signatory of the Seminary majority's protest against this resolution and resolution 3-01, which declared that all of the synod's theological and biblical interpretation and teachings must be interpreted in accord with a presumed synodical tradition as articulated in the document entitled, "A Statement of Scriptural and Confessional Principles," by Dr. Jacob A. O. Preus, President of the Lutheran Church-Missouri Synod. Piepkorn was then promoted to a strictly administrative non-teaching position at the Seminary. Later, on November 19, 1973, the Board of Control of Concordia Seminary, St. Louis, resolved to imposed a new policy of "honorably retiring" professors who had reached age 65 effective February, 1974. Professor Fredrick W. Danker a colleague, recalls Dr. Piepkorn's reaction to the action of the Board of Control: "The mere fact of retirement did not cause Piepkorn so much indignation as did the accompanying description: honorable. 'It's an insult,' he said. 'They have no theological competence. How then can they retire me honorably? What does that say for my theology? I want to be retired dishonorably.'"[1] There were six professors affected by this policy and all were signers of the protest document. Instead of "honorably retiring," Piepkorn simply tendered his resignation.

On December 13, 1973 Dr. Piepkorn wearied from the struggle of months trying to clear his name of charges of false doctrine, walked into his barber shop in St. Louis, sat down in a chair and died of a heart attack at the age of 66. The Board refused his request to clear his name, but after his death Concordia Seminary offered to declare Piepkorn "honorably retired." His family refused.

Ironically, or according to some by divine intervention, Piepkorn's death stalled the Board of Control's plan to suspend Dr. John Tietjen, President of Concordia Seminary, St. Louis, on December 17, 1973 while the students and faculty were on Christmas break. "The entire plan collapsed when God in His grace and wisdom took one of the principal actors in the whole plan to Himself in heaven. Professor Piepkorn died. The Board out of respect for him and his family postponed their meeting."[2]

His funeral was held December 17, 1973. He wore his priestly vestments, the martyr's color red and was buried with full military honors at the National Cemetery, Jefferson Barracks, Missouri.

ENDNOTES

1. Danker, Frederick W., No Room In the Brotherhood — *The Preus-Otten Purge of Missouri* (St. Louis, MO: Clayton Publishing House, Inc., 1977) p. 179.
2. *Ibid.*, p. 3. Here Danker quotes an unnamed source quoted in the *Christian News*, January 14, 1974, p. 8.

Other Sources

"Dedication of Paul M. Bretscher, Carl S. Meyer,
and Arthur Carl Piepkorn Libraries,"
Christ Seminary-Seminex, May 2, 1975.

"Close the Sem," A response to the *Affirm* article,
Christ Seminary-Seminex, n.d.

"The Collector," *Time*, August 15, 1977.

"The Arthur Carl Piepkorn Prize,"
Christ Seminary-Seminex, n.d.

⊙ Is there a Piepkorn bibliography? Why was it [or one] not included in this volume?

⊙ Why was the fine article on "Praxis Pietatis" omitted?

ACKNOWLEDGEMENTS

The publishers acknowledge with thanks permission to reproduce the following copyrighted texts:

By permission of Concordia Publishing House:
"What the Lutheran Symbols Have To Say About The Church," from *Concordia Theological Monthly* 26 (Oct, 1955) Copyright © Concordia Publishing House.

"The One Eucharist for the One World," from *Concordia Theological Monthly* 41 (Feb. 1972) Copyright © Concordia Publishing House.

"Chapel Address on the Feast of the Annunciation of the Blessed Virgin Mary," from *Concordia Theological Monthly* 42 (June 1971) Copyright © Concordia Publishing House.

"The Sacred Ministry and Holy Ordination in the Symbolic Books of the Lutheran Churches," from *Concordia Theological Monthly* 40 (1969) Copyright © Concordia Publishing House.

"Light and Glory: Devotional Reflections on the Holy Gospel for February 2," from *Concordia Theological Monthly* 32 (February 1961) Copyright © Concordia Publishing House.

By permission of The Mariological Society of America
(The Marian Library, University of Dayton):
"Mary's place within the people of God according to non-Roman Catholics," *Marian Studies* 18 (1967). Copyright © 1967 The Mariological Society of America.

By permission of the Paulist Press:
"Why Lutherans should engage in conversation with Roman Catholics," originally published in *Catholic World* 206 (November 1967) Copyright © 1967 by Paulist Press.

By permission of The American Lutheran Publicity Bureau:
"Sacrament, Sacrifice and Stewardship," originally published in *Una Sancta* Vol. 18 (No. 4, 1961) Copyright © 1961 The American Lutheran Publicity Bureau

"The Moment at Which Sacramental Union Begins," originally published in *Una Sancta* vol. 17 (No. 3, 1960) Copyright © 1960 The American Lutheran Publicity Bureau.

"Blessed are Thou Among Women," originally published in *Una Sancta*, Vol. 15 (No. 3, 1958) Copyright © 1962 by The American Lutheran Publicity Bureau.